NEOCONSERVATISM

IRVING KRISTOL

NEOCONSERVATISM

THE AUTOBIOGRAPHY OF AN IDEA

ELEPHANT PAPERBACKS

Ivan R. Dee, Publisher, Chicago

NEOCONSERVATISM. Copyright © 1995 by Irving Kristol. This book was first published in 1995 by The Free Press and is here reprinted by arrangement.

First ELEPHANT PAPERBACK edition published 1999 by Ivan R. Dee, Publisher, 1332 North Halsted Street, Chicago 60622. Manufactured in the United States of America

Library of Congress Cataloging-in-Publication Data:
Kristol, Irving.
    Neoconservatism : the autobiography of an idea / Irving Kristol.
      p. cm.
    Originally published: New York : Free Press, c1995.
    ISBN 1-56663-228-5
    1. Conservatism   United States   History   20th century. I. Title.
[JC573.2.U6K75   1999]
    973.92   dc21
                                              98-45126

The author gratefully acknowledges permission to use articles from the sources given below:

Reprinted from *Commentary*, 1949, 1950, 1951, 1970, 1972, 1991, and 1994, with permission, all rights reserved: "God and the Psychoanalysts"; "Einstein: The Passion of Pure Reason"; "Is Jewish Humor Dead?"; "Urban Civilization and Its Discontents"; "About Equality"; "The Future of American Jewry"; and "Countercultures."

Reprinted with permission of The American Enterprise Institute for Public Policy Research, Washington, D.C.: "The American Revolution as a Successful Revolution"; "Christianity, Judaism, and Socialism"; and "The Cultural Revolution and the Capitalist Future."

Reprinted, with permission, from *The American Spectator*, October 1976: "Socialism: An Obituary for an Idea."

Reprinted by permission of the New York Times Company, copyright © 1968 and 1977: "Memoirs of a Cold Warrior" and "Memoirs of a Trotskyist."

Reprinted by permission of *Foreign Affairs*, July 1967, copyright © 1967 by the Council on Foreign Relations, Inc.: "American Intellectuals and Foreign Policy."

Reprinted by permission from *Imprimis*, the monthly journal of Hillsdale College, Hillsdale, Michigan: "Utopianism, Ancient and Modern."

Reprinted with permission from *The Great Ideas Today*, 1976, copyright © 1976 by Encyclopaedia Britannica, Inc.: "Adam Smith and the Spirit of Capitalism."

Other articles, for which the author holds permission rights, originally appeared in various sources, as follow:

Wall Street Journal: "The Tragedy of 'Multiculturalism'"; "Reflections on Love and Family"; "Men, Women, and Sex"; "AIDS and False Innocence"; "Life Without Father"; "Business and the 'New Class'"; "The Frustrations of Affluence"; "On Conservatism and Capitalism"; "What Is 'Social Justice'?"; "Social Reforms: Gains and Losses"; "The Republican Future"; "'The Stupid Party'"; "The Emergence of Two Republican Parties"; "The New Populism: Not to Worry"; "The Coming 'Conservative Century'"; "The New Face of American Politics."

The Public Interest: "Capitalism, Socialism, and Nihilism" and "Corporate Capitalism in America."

Encounter: "The Adversary Culture of Intellectuals."

The Logic of Personal Knowledge: Essays by Various Contributors Presented to Michael Polanyi on His Seventieth Birthday (London: Routledge & Kegan Paul): "Machiavelli and the Profanation of Politics."

The Atlantic Monthly: "Welfare: The Best of Intentions, the Worst of Results."

The American Scholar: "American Historians and the Democratic Idea."

The National Interest: "My Cold War."

For Bill and Liz

CONTENTS

Preface ix

PREFACE

The writings in this volume are selected from my essays and journalism of the past half century. About two thirds have been published in previous books, all now out of print. One third have never appeared in book form. And the long autobiographical memoir that opens the volume, together with the essay "America's 'Exceptional' Conservatism," has never before been published. Within each section, the order is chronological. Omitted from the collection is the bulk of my more transient journalism.

In sum, this anthology traces the intellectual evolution of one American from a brief, youthful socialism, through a long period of ever more skeptical and self-critical liberalism, to something that became known as "neoconservatism." Since I am generally thought to be the "godfather" of the neoconservative "movement"—though I think the term "impulse" or "persuasion" would be more accurate—I presume to think that the intellectual evolution that is evident in this book may be of interest to others.

Inevitably, there are differences of emphasis, even occasional contradictions, to be found in these writings. I have made no effort to smooth them out, and wouldn't know how, since it is not always clear to me which emphasis or which side of a contradiction is to be favored. Later ("more mature") writings are not necessarily superior in the eyes of a reader, though the author will surely think so. There is also some overlapping—but then, some things cannot be said too often. In any case, it is the homogeneity of approach, the consistency of a certain cast of mind, that impresses (and even surprises) me, as I look over this collection. I think it fair to say that what might be called a "neoconservative imagination" is something that I have always possessed, long before the very term itself was invented, and long before there was any kind of neo-conservative "movement."

What, exactly, is neoconservatism anyway? I would say it is more a descriptive term than a prescriptive one. It describes the erosion of liberal faith among a relatively small but talented and articulate group of scholars and intellectuals, and the movement of this group (which gradually gained many new recruits) toward a more conservative point of view: conservative, but different in certain important respects from the traditional conservatism of the Republican party. We were, most of us, from lower-middle-class or working-class families, children of the Great Depression, veterans (literal or not) of World War II, who accepted the New Deal in principle, and had little affection for the kind of isolationism that then permeated American conservatism. We regarded ourselves originally as dissident liberals—dissident because we were skeptical of many of Lyndon Johnson's Great Society initiatives and increasingly disbelieving of the liberal metaphysics, the view of human nature and of social and economic realities, on which those programs were based.

Then, after 1965, our dissidence accelerated into a barely disguised hostility. As the "counterculture" engulfed our universities and began to refashion our popular culture, we discovered that traditional "bourgeois" values were what we had believed in all along, had indeed simply taken for granted. Suddenly, discussion of all social and economic issues, hitherto abstract, technical, and based largely on the findings of the social sciences, was infused with a controversy over "values." The "transvaluation of values" (Nietzsche's phrase) then merrily under way appalled many scholars and intellectuals who had always defined themselves as liberals, and a portion of them almost insensibly and in varying degrees found themselves to be "neoconservative," often protesting, furiously or feebly, against this identification. The spectrum of neoconservatism became ever broader, even as the spectrum of liberalism became ever narrower, even more dogmatically left-leaning. In 1972, the nomination of Senator George McGovern, an isolationist and a candidate of the New Left, signified that the Democratic party was not hospitable to any degree of neoconservatism. Only a few of us drew the obvious conclusion that we would have to try to find a home in the

Republican party, which had always been an alien political entity, so far as we were concerned. But with every passing year our numbers grew.

The traditional Republican party that was so alien to us was a party of the business community and of smaller-town America. It had, traditionally, little use for intellectuals, whom it regarded (with some justification) as more foolish than wise; its economic policy stopped short at the ideal of a balanced budget; it was still campaigning against the New Deal; and, in foreign policy, its inclination was almost always isolationist. It also tended to ally itself with the southern Democrats in opposition to civil rights for black Americans. This is why, in 1964, only a few neoconservatives supported Barry Goldwater while the rest of us went along with Hubert Humphrey. In the course of the 1970s and 1980s, however, the Republican party gradually "modernized" itself to some degree, in part because of the writings of neoconservatives. This was most clearly seen in the case of Ronald Reagan, the first Republican president to pay tribute to Franklin D. Roosevelt, and the first Republican president since Theodore Roosevelt whose politics were optimistically future-oriented rather than bitterly nostalgic or passively adaptive. The congressional elections of 1994 ratified this change, just as the person of Newt Gingrich exemplified it. As a consequence, neoconservatism today is an integral part of the new language of conservative politics.

What will future historians of American politics make of the neoconservative episode, now drawing to a conclusion? I do not presume to guess, or even to imagine. But I do believe, as someone who has been at the center of this episode, that if they are even minimally interested, the writings collected in this volume will be worth reading. Whether they—or some of them—will be worth the reading on their own more enduring merits is not for me to say.

SECTION I

1

An Autobiographical Memoir

Is there such a thing as a "neo" gene? I ask that question because, looking back over a lifetime of my opinions, I am struck by the fact that they all qualify as "neo." I have been a neo-Marxist, a neo-Trotskyist, a neo-socialist, a neoliberal, and finally a neoconservative. It seems that no ideology or philosophy has ever been able to encompass all of reality to my satisfaction. There was always a degree of detachment qualifying my commitment.

One "neo," however, has been permanent throughout my life, and it is probably at the root of all the others. I have been "neo-orthodox" in my religious views (though not in my religious observance). This is something of a puzzle to me, for my own religious background was not at all conducive to such a perspective. It is true that my parents' household in Brooklyn was Orthodox Jewish, but only in observance—belief seemed to have nothing to do with it. My father would go to synagogue only once a year, on the High Holidays; my mother never went, though she kept a strictly kosher household. We took notice of the other main Jewish holidays too, but we never "celebrated" them. I received absolutely no Jewish instruction at home, nor did my parents seem to care very much about my own observance. It is true that they dutifully sent me to an old-fashioned yeshiva—two afternoons a week and Sunday mornings—so that I could learn to read the prayer book and qualify for my bar mitzvah. There we also read the first five books of the Bible, translating from Hebrew into Yiddish—two languages I didn't know. (My parents spoke Yiddish to each other, but only English to the children.) I dutifully participated, learning to read the Hebrew and memorizing the Yiddish translations. Discipline was strict—if we misbehaved in any way, the rabbi would order us to stand up and then give us a stinging slap in the face. He also taught us to hate the *goyim* and to spit whenever we passed a church.

If ever there was a regimen that might have provoked rebelliousness, this was it. But though I obviously had not the faintest interest in my Jewish studies, I felt no impulse to rebel. I was duly bar-mitzvahed, making the conventional speech (in a memorized Yiddish) in which I thanked the rabbi and my parents for bringing me to this glorious day. I even continued to attend the yeshiva for at least six months afterwards, though I was not required to and my parents never encouraged me to. Then when I was sixteen my mother died of stomach cancer, and for the next six months I would get up at dawn, just when my father was setting off to work, and go to the synagogue to say the morning prayers, which included a prayer for one's recently deceased loved one. Again, my father never urged me to do this, and he himself seems never to have considered doing it. So why did I do it?

I don't know the answer to that. Though I took some adolescent pride in being a member of the "chosen people," I felt no passionate attachment to Judaism, or to Zionism, or even to the Jewish people. I had read nothing on any of these matters, and the only magazine that entered our house was *The New Masses*, to which my older sister, Lillian, subscribed as a consequence of attending City College at night. (She was an office worker during the day.) I did not think of myself as religious. On the other hand, one thing becomes clear in retrospect: There was something in me that made it impossible to become antireligious, or even non-religious, though my subsequent intellectual commitments kept trying to steer me in that direction. I was born "theotropic," and not even my dismal experience of a decadent Orthodoxy could affect this basic predisposition.

Even while I was a young Trotskyist at City College, I was a dissident in this respect. I read Plato and was immediately persuaded that it made sense for a suprasensible universe of ideas to exist. I read the King James Bible, and was immediately persuaded that the Book of Genesis was, in some nonliteral sense, true. Later in my college days I read

Niebuhr, Tillich, and Maritain, along with Trotsky, Lenin, Rosa Luxemburg et al., and found myself sympathetic to all of them. There were then no serious Jewish theologians available in English; it was not until after World War II that Buber, Rosenzweig, and Scholem began to be translated from the German. By that time, the Holocaust had touched my Jewish nerve and I was delighted to discover that there really could be an intellectual dimension to Judaism.

What impressed me most about the Christian theologians was their certainty, derived from the Bible, that the human condition placed inherent limitations on human possibility. Original Sin was one way of saying this, and I had no problem with that doctrine—though how to reconcile it with my youthful utopian socialist hopes and beliefs was beyond me. In fact no reconciliation was possible, and the "neo" worm was already eating away at my socialist certitudes. It is interesting that the Jewish prophets have never much interested me—their religious utopianism was too close to the political utopianism I was already becoming disenchanted with. I was more affected by the law-giving books of the Bible, and to this day I believe that this difference in emphasis will determine one's attitude toward traditional Orthodox Judaism as against modern reformed versions—which usually means "liberal" versions. Even as a socialist I had more respect for "tradition-bound" religion than for a modernized and liberalized one. This respect, however, did not necessarily extend to all traditional rituals and ways of behavior. I was a nonobservant Jew, but not a nonreligious one. Hence the "neo" in my religious orientation.

For decades, and even now, some of my closest friends will occasionally wonder aloud whether I really believe in God's existence. My wife tells me that back in the 1950s, my revered teacher, Sidney Hook, took her aside on several occasions and asked her precisely that question. He, as a pragmatist and a rationalist, just didn't see how it was possible. The problem with that question, of course, is that "existence"—in the normal usage of the term—is not a divine attribute. The mysterious term "being" is more appropriate. And a religious person doesn't "believe" in God, he has faith in God. One's relation to God is existential, not rationalist. As I learned later from a reading of Kant, pure reason will never get you beyond—pure reason. But the more you pray, the more likely you are to have faith. That is why children are taught to pray, rather than being instructed in "proofs" of God's "existence."

I have emphasized the importance of religion in my personal and intellectual development because, in my own writings, it is only on rare occasions evident. I am not a theologian, after all, though reading theology is one of my favorite relaxations. Other nonreligious thinkers, however, have had a more direct influence in shaping my mind. I have already mentioned Sidney Hook, whose writings revealed to me the power of logical, coherent analysis, something my formal education had neglected. He certainly helped me perceive the fallacies of Marxism—though, ironically, Hook always remained far more respectful of Marx, and of the socialist ideal, than I was. I sometimes think he taught me more than he intended. But that is the sign of a truly great teacher, which he was.

The two thinkers who had the greatest subsequent impact on my thinking were Lionel Trilling in the 1940s and Leo Strauss in the 1950s. Trilling was, in contemporary terms, a skeptical liberal, Strauss a skeptical conservative. Trilling was an elegant and subtle literary critic, Strauss a powerful Germanic, supersubtle political philosopher. In both cases, their skepticism went to the very roots of modern liberalism and modern conservatism, respectively.

I still remember vividly first reading Trilling's essays in *Partisan Review*, later collected and published under the title *The Liberal Imagination*. They hit me with the force of a revelation. Though I had by then read widely in the modernist writers—D. H. Lawrence, T. S. Eliot, W. B. Yeats, Franz Kafka, Faulkner—it had simply never occurred to me that their vision was incompatible with the dominant socialist and liberal worldviews shared by all New York intellectuals, a group whom I regarded as a Sanhedrin of wisdom and sensibility. The "modern," it turned out, was not all of a piece; artistic sensibility and political reason were in conflict. To put it another way: the *metaphysics* of modern "avant-garde" art and the metaphysics of modern "progressive" politics were at odds with one another. Given my metaphysical bent, I took this very seriously indeed. No politics, I sensed, was viable if its own culture was radically subversive of it. The "neo" part of me was quickened and invigorated.

Trilling himself spent the rest of his life trying to reconcile "reactionary" modernism in literature with a secular liberalism. He was not a religious man, but—like Matthew Arnold, whom he so much admired—his commitment to great literature was a kind of religious commitment. His "great books" had a biblical authority for him—the Bible, after all, was one of those great books. His Arnoldian liberalism kept him out of step with the "progressive" liberal community. After an early flirtation with the Left, the one certain thing about Lionel Trilling was that he was not a politically correct "progressive"—not in politics, not in education, not in cultural matters, not in manners and morals. At the same time, there existed no conservative intellectual body of thought worth noting, so that to the end Trilling remained a skeptical, out-of-step liberal, whom his students in later years would simply describe as "conservative." This lent a certain pathos to his life and thought, but it was a pathos that never came close to the pathetic. His luminous intelligence was as striking as ever as the years passed, and he coped with the disharmony of his condition by writing admiringly about Jane Austen and even Kipling instead of D. H. Lawrence or Kafka.

Leo Strauss—"Mr. Strauss," as his students called him, and still call him, posthumously—was from a different planet. A German-Jewish émigré who had been a student of medieval Jewish and Arabic philosophy, he was the quintessential philosopher, of a kind satirized in popular literature. Helpless in all practical matters, the author of very difficult and complex texts, studious and meditative, a rationalist who pressed reason to its ultimate limits, he was no kind of "intellectual"—a class he held in, at best, tolerant contempt. (I would not be surprised if he had never read a line of Trilling's.) After several years at the New School, he moved to the University of Chicago in 1949, where he became a most influential teacher. His students—those happy few who sat at his feet—became "Straussians," though they preferred to be known as "political theorists." (One such student was my dear friend, the late Martin Diamond, who helped me understand what Strauss was up to.) These students of Leo Strauss, in turn, have produced another generation of political theorists, many of whom have relocated to Washington, D.C., since the academic world of positivist "political science" has become ever more hostile to Strauss and "Straussians"—even while his mode of thought has filtered down to an ever more numerous "happy few." This was understandable, since Strauss did not disguise his disgust for what his contemporaries called "political science."

Encountering Strauss's work produced the kind of intellectual shock that is a once-in-a-lifetime experience. He turned one's intellectual universe upside down. Suddenly, one realized that one had been looking at the history of Western political thought through the wrong end of the telescope. Instead of our looking down at them from the high vantage point of our more "advanced" era, he trained his students to look at modernity through the eyes of the "ancients" and the premoderns, accepting the premise that they were wiser and more insightful than we are. One read the premoderns, therefore, in order to understand them as they understood themselves, not to understand them better than they understood themselves. In addition, one read them in order to understand ourselves, products of the modern age, better than we are able to do on our own. In the battle between the "ancients" and the "moderns," he was on the side of the "ancients."

What made him so controversial within the academic community was his disbelief in the Enlightenment dogma that "the truth will make men free." He was an intellectual aristocrat who thought that the truth could make *some* minds free, but he was convinced that there was an inherent conflict between philosophic truth and the political order, and that the popularization and vulgarization of these truths might import unease, turmoil, and the release of popular passions hitherto held in check by tradition and religion—with utterly unpredictable, but mostly negative, consequences. Strauss was respectful of the common sense of the common man when this was guided by tradition, itself the heir to generations of practical wisdom when it came to the art of living a humane life. He was contemptuous of the modern demagogic idolatry of the common man.

Moreover, he was persuaded that the great philosophers prior to the Age of Reason, and many of the greatest poets, shared this point of view. As a result, they took the greatest care in their writing so as not, as the British would say, to "frighten the horses." To a greater or lesser degree, they had a prudential concern for the effects of their opinions, as well as for their own safety—this in an era when the secular and temporal authorities felt an obligation to suppress heterodoxy. And in most cases, especially where religion and political philosophy were concerned, they did subscribe to some heterodox views, simply by virtue of being rigorously thoughtful men. One therefore had to study—not read—their texts with a quasi-"talmudic" intensity and care, in order to distinguish between their "esoteric" and "exoteric" views. Nothing has enraged contemporary "enlightened" academic political scientists and political philosophers more than this approach to the "great books" of the premodern era. Our contemporaries do not study to learn so much as to read and express opinion.

Because Strauss believed, along with the "greats" he revered, that prudence was the greatest of practical virtues, he never allowed his aristocratic mode of thinking to determine, in any simple and linear way, his political opinions. Himself a victim of Nazism, he defended liberal democracy as the best alternative among modern political regimes, even while keeping it intellectually at a distance. He was no right-wing ideologue, as some of his critics have claimed, nor did he fit easily into contemporary conservative discourse. He did not, for instance, much admire Edmund Burke, a modern conservative icon, because he felt that Burke's emphasis on "prescription" as the basis of a social order was too parochially British, and too vulnerable to the modern insistence that we should, in the words of Tom Paine (echoed by Jefferson), "let the dead bury the dead." Modern populist conservatism, it goes without saying, was alien to him.

But one didn't study Strauss to discover ready-made political opinions. He opened modernity to serious, critical thought, of a kind that reveals Marxist and postmodern critiques to be, as they are, the paltry offshoots of modernism itself. In a sense, the premodern political philosophers served Strauss as the modern (or modernist) novelists and poets served Trilling—as a force for liberation from the contemporary progressive, liberal, or conventionally conservative outlook that prevails among our intellectual classes. Strauss, in conversation, once remarked that it was entirely proper for a young man to think Dostoevski was the greatest novelist, but it would be a sign of maturity when he later concluded it was Jane Austen who had the most legitimate claim to that place. Lionel Trilling, I think, would have agreed.

By the time I was twenty-two, my "intellectual formation" (as the French would say) was already beginning to take shape. The seeds of my future neoliberalism and neoconservatism had been sown, but any flowering had to come with writing, not merely reading and thinking. I wanted very much to be not only an "intellectual" but a "writer," and, with the arrogance of youth, I was convinced I could be one. An intellectual who didn't write struck me as only half an intellectual. But what kind of writer? Of that I had no idea. In college, I had written only term papers, which got me good grades but which, I knew, revealed little by way of literary talent. There were, of course, the writers for *Partisan Review*—wonderful stylists like Dwight Macdonald and Mary McCarthy—but I sensed that they were not suitable models for me. They were out of my class, as it were. I recall a conversation I had with Saul Bellow, about a year later. I had then joined my wife in Chicago, where she was doing graduate work at the University of Chicago and where I was waiting to go into the Army. Saul and I were friends and neighbors. He was just publishing his first novel, and I was writing occasional book reviews for *The New Leader*, at which my college friend Daniel Bell was an indulgent editor. I confided to Saul that I thought I had the potential to be a writer. He looked at me suspiciously and asked: "What kind of writer?" (Saul has always been convinced, as most novelists are, that the world does not need more than one novelist.) I thought for a moment and then said briskly, "Well, good enough to write for *The New Yorker*." He roared. At that time, we intellectuals did not think too much of that slick magazine.

What had given me even this degree of confidence was one of those strokes of luck that shape careers. In a bookshop that sold "remainders"—I think it was the Marboro bookshop in Times Square—I picked up, for twenty-nine cents, a copy of John Crowe Ransom's *God Without Thunder*. I had never heard of Ransom but loved the title, since I too had little use for such a god. The book enchanted me, not so much for its theme, already familiar as well as congenial from my religious readings— by then I was into Charles Péguy and Léon Bloy—as for its style. That style was lucid, straightforward, unpretentious, but brightened with flashes of irony and wit. "That's the style for me," I thought, "I can do it!" Some months later, I submitted an unsolicited book review to *Kenyon Review*, which Ransom was then editing. I received a pleasant, *handwritten* rejection note, which strengthened my high opinion of him.

Another stroke of luck. At about the same time that I discovered John Crowe Ransom, I rediscovered W. H. Auden. To be sure, I had read his poems when they appeared in *Partisan Review*, had "appreciated" them, but I read them as a casual consumer of poetry, not as a writer reads, with an active intellect. Learning to read in that new way I owed to Ransom, whose other writing I hastily searched out. There, he introduced me to the New Criticism. Applying myself to Cleanth Brooks, I. A. Richards, and others, I learned to read poetry—really to read—as had never been possible for me before, simply because no one had ever told me how to do it. And then, I came across an older issue of *Partisan Review* and there I found Auden's "September, 1939," whose opening lines have echoed in my mind forever after:

I sit in one of the dives
On Fifty-second street
Uncertain and afraid
As the clever hopes expire
Of a low, dishonest decade

I was certainly vulnerable to the sentiments and mood of this poem, but what struck me forcefully was that phrase, "low, dishonest decade." What a powerful use of ordinary words! "Clever hopes" is good, too. Then I read through all of Auden's longer poems, most of them in this edgy, conversational style, savoring the language. They are uneven, of course, but a few wonderful phrases can, for me, redeem an entire poem. In later years, I have had a similar experience with a few other poets (Eliot, Yeats, Larkin), but much of modern poetry, I confess, evokes no response within me. This is poetry written for other poets, or for those engaged in the academic exegetical analysis of poems. I take it on faith that Wallace Stevens is a major poet but I cannot read him. I once had the idea of compiling a brief anthology of poems for ambitious young journalists who wished to write better, but nothing came of it. Instead, I tell them to read Shakespeare's sonnets in their spare time— wasted advice, in most cases.

I have mentioned the role of luck in the shaping of the mind, but it is clear to me that my entire life has been one instance of good luck after another. My relatively brief sojourn among the Trotskyists, for instance—I left before I was twenty-two—was immensely fruitful, and not only because I witnessed, close-up, very sharp wits in ideological conflict. My becoming a Trotskyist, rather than something else, was itself an accident. I knew nothing of radical politics when I entered City College, but I did have two friends from Boys' High who had accompanied me to college. We constituted a *troika* for the rest of our lives—the late Harold Lubin, Earl Raab, and myself. Earl was an esthete—he had, in high school, introduced me to the short stories of James Joyce and Thomas Mann; I was confused about my politics, so it devolved upon Hal Lubin to explore the ideological terrain and report back to us what kind of radicals we should be. In later life, as it happens, both Earl and I remained politically involved, while Hal opted out and became a professor of literature. But at the time, he was more serious, more passionate, and more optimistic about "creating a better world" than we were. When he explained to us that the Trotskyist student group was the most interesting and least tarred with the sins of Stalinism—it was the first I had heard of such sins—we promptly followed him into the Trotskyist "movement," as we then called the dozen or so young men who sat around, reading and arguing about radical politics. Young men, because City College in those days was an all-male institution, with our sexual energies finding an outlet in either study or politics.

But the larger Trotskyist organization was, thank goodness, coed. Shortly after I was graduated from City College, I was assigned to attend meetings of a "branch" of young Trotskyists in Bensonhurst, in Brooklyn, at the opposite end of the borough where I lived. I dutifully attended the meetings, which were quite farcical since we were trying to recruit young blacks in the neighborhood who were sensible enough not to take us seriously. But at these meetings I noticed a girl—she was eighteen, it turned out—who sat quietly at the other end of the small room. Her name was Gertrude Himmelfarb, but she was called "Bea." She had a trim figure and a strong, handsome face that radiated intelligence and sensibility. I noticed her for some weeks before approaching her and asking her out. In truth, I was already in love with her without even knowing her. She said "yes," quietly. And so we "went out," which is to say we went to the Saturday-night movies—in cosmopolitan Manhattan rather than provincial Brooklyn, and saw only foreign movies since we were cultural snobs. After our first excursion, I already knew that this was the girl I wanted to marry. After the third or fourth movie, I finally asked her to marry me; perhaps because she was weary of subtitles, she said yes. Thus began what my friend, Daniel Bell, later described as "the best marriage of our generation," a judgment I have no quarrel with. We are about to celebrate our fifty-third wedding anniversary.

In retrospect, it is interesting that it never even crossed my mind to suggest a "love affair," or a "relationship," or whatever other connection young people experiment with these days. Many of the young Trotskyists were bohemian in their "lifestyles," but that was not for me. Trotskyist or no, radical socialist or no, I was bourgeois to the core. I sought no sexual adventures or experiments, but wanted a girl to love and marry. Bea was of a like mind. We even waited a year to get her parents' consent—a consent withheld on the grounds that they were not about to permit their lovely and brilliant daughter to marry a young man who was earning $13.89 a week as an apprentice machinist. But when the Japanese bombed Pearl Harbor, and my salary had reached $22 a week, they relented. We were married on January 18, 1942, when she was nineteen and I was just short of my twenty-second birthday.

With such a bourgeois character, one which I seem to have been born with, it is not surprising that, shortly before this twenty-second birthday, I (and Bea) had left the Trotskyists—in a state of pleasant and intellectually productive disaffection, but with no regrets. I had received an excellent political education of a special kind. I made several lifelong friends. And I had gained a lifelong wife. That is why I don't really mind when some journalist, even today, a half-century later, casually refers to me as an "ex-Trotskyist." I regard myself as lucky to have been a young Trotskyist and I have not a single bitter memory. Even when Irving Howe "expelled" us for having had the ideological impudence to resign, I regarded it—and still do—as comic relief. Oddly enough, he never quite forgave me for leaving so many years before he did.

My subsequent army experience, as an infantryman in Western Europe, also had some significant, and on the whole benign, influences on me. I was shot at but not hit and, in what military historians call "battles," did my share of shooting, though in the confusion I doubt that I ever hit anyone or anything. When V-E day came, and I was transported to Marseilles for shipment to the Far East, so as to help conquer Japan, the atom bomb was dropped and such shipments ceased. My wartime experience in Germany, however, did have the effect of dispelling any remnants of antiauthority sentiments (always weak, I now think) that were cluttering up my mind. My fellow soldiers were too easily inclined to loot, to rape, and to shoot prisoners of war. Only army vigilance kept them in check. At the same time, observing German women and young girls, living among the rubble and selling their bodies for a few packs of cigarettes—the currency of the day—rid me of any anti-German feelings which, as a Jew, might otherwise have been present in me. Even the subsequent revelation of the Holocaust could not make me feel differently about ordinary Germans. They, too, had suffered—more than most Americans realize. And I was not so convinced that the American soldiers I knew were a different breed of humanity from their German counterparts.

I spent about a year in Marseilles, and it was a kind of postgraduate sabbatical. Because I was a college graduate I was assigned to headquarters, first in the library, where I pretended to understand the Dewey Decimal System, and then as chief company clerk. It was a small headquarters, a point of transshipment of American GIs going home, and I was assigned two young, intelligent prisoners of war who had been clerks in the German army. They were so much better than I in clerking that they were soon doing all the paperwork, leaving me to pursue my studies. My high school and college French stood me in good stead, needing only some refreshing to become usable. I spent my days reading French journals—*Les Temps Modernes, Critique, L'Esprit, Les Cahiers du Sud*, and others. I was especially fond of *Critique*, which gave excellent critical accounts of authors who were worth reading about but not worth reading. This went along with various philosophical-theological books by the likes of Jean Wahl, Rachel Bespaloff, and Lev Shestov, who made Kierkegaard's leap of faith seem like a modest hop. French intellectual life was then boiling over with a passionate interest in ideas. Existentialism was the rage and I became quite knowledgeable about that depressing philosophy, without however being depressed by it since it was intellectually so exciting. I even read a novel by Simone de Beauvoir that set my teeth on edge, which may have been her existentialist intention. Enjoying *anything*, including existentialism itself, seemed to represent for existentialists some kind of spiritual transgression.

When I returned, once again a civilian, to the States, where Bea was finishing her graduate studies at the University of Chicago, I was immediately informed that another sabbatical was in prospect. Bea had received a fellowship to go to the University of Cambridge to work on the papers of Lord Acton, the subject of her thesis. But before we left, one small thing happened that was to be of considerable importance to me. Bea told me of this new magazine that had been born in my absence, a "serious" (i.e., quite highbrow) Jewish magazine called *Commentary*, which actually paid as much as $100 for a contribution. I read what issues were available and decided that there was no reason I should not be a contributor. So I sat down and quickly wrote a very short story about my encounter with a young Jewish survivor in a Displaced Persons camp outside Marseilles. To my delight and astonishment, they immediately accepted it and promptly paid as well. This last was not unimportant, because we had calculated that Bea's fellowship money and what she had saved from my army allotment would give us a budget of $12 a week in Cambridge. *Commentary*'s fee added another $1.50 a week. What I could not foresee at the time was that the *Commentary* connection was to play such a crucial part in my life.

We really need not have worried about our English budget, since there was nothing to buy in Cambridge. Food was still stringently rationed, and we mostly lived on fish and chips or cheese sandwiches. Rent was cheap too, for our furnished room with toilet upstairs and a sink in the backyard. But this was the year of the coal shortage and the Great Freeze, so we slept in our overcoats and poor Bea, who had developed chilblains, had to wear gloves when she worked on the Acton papers lest her bloody fingers stain them. Being young, we shrugged all this off. Cambridge was lovely, positively exotic to our eyes, and we were leading the kind of bookish life that suited us. I started writing again, pieces on English affairs for *The New Leader* and a couple of book reviews for *Commentary*. I also wrote a novel, in a style that was a bastard mixture of Saul Bellow and Jean Giraudoux, whose novels I was then enchanted by. Fortunately, I never tried to get it published and eventually incinerated it. I knew in my bones that I was not born to be a novelist. Indeed, had it been published it would have been a major disaster for me, since I then almost surely would have wasted some years (perhaps even a lifetime) doing something I was not really suited for.

We returned to New York in 1947 with a couple of hundred dollars in the bank and no visible prospects. Bea wanted to write her thesis and I wanted a job that enabled me—in my spare time, if necessary—to keep on writing. Once again, my luck held out. My brother-in-law, Milton Himmelfarb, then a researcher at the American Jewish Committee (which published *Commentary*), told me that he had heard that *Commentary* was looking for a couple of junior editors. I promptly applied and was thrilled to learn that I had been accepted. My salary was $3,600 a year, more than enough to allow us to rent a dark two-room apartment on Broadway and 96th Street, immediately above a Bickford's cafeteria (now long since gone). The smells were awful but the neighborhood was fine—at last we had our own apartment, and in the heart of Manhattan, no less! Interestingly, it never occurred to us to look for an apartment in Greenwich Village. Bohemia held no attractions for us, though we were then childless.

My colleagues at *Commentary* were an extraordinary group:

• Elliot Cohen, the editor and founder, had edited *The Menorah Journal* at Columbia, to which his classmate Lionel Trilling contributed, and he then spent two decades in the bureaucratic wilderness of Jewish philanthropy. He was a thoroughly assimilated Southern Jew whose interest was in Jews, not Judaism. He was very intelligent and wrote well, in a somewhat florid style. I liked and respected him, while he had a kind of fatherly affection for me.

• Clement Greenberg, ten years older than I, was even then a prominent art critic. Clem, like Elliot, was interested in Jews (though not *very* interested) as distinct from Judaism. He wrote for *Partisan Review*, not for *Commentary*, and was our main link with the intellectual community around *P.R.* Because he could read German, he became the editor for a brilliant group of German-Jewish émigré writers (most notably Hannah Arendt). Though he had a reputation as having a terrible temper, leading even to an occasional brawl, we saw none of that. Toward his younger colleagues he was always genial, if distant. I recall vividly, for obvious reasons, his once offering to acquire for me a large Jackson Pollock painting for $10,000. It was a friendly gesture, but I declined. I didn't have ten thousand dollars, we didn't have space in our apartment for so large a painting, and I didn't like (still don't like) "abstract expressionist" art. That painting would today be worth millions. But, since I still don't like abstract expressionist art, I have never felt particularly regretful.

• Robert Warshow was, for me, the most troubling of my colleagues. We got along well enough—played poker together, that sort of thing—but he always made me feel uncomfortable. There was a hard, cold, almost affectless streak in him, clothed in the purest rationalism. Like Elliot and Clem, his interest in Jews was "ethnic" though, I always felt, as minimal as such an interest could be for an editor on a Jewish magazine. But he was a truly brilliant writer, with a cool, chiseled, powerful style that suited his talent and personality perfectly. He would write in longhand, in pencil, on a yellow pad, in a very large handwriting that permitted only six or seven lines a page, and when he brought in his essays to be typed they were letter perfect—no deletions, no additions, not even a correction in punctuation. I have never seen anything like it—it's as if every single word in the essay was preformed in his mind before he sat down to write. Several of those essays, mainly on popular culture—and there was very little serious writing about popular culture then—are deservedly famous today.

• Nathan Glazer, whom I had known at City College—he was a couple of years behind me—became one of my closest friends and remains so to this day. (He was later to succeed Daniel Bell as my coeditor of *The Public Interest*.) Intelligent, amiable, intellectually curious, he was a sociologist who was skeptical of most of what then passed for sociology, and established a valuable department, "The Study of Man," which summarized and criticized new trends in the social sciences. He also had a more intense Jewish background than Clem or Bob, and together we constituted the "Jewish" editors; I specialized in Jewish religious writing and he in the secular life of the Jewish community. We were also both more "political" than the others, having emerged from the ideological hothouse of City College.

• Richard Clurman, fresh from the University of Chicago, joined *Commentary* the same day I did. Bright and articulate, he was more interested in journalism than Judaism. We were not surprised when he left to work for *Time* magazine, where he had a distinguished career.

My position at *Commentary* brought me to the margin of the world of *Partisan Review*, since the two magazines overlapped one another on the political spectrum. Only on the margin, because the *P.R.* crowd was older than we were and far less bourgeois in what we now call their "lifestyle." Still, it was exciting to meet and get to know all these famous people I had been reading for the past ten years. My most vivid memory of our excursion into the world of *P.R.* occurred at a cocktails-and-buffet party at the apartment of William Phillips, the coeditor of the magazine. I had piled my plate with food and sat down in the middle of a couch, assuming Bea would join me there. Instead, what happened was this: Mary McCarthy sat down on my right, Hannah Arendt on my left, and then Diana Trilling pulled up a chair and sat directly opposite me. I was trapped, and I remember thinking, as I sank into a terrified paralysis of body and mind, that this was an event to remember. For the next hour, they argued about Freud and psychoanalysis while I sat there mute, not even touching my food lest eating seem like a rude intrusion into their high conversation. I kept wondering why my wife wasn't rescuing me, but she sat across the room eating and giggling. When the conversation finally broke up, I had not the faintest recollection of anything that had been said.

During my first years at Commentary, I wrote only on philosophy, religion, and occasionally on literature. My political views were what we would now call neoliberal, but I had no interest in expressing them. What brought me back into the world of political controversy was the extraordinary profusion of opinions sympathetic to, even apologetic for, the Stalinist regime in Russia among so many leading liberals. These opinions were dominant in The Nation, The New Republic, The New York Times, and Hollywood, so that anti-Stalinist liberals came to feel, as they were, an isolated group within the larger intellectual community. Eventually, I was sufficiently irritated to write a short political piece.

The occasion was a book by Carey McWilliams, a leading "progressive" and a very stylish writer. We had actually published an article by him in Commentary, on how "social discrimination"—e.g., barring Jews from membership in country clubs—was part of a larger pattern of discrimination that sustained the hegemony of a ruling class. I did not like the piece because I did not see why any Jew should want to join a country club where Jews were not welcome. (In truth, at that time I didn't see the point of anyone belonging to a country club.) But Elliot, the editor, understood that this was an issue that did matter to those wealthy Jews who, as leaders of the American Jewish Committee, financed Commentary. He was quite right; the article evoked a chorus of appreciative approval from the A.J.C. Since relations between the A.J.C. and Commentary were always under strain, our political posture being too anti-Communist for the more "mainline" liberal A.J.C. members, this was no small matter.

McWilliams' book was a slick, prototypical exposition of this "mainline" liberalism, studded with a disingenuous rhetoric that cleverly wedded this liberalism, in the most natural way, with a discrete apologia for Stalinist fellow-traveling. My Trotskyist background, as well as my reading in literary criticism, made it easy for me to dissect his rhetoric and reveal its underlying purpose. To my astonishment, the review was enthusiastically received by people whose opinions I respected. I was astonished because political writing was so easy that I had no idea it was, as seemed to be the case, in scarce supply—at least so far as "our side" was concerned.

Well, one thing leads to another. Encouraged by the reception of that book review, I wrote what was to be the most controversial essay of my career. It was 1952, and McCarthyism was the issue of the day. The problem for liberal intellectuals was to define an attitude toward the civil liberties of Communists. (There was, so far as I was concerned, no problem in defining one's opposition to Senator McCarthy.) Most "mainline" liberals, many of them "fellow travelers" in varying degrees, did not argue in favor of toleration of Communists as Communists—a perfectly acceptable opinion which I respected even if I didn't fully agree with it. They preferred to regard the question of whether anyone was or was not a Communist as an irrelevancy, since for them Communists were simply "progressives" who were more outspoken and militant than the rest of the breed. It was the disingenuousness, the hypocrisy, even the intellectual cowardice of such people that moved me to write my article in *Commentary*. In that article, I had a passing reference to Senator McCarthy as a "vulgar demagogue" who was making an impression on the American people because they knew him to be anti-Communist (as they were), whereas they knew no such thing about most of the leading spokesmen of the American liberal community. This was during the Korean war, a war in which as many American soldiers died as were later to die in Vietnam, and popular passions were high. And here were our leading liberals, many of whom were publicly suspicious of American motives in this war (though not of Communist motives), becoming passionate only in the defense of the civil liberties of American Communists, who openly supported the North Korean regime. My article dissected some of these leading liberal spokesmen, demonstrating that their ostensible concern for the civil liberties of Communists arose, more often than not, out of an ideological sympathy for Communists as "fellow progressives."

What a storm my article created! In truth, American liberals were so hysterical about McCarthy that they simply could not think straight about the issue I was addressing. My unforgivable sin, I subsequently realized, was in *not* being hysterical about McCarthy, whom I assumed to be a transient, ugly phenomenon with no political future. That I had no use for "witch-hunting" I assumed the readers of *Commentary* would take for granted. On the other hand, I did have the temerity to suggest that, while the American Communists had their civil rights under the Constitution, no American had a "right" to government employment, and the idea of "civil liberties" could not be stretched to give Communists, or even their loyal fellow travelers, such a right. Nor did anyone's civil liberties make him immune to public opprobrium. The Communists, after all, were a totalitarian group hostile to our constitutional democracy. How we defined their civil liberties was a matter of prudence, not principle. After the experience of the Weimar Republic this seemed to me a reasonable approach. Perhaps I didn't express these thoughts with the clarity they needed. But it would not have mattered, since most of my infuriated critics had an agenda of their own.

I survived the tumult and the shouting that article provoked because many prominent liberals thought that I had made a point worth making, one not at all offensive to an authentic liberalism which understood that there were indeed enemies on the left. The main effect was to define me publicly, for the first time, as a political writer with a voice of my own. The timing, as it happened, was not of the best. My situation at *Commentary*, after five wonderful years, had become intolerable. Elliot Cohen was in the process of having a nervous breakdown that would later cost him his life. I didn't understand the tragedy that was happening; all I knew was that his editorial interventions had become ever more capricious and arbitrary. As the managing editor, I found myself pinned between authors and editor, trying to negotiate acceptable solutions to the problems he was causing. Finally I felt so miserable that I had to resign. I came home and broke the news to Bea. She had news of her own: She was pregnant.

Job hunting was a new experience for me, and fortunately it did not last long. I applied for a position on *Fortune*, where a senior editor was an old friend of Elliot's who had become an acquaintance of mine. (He, too, had once been a Trotskyist!) He gently turned me down, essentially on the grounds that my kind of writing was too "highbrow" for them. Occasionally I wonder, with a shudder, what my life would have been like had they hired me.

It was Sidney Hook who came to my rescue, a practice he made a habit of doing for the rest of my life. Something called the American Committee for Cultural Freedom had recently been formed, associated with the Congress for Cultural Freedom in Paris. It was an organization of anti-Communist liberals with the mission of counterbalancing the pro-Communist liberals and *gauchistes* who were then so active in the intellectual worlds of the Western democracies, including our own. The position of executive director of the A.C.C.F. was then vacant and Hook, who liked my political writing, campaigned successfully to get the job for me. Apparently I was acceptable even to those liberals on the Committee who thought my *Commentary* article had gone somewhat overboard.

The next ten months or so were tedium interspersed with crises. The tedium was the administrative chores, which I coped with easily enough. (I have always found administration a much-overrated skill.) The crises were internally generated by a heterogeneous group of intellectuals whose common cause turned out to be not quite common enough. There was a small group on the right, led by James Burnham, who if not pro-McCarthy was certainly anti-anti-McCarthy. There was a much larger group on the center-left, led by Arthur Schlesinger Jr. and Richard Rovere, who believed the Committee should be, above all, actively anti-McCarthy. Somewhere in the middle were a handful of very articulate people, led by Diana Trilling, who were unhappy with the ideological posture of the Congress in Paris, which was anti-Communist but which, in an effort to appeal to the anti-Communist left, was not simply or belligerently pro-American. I mediated between these groups, not fully sharing the views of any in this respect—my guide was Sidney Hook, who was the Committee's moving spirit—but all such mediation could do was to put out one firestorm of controversy and prepare for the next. My only satisfaction was the organization of two public debates, the first (naturally) on the relation of religion to democracy (Paul Tillich vs. Sidney Hook), the second on "containment" vs. "liberation" in American foreign policy (Arthur Schlesinger vs. James Burnham). They were very good debates, attended by some five hundred people, and the Committee actually made some money on them. In the end, however, the spirit of factionalism was bound to prevail, as it always does among intellectuals with ideological passions and little political common sense.

I was about at the end of my tether and tenure when Sidney, once again, came to the rescue. The Congress, he informed me, was interested in starting an English-language cultural-intellectual-political magazine in Paris to counteract the predominant influence of anti-American and often Communist fellow-traveling magazines in all the democracies, not only of Western Europe but in Asia as well. Would I like to be considered for the position of editor? That question answered itself. The prospect of editing such a magazine, in Paris no less, made my head spin with anticipation.

I had not, at that time, met anyone from the Congress, so some interviewing was in order. I flew to Paris—well, from there on it's something of a blur. On either the first or second night Michael Josselson, the Congress's executive director, took me to dinner at the home of the ex-Communist novelist and critic Manès Sperber. I no longer recall who was there because after the appetizer of garlic-packed snails I passed out. (It turned out that I am allergic to garlic in large doses.) They laid me out on a dining-room couch, Sperber fed me some pills, and they proceeded to an evening of fine food and animated conversation while I lay on that couch, regaining consciousness intermittently in order to throw up. For the rest of my trip I was violently sick. I do recall going to London with Mike to have lunch at the Savoy with the leaders of the British Committee for Cultural Freedom, among them Malcolm Muggeridge, T. R. Fyvel, George Lichtheim, and Fred Warburg, the publisher (Secker and Warburg, as it then was). I recall, while at the table rather than the "loo," their making a very strong pitch for locating the magazine in London—bereft of a good literary magazine since the death of Cyril Connolly's *Horizon*—and for making Stephen Spender (a member of the British Committee but then away teaching in Cincinnati) my coeditor. Mike found their case very persuasive, especially after Muggeridge offered to raise the money for Spender's salary. So did I, though I really would have preferred Paris. Anyway, I staggered home to inform my wife that we would be living in London after all. She, being as much an Anglophile as I was a Francophile, was happy to hear the news. A month or so later, I flew to London to find a place for us to live, to rent a temporary office, and to hire someone to help put out the magazine.

That was early in 1953, shortly before the Coronation. I had committed myself to a first issue in October—for an untitled magazine that wasn't even on a drawing board. I recall T. S. Matthews of *Time*, then in London ostensibly to fund some kind of highbrow British magazine, telling me that I was being wildly unrealistic. In the event, my magazine came out on schedule; his never did.

I rented a shabby two-room office and hired a secretary-assistant, in the person of Margot Walmsley—a splendid woman, prematurely widowed, who stayed with the magazine until the bitter end, by which time she had become managing editor. (It also turned out that, on practically no money at all, she gave the liveliest cocktail parties at which all sorts of people showed up—some very interesting, some merely important.) The two of us put out our first issue. I solicited articles from my friends in the United States, Stephen—still in Cincinnati—wrote to his friends in London, we agreed on a title after much bickering, I found a printer and distributor, I designed a magazine modeled (with variations) on *Commentary*, and in the fall of 1953 the first issue did come out, as promised. The history of *Encounter*—including the CIA connection—has by now been well told by Peter Coleman in *The Liberal Conspiracy*, and told less well by others, so I shall say little about it. I do feel compelled to say, however, that my relations with Stephen Spender were, against the odds, quite good, all things considered. After all, he was ten years older than I, infinitely more distinguished, and was far more sensitive to the opinions of British literary circles than I was. So there was always the possibility of friction, a possibility that was realized less often than I had feared. A poet, a man of letters, and a gentleman, Stephen was absolutely no kind of editor. I ran the magazine, he made major contributions to it. He brought W. H. Auden and Isaiah Berlin to *Encounter*, and the imprimatur that resulted was significant. He also solicited the most famous article ever printed in *Encounter*—Nancy Mitford's "U and Non-U," which provoked the popular press to a frenzy of "research" into the class-specific usages of the British vocabulary. This was not exactly the kind of article that our publishers in Paris had in mind for the magazine, and they, like all non-Brits, were mystified by the commotion it caused.

The 1950s were, despite Suez, the golden decade of England's post-war history, and we were lucky to be there then. The dollar was strong and my modest salary—less so by British standards—went a long way. We lived in a succession of furnished houses and could even afford an *au pair* girl, which permitted Bea to continue her research and writing. Her biography of Lord Acton had already been published, to a laudatory review in the *Times Literary Supplement*, so she was of interest to the British in her own right. We made many friends, amid a host of acquaintances.

Very few of our friends and acquaintances came from Stephen's circle, the literary establishment. They were simply not my kind of people. There was never any serious intellectual or political talk at their parties, just malicious, witty—often brilliantly witty—gossip. I never felt more solemnly New York-Jewish than at one of these occasions, and never more bourgeois. They all seemed to have more money than we had, or at least lived more extravagantly and adventurously than we did. Many of them could fairly be called upper class, but those who weren't affected upper-class mannerisms and modes of speech. As an American, I was to some degree outside the British class system—but only to a degree. The thought of attempting an entry never crossed my mind.

Our closest friends, almost inevitably, were older Jewish ex-radicals who were now on *Encounter's* ideological wavelength and among whom we felt at home. These included Jane Degras, historian of the Comintern at the Royal Institute of International Affairs; T. R. Fyvel, who had been a close friend of George Orwell and who was now at the BBC; George Lichtheim, the fiercely independent neo-Marxist and anti-Communist; and Mark Abrams, who introduced opinion polling and market research to Britain. In addition, among the Labour M.P.'s—the very first politicians I had ever met in the flesh—there was Woodrow Wyatt, now a prominent conservative journalist who sits in the House of Lords; Anthony Crosland, who was trying to redefine socialism in terms of simple social and economic equality, and who was fascinated by the "City College sociologists," especially my friends Daniel Bell and Seymour Martin Lipset; and Denis Healey, who transfixed the visiting Lionel Trilling at dinner one night with his knowledge of contemporary literature, leaving me to disabuse Trilling of the notion that all Members of Parliament were like Healey. The only conservative M.P. we were friendly with was Angus Maude, who should have been Prime Minister, but his fellow Tories thought him to be far too intelligent for that responsible position.

There were, however, conservatives not in Parliament with whom we established ties of friendship. They included Malcolm Muggeridge, then editor of *Punch* and the *enfant terrible* of British journalism, and Michael Oakeshott, who succeeded Harold Laski in his chair at the London School of Economics and who was already on his way to becoming one of the most distinguished conservative thinkers of this century. By marrying, as it were, Oakeshott to Muggeridge, three gifted young Conservative journalists were born. They were Peregrine Worsthorne, Colin Welch, and Henry Fairlie, with all of whom we became fast friends. They had no counterparts in America at the time. And, of course, there was the steady stream of American visitors to enliven our days: Dan Bell, the Glazers, the Sidney Hooks, the Trillings, the Jason Epsteins, and numerous others.

In London, though our social life was politically ecumenical, my (and Bea's) evolving discontent with social democracy and liberalism continued. As an American and a coeditor of *Encounter*, I kept aloof from British politics—my writing for *Encounter* consisted of essays on Machiavelli, Tacitus, and the Marquis de Sade—but I found my conservative friends far more interesting than the others. I hadn't known any conservatives—as distinct from ex-radicals with budding right-wing opinions—in New York, and I was fascinated by the fact that they felt perfectly at ease with themselves as conservatives, neither apologetic nor unduly contentious. They were, after all, heirs to a long tradition of conservative politics and conservative thought in Britain, whereas there was no such tradition in the United States. Though in a distinct minority, they were accepted by society at large as having a legitimate place on the political spectrum. More than that, their claim to government could hardly be dismissed, with Winston Churchill still the overpowering figure that he was.

My discontent with social democracy *cum* liberalism had absolutely nothing to do with economics, of which I was perfectly ignorant. It did have to do with foreign policy, where I was, on general principles, a "realist" to the core, contemptuous of the Left's bland assumption that the class struggle was natural but that national or purely ideological conflicts were not. I was equally contemptuous of the Left's predisposition to see Communists as, in some sense, a wayward extremity of the Left, ultimately redeemable by therapeutic strategies. (My Trotskyist background stood me in good stead here.) The Cold War seemed to me not deplorable but inevitable. In contrast, the kind of liberal sentiments and thinking that went into the formation of the United Nations struck me as not at all inevitable and certainly deplorable. Even the so-called "right-wing" Labourites, who were friendly to *Encounter*, felt they had to be cautious in their anti-Communism, lest they appeared to be impugning their own socialist beliefs. For my own part, I found their socialist beliefs—especially the blind commitment to egalitarian politics across the board—ever more questionable. The prospect of the entire world evolving into a cheerless global Sweden, smug and unhappy, had no attraction for me.

Though we felt truly privileged passing these years in London, we had every intention of returning to America when the first opportunity presented itself. The longer we lived in Britain, the more American we felt. When our son, William, reached school age, we sent him to the French Lycée; we did not want him to return an imitation Brit. And when our daughter, Elizabeth, was born, we promptly registered her at the American Embassy. I sensed that, though life in England could then be more pleasant, in so many ways, than coping with the tensions of American life, I also sensed that British politics and British culture were becoming ever more provincial. The United States, it was easy to foresee, was going to be the place where the action was, and—somewhat to my own surprise—I felt keenly that I wanted somehow to participate in that action. We had good friends in London who, as American expatriates, made very decent lives for themselves. But not for a moment did we have even the most fleeting idea of emulating them. Oddly enough, the sphere of action I had in mind for myself was domestic politics rather than foreign affairs. I intuited, rather than knew, that after the Eisenhower interregnum we were living through, American politics was going to become a lot more interesting.

The opportunity to return came as the result of an intervention in our lives of an old friend, Paul Jacobs, then a staff writer for *The Reporter*. The editor of that magazine—I think it was Theodore Draper—had just left and the publisher and editor-in-chief, Max Ascoli, was seeking a replacement. Paul, then more sympathetic to *Encounter* then he was later to be, recommended me to Max, who was intrigued enough to bring me to New York for an interview. I went with trepidation because editors of *The Reporter* seemed to come and go, and Max was reputed to be a difficult man to work with. The meeting went well. I liked him. He was an Italian antifascist émigré who had taught at the New School for Social Research in New York before marrying Marian Rosenwald, a very wealthy woman whose family had founded Sears, Roebuck. I was actually familiar with some academic articles he had written, which pleased him. He was also pleased by my European experience and my personal acquaintance with Raymond Aron, Ignazio Silone (who coedited the Italian counterpart to *Encounter*), and Isaiah Berlin. He made me a generous offer and, eager to return home, I accepted. However things worked out, I reckoned, at least I would have some kind of head start in a career in the States.

We arrived in New York at the very end of 1958, rented a large, old apartment on Riverside Drive for $270 a month—Marian was shocked to learn that rents were so high—and quickly settled in. It did not take me long to learn that working with—in truth, under—Max Ascoli was as difficult as the reports would have it. He was kind, generous, and intelligent, but he was also egomaniacal, and sometimes tyrannical in behavior. He was also extremely snobbish. When I solicited and received a book review by George Steiner, then a young writer on the London *Economist*, Max was reluctant to publish it. But when he discovered that Steiner was the son of a well-known international banker, his attitude changed radically. We agreed that I was to be "reintroduced to America" by focusing at first on "the back of the book"—book reviews, the arts, cultural reportage—which seemed sensible enough. The trouble was that he wanted to keep me there. The political articles were his domain, over which he exercised a lordly sovereignty. Unfortunately, he was not really a good editor—his command of the English language left much to be desired—and in general he preferred second-rate contributors whose copy he could regard as raw material. Even more unfortunately, he regarded his long editorials, usually on the importance of NATO, as the magazine's centerpiece and very reason for being. Indeed, he bitterly resented any article that caused too much comment because it distracted attention from his editorials. He was always competing with his writers, and the only way he could win was to prefer the second-rate to anything better.

I first understood this clearly in the case of Daniel Patrick Moynihan. I was introduced to Pat, who was then teaching at Syracuse, by Bob Bingham, our managing editor, who had worked with Pat in the Democratic reform movement in New York City. He thought Pat might be a possible contributor, and so we had lunch. I was overwhelmed. Pat had enough wonderful ideas for articles to fill up his own magazine. We finally agreed that he would write a 4,000-word piece on automobile safety, an issue he had worked on when he was an assistant to Governor Averell Harriman. I had high hopes, but they fell far short of the reality when, a little more than a week later, I received a 10,000-word article on automobile safety that was an editor's dream. I wanted to publish it *in toto* and feature it, but Max wouldn't have it. The article was cut to perhaps 6,000 words and, when it attracted a lot of attention and won all sorts of prizes, Max was not at all happy. He soon made it clear that while he was willing to publish more Moynihan, it should not be too often and not at too great length.

I don't want to paint too bleak a picture. *The Reporter* was a better magazine than my own frustrating experience would suggest. It just wasn't a magazine where I could play a significant editorial role. The staff was friendly and I liked them. My friendship with Pat Moynihan flourished, and there was also this young researcher, Meg Greenfield, in whom I had an ally in trying to enliven the magazine. But after one year, I felt trapped and decided to leave. Max was understanding and gracious, gave me a generous severance payment, and once again I was without employment.

I knew exactly what I wanted to do next—to write a book that would be a critical examination of the evolution of the American democracy, a kind of sequel to Tocqueville and Henry Adams. For three months I read furiously, took a large bundle of notes, and then realized it was all an exercise in futility. I was not a book writer. I did not have the patience and I lacked the necessary intellectual rigor to bring my ideas into some kind of consistent thesis. I learned a lot in those three months, and it stood me in good stead in the years to follow. But I needed a job—and, fortunately, soon found a congenial one. Through a mutual friend, I was introduced to Arthur Rosenthal, publisher and editor-in-chief at Basic Books, a small publishing house specializing in psychoanalytical works. Arthur wanted to expand the list to include the social sciences, and that was my mission, first on a part-time basis but in the course of the next ten years as executive vice president of the firm.

Arthur was a wonderful man to work for, and never in those ten years did we have a serious argument. I did what I was supposed to do and I think I did it well. But it did not take me long to realize that though publishing was a business I could be passably good at, I lacked the kind of patience, passion, and commitment that is the mark of an authentic editor-publisher. Arthur had it; I didn't. I was exasperated by the fact that once you had wed a good idea to its potential author, it took two years at least for him to deliver a manuscript (often not the book you had had in mind in the first place), another year to get it edited and published, and then it might or might not sell for reasons which, so far as I could see, had little to do with its intrinsic merit or lack thereof. The cure for such exasperation was for me to do some writing on the side.

At that time, the Great Society was getting into full swing and I found myself increasingly skeptical of the liberal ideas behind it and of the programs they spawned. I started to write occasional "op-ed" pieces for *The New Leader*, making the arguments in support of my skepticism; but, increasingly, I felt that something more was needed. Not surprisingly, that "something more" took shape in my mind as another magazine. The only existing conservative journal, the *National Review*, was not to our tastes—at that time insufficiently analytical and "intellectual," too stridently hostile to the course of American politics ever since 1932. I discussed these thoughts with my friend Dan Bell, then at Columbia, who shared my skepticism though less from an ideological point of view than from that of a scrupulous social scientist. We even went around to a few wealthy individuals someone or other had put us in touch with, but they were immune to our enthusiasm.

It was not until the beginning of 1965 that a potential publisher appeared on the scene. At a dinner at Sidney Hook's, we found ourselves in the company of Warren and Anita Manshel. We had known Warren when, as a newly minted Ph.D. from Harvard, he had come to work in Paris for the Congress for Cultural Freedom. There he had met and married Anita, the daughter of a very successful Wall Street investor. He was now himself on Wall Street, struggling with boredom because his heart belonged to politics. I mentioned the magazine idea and he was interested. How much would it cost, he asked? I explained that, by my calculations, $10,000 could see us through the first year (i.e., four issues). The editors—Dan Bell and myself—would work *pro bono* (as they have ever since). He agreed to put up the money and became our publisher. Over time, in the following years, he invested much larger sums in what became *The Public Interest*, until such times as some foundations became interested in us.

I edited the magazine, the first issue of which came out in the fall of 1965, out of my office at Basic Books, with my secretary constituting the rest of the staff. For the first issues, I asked friends to contribute— Daniel Bell (my coeditor), Pat Moynihan, Nathan Glazer, James Q. Wilson, and others who I had reason to think were upset by the frothy ideological climate of the mid-1960s. One forgets just how frothy this climate was. The centerpiece of the War on Poverty was the sociological fantasy that if one gave political power to the poor, by sponsoring "community action," they would then lift themselves out of poverty at the expense of the rich and powerful. All of us at the core of *The Public Interest* had grown up in lower-middle-class or working-class households— unlike the academics who had authored the War on Poverty—and we knew that becoming politically militant was no way for poor people to lift themselves out of poverty. This, it seemed to us, was just a sociological echo of an older socialist idea that a "Great Society" could only come about as a consequence of class struggle.

There were many other such fantasies floating about at that time. One involved the threat and promise of "automation." We were, it seems, entering a "push-button" phase of human history, in which the economy would mechanically (or electronically) produce abundance, but in which no one would have steady work. What would all these people do? Thus arose the problem of "leisure" and how tens of millions of people, with time on their hands, could spend that time fruitfully. The Ford Foundation ran many conferences on this problem, and some very big books on "leisure" duly appeared. Lyndon Johnson even appointed a Commission on Automation. Fortunately, Dan Bell and the M.I.T. economist Robert Solow became members, and they shaped the final report to suggest that things would never be as good or as bad as imagined. It was his experience on this Commission that persuaded Dan there was urgent need for a journal like *The Public Interest*, and Bob Solow contributed a piece on "automation" to our first issue.

I designed the magazine the way I had designed *Encounter*: by borrowing from the format of existing or previous magazines and changing things around a little. What was important was that, given our lack of staff, it should be as "idiot proof" as possible. So the articles for the first issue came in, the printer delivered as promised, and there we were, with two thousand copies ready to be mailed to subscribers who had answered our ads as well as to a list of people who ought to have been interested. My secretary, Vivian Gornick, was an intelligent, pleasant young woman who had done graduate work in English literature. She had done the proofreading, dealt with the printer, and now she went down to the post office with a small truckload of copies to be mailed. But the post office refused to mail them—it turned out we had failed to get some necessary permits. Vivian came back in despair, and I was stumped. Then Vivian said that we should try again. It worked this time. Vivian simply sat on the loading dock, burst into tears, and the kindly older supervisor was so touched that he waived his objections. Shortly thereafter, Vivian wrote her first article for *The Village Voice* which launched her career as a feminist—an increasingly radical feminist—writer.

Though the founding of *The Public Interest* is generally seen in retrospect as the origin of "neoconservatism" (a term that had not yet been invented), the core group around the magazine still regarded themselves as liberal, if of a dissenting and revisionist bent. I was the most conservative of the lot, my British experience having exposed me to intelligent, thoughtful, and lively conservatives. But conservatism in the States at that moment was represented by the Goldwater campaign against the New Deal, with which none of us had any sympathy, and by *National Review*, which we regarded as too right-wing. The spectrum of opinion within our group was very narrow, with me slightly on the right, Dan Bell (ever loyal to his right-wing social-democratic background) on the left, and the rest somewhere in the middle. We considered ourselves to be realistic meliorists, skeptical of government programs that ignored history and experience in favor of then-fashionable left-wing ideas spawned by the academy. This was the original idea of the magazine, but events soon overtook us.

The major event of that period was the student rebellion and the rise of the counterculture, with its messianic expectations and its apocalyptic fears. It certainly took us by surprise, as it did just about everyone else. Suddenly we discovered that we had been cultural conservatives all along. This shock of recognition was to have profound consequences. We were bourgeois types, all of us, but by habit and instinct rather than reflection. Now, we had to decide what we were for, and why. Cool criticism of the prevailing liberal-left orthodoxy was not enough at a time when liberalism itself was crumbling before the resurgent Left. Nor were we the only ones to experience this sea change. The editor of *Commentary*, Norman Podhoretz, and most of the contributors to it, who had been moving left until 1965, now became our allies. As the New Left and the counterculture began to reshape liberalism—as can be seen by a perusal of *The New York Review of Books* and even *The New Yorker*—and, eventually, to reshape the Democratic party, disenchanted liberals began to find themselves harboring all kinds of conservative instincts and ideas. Something like a "movement" took shape, with *The Public Interest* at (or near) the center. It never really was a movement, however, since no organizational efforts were made or even thought of. It would more fairly be described as a current of thought, represented by not more than a few dozen people who were rather more articulate and familiar with ideological controversy than most conservatives at the time. The political implications of this current of thought were gradually to reveal themselves under the pressure of events. One such key event was the nomination of Senator George McGovern as the Democratic candidate in 1972, which in effect sent us—most of us, anyhow—a message that we were now off the liberal spectrum and that the Democratic party no longer had room for the likes of us. Though none of us was a Republican, and few of us even knew any Republicans, our political landscape was in the process of being transformed.

One important agent in this transformation was *The Wall Street Journal*, a newspaper that, at the time, few American intellectuals had ever seen, much less read. But it turned out that a young conservative journalist in their Washington bureau, Robert Bartley, had been reading *The Public Interest* and sensed that something of interest to conservatives—a fresh wind, as it were—was happening. He rang me up for an interview and in May of 1972 his article about *The Public Interest*, "Irving Kristol and Friends," appeared. It was favorable almost (but not quite) to the point of embarrassment, and suddenly we had national exposure. A few years later, Bob was appointed editor of the editorial and op-ed pages, and I became a frequent contributor to those pages. More important, the editorials themselves began to reflect, in some degree, the mode of thinking to be found in *The Public Interest*—analytical, skeptical, and implicitly ideological in a way we did not ourselves at the time appreciate.

At that time, I had already left Basic Books to become a Luce professor at New York University. (The appointment was largely due to vigorous lobbying by Sidney Hook.) I spent eighteen years as a professor there, as Luce professor and then John M. Olin Professor, and enjoyed it immensely—lots of free time, long vacations, and if one can avoid entanglement with departmental or faculty politics (as I was able to do), a generally easy life. I also found teaching to be a useful exercise, because it forced me to seek more coherence in my thinking than I was accustomed to. The title of "professor" was desirable too, because otherwise I ran the danger of being labeled a "journalist." But it will not come as a surprise to NYU to learn that most of my energy and attention were focused on the "real world," of which academia these days is a creaking and reluctant part.

Washington, D.C., on the other hand, is very much in the real world, in the sense that what it does matters a lot even though what it thinks can often be extraterrestrial. At that time, when I had already marked my fiftieth birthday, I had been to Washington only once in my life, and that was a one-day visit while I was on home leave from *Encounter*. (The goal was to persuade Walter Lippmann to contribute an article to the magazine; he was friendly but unobliging.) I was still very much a New Yorker, still as much a free-floating intellectual as a serious "policy wonk" in my thinking. But Bill Baroody Sr., head of the American Enterprise Institute, a small conservative "think tank" in Washington, had been reading *The Public Interest* and *The Wall Street Journal* and sensed that something new and enlivening was occurring. He got in touch with me, offered me an honorary title of "associate fellow" (or some such thing), and a connection was established.

At that time, AEI was concerned solely with economics and a defense of the "free enterprise system." But Bill himself had a much broader range of interests, which included religion, political philosophy, and the social sciences generally. The emergence of a new group of "neoconservative" intellectuals—the term was invented, in a spirit of contempt for "renegades," by the socialist Michael Harrington—intrigued and excited him. He calmly ignored the fact that not a single one of us was at that time a Republican, a fact that caused much outrage among Goldwater conservatives who were the main financial support for AEI. In the course of the 1970s and 80s, Bill made a determined effort to recruit "neoconservatives" to AEI, and did in fact recruit, early on, Jeane Kirkpatrick, Michael Novak, Ben Wattenberg, as well as many others as the years proceeded. His task was facilitated by the appearance on the scene of a rejuvenated Bradley Foundation and John M. Olin Foundation, now staffed by younger men and women who had been exposed to, and influenced by, "neoconservative" thinking. Among them special note has to be made of Michael Joyce of Bradley, who turned out to be an accomplished neoconservative thinker in his own right.

This was all taking place during the Cold War—a war, it is often forgotten, that was not so cold for the United States, which lost over 100,000 soldiers killed in Korea and Vietnam. On the whole, though I wrote critically of the liberal illusions embedded in the thinking of our State Department and the foreign policy establishment—illusions about the nature of foreign affairs generally and of Communist intentions in particular—it was writing done with my left hand, as it were. The illusions were so simpleminded, and the whole controversy over foreign policy so *intellectually* unchallenging. (*The Public Interest* dealt only with domestic policy, as a consequence.) I had had an excellent education in communism at City College and in my Trotskyist youth group, and I knew that if you took Marxist-Leninist doctrine as seriously as the Soviet leadership did, the broad outline of an appropriate American foreign policy almost designed itself. To be a "hard-liner" vis-à-vis the Soviet Union or another Communist regime meant that you were likely to be right far more often than wrong. Only people who believed themselves so clever as to be able to outwit those odds could come up with original views on the Cold War. Unfortunately, our universities are well populated by such types. More unfortunately, some of them ended up micromanaging American policy in Vietnam, with disastrous results.

My intellectual perplexities in the 1970s began to focus rather on economics. Until that time I took it for granted that John Maynard Keynes had discovered the secret of the "boom-and-bust" cycle that seemed to characterize a market economy, and I assumed that astute fiscal management by the government could reconcile economic growth and economic equilibrium. This assumption certainly seemed validated by the postwar experience—until the 1970s, that is. Then we found ourselves confronting simultaneous inflation and depression, and no one seemed to be able to explain it, much less know what to do about it. I decided with the greatest reluctance that "neoconservatism" could not blandly leave the economy to the economists, and that I personally had to become economically literate. So I took a sabbatical leave from NYU in the academic year 1976–1977, and we moved to Washington, where I became a visiting fellow at AEI while Bea formed a similar relationship with the Woodrow Wilson Center.

The timing was most fortuitous. The Ford Administration was winding down and, for the first time, I was able to see close-up the basic political impotence of traditional conservatism, which lived off Democratic errors but had no governing philosophy of its own—at least none that could strike a popular nerve among the electorate. There were many fine people in the Ford Administration, and by election time they were all defeatist, in the sense that they thought the Republican party would be better off out of office than in it. Their party had reached the end of the road—the post-New Deal road—and was floundering in a blind alley.

A fair number of these people came to AEI, as a kind of temporary haven. The economists among them were useful for my purposes, since they could help me understand the economic literature, old and new, that I was assiduously studying. But the men I formed the closest ties with were three newly unemployed lawyers—Robert Bork, Antonin Scalia, and Laurence Silberman—who have remained close friends to this day. AEI had no lunchroom at that time and so we "brown-bagged it" every day, munching on our hamburgers or sandwiches while talking about everything but law, for this would have excluded me from the conversation. Our main topics for discussion were religion (my permanent favorite) and economics, about which none of us knew as much as we would have liked. But it was clear to all of us that the Republican party would have to become more than the party of a balanced budget if it was to be invigorated. As it happens, there was an apostle of a new conservative economics right at hand, also spending a year at AEI. He was Jude Wanniski, and something called "supply-side" economics was his theme. He became a frequent member of our little luncheon group.

I had known Jude, then an editorial writer for *The Wall Street Journal*, for a couple of years previously, and had been largely responsible for his getting the foundation grant that brought him to AEI to write his book on supply-side economics. Jude had tried very hard to indoctrinate me in the virtues of this new economics, with partial success: I was not certain of its economic merits but quickly saw its political possibilities. To refocus Republican conservative thought on the economics of growth rather than simply on the economics of stability seemed to me very promising. Republican economics was then in truth a dismal science, explaining to the populace, parent-like, why the good things in life that they wanted were all too expensive. In the course of my new studies in economics, I had become aware that this naysaying economics originated with Ricardo and represented nothing less than a perversion of the optimistic economics of Adam Smith, an economic idea of capitalism I found far more congenial. It was Jude who introduced me to Jack Kemp, a young congressman and a recent convert. It was Jack Kemp who, almost single-handed, converted Ronald Reagan to supply-side economics. Ideas do have consequences, but in mysterious ways.

Economists, most of them Keynesian or neo-Keynesian, have given supply-side economics a bad name. That is because, with its emphasis on microeconomic incentives and disincentives, supply-side economics calls into question the entire structure of macroeconomic analysis and forecasting developed since World War II. Since something like half the economists in the United States today are macroeconomists—in academia, industry, and government—they are understandably irked when someone comes along to suggest that their intellectual efforts, some of them technically brilliant, are largely in vain when it comes to "guiding" the economy or making short-term forecasts. Such forecasts are right only by accident; if it were otherwise, Wall Street would be an infallible mechanism for making all investors rich. The essential goal of supply-side economics is to keep increases in government spending below the historical rate of growth of the economy, avoid needless government regulations, and keep tax rates low so as to encourage investment and sustain growth. After that is done, particular circumstances will intervene in unpredictable ways, but the preconditions for enduring, long-term growth will exist.

Neo-Keynesian orthodoxy has persisted in claiming that supply-side economics was tried and failed during the Reagan years, during which the budget deficit ballooned alarmingly. This is a false accusation. To begin with, the Democratic Congress, in a political frenzy, enacted much larger tax cuts than President Reagan originally requested. Then, for the rest of the decade the same Congress proceeded to make expenditures at a rate far above the rate of growth of the economy, so that even as government's revenues increased—as they did, despite the tax cuts—the deficit increased more rapidly. The reason these facts are either ignored or distorted is that liberal politicians, the liberal media, and a substantial segment of professional economists do not want to encourage people to think that the activities of government ought to be considerably more limited than they now are.

There is nothing wrong with supply-side economics but there is often something wrong with people attracted to it. These people are all too likely to think that if you follow the correct economic prescriptions, the polity will bloom with social and political health as well as greater economic well-being. But there is a lot more necessary for a healthy society and a healthy polity than solid economic growth—as we have discovered in the post-World War II decades. Just as erroneous economic actions by government can wreck a society and a polity, so erroneous moral and political beliefs can accomplish the same end, more indirectly but just as effectively.

And here, I think, is where what we call "neoconservatism" has made its major contribution in these past two decades. By enlarging the conservative vision to include moral philosophy, political philosophy, and even religious thought, it helped make it more politically sensible as well as politically appealing. Supply-side economics, in one version or another, offered neoconservatism an economic approach that promised steady economic growth—a *sine qua non* for the survival of a modern democracy. Neoconservatism, for its part, has provided traditional conservatism with an intellectual dimension that goes beyond economics to reflections on the roots of social and cultural stability. If the Republican party today is less interested in the business community than in the pursuit of the happiness of ordinary folk, and if—as I think is the case—this has made the party more acceptable and appealing to the average American, then I believe the work of neoconservative intellectuals has contributed much to this change.

In 1987, Bea and I made another major decision: to retire from our professorships, at the City University of New York and New York University, respectively, and move—along with *The Public Interest*—to Washington, D.C., where I would become a senior fellow at AEI. We were, and to a large extent remain, New Yorkers, but we found life in New York not only disagreeable in the details of daily living but boring as well. That our children and grandchildren were in D.C. was surely a large consideration, but I do believe we would have made the move anyhow. New York is the national center of the arts, the communications media, and finance, but if you are keenly interested in public policy, as we had gradually become, D.C. is the place to be—especially since public policy these days has its own cultural and intellectual aspects.

There were two other reasons behind the move. First, most of our New York friends in the academic and journalistic worlds had exited our lives, through either retirement or death, and we had little contact with the generation that replaced them. Second, we found ourselves more and more isolated politically, as a result of our shift toward conservatism. New York is a one-party town, where liberalism and the Democratic party unite to establish a regnant orthodoxy. Conservatives are mainly found in the financial community, and their outlook tends to be narrow.

We found ourselves more and more uncomfortable at dinner parties, where we were regarded as exotic curiosa. In Washington, there is no shortage of conservatives and Republicans, and of necessity there is a degree of comity between liberals and conservatives that is unknown to New York. Perhaps this situation will change, but it is my perception that while Washington is a pleasant place in which to live, New York has become ever more unpleasant. And while New York intellectual and cultural life becomes ever more parochial and sterile—witness what is happening to the *New York Times*, which used to be a national newspaper— Washington inches along toward greater hospitality toward the life of the mind. Or so it seems to me. So today we are "Washingtonians," joining a growing population of New York transplants.

Even before moving to Washington, however, I did have one final idea for a new magazine I would like to be involved in, one that was to be located in Washington. As I have noted, *The Public Interest* dealt only with domestic affairs. But as the Soviet regime showed signs of unraveling, it became clear to me that some kind of post-Cold War foreign policy would be needed. Such a policy would have to steer its own course between Wilsonian internationalist utopianism and a "pragmatism" that was little more than opportunism. In short, I foresaw a "neorealist" foreign policy journal that would complement the "neoconservatism" of *The Public Interest*. The idea for such a magazine took shape in the course of discussions with Owen Harries, an Australian political scientist, former Australian Ambassador to Unesco, now an American resident, and one of the wisest analysts of foreign policy. He was willing to be the editor of *The National Interest* (as it was to be called), while I would be merely the publisher, watching over the budget. The first issue appeared in the fall of 1985, and it is now, together with the long-established *Foreign Affairs*, the leading journal in its field.

Washington is not only the political center of the nation, but the government center as well. This is both good and bad. To see close-up how government operates in both domestic and foreign affairs—how it must operate under the rule of law—is to appreciate how complex modern government is and how difficult it is to bring about political change. That's good, since to listen to the TV news or read the newspapers is to experience a radical simplification. What is bad is the natural tendency to get too closely involved in the problems of government and lose sight of the larger issues of politics, issues concerning what kind of country we want to be and what kind of lives we want to live in it.

In the past three decades, Washington has witnessed a surge of intellectual vitality. This is largely the result of the formation and growth of "think tanks"—conservative, liberal, and left-of-center. Washington's universities play only an ancillary role in this, since they are more teaching universities than research centers. And, it has to be said, the tendency among the think tanks is to focus on governmental activities, especially those affecting the economy. Still, with every passing year this focus is of necessity broadened to include such social issues as crime, illegitimacy, family problems, education and other such matters that neoconservative social scientists have been especially prominent in highlighting. There is even a growing attention to cultural issues (e.g., the condition of the humanities and the arts). AEI, under Christopher DeMuth, exemplifies this wider focus. So it is far more possible than it used to be to lead a perfectly civilized life as well as an active life in Washington. And, of course, it is still the most gracious and beautiful city in the nation, which is why people hate to leave it. The recent modest decline in Washington's population is exclusively the result of middle-class black people moving to the suburbs.

So here I am and here we are. I conclude this memoir on my seventy-fifth birthday and a few days after our fifty-third wedding anniversary. Looking back, I am astonished how intellectually twinned Bea and I have been over the years—pursuing different subjects while thinking the same thoughts and reaching the same conclusions. And not only Bea and I but our children. An intellectual memoir like this necessarily short-changes some of the most important and engrossing facts of life, such as children. I have been fortunate to have children, Bill and Liz, who are not only dear to me because they are my children, but who also happen to be gifted, interesting, and—even more remarkable—intellectually and politically congenial. And they, in turn, have managed to marry spouses who are equally gifted, interesting, and congenial. Susan Scheinberg Kristol is a classicist by training and a magnificent mother to her three children. And Liz, who still manages an occasional piece of sparkling criticism while caring for her two very young children, is married to Caleb Nelson, currently a law clerk for Clarence Thomas.

If I am, as is sometimes said of me, a cheerful conservative, it is because I have much to be cheerful about. So far at least, all of our family is right here with us in Washington. Bea has just published her tenth book and only a cataclysm of some kind will slow her down. I, on the other hand, have definitely slowed down simply because writing commentaries about current affairs interests me less. I am happy to leave such work to my son Bill, who is in any case the better political scientist. I find myself far more interested in the problems of American civilization, or even Western civilization, than in American politics as conventionally defined, and I am more intrigued by the problematical aspects of modernity itself than in our current social issues. One of these problematical aspects is the relation of our religious-moral traditions to the secular-rationalist culture that has been imposed upon them.

And where stands neoconservatism today? It is clear that what can fairly be described as the neoconservative impulse (or, at most, the neoconservative persuasion) was a generational phenomenon, and has now been pretty much absorbed into a larger, more comprehensive conservatism. My son and daughter and son-in-law and daughter-in-law, along with dozens of young "interns" who have worked at *The Public Interest* over the past thirty years, are now all conservatives without adjectival modification. They have, I should like to think, keener intellectual and cultural interests than was once common among conservatives. There are even "conservative intellectuals" today to whom the media pay attention, something that didn't exist fifty years ago.

So I deem the neoconservative enterprise to have been a success, to have brought elements that were needed to enliven American conservatism and help reshape American politics. But my personal opinion is hardly authoritative, and I am well aware that the unanticipated consequences of ideas and acts are often very different from what was originally intended. That, I would say, is the basic conservative axiom, and it applies to conservatives as well as liberals and radicals.

1995

SECTION II

Race, Sex, and Family

2

Welfare: The Best of Intentions, the Worst of Results

In 1835, Alexis de Tocqueville submitted an *Essay on Pauperism* to the Royal Academic Society of Cherbourg. The *Essay* addressed itself to a striking contemporary paradox: Why, in the most "opulent" (we would say, more timidly, "affluent") nation in the world—that is, England—was there such an extraordinary problem of "pauperism" (what we would now call "welfare": poor people on poor relief)? In France and Spain and Portugal, he pointed out, the people were all much poorer than in England; and the average Spaniard was poor even in comparison with the English pauper on poor relief. But in none of these poorer countries was there a "pauper problem" of the kind that agitated English society and English politics. How could one account for that "apparently inexplicable" phenomenon?

"ENOUGH"

Tocqueville's answer was twofold. First, urbanization and industrialization made the poor more dependent on public charity for a minimum level of subsistence. In an agrarian economy, it was only in rare periods of famine that the poorest rural laborer could not get enough to eat—"enough" meaning here simply a diet that would avert starvation. In contrast, the poor in a modern city have no such normal, minimum

43

guarantee; they are therefore in frequent need of public assistance, if they are to keep body and soul together.

Second, in an "opulent" society, the idea of poverty itself undergoes a continual redefinition. The poor experience not only the need for a guaranteed minimum; they also suffer from what a modern sociologist would call "relative deprivation." Tocqueville puts the matter this way:

"Among civilized peoples, the lack of a multitude of things causes poverty. . . . In a country where the majority is ill-clothed, ill-housed, ill-fed, who thinks of giving clean clothes, healthy food, comfortable quarters to the poor? The majority of the English, having all these things, regard their absence as a frightful misfortune; society believes itself bound to come to the aid of those who lack them. . . . In England, the average standard of living a man can hope for in the course of his life is higher than in any other country of the world. This greatly facilitates the extension of pauperism in that kingdom."*

But Tocqueville did not stop with this explanation—a persuasive and not particularly controversial explanation—of why wealthy nations have so many "paupers." He went on to assert that public assistance and "pauperdom" existed in a symbiotic relationship, and he predicted that each would nourish the other, that both would inexorably grow. Behind this remarkable prediction was a view of human nature. "There are," he wrote, "two incentives to work: the need to live and the desire to improve the conditions of life. Experience has proven that the majority of men can be sufficiently motivated to work only by the first of these incentives. The second is only effective with a small minority. . . . A law which gives all the poor a right to public aid, whatever the origin of their poverty, weakens or destroys the first stimulant and leaves only the second intact."

At this point, we are bound to draw up short and take our leave of Tocqueville. Such gloomy conclusions, derived from a less than benign view of human nature, do not recommend themselves either to the twentieth-century political imagination or to the American political temperament. We do not like to think that our instincts of social compassion might have dismal consequences—not accidentally but inexorably. We simply cannot believe that the universe is so constituted. We much prefer,

---

*Tocqueville and Beaumont on Social Reform, edited by Seymour Drescher, Harper Torchbooks.

if a choice has to be made, to have a good opinion of mankind and a poor opinion of our socioeconomic system. We shall, for instance, be more sympathetic, if not to the specific argument, then at least to the general approach of *Regulating the Poor: The Function of Public Welfare* by Frances Fox Piven and Richard A. Cloward, recently published by Pantheon.

MYSTERY

Professors Piven and Cloward, both leading "activists" in the Welfare Rights Movement, have written a valuable book—but, alas, a confusing one. The confusion results from the two purposes they have in mind.

The first purpose, which they achieve in an excellent and even masterly way, is to answer the same question that perplexed Tocqueville: Why has there been such a fantastic "welfare explosion" in the United States? Specifically, why has there been such an extraordinary growth in our welfare population *after* 1964—after, that is, unemployment began to move down toward the unprecedented (in peacetime, anyway) low level of 3.5 percent? Between 1964 and 1968, we had general prosperity of a kind not known since World War II.

This prosperity was not, of course, shared equally by rich and poor, white and black; but all did demonstrably and substantially share in it. Nevertheless, it was precisely during those years that the "welfare explosion" took place.

I do not think it is sufficiently appreciated by the public at large just how baffling this event was to our scholars and our policymakers in Washington. For half a decade, our best minds puzzled over the statistics, held innumerable conferences to discuss them, and got nowhere. The only serious effort at explanation was made by Daniel Patrick Moynihan, in his famous and brilliant memorandum on the Negro family, in 1965. He called attention to the fact that most of the new welfare recipients were in the Aid to Dependent Children category, that a growing proportion of families in this category were black and fatherless, and that the disorganization of the Negro family seemed to have gathered a sociological momentum of its own—a momentum impervious to the effects of improving economic circumstances. *Why* this was happening to the Negro family, however, Mr. Moynihan could not convincingly explain. This permitted a great many liberal-minded scholars to spend all of their energies attacking him rather than the problem.

But, eventually, any social phenomenon yields up its mystery. Or, to put it another way: Eventually, all social observers, no matter how blurred their vision may be by tacit ideological presuppositions, come to see the obvious. We now know what caused the "welfare explosion." I would also say—though this topic is still exceedingly controversial—that we are coming to realize what has been causing the disorganization of the Negro family.

All the facts are lucidly and authoritatively presented by Professors Piven and Cloward. Unfortunately, they have felt compelled to wrap their findings in a thin, transparently false general theory of welfare in a capitalist society.

This general theory is so simpleminded, so crude in a quasi-Marxist way, that one is embarrassed to summarize it. I will therefore let the authors state it for themselves:

> . . . Relief arrangements [under capitalism] are not shaped by the impulse to charity . . . [they are] created and sustained to help deal with the malfunctions inherent in market economies.
>
> Relief arrangements are usually initiated or expanded in response to the political disorders that sometimes follow from the sharp economic downturns or dislocations that periodically beset market systems. The purpose of relief-giving at such times is not to ease hunger and want but to deal with civil disorder among the unemployed. Once stability is restored, however, the relief system is not ordinarily eliminated. Instead, it is reorganized to buttress the normal incentives of the labor market. This is done in two ways. The main way is by cutting the "able-bodied" off the rolls, whether or not there are jobs, and whether or not the wages offered are sufficient for survival. Second, some of those who cannot work or who are not needed in the labor market are allowed to continue on the relief rolls, but they are treated so barbarously as to make of them a class of pariahs whose degradation breeds a fear and loathing of pauperism among the laboring classes.

Now, the objections to this theory—on historical, sociological, and economic grounds—are too numerous to mention. But one objection ought to be definitive: It does not explain what Piven–Cloward elsewhere in the book explain so well—that is, the "welfare explosion" of the 1960s. True, this "welfare explosion" coincided with rioting in the black slums. But according to the general theory, the poor in the black

slums should not have been rioting at all, since the economy was boom-
ing and black unemployment was at an all-time low; and if they did riot,
it should have been because they were being pushed off welfare into low-
paying jobs. In fact, they were rioting while they were going *on* welfare in
ever-increasing numbers—and while welfare payments were being
increased, not while they were being cut back.

The true explanation of the "welfare explosion" is available to any
reader of *Regulating the Poor* who will ignore the authors' general theory.
(This is easily done: Once they have stated the theory, they happily forget
all about it when discussing the 1960s.) This "explosion" was created—
in part intentionally, in larger part unwittingly—by public officials and
public employees who were executing public policies as part of a "War
on Poverty." And these policies had been advocated and enacted by many
of the same people who were subsequently so bewildered by the "welfare
explosion." Not surprisingly it took them awhile to realize that the problem they were trying to solve was the problem they were creating.

Here, as related in Piven–Cloward's book, are the reasons behind the
"welfare explosion" of the 1960s:

1. The number of poor people who are eligible for welfare will
increase as one elevates the official definitions of "poverty" and "need."
The War on Poverty elevated these official definitions; therefore, an
increase in the number of "eligibles" automatically followed.

2. The number of eligible poor who actually apply for welfare will
increase as welfare benefits go up—as they did throughout the 1960s.
When welfare payments (and associated benefits, such as Medicaid and
food stamps) compete with low wages, many poor people will rationally
prefer welfare. In New York City today, as in many other large cities, welfare benefits not only compete with low wages; they outstrip them.

3. The reluctance of people actually eligible for welfare to apply for
it—a reluctance based on pride or ignorance or fear—will diminish if an
organized campaign is instituted to "sign them up." Such a campaign was
successfully launched in the 1960s by (a) various community organizations sponsored and financed by the Office of Economic Opportunity, (b)
the Welfare Rights Movement, and (c) the social work profession, which
was now populated by college graduates who thought it their moral duty
to help people get on welfare—instead of, as used to be the case, helping

them get off welfare. In addition, the courts cooperated by striking down various legal obstacles (for example, residence requirements).

In summary, one can say that the "welfare explosion" was the work, not of "capitalism" or of any other "ism," but of men and women like Miss Piven and Mr. Cloward—in the Welfare Rights Movement, the social work profession, the office of Economic Opportunity, and so on. It would be nice to think that the "general theory" in *Regulating the Poor* was devised mainly out of an excess of modesty.

CONNECTION

It should be emphasized that Piven–Cloward think the "welfare explosion" is a good thing. They believe more people should be on welfare and that these people should get far more generous benefits than now prevail. One would expect, therefore, that this book would have a triumphant tone to it. Yet it does not. Indeed, it ends rather abruptly, in a minor key.

The reason, one suspects, is that even Piven–Cloward must be less than certain about what they have accomplished. Somehow, the fact that more poor people are on welfare, receiving more generous payments, does not seem to have made this country a nicer place to live in—not even for the poor on welfare, whose condition seems not noticeably better than when they were poor and off welfare. Something appears to have gone wrong: A liberal and compassionate social policy has bred all sorts of unanticipated and perverse consequences.

One such perverse consequence, and surely the most important, is the disorganization and demoralization of the Negro family. It used to be thought that a generous welfare program, liberally administered, would help poor families stick together. We now find that as many poor black families are breaking up *after* they get on welfare as before they got on; and that, in general, the prospect of welfare does nothing to hold a poor family together. Mr. Moynihan was percipient in emphasizing, back in 1965, that there was a connection between family disorganization and the influx of poor black female-headed families to welfare. What we can now see is that the existence of a liberal welfare program might itself have been responsible, to a significant extent, for this family disorganization.

UNMANNED

One must emphasize here that the question of race or ethnicity is of secondary importance. It is true that the Negro family has experienced historical vicissitudes that make it a relatively vulnerable institution. But it is also probable—I would go so far as to say certain—that if the Irish immigrants in nineteenth-century America had had something comparable to our present welfare system, there would have been a "welfare explosion" then, and a sharp increase in Irish family disorganization, too. The family is, in our society, a vital economic institution. Welfare robs it of its economic function. Above all, welfare robs the head of the household of *his* economic function, and tends to make of him a "superfluous man." Welfare, it must be remembered, *competes* with his (usually low) earning ability; and the more generous the welfare program, the worse he makes out in this competition.

Is it surprising, then, that—unmanned and demoralized—he removes himself from family responsibilities that no longer rest on his shoulders? That he drifts out of his home—or is even pushed out of his home—into the male street corner society of the slum? One wonders how many white middle-class families would survive if mother and children were guaranteed the father's income (or more) without the father's presence? And how many white middle-class fathers would, under these circumstances, persist at their not-always-interesting jobs?

To raise such questions is to point to the fundamental problems of our welfare system, a vicious circle in which the best of intentions merge into the worst of results. It is not easy to imagine just how we might break out of this vicious circle. One might suggest, however, that we begin by going back and reading Tocqueville more respectfully. We may not find the truth in him; but the exercise may help liberate us from our own twentieth-century illusions.

1971

3

The Tragedy of "Multiculturalism"

It is difficult, and even dangerous, to talk candidly about "multicultural-ism" these days. Such candor is bound to provoke accusations of "insen-sitivity" at least, "racism" at worst.

Even some of the sharpest criticisms of multiculturalism are content to limit themselves to demonstrating how "illiberal" it is, how it violates traditional ideas about the substance of liberal education, and how it represents a deplorable deviation in the way our young Americans, so heterogeneous in their origins, are to be educated to live together. This criticism is certainly valid and welcome. But it also implicitly concedes too much by going along with the assumption that there really is such a thing as multiculturalism—i.e., a sincere if overzealous effort by well-meaning educators to broaden the horizons of the conventional curricu-lum. Such educators doubtless exist, but their efforts end up being the victims of a far more aggressive mode of multiculturalism.

Though the educational establishment would rather die than admit it, multiculturalism is a desperate—and surely self-defeating—strategy for coping with the educational deficiencies, and associated social patholo-gies, of young blacks. Did these black students and their problems not exist, we would hear little of multiculturalism. There is no evidence that a substantial number of Hispanic parents would like their children to know more about Simon Bolivar and less about George Washington, or that Oriental parents feel that their children are being educationally deprived because their textbooks teach them more about ancient Greece than about ancient China.

AFTER-SCHOOL INSTRUCTION

To the degree that there is any such sentiment in these minority groups, it can be coped with in the traditional way—by a few hours a week of after-school instruction for their children, privately arranged. (At the college level, of course, instruction in the relevant languages, literature, and history has always been available.) But most adult Hispanics and Orientals do not have any such concern. They are fully preoccupied with the process of "Americanization." The "roots" these groups seek are right here in the U.S., not among the Aztecs or in the Ming dynasty.

Most Hispanics are behaving very much like the Italians of yesteryear; most Orientals, like the Jews of yesteryear. Because of differences in cultural background, their integration into American society proceeds at different rates—but it does proceed. The process is not without pain and turmoil, but it works. Ironically, and sadly, it has not worked so well for American blacks, among the earliest arrivals. Hence, out of desperation, the turn to multiculturalism.

Multiculturalism comes in varying kinds and varying degrees of intensity. A child may come home from elementary school knowing more about Harriet Tubman than about Abraham Lincoln. This can be disconcerting to white parents and baffling to Hispanics or Orientals, but presumably they can shrug it off as a transient phenomenon. The question is: Do such trivial pursuits of worthy but relatively obscure racial ancestors really help black students? There is no evidence that it does. In theory, it is supposed to elevate their sense of "self-esteem," as individuals and as blacks. But genuine self-esteem comes from real-life experiences, not from the flattering attention of textbooks.

In fact, as is well known by now, the problems of young blacks do not arise in our schools, nor are they remediable there. They are the product of their homes and environments—a terrible social problem, not an educational problem. But this does not prevent our overly ambitious educational establishment from engaging in a pretense of offering "solutions." In addition to promoting self-esteem among young blacks—our white students already have a wildly inflated notion of their academic capabilities, as researchers have demonstrated—it seeks to promote appropriate "role models" in the school. "Role models" and "self-esteem" are now crucial terms in the psychobabble of the educational world.

Actually, hiring more black male teachers is a good idea. But it has nothing to do with the provision of role models. Just as fathers in the home are very important as a source of moral authority, so black male teachers can be a useful source of authority in the school—especially when the home has no father. They can help make a school a more orderly and decent place. But just as fathers play their part without a thought of being role models, so do black male teachers play an equivalent part.

Role models are largely a sociological fantasy. We all, when young, have known (or have known of) adults whom we respected and admired—until, with time, their images fade as our interests shift. Very few of us have gone through life gazing at role models we have known. And, unfortunately, there is as yet little evidence that black teachers have a significant, differential effect on the academic achievements of black students.

It is in its most intense and extreme form, however, that multiculturalism is on its way to being a major educational, social, and eventually political problem. This version is propagated on our college campuses by a coalition of nationalist-racist blacks, radical feminists, "gays" and lesbians, and a handful of aspiring demagogues who claim to represent various ethnic minorities. In this coalition, it is the blacks who provide the hard core of energy, because it is they who can intimidate the faculty and the administration, fearful of being branded "racist." This coalition's multiculturalism is an ideology whose educational program is subordinated to a political program that is, above all, anti-American and anti-Western.

It is no exaggeration to say that these campus radicals (professors as well as students), having given up on the "class struggle"—the American workers all being conscientious objectors—have now moved to an agenda of ethnic-racial conflict. The agenda, in its educational dimension, has as its explicit purpose to induce in the minds and sensibilities of minority students a "Third World consciousness"—that is the very phrase they use. In practice, this means an effort to persuade minority students to be contemptuous of and hostile to America and Western civilization as a whole, interpreted as an age-old system of oppression, colonialism, and exploitation. What these radicals blandly call multiculturalism is as much a "war against the West" as Nazism and Stalinism ever were.

Under the guise of multiculturalism, their ideas—whose radical substance often goes beyond the bounds of the political into sheer fantasy—are infiltrating our educational system at all levels. Just as bad money drives out good, so the most intense versions of an ideology tend to color and shape the less intense.

CONCESSION AFTER CONCESSION

It is now becoming ever more common within the American educational system for increasing numbers of young blacks to learn that what we call "Western civilization" was invented by black Egyptians and feloniously appropriated by the Greeks, or that black Africa was a peaceful, technologically advanced continent before the white Europeans devastated it. Such instruction can only inflame an already common belief among blacks that "white America" and its government are deliberately fostering drug addiction and diabolically tolerating the AIDS virus in the black community. Multiculturalism, as its most ardent proponents well understand, is a technique for "consciousness raising" by deliberately stroking this kind of paranoia.

One does not wish to be apocalyptic—though thoughtful and honest teachers may be forgiven for thinking their world is coming to an end. Most of those who tolerate or even advocate multiculturalism in our schools and colleges have educational, not ideological, intentions. But the force is with the extremists, who ride roughshod over the opposition by intimidating it with accusations of "racism." So the opposition timidly makes concession after concession, while seeking shelter in anonymity.

Recently, a journalist telephoned five leading professors of Egyptology, asking them what they thought about the claim of a black Egyptian provenance for Western civilization. They all said it is nonsense. At the same time, they all withheld permission for their names to be attached to this risky, "politically incorrect" position.

There is no doubt that today, multiculturalism is beclouding and disorienting the minds of tens of thousands of our students—mainly black students. It is not an educational reform. It is an educational—and an American—tragedy.

1991

4

Reflections on Love and Family

The *Washington Post* struck a new note in American journalism on Dec. 27. Its lead front-page story, reporting President Bush's appointment of Barbara Franklin as Secretary of Commerce, ended its opening sentence with the observation that he was "adding a third woman to his male-dominated Cabinet as he begins his reelection campaign."

A male-dominated Cabinet? I have had many thoughts about President Bush's cabinet, not all of them complimentary, but I confess to not having noticed that it is "male-dominated." Even now that this fact has been called to my attention, I don't know quite what to make of it. Does the current composition of the cabinet mean that it is "biased" in favor of males and against females? Are we all supposed to share the radical feminist view that the relation between the sexes can be reduced to a struggle for power, whose goal, in the case of men, is domination, while for women it is "equal representation" via "affirmative action"?

THIRD WOMAN

In any case, Ms. Franklin is now the third woman in the Cabinet. Quick: Name the other two! Well, never mind, it's the numbers that count, not the mere human identities. At least that is what the White House seems to have been intimidated into thinking. For, as the *Post* also noted, the appointment is surely linked to President Bush's reelection campaign.

54

Incredibly enough, there are highly paid professional politicos in the White House who do think along such "affirmative action" lines, and who believe that adding a woman to the Cabinet will attract female votes, that appointing a black will attract black voters, that a Hispanic appointee will attract Hispanic voters, and so on down the line.

The media myth of "multiculturalism" has so overpowered their political imagination that they are oblivious to both experience and common sense. Experience tells us that the media will broadcast its own interpretation of such appointments, to the effect that conservative women do not really represent their sex, any more than conservative blacks or Hispanics really represent their respective racial and ethnic groups. And common sense informs us that the overwhelming majority of Americans are much too busy with their own lives to pay attention to the sexual, racial, or ethnic identity of cabinet appointees, most of whom will soon lapse into invisibility. Where are the Cavazoses of yesteryear? He was, you will surely not recall, President Reagan's Secretary of Education.

Though I clearly have no sympathy with the militant (by now conventional) feminist notion that relations between the sexes are, above all, power relations, there are aspects of contemporary feminism that do evoke a sympathetic response in me. I do believe that it is a good idea for men to learn, once again, how to be gentlemen and to treat women as ladies—with courtesy and sensitivity. I think men should behave this way even to feminists who are appalled at the thought of being considered ladies.

In that same issue of the *Post*, Nat Hentoff has a most interesting column that touches on this issue. It seems that, in a classroom at the Schuylkill campus of Pennsylvania State University, there hangs a large reproduction of Goya's "Naked Maja," a beautiful nude woman lying on a couch. An English professor, Nancy Stumhofer, has had the painting removed because, she says, she felt embarrassed and uncomfortable teaching with that painting behind her. Actually, the painting was simply moved to the TV-reading room of the student center, where it will presumably help students concentrate on their studies.

It seems to me that Professor Stumhofer's feelings were perfectly understandable and her reaction—removing the painting—perfectly justifiable. But various members of the faculty and a number of students attacked the removal as a species of "censorship." Mr. Hentoff himself, who is a fanatic on the First Amendment, feels that any discomfort to female students caused by the painting, and any erotic fantasies provoked among the males, "might have been an opportunity for the professor . . . to get a class discussion going as to why a painting of a nude woman led certain members of the class to behave that way." Can it really be that he doesn't know?

The interesting question is how on earth that painting got there in the first place. Apparently it was placed in the classroom 10 years ago, as part of a ripple on the tide of "sexual liberation." This impulse toward regarding sex as something "perfectly natural" and nonproblematic had its origins in certain superficial dogmas about human nature sanctioned by pop psychology.

"Sexual liberation," as it emerged in the 1950s, has turned out to be—as it was destined to be—a male scam. Easy, available sex is pleasing to men and debasing to women, who are used and abused in the process. Nevertheless, the agenda of a candid, casual attitude toward sex was vigorously sponsored by feminists who mistakenly perceived it as a step toward "equality." Even today there are some laggard feminists who are firmly persuaded that mixed dormitories and mixed bathrooms on a university campus represent such a step. But true equality between men and women can only be achieved by a moral code that offers women some protection against male predators—and all men are, to one degree or another, natural predators when it comes to sex.

It is not surprising, therefore, that we are witnessing today a new feminism that is a reaction to "sexual liberation." One of the forms it takes is the lesbian movement, now so extraordinarily popular on some college campuses. Another such form is a hostility toward pornography as well as a keen sensitivity to a phenomenon known as "date rape." This reaction, like all such reactions against an extremist social absurdity, has its own ugly features and is capable of distorting and destroying lives. But, then, so did the "sexual liberation" against which it is in rebellion.

Having survived several decades of ridicule and scorn by the same people who brought us "sexual liberation," the nuclear family is now once again respectable, even popular. Unfortunately, this popularity is promoted by those same (or similar) pop psychologists and their Hollywood screenwriters who haven't the foggiest idea of what real family life is about but are determined to counsel us as to its virtues. Inevitably, their counsel is specious and has a particular political spin.

The new pop gospel for the family is all about "love." Parents are supposed to go around telling their children, "I love you," and children are supposed to respond in kind. The other night, I saw on a television sitcom a 10-year-old boy come down for breakfast and kiss his mother and father before sitting down to eat. Surely not even in Hollywood do 10-year-old boys behave that way. Had I ever tried it, my mother promptly would have taken my temperature.

Families are not about "love," but about sensed affection plus, above all, absolute commitment. Children do not yearn for "love," they desire and need the security that comes from such an absolute commitment, spiced with occasional demonstrations of affection. That is why children are so incredibly loyal to parents and grandparents who, by Hollywood standards, may seem to be unloving. My grandfather's household was Orthodox Jewish, and he showed affection for us by sometimes putting a hand on our shoulder and smiling, while saying absolutely nothing. His children and grandchildren were in awe of him and thought him to be the finest man in the world. The commitment on both sides was unconditional. Was that an "unhealthy family?"

SENSE OF PIETY

Why this sentimental emphasis on "love" in the household? My guess is that our popular culture, having spent years disassembling the family as a sociological institution, is now trying to reconstitute it as a purely voluntary association based on personal feelings. But the family in real life is based on impersonal feelings. We do not honor our father and mother because of the kinds of persons they are, but because they are our father and mother. We do not recognize their authority because they, in any sense, "deserve" it. We do so—and we are pleased to do so—out of a natural sense of piety toward the authors of our being.

But natural authority and natural piety are anathema to our culture, both popular and "highbrow." To take them seriously is inherently "traditional," and this could lead to—well, a conservative predisposition, God forbid. That is why our culture today is trying so desperately to re-create the family as a lifelong love affair. Alas, lifelong love affairs are even rarer than lifelong marriages.

1992

5

Men, Women, and Sex

When one's ideological certitudes give birth to a world that is different
from what one anticipated, this is normal and consistent with the natural
order of things. For the world is always recalcitrant about our certitudes,
and our ability to shape the future is never as powerful as we think. Even
Madison and Jefferson, at the very end of their lives, had cause to worry
whether the nation they had helped create four decades earlier had not
wandered from its original destiny. But the Americans of the 1830s had
few such doubts. The American republic was a popular success, even if it
wasn't quite the republic Jefferson and Madison had dreamed of. If an
ideology is robust and realistic enough, the eventual imperfections in its
realization are no cause for disillusionment.

But what happens when one's ideological certitudes give birth to a
world that is the *opposite* of what was anticipated? That is what happened
to 20th-century communism, with results we are now familiar with. And
that is what is happening to our liberal certitudes about sex—about the
proper relations between the sexes, and the role of sex in a civilized
community.

A CONTRARY REALITY

Who would have thought, back in 1950, that we would today be handing
out condoms to high school students in a desperate (and surely doomed)

58

attempt to stem the astounding increase in teenage pregnancies? Is that what "sex education" has come to? Who would have thought we would be witnessing an alarming increase in venereal disease (including a fatal venereal disease, AIDS)? Who anticipated an incredible upsurge in male homosexuality and lesbianism? Who could have imagined that our sexually liberated popular culture would be featuring movies of sexual aggression, with men engaged in serial murders of women and women killing men to protest sexual oppression? This is entertainment?

If one goes back and reads the "progressive" literature on sex from 1900 on, none of this was anticipated and all of it would have been regarded as impossible. Moving closer to our own time, if one goes back and consults the extensive literature on "sexual liberation" that emerged in the 1950s and 1960s, one can say flatly that this set of ideological certitudes has produced an absolutely contrary reality. "Repressions" and "taboos" are gone, and free sex seems to be generating anxiety and anger and misery without end. A century of liberal social thought about men, women, and sex lies in ruins about us.

One can understand and even sympathize with the fervor of this "progressive" movement when it is seen against the background of Victorian repressiveness of sexuality, and especially of women's sexuality. But if one limits oneself to this perspective, one fails to understand that Victorian morality, which actually antedated Victoria's inauguration by several decades, was in its own way a phenomenon of "women's liberation"— which is why Victorian women were so much more insistent on this morality than were the men. There were rebels, of course—modern feminism was born in the Victorian era. But this feminism was focused on a demand for equality of legal and political rights. When it came to sex, most Victorian feminists—always a minority—were just as "prudish" as their nonfeminist sisters.

Victorian women were close enough to the pre-Victorian age to see, as we cannot, the clear benefits the Victorian ethos bestowed on women generally. True, this ethos idealized women in an absurdly unrealistic way—put them, in theory at least, on a pedestal. And living on a pedestal is the kind of life sentence that real women can find intolerable. On the other hand, it has its advantages over living in the gutter, which is where most women struggled to survive prior to the Victorian elevation.

From the plays of Shakespeare to the novels of Fielding, the distinction between a tiny minority of aristocratic "ladies" and a vast majority of "women"—if young enough, "wenches"—was accepted as a matter of course. "Ladies" were never beaten by their husbands. "Women" commonly were. What the Victorians did was extend the category of "lady" so that all women could potentially enter it, and so that all middle-class and lower-middle-class women were in fact automatically enrolled. That all women could be "ladies" was a bold Victorian invention. So, indeed, was the parallel notion that you didn't have to be born a gentleman to be one. You could become one by education and self-improvement. And one of the marks of a gentleman was to treat ladies with respect.

There are still remnants of this Victorian ethos occasionally to be seen today, though mainly among those beyond a certain age. When men stand up when a lady enters the room, when they offer their seats on a bus or train to a standing lady, when they hold the door for a lady to precede them—all those little acts of deference define a relationship between a "lady" and a "gentleman." It is a relationship that our younger, more "liberated" generations find close to incomprehensible, even indefensible. Women today are keenly interested in "equal" rather than deferential treatment. As for men—well, let a college president announce what used to be a cliche, that one of the purposes of a university is to produce "gentlemen," and he will be laughed out of his profession.

But what has replaced the ladies–gentlemen relationship as a norm for relations between the sexes? Freedom, confusion, and disorientation, all embellished with a veneer of "equality." Sex is indeed natural, as our progressives keep telling our young. But the equation, natural = innocent, is a modern fantasy. In reality, sex is the least innocent of human transactions. That is why it needs to be guided by rules that circumscribe this relationship in a civilized way.

It is a fact of our human nature that casual sex is likely to be demeaning to women—at least to most women, most of the time. The "dating game" as it is now played is rigged in favor of men. For men, the sexual act can represent a neat combination of power and pleasure, with the woman an agreeable "sex object." For women, it tends to be suffused with more generalized human emotions, and there are not many women who want to go to bed with sex objects—though, if they feel they have no choice, they will.

Our media, trapped in a progressive mode of thinking about sex, keep desperately trying to pretend that this difference does not exist. So do our universities, as they blithely crowd their students into mixed dorms, even mixed shower rooms. In both cases, we are presented with the myth of modern, liberated women, usually pursuing a professional career, who can "handle" sex as easily, as calmly, as confidently as their male counterparts are presumed to do. It is a myth that has ruined countless lives.

It is the unreality of this myth that fuels the energy of a radical feminism—i.e., antimale feminism—so that the sexual act itself appears as a form of sexual oppression. It also helps inspire the lesbian movement, about which there is little that is gay. Both are reactions against the ideology of "sexual liberation"—but, still imprisoned as they are within this ideology, they dare not say so.

Take the current fuss about "sexual harassment." Those of us who have memories of an earlier time have no trouble understanding that women are insisting that men should behave more like gentlemen, less like predatory boors. But our modern women can't say this, because it suggests that they might wish to be treated like "ladies," and they have been taught that there is something invidious in the categories of "ladies" and "gentlemen." Instead, they fall back on their "right" as individuals not to be subject to sexual aggressiveness.

"Rights" seems to be the only acceptable language today. The trouble with this rhetoric is that it creates confusion. It tells men that they are to treat women with respect and circumspection—but without explaining why women's sexual identity merits such treatment.

Or take the issue of pornography, which has split the feminist movement wide open precisely because no one can figure out what "rights" are being violated by it, while the apologists for pornography can point to their rights under the First Amendment. Now, no one can doubt that pornography is degrading to women. It does not, however, violate their "rights." What it does is debase the womanhood of women. But within the dominant ideology this too is unsayable.

THE TWO FREUDS

The history of the ideology of "sexual liberation" remains to be written. But there is no question that the popularization and vulgarization of the writings of the early Freud played a major role. It is he who taught us that our sexual discontents were distortions inflicted upon us by our

older inhibitions and taboos. Most Americans, and certainly all "enlightened" Americans, still seem to believe that. It is too bad that they have
never consulted the writings of the later Freud—notably "Civilization
and Its Discontents."

Freud reversed himself as he came to the realization that a degree of
sexual repression was the very source of civilization itself. He still distinguished, to be sure, between neurotic repression and rational social
repression. But our culture seems to have lost the intellectual and moral
capacity to make (and live with) such fine distinctions.

1992

6

AIDS and False Innocence

Why is Magic Johnson regarded by our media as some kind of moral hero, even a role model for the young? Mr. Johnson, a basketball player of extraordinary talent, has tested HIV positive, as a result—he tells us—of having been sexually promiscuous with more than 200 women. One or some of these women were infected with the HIV virus. As a result, a brilliant career has been cut short, as has a life. It is a sad story, to which compassion and pity are appropriate responses. But it is also a sordid story of a man defeated by his unruly sexual appetite. So why are we being asked to see him as an innocent victim, courageously coping with adversity?

There are such innocent victims, to be sure. There are people who have been infected with the AIDS virus as a result of receiving a tainted blood transfusion. There are some who have contracted the disease from their bisexual husbands or lovers and have then transmitted it to their children. And then there are all those drug addicts who have used tainted needles—though, since they are also active purveyors of the virus to their sexual partners, there is some reason to question their innocence.

A FOOLISH, RECKLESS MAN

In any case, Magic Johnson cannot claim the status of an innocent victim. He knew, or should have known, the risk he was running. Moreover, it is very probable that, in the course of his promiscuous pursuits, he has infected others, either directly or indirectly. He is a foolish, reckless man who does not merit any kind of character reference. So why is he being presented as such a glamorous person, worthy of respect—even of adulation?

This question is part of a larger question. Why are all victims of AIDS treated as innocent victims when so many are responsible for their condition by their own actions? It is this idea of innocence, associated with AIDS, that legitimates all those celebrity fundraising parties to help the victims of the disease. It is, similarly, this idea of innocence that encourages the victims themselves to organize public demonstrations, exhibitions, and protests—all of which receive respectful attention from the media, our politicians, our educators. And, of course, it is this idea of innocence that stimulates the strident demands that government spend more and more money on AIDS research, even though research on AIDS is now more generously funded than research on cancer, which claims a far greater number of victims.

What, it is time to ask, is so special about AIDS that its victims are automatically cocooned in innocence and endowed with indignant self-righteousness? After all, AIDS is not some kind of exotic disease striking at random. The AIDS epidemic has its roots in certain forms of human behavior, and it is this behavior that sustains and magnifies the epidemic.

AIDS is a venereal disease that seems to have been born out of homosexual anal intercourse. Just why and how this happened remains a puzzle, since such a sexual practice has been with us forever while the disease is (or at least seems to be) new. But what is not a puzzle is why we have an AIDS epidemic—why the disease has spread so fast and is claiming so many victims.

The epidemic character of the disease was first established by reason of homosexual promiscuity, and has since been accelerated by sexual promiscuity in general, as victimized women became carriers in their turn. Absent such sexual promiscuity there would still be AIDS, but nothing like an AIDS epidemic.

The arithmetical connection between AIDS and promiscuity—what in the 19th century would have been called the "arithmetic of woe"—is obvious. The more promiscuous you are, the greater the risk of finding yourself, one day, testing HIV positive. Couples who are monogamous—and this holds true whether they are homosexual or heterosexual—are at little risk. A few sexual encounters increase the risk noticeably, but still keep it at a modest level. A larger number of sexual encounters means a much larger risk. A very large number of sexual encounters is a near-certain prescription for AIDS. One of the reasons homosexuals are so much more vulnerable to the AIDS virus is that, for reasons that remain unclear, homosexuals tend to be significantly more promiscuous than heterosexuals. Or at least they used to be. Today, one has the impression that heterosexuals are trying to catch up.

Nevertheless, any pointed reference to the relation of sexual promiscuity to AIDS is not to be found in the media or among our educators. It is repressed because it might seem to be "judgmental"—i.e., having a moral connotation. When *Newsweek* recently had a cover story on AIDS among teenagers, it recounted the sad tale of an 18-year-old girl, a high school graduate, who aimed at a career in the military. Tests, however, revealed that she was HIV positive. Further inquiries by the doctors revealed that, in the previous twelve months, she had had sexual encounters with 24 different men! This is a seemingly average, cheerful, ambitious girl. And what did *Newsweek* have to say about such promiscuity? Nothing, absolutely nothing. It reported the facts but strenuously avoided any suggestion that she had been wrong in her behavior. The tone of the story was such as to imply that her mistake was in not insisting that those men practice "safe sex."

Is it any wonder that the HIV virus is spreading among teenagers? In Washington, D.C., two thirds of tenth-grade boys and one fifth of tenth-grade girls report that they have recently had four or more sex partners. These youngsters are a recruiting pool for our AIDS population. Confronted with the grim shadow of AIDS, educators can think only of distributing condoms and appealing for "safe sex." But promiscuity, especially among the young though among adults as well, will always overwhelm "safe sex." Men and women who are casual about sex are not likely to be scrupulous about the details.

In general, the notion that men and women, especially young men and women, in the midst of sexual arousal, will always remember to disengage and observe some moments of clinical detachment leading to precautionary action—well, one suspects that propagandists for "safe sex" have lost touch with the real world of passionate behavior. Such a businesslike attitude toward sex may prevail among some (though surely not all) adults. It has little to do with the majority of Americans, who practice "safe sex" by limiting the numbers of their sexual partners.

Why is it, then, that in our sex education programs, and in our popular culture as well, the dangers of promiscuity are hardly ever mentioned? The argument against teaching chastity, that it is "unrealistic" in today's "liberated" cultural climate—a debatable thesis, some would say—does not hold for promiscuity, after all. One could have a tolerant, benign view of sex among the young—as all teachers of sex education do—while stressing the advantage of fidelity over promiscuity. But the idea of fidelity, like the idea of promiscuity, has no place in education for "safe sex." The words themselves are meticulously avoided, along with the ideas.

What is at work here is not science, and not education properly understood, but ideology. For a century now, the liberal-progressive point of view has had, as one of its basic premises, a belief in the original innocence of human nature and a profound resentment against the "distortions" that society and its traditional values have imposed upon it. One such distortion is "sexual repression," which leads to all sorts of neuroses, all sorts of aberrant behavior, all sorts of social problems. Since it is society that causes this state of affairs, it is pointless to expect individuals to be capable of responsible behavior. We would then be "blaming the victim."

LIBERATION FROM VALUES

Similarly, the well-established connection between homosexual promiscuity and AIDS must be ignored, lest a bias toward "traditional family values" filter into public discourse. Liberation from such values and a rediscovery of humanity's original innocence are necessary preconditions for achieving the liberal-progressive vision of a more decent and humane world.

It is to secure this vision that otherwise sensible people are frantically handing out condoms to fourteen-year-old kids—something that, only yesteryear, they would have regarded as absurd. But AIDS has imported a new, destructive element into this vision, one that could challenge one of the very foundations of progressive liberalism itself. And that is why AIDS has become a special object for compassionate, generous treatment in our culture and politics. The victims of AIDS are, in truth, the victims of the liberal-progressive ideology, which is now mobilizing opinion in its self-defense.

It is fair to say that never has "liberal guilt" been so honestly earned.

1992

7

Life Without Father

One of the incontestable findings of modern social science is that fathers are Very Important People. I confess to having been astonished to discover just how important we are. Important in all sorts of unexpected ways. Thus, it turns out that almost two thirds of rapists, three quarters of adolescent murderers, and the same percentage of long-term prison inmates are young males who grew up without fathers in the house. I doubt that many fathers have understood that their mission in life had anything to do with the prevention of rape, murder, or long-term imprisonment among their sons.

There are other pertinent statistics. When a father is present in the household, teenage girls get pregnant 50 percent less frequently than their fatherless counterparts. Just why this is so is not clear, though it is highly doubtful that it results from heart-to-heart, educational talks about sex. In addition, children in a mother–father household are less likely to drop out of school, get involved with drugs, be delinquent, or—and this is a surprise—suffer child abuse.

The new focus on the father derives mainly from the realization that the social pathologies exhibited by families on welfare, or in the "underclass" generally, have a lot to do with the fact that these are so often fatherless families. (It may also flow from a sense of disquiet among the middle classes at the discovery, from our statistical data, that even divorced parents—even when they are remarried—create problems for their children.)

"YEAR OF THE FATHER"

So it is that *Newsweek* has declared this to be "The Year of the Father," explaining that "fathers have become almost mythic figures—manning (as it were) the barricade safeguarding America against further decay." It then goes on to quote Vice President Al Gore urging us to "instill in the next generation of fathers the belief that fatherhood is a sacred trust." Just how this is to be done goes unmentioned; except for *Newsweek's* pious exhortation on the need for fathers to be more like mothers, to "nurture" their families and to appreciate the need for "paternal love."

But just how do fathers "nurture" their families? What does that mean in practice? And how are fathers to generate and display the necessary "paternal love"? Television, of course, has not hesitated to give us the answer.

On its family series and soap operas, television portrays the ideal father envisaged by the liberal imagination. He hugs his children, assures them that he loves them, guides them through their homework, is actively involved in all their extracurricular activities, etc. These fathers, of course, are generally upper-middle-class professionals, with the ability to share "quality time" with their children. Such fathers, when they exist, are to be treasured. But in no sense are they "ideal" fathers, against which all other versions of fatherhood are to be judged. Too many fathers are exhausted and/or distracted by their work, or simply lack the requisite gregarious personality. But they can be, and usually are, "good fathers."

A good father has two characteristics. First, he is *there*, a loyal member of the household. Second, he works to help support his family. The fact that his wife may also work, part-time or full-time, is irrelevant. While she *may* work, he *must* work, because fatherhood and work go together. Whether he spends "quality time" with his children, "nurturing them," loving them, is of far lesser importance. We do not live in a unisex world. Children may adore their fathers, but if it is love they seek, they will usually prefer to go to mother.

To be sure, it presumably makes a difference to the quality of life in a household whether the father is frequently away from home, whether he has time to spend with his children, whether he accompanies them on family excursions. All of this will surely matter to his marriage, but seems to matter less to his role as father. So far as his children are concerned, the basic issue is whether or not he visibly exists, a presence in the household, a symbol of security and stability, even if he is a traveling salesman or an executive who is away from home a good part of the time.

As the son of immigrant parents, I—like others of my generation—can offer personal testimony on this point. My father never did any of the things that, according to the "parenting" wisdom of today, are supposed to be so important. I don't recall him ever hugging me, or kissing me, or telling me that he loved me. (Had he done so, I would have been embarrassed.) I don't recall ever having an extended conversation with him. He never read to me—his command of English was too imperfect and, in any case, there were no children's books in our house. He worked long hours, leaving the house before 6 a.m. and returning at 7 p.m.; in the evening, he was too tired to do more than chat with my mother, leaf through the newspaper, and listen to the radio while dozing off. He was always calm and genial—but distant—in demeanor, and was thought by all our relatives and his fellow workers to be wise, and fair, and good. I thought so, too. He was, and remains in memory, a version of the good father. And I never felt the need for a better one.

Fathers must work—in a sense, that is the most "fatherly" thing a father does. And the reason there is now so much discussion of "welfare reform" is the dawning realization that welfare edges the father out of his role as "breadwinner."

As things now stand, welfare benefits are so high that it is very difficult for a potential father without a high school education to compete with them. (And it is also important to remember that the job market may not find today's high school diploma to be the equivalent of a high school education.) It's not that those welfare benefits are high by middle-class standards; they are not. Most people on welfare are truly poor. The trouble is that they are no longer among the working poor, which is why their families are aborted or disintegrate.

In many of our larger states, welfare literally outbids the biological father for the responsibility—and privilege, as it was once thought to be—of supporting his wife and child. A beginning salary of $5 an hour, or $6 an hour, or even $7 an hour, will not support his "family" as well as welfare does. Unless he is passionately and independently committed to a "work ethic," he will opt out. In every society we know of, the work ethic tends to crumble before such competition. The potential fathers and husbands are "unmanned," and they then assert their manliness by fathering more out-of-wedlock children.

Moreover, it is important to realize that even in those states where the level of welfare is lower, the difference between what a father can earn and the income from welfare is too small. If welfare (with associated benefits) comes to $8,000 a year, and the father earns $10,000 a year, that means, in effect, that he is working—often at a not very agreeable job—for $2,000 a year. Unless the father has a prior, powerful commitment to the family, he is unlikely to take his job all that seriously.

Such a prior, powerful commitment to the family is most notable among many of the newer immigrants. The father works (sometimes at two jobs), the mother may work part-time, and the children, if they are of age, add marginally to the family's income by working after school. Welfare is avoided as shameful. It all adds up to the traditional American story, from poverty to somewhere in the middle class in one generation. Where on earth do these people get the perseverance to climb this hard and rocky road?

HEALTHY SKEPTICISM

The answer is twofold. Most of these immigrants come from poor nations where a welfare state is embryonic, if it exists at all, and a "welfare psychology" has not yet emerged. They believe in the old cliche, which my mother used to say to me: "Remember, the world doesn't owe you a living." They are therefore skeptical of those politicians and advocates of the "helping professions" who assure them of the opposite. They suspect a trap—and, of course, they are right.

Second, they come from more traditional societies where American popular culture, with its contempt for any kind of deferred gratification, has not yet shaped their imagination. They may watch television but remain well aware of the difference between seductive fantasy and recalcitrant reality, and are still capable of enjoying the one without losing sight of the other—as Americans used to be. Their children inevitably will be "Americanized," but by then they will be on their way to a self-supporting life.

This symbiosis of a welfare state and a popular culture basically hostile to the "work ethic," the savings ethic, and other such "bourgeois" virtues, is what is ravaging American society today. Welfare reform, if it is to be meaningful, will have to cope with both these forces. One cannot simply rely on economists for guidance, nor can one rely on those who are simply (or passionately) concerned with "social issues" and moral reformation. To cope with this terrible problem we have created for ourselves, we shall need some kind of political union between these two forces. Such a union, were it to occur, would create a powerful—probably irresistible—agenda for American politics.

1994

SECTION III

From Adversary Culture to Counterculture

8

American Intellectuals and Foreign Policy

A recent letter to the *New York Times*, complaining about the role of the academic community in opposing President Johnson's Vietnam policy, argued that "it is not clear why people trained in mathematics, religion, geology, music, etc., believe their opinions on military and international problems should carry much validity." And the letter went on: "Certainly they [the professors] would oppose unqualified Pentagon generals telling them how to teach their course."

One can understand this complaint; one may even sympathize with the sentiments behind it. The fact remains, however, that it does miss the point. For the issue is not intellectual competence or intellectual validity—not really, and despite all protestations to the contrary. What is at stake is that species of power we call moral authority. The intellectual critics of American foreign policy obviously and sincerely believe that their arguments are right. But it is clear they believe, even more obviously and sincerely, that *they* are right—and that the totality of this rightness amounts to much more than the sum of the individual arguments.

An intellectual may be defined as a man who speaks with general authority about a subject on which he has no particular competence. This definition sounds ironic, but is not. The authority is real enough, just as the lack of specific competence is crucial. An economist writing about economics is not acting as an intellectual, nor is a literary critic when he explicates a text. In such cases, we are witnessing professionals

75

at work. On the other hand, there is good reason why we ordinarily take the "man of letters" as the archetypical intellectual. It is he who most closely resembles his sociological forebear and ideal type: the sermonizing cleric.

Precisely which people, at which time, in any particular social situation, are certified as "intellectuals" is less important than the fact that such certification is achieved—informally but indisputably. And this process involves the recognition of the intellectual as legitimately possessing the prerogative of being moral guide and critic to the world. (It is not too much of an exaggeration to say that even the clergy in the modern world can claim this prerogative only to the extent that it apes the intellectual class. It is the "writing cleric," like the "writing psychoanalyst," who achieves recognition.) But there is this critical difference between the intellectual of today and the average cleric of yesteryear: the intellectual, lacking in otherworldly interests, is committed to the pursuit of temporal status, temporal influence and temporal power with a single-minded passion that used to be found only in the highest reaches of the Catholic Church. Way back in 1797, Benjamin Constant observed that "in the new society where the prestige of rank is destroyed, we—thinkers, writers, and philosophers—should be honored as the first among all citizens." The only reason Constant did not say "we intellectuals" is that the term had not yet come into common usage.

It is simply not possible to comprehend what is happening in the United States today unless one keeps the sociological condition and political ambitions of the intellectual class very much in the forefront of one's mind. What we are witnessing is no mere difference of opinion about foreign policy, or about Vietnam. Such differences of opinion do exist, of course. Some of the most articulate critics believe that the United States has, through bureaucratic inertia and mental sloth, persisted in a foreign policy that, whatever its relevance to the immediate postwar years, is by now dangerously anachronistic. They insist that the United States has unthinkingly accepted world responsibilities which are beyond its resources and that, in any case, these responsibilities have only an illusory connection with the enduring national interest. These men may be right; or they may be wrong. But right or wrong, *this* debate is largely irrelevant to the convulsion that the American intellectual community is now going through—even though occasional references may be made to it, for credibility's sake. One does not accuse the President of the United

States and the Secretary of State of being "war criminals" and "mass murderers" because they have erred in estimating the proper dimensions of the United States' overseas commitments. And it is precisely accusations of this kind that are inflaming passions on the campus, and which are more and more coming to characterize the "peace movement" as a whole.

What we are observing is a phenomenon that is far more complex in its origins and far-reaching in its implications. It involves, among other things, the highly problematic relationship of the modern intellectual to foreign affairs, the basic self-definition of the American intellectual, the tortured connections between American liberal ideology and the American imperial republic, and the role of the newly established academic classes in an affluent society. Above all, it raises the question of whether democratic societies can cope with the kinds of political pathologies that seem to be spontaneously generated by their very commitment to economic and social progress.

II

No modern nation has ever constructed a foreign policy that was acceptable to its intellectuals. True, at moments of national peril or national exaltation, intellectuals will feel the same patriotic emotions as everyone else, and will subscribe as enthusiastically to the common cause. But these moments pass, the process of disengagement begins, and it usually does not take long for disengagement to eventuate in alienation. Public opinion polls generally reveal that the overwhelming majority of ordinary citizens, at any particular time, will be approving of their government's foreign policy; among intellectuals, this majority tends to be skimpy at best, and will frequently not exist at all. It is reasonable to suppose that there is an instinctive bias at work here, favorable to government among the common people, unfavorable among the intellectuals.

The bias of the common man is easy to understand: He is never much interested in foreign affairs; his patriotic feelings incline him to favor his own government against the governments of foreigners; and in cases of international conflict, he is ready to sacrifice his self-interest for what the government assures him to be the common good. The persistent bias of intellectuals, on the other hand, requires some explaining.

We have noted that the intellectual lays claim—and the claim is, more often than not, recognized—to moral authority over the intentions and actions of political leaders. This claim finds concrete rhetorical expression in an ideology. What creates a community of intellectuals, as against a mere aggregate of individuals, is the fact that they subscribe—with varying degrees of warmth, or with more or less explicit reservations— to a prevailing ideology. This ideology permits them to interpret the past, make sense of the present, outline a shape for the future. It constitutes the essence of their rationality, as this is directed toward the life of man in society.

Now, it is the peculiarity of foreign policy that it is the area of public life in which ideology flounders most dramatically. Thus, while it is possible—if not necessarily fruitful—to organize the political writings of the past three hundred years along a spectrum ranging from the ideological "left" to the ideological "right," no such arrangement is conceivable for writings on foreign policy. There is no great "radical" text on the conduct of foreign policy—and no great "conservative" text, either. What texts there are (e.g. Machiavelli, Grotius, in our own day the writings of George Kennan and Hans Morgenthau) are used indifferently by all parties, as circumstance allows.

And we find, if we pursue the matter further, that the entire tradition of Western political thought has very little to say about foreign policy. From Thucydides to our own time, political philosophy has seen foreign affairs as so radically affected by contingency, fortune and fate as to leave little room for speculative enlightenment. John Locke was fertile in suggestions for the establishment and maintenance of good government, but when it came to foreign affairs he pretty much threw up his hands: "What is to be done in reference to foreigners, depending much upon their actions and the variation of designs and interests, must be left in great part to the prudence of those who have this power committed to them, to be managed by the best of their skill for the advantage of the Commonwealth."

The reasons why this should be so are not mysterious. To begin with, the very idea of "foreign policy" is so amorphous as to be misleading. As James Q. Wilson has pointed out, it is not at all clear that a state department can have a foreign policy in a meaningful sense of that term—i.e. one "policy" that encompasses our economic, military, political and sentimental relations with nations neighborly or distant, friendly or inimical. Moreover, whereas a national community is governed by principles by which one takes one's intellectual and moral bearings, the nations of

the world do not constitute such a community and propose few principles by which their conduct may be evaluated. What this adds up to is
that ideology can obtain exasperatingly little purchase over the realities
of foreign policy—and that intellectuals feel keenly their dispossession
from this area. It is not that intellectuals actually believe—though they
often assert it—that the heavy reliance upon expediency in foreign
affairs is intrinsically immoral. It is just that this reliance renders intellectuals as a class so much the less indispensable: to the extent that expediency is a necessary principle of action, to that extent the sovereignty of
intellectuals is automatically circumscribed. It is only where politics is
ideologized that intellectuals have a pivotal social and political role. To be
good at coping with expediential situations you don't have to be an intellectual—and it may even be a handicap.

It is this state of affairs that explains the extraordinary inconsistencies
of intellectuals on matters of foreign policy, and the ease with which they
can enunciate a positive principle, only in the next breath to urge a contrary action. So it is that many intellectuals are appalled at our military
intervention in Southeast Asia, on the grounds that, no matter what happens there, the national security of the United States will not be threatened. But these same intellectuals would raise no objection if the United
States sent an expeditionary force all the way to South Africa to over-
throw apartheid, even though South Africa offers no threat to American
security. So it is, too, that intellectual critics are fond of accusing American foreign policy of neglecting "political solutions" in favor of crude
military and economic action—thereby demonstrating their faith that, if
foreign policy were suffused with sufficient ideological rationality, it
would dissolve the recalcitrance that mere statesmen encounter. And
when the statesman candidly responds that he is coping, not with problems, but with an endless series of crises, and that he really has no way of
knowing beforehand what "solution," if any, is feasible, he is simply rein-
forcing the intellectual's conviction that the managers of foreign affairs
are, if not more wicked than he is, then certainly more stupid. Usually,
he will be willing to think they are both.

Charles Frankel has written that "international affairs are peculiarly
susceptible to galloping abstractions"* and has stressed that "intellectu-

---

*Charles Frankel, "The Scribblers and International Relations," *Foreign Affairs*, October 1965.

als, more than most other groups, have the power to create, dignify, inflate, criticize, moderate or puncture these abstractions." In the event, intellectuals rarely moderate or puncture, but are diligent in inflation. Abstractions are their life's blood, and even when they resolutely decide to become "tough-minded" they end up with an oversimplified ideology of Realpolitik that is quite useless as a guide to the conduct of foreign affairs and leads its expounders to one self-contradiction after another. But the important point is not that intellectuals are always wrong on matters of foreign policy—they are not, and could not possibly be, if only by the laws of chance. What is striking is that, right or wrong, they are so often, from the statesman's point of view, irrelevant. And it is their self-definition as ideological creatures that makes them so.

III

In the United States, this ideological self-definition has taken on a very special form, and the relation of the American intellectual to foreign policy has its own distinctive qualities. Just how distinctive may be gathered from asking oneself the following question: Is it conceivable that American intellectuals should ever disapprove of any popular revolution, anywhere in the world—whatever the express or implicit principles of this revolution? One can make this question even sharper: Is it conceivable for American intellectuals ever to approve of their government suppressing, or helping to frustrate, any popular revolution by poor people—whatever the nature or consequences of this revolution? The answer would obviously have to be in the negative; and the implications of this answer for American foreign policy are not insignificant. This policy must work within a climate of opinion that finds the idea of a gradual evolution of traditional societies thoroughly uninteresting—which, indeed, has an instinctive detestation of all traditional societies as being inherently unjust, and an equally instinctive approval, as being inherently righteous, of any revolutionary ideology which claims to incorporate the people's will.

As a matter of fact, even though official policy must obviously be based on other considerations, the makers of policy themselves find it nearly impossible to escape from this ideological framework. The State Department, for example, is always insisting that the United States is a truly revolutionary society, founded on revolutionary principles and offering a true revolutionary promise—as contrasted with the communists' spurious promises. The intellectual critics of American foreign policy deny that any such revolutionary intention or program exists—but think it ought to. There are precious few people in the United States who will say aloud that revolutionary intentions are inconsistent with a prudent and responsible foreign policy of a great power. Oddly enough, to hear this point made with some urgency these days, one has to go to the Soviet Union.

The American intellectual tradition has two profound commitments: to "ideals" and to "the people." It is the marriage of these two themes that has made the American mind and given it its characteristic cast— which might be called *transcendentalist populism*.

The "transcendentalist" theme in American thought is linked to a disrespect for tradition, a suspicion of all institutionalized authority, an unshakable faith in the "natural" (what once was called "divine") wisdom of the sincere individual, an incorruptible allegiance to one's own "inner light." The American intellectual sees himself as being in perpetual "prophetic confrontation" with principalities and powers. (That very phrase, "prophetic confrontation," has lately been used by Hans Morgenthau to define the proper stance of the intellectual vis-à-vis his government's policies.) Tell an American intellectual that he is a disturber of the intellectual peace, and he is gratified. Tell him he is a reassuring spokesman for calm and tranquillity, and he will think you have made a nasty accusation.

This transcendentalist "protestantism" of the American intellectual derives from the history of American Protestantism itself—as does his near-mystical celebration of "the people." Indeed, the two themes have evolved as part of one historical process, which has been concisely described by the historian Russell B. Nye:

From the mid-18th century to the mid-19th in American thought . . . the accepted version of the individual's power to grasp and interpret God's truth underwent a complete change—from Calvin's dependence on the Bible . . . to Deism's grant to man of equal sovereignty in a universe of reason, to Channing's transfer of sovereignty from Bible and church to man, and finally to the self-reliance of Emerson, Parker, and Thoreau. The lines of thought moved from Mather's distrust of man, to Jefferson's qualified confidence in him, to Emerson's and Jackson's deep and abiding faith in his capacity to find out and act upon divine truth.*

This evolution, which might be called the democratization of the spirit, has created an American intellectual who is at one and the same time (a) humble toward an idealized and mythical prototype of the common man (if the people have a quasi-ecclesiastical function, to oppose them in any consistent way partakes of heresy) and (b) arrogant toward existing authority, as presumptively representing nothing but a petrified form of yesteryear's vital forces. It has also had a peculiar effect upon the politics of American intellectuals, which is more often than not a kind of transcendentalist politics, focusing less on the reform of the polity than on the perfection and purification of self in opposition to the polity. Just as the intellectual opposition to slavery in the 1830s and 1840s paid little attention to the reform of particular institutions but focused primarily on the need for the individual to avoid being compromised and contaminated by this general evil, so in the 1960s what appears most to torment our academic intellectuals is the morality of their own actions—whether they should coöperate with Selective Service, accept government contracts, pay taxes, etc. At both times, the issue of individual, conscientious "civil disobedience" has become acute. It is instructive to note that, though the British Labor Party bitterly opposed British imperialism for over five decades, its opposition never took any such form. This is some measure of the difference between a political tradition and one that transcends mere politics.

The United States, to be sure, does have its own political tradition. And though the American intellectual tradition has suffused all areas of American life, it has never completely overwhelmed the political. This latter, mainly the creation of American Whiggery, is incarnated in our major institutions and finds its literary expression in such documents as the Constitution, the Federalist Papers, some presidential addresses, judicial decisions, etc. This tradition is still very much alive in our law schools and helps explain why these schools play so singular a role in our political life. But among intellectuals it has never enjoyed much favor,

*Russell B. Nye, "The Search for the Individual, 1750–1850," *The Centennial Review*, Winter 1961.

being thought to be inherently conservative and nondemocratic. The American intellectual of today is far more comfortable listening to a "protest folk song"—the truly indigenous art form of transcendental populism—than he is listening to a grave and solemn debate over a matter of policy. Witness the way in which the one genre has overwhelmed the other in the "teach-in."

Precisely what an American intellectual does *not* believe was most elegantly expressed by Sir Thomas More, in the discussion of an intellectual's obligation in his "Utopia":

> If evil persons cannot be quite rooted out, and if you cannot correct habitual attitudes as you wish, you must not therefore abandon the commonwealth. . . . You must strive to guide policy indirectly, so that you make the best of things, and what you cannot turn to good, you can at least make less bad. For it is impossible to do all things well unless all men are good, and this I do not expect to see for a long time.

There have been, of course, some American intellectuals who have followed Sir Thomas More's direction. For their efforts and pains, they have been subjected to the scorn and contempt of the intellectual community as a whole. (Arthur Schlesinger Jr., Eric Goldman, and John Roche could provide us with eloquent testimony on this score.) This community, unlike Sir Thomas More, is quite convinced that all men are indeed good and that any such modest and compromising involvement with political power can represent only a corruption of the spirit.

IV

The transformation of the American republic into an imperial power has sharply exacerbated the relations between the intellectual and the makers of foreign policy. The term "imperial power" is merely a synonym for "great power" and is not necessarily the same thing as "imperialistic" power. But there would seem to be a gain in clarity, and a diminution of humbug, in insisting on the use of the more provocative phrase. There are a great many people who appear to think that a great power is only the magnification of a small power, and that the principles governing the actions of the latter are simply transferable—perhaps with some modification—to the former. In fact, there is a qualitative difference between the two conditions, and the difference can be summed up as follows: A great power is "imperial" because what it does *not* do is just as significant, and just as consequential, as what it does. Which is to say, a great power does not have the range of freedom of action—derived from the freedom of inaction—that a small power possesses. It is entangled in a web of responsibilities from which there is no hope of escape; and its policymakers are doomed to a strenuous and unquiet life, with no prospect of ultimate resolution, no hope for an unproblematic existence, no promise of final contentment. It is understandable that these policymakers should sometimes talk as if some particular redirection of policy, of any great power, is capable of terminating the tensions inherent in this imperial condition. But it is foolish for us to believe them; and it is even more foolish for them to believe themselves. It is no accident that all classical political philosophers, and all depicters of utopia, have agreed that, to be truly happy, a human community should be relatively small and as isolated as possible from foreign entanglements.

Indeed, this utopian ideal is a major historic theme of American foreign policy, being at the root of what we call "isolationism." And so long as the United States was not a great power, it was not entirely utopian. The American republic, until the beginning of the twentieth century, was genuinely isolationist, and isolationism made both practical and idealistic sense. Practical sense, because the United States was geographically isolated from the main currents of world politics. Idealistic sense, because the United States could feel—and it was no illusion—that it served as a splendid and inspiring example to all believers in popular government everywhere, and that this exemplary role was more important than any foreign actions it might undertake, with the limited resources at its command. True, at the same time that the United States was isolationist, it was also expansionist. But there is no necessary contradiction between these two orientations, even though some modern historians are shocked to contemplate their coexistence. Most of the territories that the United States coveted, and all that were acquired, prior to the Civil War, were thinly populated—there was no subjugation of large, alien masses. And the intent of this expansion was always to incorporate such territories into the United States on absolutely equal terms, not to dominate them for any reasons of state. The idea of "manifest destiny" was therefore easily reconcilable to the isolationist idea. This reconciliation became troublesome only when expansion threatened to disturb the regional balance of power within the republic. Thus, the opposition to the Mexican War among some Northerners was intense, because it meant a possible accretion to the power of the "slavocracy." But there would otherwise have been little opposition to westward and southwestern expansion; and, once the war was over, no one thought for a moment of giving these territories back to Mexico or permitting them to evolve into independent national entities.

In the end, of course, "manifest destiny" did write an end to American isolationism, by establishing the material conditions for the emergence of the United States as a great power. But the isolationist idea, or at least crucial aspects of it, survived—not simply as some kind of "cultural lag," but by reason of being so intimately conjoined to "the American way of life," and to the American intellectual creed. This way of life insisted upon the subordination of public policy to private, individual needs and concerns. It had little use for the idea of military glory, which Abraham Lincoln called "that attractive rainbow that rises in showers of blood—that serpent's eye that charms to destroy." It was intensely patriotic, but allergic to all conceptions of national *grandeur*. The United States was tempted to a brief fling at European-style imperialism under Presidents McKinley and Theodore Roosevelt, but found the experience disagreeable, and that enterprise was gradually liquidated. When the American democracy entered World War I, it was in no imperial frame of mind. On the contrary, the whole point of the Wilsonian "crusade" was to rid the world of imperial politics. One can almost say that this crusade was a penultimate outburst of the isolationist spirit, in that its goal was a happy, self-determined existence for all the individuals on this earth—*une vie à l'Américaine*—without any further cruel violations of it by international power politics.

The disillusionment consequent upon this crusade prepared the way for the United States to enter history as an imperial power. To be sure, its most immediate effect was to stimulate a purely geographic isolationism that was shot through with streaks of xenophobia. But this attitude simply could not withstand the pressure of events and the insistent demands of world realities. In retrospect, the spectacle of the United States entering World War II has an almost dreamlike, fatalistic quality. There was never, prior to Pearl Harbor, any literal threat to the national security of the United States. And there was no popular enthusiasm, except among a small if influential group of "internationalists," for the United States' accepting responsibility for the maintenance of "world order." It all just seemed inescapable, and the alternative—retiring into a Fortress America—just too unmanly. The dominant mood was resignation, tinged with outrage at the Japanese bombardment of American soil. And resignation—sometimes sullen, sometimes equable—has remained the dominant popular mood ever since.

Strangely enough, this resigned acceptance of great-power responsibilities by the American people has been accompanied by a great unease on the part of the intellectuals. It is strange, because one had expected the reverse of this situation. During the two postwar decades, many commentators expressed doubt whether the American people could sustain the frustrations and sacrifices inherent in an imperial role. Such doubts were given point by the upsurge of extremist sentiments associated with the late Senator McCarthy, and unquestionably incited by popular resentment at the Korean War. But Korea can now be seen to have been a kind of baptism-by-fire; and the war in Vietnam has been borne with greater patience than might have been expected. It is not a popular war—how could it be?—but the general feeling is that it has to be endured. It is among the intellectuals—including some of the aforementioned commentators—that extreme dissatisfaction, sometimes extremist dissatisfaction, is rife. It is among American intellectuals that the isolationist ideal is experiencing its final, convulsive agony.

Though this dissatisfaction affects only a minority, it is nevertheless a most serious matter. It is much to be doubted that the United States can continue to play an imperial role without the endorsement of its intellectual class. Or, to put it more precisely: Since there is no way the United States, as the world's mightiest power, can avoid such an imperial role, the opposition of its intellectuals means that this role will be played out in a domestic climate of ideological dissent that will enfeeble the resolution of our statesmen and diminish the credibility of their policies abroad.

What is to be done? It is always possible to hope that this intellectual class will come to realize that its traditional ideology needs reformation and revision. It is even possible to argue plausibly that, in the nature of things, this is "historically inevitable." One can go so far as to say that, on intellectual grounds alone, this intellectual class will feel moved to desist from the shrill enunciation of pieties and principles that have little relevance to the particular cases our statesmen now confront, and to help formulate a new set of more specific principles that will relate the ideals

which sustain the American democracy to the harsh and nasty impera-
tives of imperial power. All of this is possible. But one must add that
none of these possibilities is likely to be realized in the immediate or
even near future.

It is unlikely for two reasons. The first is that the burden of guilt such
a process would generate would be so great as to be insupportable. It
took three centuries to create the American intellectual as we know him
today; he is not going to be re-created in one generation. He is committed in the most profound way to a whole set of assumptions and ideas
that are rooted in the "isolationist" era of American history, and he cannot depart from these assumptions and ideals without a terrible sense of
self-betrayal. Our State Department may find it necessary, if disagreeable, to support military dictatorships in certain countries, at certain
times. It is hard to see our intellectuals swallowing this necessity. They
might agree in the abstract that alternatives are not available. They might
even grant to certain dictatorships the kind of dispensation that is often
extended to heathens by an otherwise dogmatic orthodoxy. But they will
gag at extending such a dispensation to "our" dictators—this would be
too subversive of the dogmas by which they define their existence as a
class. The furthest that American intellectuals can go toward coping with
the realities of imperial power is to erect a double standard that under-
mines the moral basis of American diplomacy.

Secondly, this crisis of the intellectual class in the face of an imperial
destiny coincides with an internal power struggle within the United
States itself. Our intellectuals are moving toward a significant "confrontation" with the American "establishment" and will do nothing to
strengthen the position of their antagonist. Which is to say that the
American intellectual class actually has an interest in thwarting the evolution of any kind of responsible and coherent imperial policy. Just what
this interest is, and what this confrontation involves, we are only now
beginning to discern. Behind the general fog that the ideology of dissent
generates, the outlines of a very material sociological and political problem are emerging.

V

It has always been assumed that as the United States became a more
highly organized national society, as its economy became more manageri-

al, its power more imperial and its populace more sophisticated, the intellectuals would move inexorably closer to the seats of authority—would, perhaps, even be incorporated en masse into a kind of "power élite." Many writers and thinkers—and not only on the political left—have viewed this prospect with the greatest unease, for it seemed to them to threaten the continued existence of intellectuals as a critical and moral force in American life.

Well, it has happened here—only, as is so often the case, it is all very different from what one expected. It is true that a small section of the American intellectual class has become a kind of permanent brain trust to the political, the military, the economic authorities. These are the men who commute regularly to Washington, who help draw up programs for reorganizing the bureaucracy, who evaluate proposed weapons systems, who figure out ways to improve our cities and assist our poor, who analyze the course of economic growth, who reckon the cost and effectiveness of foreign aid programs, who dream up new approaches to such old social problems as the mental health of the aged, etc. But what has also happened, at the same time, is that a whole new intellectual class has emerged as a result of the explosive growth, in these past decades, of higher education in the United States. And these "new men," so far from being any kind of élite, are a mass—and have engendered their own mass movement.

As a matter of courtesy and habit, one refers to these professors as "intellectuals." Some of them, of course, are intellectuals, in the traditional sense of the term. The majority unquestionably are not—no population, no matter how elevated, could produce that many intellectuals. Professor Robert Nisbet, as shrewd an observer of the academic scene as we have, has estimated that "at the present time not less than sixty percent of all academics in the universities in this country have so profound a distaste for the classroom and for the pains of genuine scholarship or creative thought that they will seize upon anything . . . to exempt themselves respectably from each."*

In most instances, whether a man these days ends up a college professor or, say, a social worker or a civil servant is largely a matter of chance. Nevertheless, this academic mass has taken over not only the political metaphysics of the American intellectual, but also his status and preroga-

---

*Robert A. Nisbet, "What Is an Intellectual?" *Commentary*, December 1965.

tives. Americans have always had a superstitious, if touching, faith in the importance of education. And the American people have quickly conceded to the professoriat of our affluent society the moral authority that intellectuals have always claimed as their peculiar endowment.

Now, this new intellectual class, though to outsiders appearing to be not at all badly off, is full of grievance and resentment. It feels discriminated against—opinion polls reveal that professors, especially in the social sciences and humanities, invariably tend drastically to underestimate the esteem in which public opinion (and, more particularly, the opinion of the business community) holds them. It feels underpaid; you'll not find any credence on the campus for the proposition (demonstrably true) that the salaries of professors do not compare unfavorably with the salaries of bank executives. It feels put upon in all sorts of other familiar ways. The symptoms are only too typical: Here is a new class that is "alienated" from the established order because it feels that this order has not conceded to it sufficient power and recognition.

The politics of this new class is novel in that its locus of struggle is the college campus. One is shocked at this—we are used to thinking that politics ought not to intrude on the campus. But we shall no doubt get accustomed to the idea. Meanwhile, there is going to be a great deal of unpleasant turbulence. The academic community in the United States today has evolved into a new political constituency. College students, like their teachers, are "new men" who find the traditional student role too restrictive. Students and faculty therefore find it easy to combine their numbers and their energies for the purpose of social and political action. The first objective—already accomplished in large measure—is to weaken control of the administration and to dispossess it of its authoritative powers over campus activities. From this point the movement into politics proper—including elections—is about as predictable as anything can be.

Just what direction this movement into politics will follow it is too early to say with certainty. Presumably, it will be toward "the left," since this is the historical orientation of the intellectual class as a whole. It is even possible that the movement will not be calmed until the United States has witnessed the transformation of its two-party system to make room for a mass party of the ideological left, as in most European countries—except that its "grass roots" will be on the campus rather than in the factory. But what is certain is that the national prestige and the international position of the United States are being adversely affected by this *sécession des clercs*. Imperial powers need social equilibrium at home if they are to act effectively in the world. It was possible to think, in the years immediately after World War II, that the United States had indeed achieved this kind of equilibrium—that consensus and equipoise at home would permit our statesmen to formulate and pursue a coherent foreign policy. But the "academic revolution" of the 1950s and 1960s raises this issue again, in a most problematic and urgent way.

VI

Though there is much fancy rhetoric, pro and con, about "the purpose of American foreign policy," there is really nothing esoteric about this purpose. The United States wishes to establish and sustain a world order that (a) ensures its national security as against the other great powers, (b) encourages other nations, especially the smaller ones, to mold their own social, political and economic institutions along lines that are at least not repugnant to (if not actually congruent with) American values, and (c) minimizes the possibility of naked, armed conflict. This is, of course, also the purpose of the foreign policies of such other great powers as Soviet Russia and Maoist China. Nor could it be otherwise, short of a fit of collective insanity on the part of the governing classes of these powers. Without the conflict, tension and reconciliation of such imperial purposes there would be no such thing as "foreign affairs" or "world politics," as we ordinarily understand these terms.

But for any imperial policy to work effectively—even if one means by that nothing more than doing the least possible mischief—it needs intellectual and moral guidance. It needs such guidance precisely because, in foreign affairs, one is always forced to compromise one's values. In the United States today, a relative handful of intellectuals proffers such guidance to the policymaker. But the intellectual community en masse, disaffected from established power even as it tries to establish a power base of its own, feels no such sense of responsibility. It denounces, it mocks, it vilifies—and even if one were to concede that its fierce indignation was justified by extraordinary ineptitude in high places, the fact remains that its activity is singularly unhelpful. The United States is not going to cease being an imperial power, no matter what happens in Vietnam or elsewhere. It is the world situation—and the history which created this situation—that appoints imperial powers, not anyone's decision or even anyone's overweening ambition. And power begets responsibility— above all, the responsibility to use this power responsibly. The policy- maker in the United States today—and, no doubt, in the other great powers, too—finds this responsibility a terrible burden. The intellectu- als, in contrast, are bemused by dreams of power without responsibility, even as they complain of moral responsibility without power. It is not a healthy situation; and, as of this moment, it must be said that one cannot see how, or where, or when it will all end.

1967

9

Capitalism, Socialism, and Nihilism

Whenever and wherever defenders of "free enterprise," "individual liberty," and "a free society" assemble these days, one senses a peculiar kind of nostalgia in the air. It is a nostalgia for that time when they were busily engaged in confronting their old and familiar enemies, the avowed proponents of a full-blown "collectivist" economic and social order. In the debate with these traditional enemies, advocates of "a free society" have, indeed, done extraordinarily well. It is therefore a source of considerable puzzlement to them that, though the other side seems to have lost the argument, their side seems somehow not to have won it.

Now, I am aware that within this group itself there are different ideological and philosophical tendencies. Friedrich Hayek is not Milton Friedman, for instance, nor vice versa, and there are interesting differences between the 19th-century liberal individualism of the one and the 19th-century radical individualism of the other. Still, these twain do meet—and not only in Switzerland. There can be little doubt, for instance, that their thinking has converged into a powerful attack on the traditional socialist notions of central economic planning and a centrally administered economy. And there is absolutely no doubt, in my own mind, that this attack has been enormously successful—far more successful than one would have dreamed possible 25 years ago.

This attack, like so many successful attacks, has taken the form of a pincer movement. On the one hand, Professor Hayek has explored, in *The Counterrevolution of Science*, the ideological origins in the 19th century of the notion of large-scale "social engineering," and his critical history of what he calls—and of what we now call, after him—"scientism" is a major contribution to the history of ideas. It is in good part because of Professor Hayek's work in this area, and also because of his profound insights—most notably in *The Constitution of Liberty*—into the connection between a free market, the rule of law, and individual liberty, that you don't hear professors saying today, as they used so glibly to say, that "we are all socialists now." They are far more likely to say that the question of socialism is irrelevant and they would prefer not to discuss it.

Milton Friedman, on the other hand, has launched his main attack on "the planned society" through the jungles of social and economic policy, as distinct from the highlands of theory. No other thinker of our time has so brilliantly exposed and publicized the perversities that can be engendered by governmental intervention in the economic life of a nation. Whereas Hayek demonstrated why large-scale, centralized planning does not have the wonderful results it is supposed to, Friedman shows us how governmental rules and regulations so frequently get results that are the opposite of those intended. In addition, Friedman has instructed us all—including most socialists and neosocialists—in the unsuspected, creative powers of the market as a mechanism for solving social problems. Indeed, we have now reached the stage where planners will solemnly assemble and contemplate ways of using the powers of government *to create markets* in order to reach their goals.

As a result of the efforts of Hayek, Friedman, and the many others who share their general outlook, the idea of a centrally planned and centrally administered economy, so popular in the 1930s and early 1940s, has been discredited. Even in the socialist nations, economists are more interested in reviving the market than in permanently burying it. Whether they can have a market economy without private property is, of course, an issue they will shortly have to face up to.

The question then naturally arises: If the traditional economics of socialism has been discredited, why has not the traditional economics of capitalism been vindicated? I should say that the reasons behind this state of affairs are quite obvious and easily comprehensible—only they are terribly difficult to explain to economists.

ON "THINKING ECONOMICALLY"

The original appeal of the idea of central economic planning—like the traditional appeal of socialism itself—was cast primarily in economic terms. It was felt that such planning was necessary to (a) overcome the recurrent crises—i.e., depressions—of a market economy, and (b) provide for steady economic growth and greater material prosperity for all. This importance which traditional socialism—the Old Left, as we would call it today—ascribed to economics was derived from Marxism, which in turn based itself on the later writings of Marx. But the socialist impulse always had other ideological strands in it, especially a yearning for "fraternity" and "community," and a revulsion against the "alienation" of the individual in liberal-bourgeois society. These ideological strands were prominent among the "utopian socialists," as Engels was to label them, and in the early thought of Karl Marx himself, in which economics received much less attention than religion and political philosophy. They are prominent again today, in the thinking of what is called the "New Left."

The Old Left has been intellectually defeated on its chosen battleground, i.e., economics. But the New Left is now launching an assault on liberal society from quite other directions. One of the most astonishing features of the New Left—astonishing, at least, to a middle-aged observer—is how little interest it really has in economics. I would put it even more strongly: The identifying marks of the New Left are its refusal *to think economically* and its contempt for bourgeois society precisely because this is a society that does think economically.

What do I mean by "thinking economically"? I have found that it is very hard to convey this meaning to economists, who take it for granted that this is the only possible way for a sensible man to think—that, indeed, thinking economically is the same thing as thinking rationally. Economics is the social science *par excellence* of modernity, and economists as a class find it close to impossible to detach themselves from the philosophical presuppositions of modernity. This would not be particularly significant—until recently has not been particularly significant— were it not for the fact that the New Left is in rebellion against these philosophical presuppositions themselves.

Let me give you a simple illustration. One of the keystones of modern economic thought is that it is impossible to have an *a priori* knowledge of what constitutes happiness for other people; that such knowledge is incorporated in an individual's "utility schedules"; and this knowledge, in turn, is revealed by the choices the individual makes in a free market. This is not merely the keystone of modern economic thought; it is also the keystone of modern, liberal, secular society itself. This belief is so deeply ingrained in us that we are inclined to explain any deviation from it as perverse and pathological. Yet it is a fact that for several millennia, until the advent of modernity, people did not believe any such thing and would, indeed, have found such a belief to be itself shockingly pathological and perverse. For all premodern thinkers, *a priori* knowledge of what constituted other people's happiness was not only possible, it was a fact. True, such knowledge was the property of a small elite—religious, philosophical, or political. But this was deemed to be altogether proper: Such uncommon knowledge could not be expected to be found among common men. So you did not need a free market or a free society to maximize individual happiness; on the contrary, a free market, not being guided by the wisdom of the elite, was bound to be ultimately frustrating, since the common people could not possibly know what they *really* wanted or what would really yield them "true" happiness.

Now, we know from our experience of central economic planning that this premodern approach is fallacious—but if, and only if, you define "happiness" and "satisfaction" in terms of the material production and material consumption of commodities. If you do not define "happiness" or "satisfaction" in this way, if you refuse to "think economically," then the premodern view is more plausible than not. It is, after all, one thing to say that there is no authentically superior wisdom about people's tastes and preferences in commodities; it is quite another thing to deny that there is a superior wisdom about the spiritual dimensions of a good life. Even today, that last proposition does not sound entirely ridiculous to us. And if you believe that man's spiritual life is infinitely more important than his trivial and transient adventures in the marketplace, then you may tolerate a free market for practical reasons, within narrow limits, but you certainly will have no compunctions about overriding it if you think the free market is interfering with more important things.

THE SHAMEFACED COUNTERREVOLUTION

Modern economists are for the most part unaware that their habit of "thinking economically" only makes sense within a certain kind of world, based on certain peculiarly modern presuppositions. They insist that economics is a science, which is certainly true, but only if you accept the premises of modern economics. Thus, one of our most distinguished economists, Ludwig Von Mises, wrote:

> Economics is a theoretical science and as such abstains from any judgment of value. It is not its task to tell people what ends they should aim at. It is a science of the means to be applied for the attainment of ends chosen, not . . . a science of the choosing of ends.

That statement sounds terribly modest and uncontroversial and platitudinous. But is it? Is it really so easy to separate means from ends? What, for example, if we are members of a monastic community and our end is holy poverty—not just poverty but holy poverty, a poverty suffused with a spiritual intention? Can economics help us attain this end? Or, to take a somewhat less extreme instance: What if we are loyal members of the kind of Orthodox Jewish community that even today is to be found in sections of New York City? In such a community, where most people are engaged in business, there unquestionably is some role for an economist—but only within narrow limits. In the end, the superior purpose of such a community is obedience to sacred Law and meditation on the meaning of this Law. For the maximization of such an end, economics is of little use.

Modern, liberal, secular society is based on the revolutionary premise that there is no superior, authoritative information available about the good life or the true nature of human happiness, that this information is implicit only in individual preferences, and that therefore the individual has to be free to develop and express these preferences. What we are witnessing in Western society today are the beginnings of a counterrevolution against this conception of man and society. It is a shamefaced counterrevolution, full of bad faith and paltry sophistry, because it feels compelled to define itself as some kind of progressive extension of modernity instead of, what it so clearly is, a reactionary revulsion against modernity. It is this failure in self-definition that gives rise to so much irrelevant controversy.

The debate provoked by the writings of John Kenneth Galbraith is, it seems to me, a case in point. Galbraith thinks he is an economist and, if one takes him at his word, it is easy to demonstrate that he is a bad one.

But the truth is that Galbraith is not really an economist at all; he can be more accurately described as a reluctant rabbi. His essential thesis is one familiar to premodern moralists and theologians: Consumption *ought not to be* a constant function of relative income. Implicit in this thesis are the corollaries that (1) Galbraith knows better than any common man what "utility schedule" will provide all common men with enduring and meaningful satisfaction, and (2) if common men were uncorrupted by capitalist propaganda, they would permit Galbraith to prescribe "utility schedules" for them. Some of Galbraith's critics think they have refuted him when they make all this explicit. What they have done, I should say, is to enlighten him as to his own true purpose. That he so stubbornly resists such enlightenment is to be explained by his naive conviction that, because he is attacking bourgeois society, he must be a "progressive" thinker.

THE NEW LEFT VS. "ECONOMIC MAN"

A similar confusion, I should say, arises in connection with what we call the "environmentalist" movement. Economists and politicians both—the one with naiveté, the other with cunning—have decided to give a literal interpretation to the statements of this movement. And, given this literal interpretation, the thrust of environmentalism is not particularly subversive. If people today are especially concerned about clean air and clean water, then economic analysis can show them different ways—with different costs and benefits—of getting varying degrees of clean air and clean water. But it turns out that your zealous environmentalists do not want to be shown anything of the sort. They are not really interested in clean air or clean water at all. What does interest them is modern industrial society and modern technological civilization, toward which they have profoundly hostile sentiments. When they protest against "the quality of life" in this society and this civilization, they are protesting against nothing so trivial as air or water pollution. Rather they are at bottom rejecting a liberal civilization which is given shape through the interaction of a countless sum of individual preferences. Since they do not like the shape of that civilization, they are moved to challenge—however indirectly or slyly—the process that produces this shape. What environmentalists really want is very simple: They want the authority, the power to create an "environment" which pleases them; and this "environment" will be a society where the rulers will not want to "think economically" and the ruled will not be permitted to do so.

Something similar is going on with the "consumer protection movement," whose true aim is not to "protect" the consumer but rather to circumscribe—and ultimately abolish—his "sovereignty." The objection to such sovereignty is that common people *do* "think economically" when they are liberated from traditional constraints and are encouraged to do whatever they think best for themselves. The "consumer protection movement," like the "environmentalist" movement, is a revulsion against the kind of civilization that common men create when they are given the power, which a market economy does uniquely give them, to shape the world in which they wish to live.

I think we can summarize our situation as follows: The Old Left accepted the idea of the common good proposed by bourgeois-liberal society. The essential ingredients of this idea were material prosperity and technological progress. Bourgeois liberalism insisted that individual liberty was a precondition of this common good; the Old Left insisted that centralized planning was a precondition but that individual liberty would be an eventual consequence. The experience of the post-World War II decades has revealed that the Old Left simply could not compete with bourgeois liberalism in this ideological debate. The result has been the emergence of a New Left which implicitly rejects both the bourgeois-liberal and the Old Left idea of the common good, and which therefore rejects (again implicitly, for the most part) the ideological presuppositions of modernity itself. This movement, which seeks to end the sovereignty over our civilization of the common man, must begin by seeking the death of "economic man," because it is in the marketplace that this sovereignty is most firmly established. It thinks of itself as a "progressive" movement, whereas its import is regressive. This is one of the reasons why the New Left, every day and in every way, comes more and more to resemble the Old Right, which never did accept the liberal-bourgeois revolutions of the 18th and 19th centuries.

THE INADEQUACIES OF LIBERALISM

One is bound to wonder at the inadequacies of bourgeois liberalism that have made it so vulnerable, first to the Old Left and now to the New.

These inadequacies do not, in themselves, represent a final judgment upon it; every civilization has its necessary costs and benefits. But it does seem to be the case that, in certain periods, a civilization will have greater difficulty striking an acceptable balance than in others, and that sometimes it arrives at a state of permanent and precarious "tilt" for reasons it cannot quite comprehend. What it is important to realize, and what contemporary social science finds it so hard to perceive, is that such reasons are not necessarily new events or new conditions; they may merely be older inadequacies—long since recognized by some critics—that have achieved so cumulative an effect as to become, suddenly, and seemingly inexplicably, intolerable.

Certainly, one of the key problematic aspects of bourgeois-liberal society has long been known and announced. This is the fact that liberal society is of necessity a secular society, one in which religion is mainly a private affair. Such a disestablishment of religion, it was predicted by Catholic thinkers and others, would gradually lead to a diminution of religious faith and a growing skepticism about the traditional consolations of religion—especially the consolations offered by a life after death. That has unquestionably happened, and with significant consequences. One such consequence is that the demands placed upon liberal society, in the name of temporal "happiness," have become ever more urgent and ever more unreasonable. In every society, the overwhelming majority of the people lead lives of considerable frustration, and if society is to endure, it needs to be able to rely on a goodly measure of stoical resignation. In theory, this could be philosophical rather than religious; in fact, philosophical stoicism has never been found suitable for mass consumption. Philosophical stoicism has always been an aristocratic prerogative; it has never been able to give an acceptable rationale of "one's station and one's duties" to those whose stations are low and whose duties are onerous. So liberal civilization finds itself having spiritually expropriated the masses of its citizenry, whose demands for material compensation gradually become as infinite as the infinity they have lost. All of this was clearly foreseen by many of the antimodern critics who witnessed the birth of modernity.

Another, and related, consequence of the disestablishment of religion as a publicly sanctioned mythos has been the inability of liberal society ever to come up with a convincing and generally accepted theory of political obligation. Liberal philosophers have proposed many versions of utilitarianism to this end, but these have remained academic exercises and have not had much popular impact. Nor is this surprising: No merely utilitarian definition of civic loyalty is going to convince anyone that it makes sense for him to die for his country. In actual fact, it has been the secular myth of nationalism which, for the past century and a half, has provided this rationale. But this secular myth, though it has evolved hand in hand with bourgeois society, is not intrinsically or necessarily bourgeois. Nationalism ends by establishing "equal sacrifice" as the criterion of justice; and this is no kind of bourgeois criterion. We have seen, in our own day, how the spirit of nationalism can be utterly contemptuous of bourgeois proprieties, and utterly subversive of the bourgeois order itself.

THE DEPLETION OF MORAL CAPITAL

Even the very principles of individual opportunity and social mobility, which originally made the bourgeois-liberal idea so attractive, end up—once the spirit of religion is weakened—by creating an enormous problem for bourgeois society. This is the problem of publicly establishing an acceptable set of rules of distributive justice. The problem does not arise so long as the bourgeois ethos is closely linked to what we call the Puritan or Protestant ethos, which prescribes a connection between personal merit—as represented by such bourgeois virtues as honesty, sobriety, diligence, and thrift—and worldly success. But from the very beginnings of modern capitalism there has been a different and equally influential definition of distributive justice. This definition, propagated by Mandeville and Hume, is purely positive and secular rather than philosophical or religious. It says that, under capitalism, whatever is, is just—that all the inequalities of liberal-bourgeois society must be necessary, or else the free market would not have created them, and therefore they must be justified. This point of view makes no distinction between the speculator and the bourgeois-entrepreneur: Both are selfish creatures who, in the exercise of their private vices (greed, selfishness, avarice), end up creating public benefits.

Let us leave aside the intellectual deficiencies of this conception of justice—I myself believe these deficiencies are radical—and ask ourselves the question which several contemporaries of Mandeville and Hume asked before us: Will this positive idea of distributive justice commend itself to the people? Will they accept it? Will they revere it? Will they defend it against its enemies? The answer, I submit, is as obvious as it is negative. Only a philosopher could be satisfied with an *ex post facto* theory of justice. Ordinary people will see it merely as a self-serving ideology; they insist on a more "metaphysical" justification of social and economic inequalities. In the absence of such a justification, they will see more sense in simpleminded egalitarianism than in the discourses of Mandeville or Hume. And so it has been: As the connection between the Protestant ethic and liberal-bourgeois society has withered away, the egalitarian temper has grown ever more powerful.

For well over a hundred and fifty years now, social critics have been warning us that bourgeois society was living off the accumulated moral capital of traditional religion and traditional moral philosophy, and that once this capital was depleted, bourgeois society would find its legitimacy ever more questionable. These critics were never, in their lifetime, either popular or persuasive. The educated classes of liberal-bourgeois society simply could not bring themselves to believe that religion or philosophy was that important to a polity. *They* could live with religion or morality as a purely private affair, and they could not see why everyone else—after a proper secular education, of course—could not do likewise. Well, I think it is becoming clear that religion, and a moral philosophy associated with religion, is far more important politically than the philosophy of liberal individualism admits. Indeed, I would go further and say that it is becoming clearer every day that even those who thought they were content with a religion that was a private affair are themselves discovering that such a religion is existentially unsatisfactory.

LIBERTARIANISM AND LIBERTINISM

But if the grave problems that secularization would inevitably produce for liberal-bourgeois society were foreseen, if only in general terms, not all the problems that our liberal society faces today were foreseen. While many critics predicted a dissolution of this society under certain stresses and strains, none predicted—none could have predicted—the blithe and mindless self-destruction of bourgeois society which we are witnessing today. *The enemy of liberal capitalism today is not so much socialism as nihilism.* Only liberal capitalism doesn't see nihilism as an enemy, but rather as just another splendid business opportunity.

One of the most extraordinary features of our civilization today is the way in which the "counterculture" of the New Left is being received and sanctioned as a "modern" culture appropriate to "modern" bourgeois society. Large corporations today happily publish books and magazines, or press and sell records, or make and distribute movies, or sponsor television shows which celebrate pornography, denounce the institution of the family, revile the "ethics of acquisitiveness," justify civil insurrection, and generally argue in favor of the expropriation of private industry and the "liquidation" of private industrialists. Some leaders of the New Left are sincerely persuaded that this is part of a nefarious conspiracy to emasculate them through "co-optation." In this, as in almost everything else, they are wrong. There is no such conspiracy—one is almost tempted to add, "alas." Our capitalists promote the ethos of the New Left for only one reason: They cannot think of any reason why they should not. For them, it is "business as usual."

And indeed, why shouldn't they seize this business opportunity? The prevailing philosophy of liberal capitalism gives them no argument against it. Though Milton Friedman's writings on this matter are not entirely clear—itself an odd and interesting fact, since he is usually the most pellucid of thinkers—one gathers that he is, in the name of "libertarianism," reluctant to impose any prohibition or inhibition on the libertine tendencies of modern bourgeois society. He seems to assume, as I read him, that one must not interfere with the dynamics of "self-realization" in a free society. He further seems to assume that these dynamics cannot, in the nature of things, be self-destructive—that "self-realization" in a free society can only lead to the creation of a self that is compatible with such a society. I don't think it has been sufficiently appreciated that Friedman is the heir, not only to Hume and Mandeville, but to modern romanticism too. In the end, you can maintain the belief that private vices, freely exercised, will lead to public benefits only if you are further persuaded that human nature can never be utterly corrupted by these vices, but rather will always transcend them. The idea of bourgeois virtue has been eliminated from Friedman's conception of bourgeois society, and has been replaced by the idea of individual liberty. The assumption is that, in "the nature of things," the latter will certainly lead to the former. There is much hidden metaphysics here, and of a dubious kind.

And Hayek, too, though obviously hostile in temperament and mood to the new nihilism, has no grounds for opposing it in principle. When

Hayek criticizes "scientism," he does indeed write very much like a Burkean Whig, with a great emphasis on the superior wisdom implicit in tradition, and on the need for reverence toward traditional institutions that incorporate this wisdom. But when he turns to a direct contemplation of present-day society, he too has to fall back on a faith in the ultimate benefits of "self-realization"—a phrase he uses as infrequently as possible, but which he is nevertheless forced to use at crucial instances. And what if the "self" that is "realized" under the conditions of liberal capitalism is a self that despises liberal capitalism, and uses its liberty to subvert and abolish a free society? To this question, Hayek—like Friedman—has no answer.

And yet this is *the* question we now confront, as our society relentlessly breeds more and more such selves, whose private vices in no way provide public benefits to a bourgeois order. Perhaps one can say that the secular, "libertarian" tradition of capitalism—as distinct from the Protestant-bourgeois tradition—simply had too limited an imagination when it came to vice. It never really could believe that vice, when unconstrained by religion, morality, and law, might lead to viciousness. It never really could believe that self-destructive nihilism was an authentic and permanent possibility that any society had to guard against. It could refute Marx effectively, but it never thought it would be called upon to refute the Marquis de Sade and Nietzsche. It could demonstrate that the Marxist vision was utopian; but it could not demonstrate that the utopian vision of Fourier—the true ancestor of our New Left—was wrong. It was, in its own negligent way, very much a bourgeois tradition in that, while ignoring the bourgeois virtues, it could summon up only a bourgeois vision of vice.

THE HUNGER FOR LEGITIMACY

Today, the New Left is rushing in to fill the spiritual vacuum at the center of our free and capitalist society. For the most part, it proclaims itself as "socialist," since that is the only tradition available to it. It unquestionably feeds upon the old, socialist yearnings for community—for a pre-individualist society—and is therefore, if not collectivist, at least "communalist" in its economics and politics. But it is also nihilistic in its insistence that, under capitalism, the individual must be free to create his own morality. The New Left is best seen as a socialist heresy, in that it refuses to "think economically" in any serious way. One might say it is a socialist heresy that corresponds to the liberal heresy it is confronting: the heresy of a "free society" whose individuals are liberated from the bourgeois ethos that used to bind them together in a bourgeois-liberal community. And as the "free society" produces material affluence, but also moral and political anarchy, so the New Left—even as it pushes individual liberty beyond anarchy itself—longs for a moral and political community in which "thinking economically" will be left to our helots, the machines. In all their imagined utopian communities, the free individual who contracts for "the good life" has to surrender both his individualism and his freedom.

It is in the nature of heresies to take a part for the whole. Thus, our version of the "free society" is dedicated to the proposition that to be free is to be good. The New Left, though it echoes this proposition when it is convenient for its purposes, is actually dedicated to the counter-belief—which is the preliberal proposition—that to be good is to be free. In the first case, the category of goodness is emptied of any specific meaning; in the second case, it is the category of freedom which is emptied of any specific meaning. In the war between these two heresies, the idea of a free society that is in some specific sense virtuous (the older "bourgeois" ideal) and the idea of a good community that is in some specific sense free (the older "socialist" ideal as represented, say, by European social democracy) are both emasculated; and the very possibility of a society that can be simultaneously virtuous and free, i.e., that organically weds order to liberty, becomes ever more remote.

And yet no society that fails to celebrate the union of order and liberty, in some specific and meaningful way, can ever hope to be accepted as legitimate by its citizenry. The hunger for such legitimacy is, I should say, the dominant political fact in the world today—in the "free" nations and among the "socialist" countries as well. It is instructive, and rather sad, to observe the enormous popularity of the recent TV serial, *The Forsyte Saga*, in both capitalist and socialist societies. Obviously, it evoked a profound nostalgia for an order—a society where virtue and freedom were reconciled, however imperfectly—which some of these nations had lost, and which others had never even known. I should say that something of the sort also explains the international popularity of *Fiddler on the Roof*, which gives us a picture of a different kind of legitimate order—a picture that has obvious appeal even to people who do not know the difference between the Talmud and the Code Napoleon.

I find even more pathetic the efforts of the governments of the "free world" and of the "socialist" nations to achieve some minimum legitimacy by imitating one another. The "free societies" move haltingly toward collectivism, in the hope that this will calm the turbulence that agitates them and threatens to tear them apart. The "socialist" nations take grudging steps toward "liberalization," for the same purpose. The results, in both cases, are perverse. Each such step, so far from pacifying the populace, further provokes them, since each such step appears as a moral justification of the turbulence that caused it.

What medicine does one prescribe for a social order that is sick because it has lost its soul? Our learned doctors, the social scientists, look askance at this kind of "imaginary" illness, which has dramatic physical symptoms but no apparent physical causes. Some, on what we conventionally call the "right," cannot resist the temptation to conclude that the patient is actually in robust health, and that only his symptoms are sick. Others, on what we conventionally call the "left," declare that the patient is indeed sick unto death and assert that it is his symptoms which are the causes of his malady. Such confusion, of course, is exactly what one would expect when both patient and doctors are suffering from the same mysterious disease.

1973

10

The Adversary Culture of Intellectuals

No sooner did the late Lionel Trilling coin the phrase "adversary culture" than it became part of the common vocabulary. This is because it so neatly summed up a phenomenon that all of us, vaguely or acutely, had observed. It is hardly to be denied that the culture that educates us—the patterns of perception and thought our children absorb in their schools, at every level—is unfriendly (at the least) to the commercial civilization, the bourgeois civilization, within which most of us live and work. When we send our sons and daughters to college, we may expect that by the time they are graduated they are likely to have a lower opinion of our social and economic order than when they entered. We know this from opinion poll data; we know it from our own experience.

We are so used to this fact of our lives, we take it so for granted, that we fail to realize how extraordinary it is. Has there ever been, in all of recorded history, a civilization whose culture was at odds with the values and ideals of that civilization itself? It is not uncommon that a culture will be critical of the civilization that sustains it—and always critical of the failure of this civilization to realize perfectly the ideals that it claims as inspiration. Such criticism is implicit or explicit in Aristophanes and Euripides, Dante and Shakespeare. But to take an adversary posture toward the ideals themselves? That is unprecedented. A few writers and thinkers of a heretical bent, dispersed at the margins of the culture, might do so. But culture as a whole has always been assigned the task of, and

106

invariably accepted responsibility for, sustaining and celebrating those values. Indeed, it is a premise of modern sociological and anthropological theory that it is the essence of culture to be "functional" in this way.

Yet ours is not. The more "cultivated" a person is in our society, the more disaffected and malcontent he is likely to be—a disaffection, moreover, directed not only at the actuality of our society but at the ideality as well. Indeed, the ideality may be more strenuously opposed than the actuality. It was, I think, Oscar Wilde who observed that, while he rather liked the average American, he found the ideal American contemptible. Our contemporary culture is considerably less tolerant of actuality than was Oscar Wilde. But there is little doubt that if it had to choose between the two, it would prefer the actual to the ideal.

The average "less cultivated" American, of course, feels no great uneasiness with either the actual or the ideal. This explains why the Marxist vision of a radicalized working class erupting into rebellion against capitalist society has turned out to be so erroneous. Radicalism, in our day, finds more fertile ground among the college-educated than among the high school graduates, the former having experienced more exposure to some kind of adversary culture, the latter—until recently, at least—having its own kind of "popular" culture that is more accommodating to the bourgeois world that working people inhabit. But this very disjunction of those two cultures is itself a unique phenomenon of the bourgeois era, and represents, as we shall see, a response to the emergence, in the nineteenth century, of an "avant-garde," which laid the basis for our adversary culture.

Bourgeois society is without a doubt the most prosaic of all possible societies. It is prosaic in the literal sense. The novel written in prose, dealing with the (only somewhat) extraordinary adventures of ordinary people, is its original and characteristic art form, replacing the epic poem, the lyric poem, the poetic drama, the religious hymn. These latter were appropriate to societies formally and officially committed to transcendent ideals of excellence—ideals that could be realized only by those few of exceptional nobility of character—or to transcendent visions of the universe wherein human existence on earth is accorded only a provisional significance. But bourgeois society is uninterested in such transcendence, which at best it tolerates as a private affair, a matter for individual taste and individual consumption, as it were. It is prosaic, not only in form, but in essence. It is a society organized for the convenience and comfort of common men and common women, not for the production of heroic, memorable figures. It is a society interested in making the best of this world, not in any kind of transfiguration, whether through tragedy or piety.

Because this society proposes to make the best of this world, for the benefit of ordinary men and women, it roots itself in the most worldly and common of human motivations: self-interest. It assumes that, though only a few are capable of pursuing excellence, everyone is capable of recognizing and pursuing his own self-interest. This "democratic" assumption about the equal potential of human nature, in this limited respect, in turn justifies a market economy in which each individual defines his own well-being, and illegitimates all the paternalistic economic theories of previous eras. One should emphasize, however, that the pursuit of excellence by the few—whether defined in religious, moral, or intellectual terms—is neither prohibited nor inhibited. Such an activity is merely interpreted as a special form of self-interest, which may be freely pursued but can claim no official status. Bourgeois society also assumes that the average individual's conception of his own self-interest will be sufficiently "enlightened"—that is, sufficiently farsighted and prudent—to permit other human passions (the desire for community, the sense of human sympathy, the moral conscience, etc.) to find expression, albeit always in a voluntarist form.

It is characteristic of a bourgeois culture, when it exists in concord with bourgeois principles, that we are permitted to take "happy endings" seriously (". . . and they lived happily ever after"). From classical antiquity through the Renaissance, happy endings—worldly happy endings—were consigned to the genre of Comedy. "Serious" art focused on a meaningful death, in the context of heroism in battle, passion in love, ambition in politics, or piety in religion. Such high seriousness ran counter to the bourgeois grain, which perceived human fulfillment—human authenticity, if you will—in terms of becoming a good citizen, a good husband, a good provider. It is, in contrast to both prebourgeois and postbourgeois *Weltanschauungen*, a *domestic* conception of the universe and of man's place therein.

This bourgeois ideal is much closer to the Old Testament than to the New—which is, perhaps, why Jews have felt more at home in the bourgeois world than in any other. That God created this world and affirmed its goodness; that men ought confidently to be fruitful and multiply; that work (including that kind of work we call commerce) is elevating rather than demeaning; that the impulse to "better one's condition" (to use a favorite phrase of Adam Smith's) is good because natural—these beliefs were almost perfectly congruent with the worldview of postexilic Judaism. In this worldview, there was no trace of aristocratic bias: Everyman was no allegorical figure but, literally, every common person.

So it is not surprising that the bourgeois worldview—placing the needs and desires of ordinary men and women at its center—was (and still is) also popular among the common people.* Nor is it surprising that, almost from the beginning, it was an unstable worldview, evoking active contempt in a minority, and a pervasive disquiet among those who, more successful than others in having bettered their condition, had the leisure to wonder if life did not, perhaps, have more interesting and remote possibilities to offer.

The emergence of romanticism in the middle of the eighteenth century provided an early warning signal that, within the middle class itself, a kind of nonbourgeois spiritual impulse was at work. Not antibourgeois; not yet. For romanticism—with its celebration of noble savages, Weltschmerz, passionate love, aristocratic heroes and heroines, savage terrors confronted with haughty boldness and courage—was mainly an escapist aesthetic mode as distinct from a rebellious one. It provided a kind of counterculture that was, on the whole, safely insulated from bourgeois reality, and could even be tolerated (though always uneasily) as a temporary therapeutic distraction from the serious business of living. A clear sign of this self-limitation of the romantic impulse was the degree to which it was generated, and consumed, by a particular section of the middle class: women.

One of the less happy consequences of the women's liberation movement of the past couple of decades is the distorted view it has encouraged of the history of women under capitalism. This history is interpreted in terms of repression—sexual repression above all. That repression was real enough, of course; but it is absurd to regard it as nothing but an expression of masculine possessiveness, even vindictiveness. Sexual repression—and that whole code of feminine conduct we

---

*This generalization, skimming over differences in national traditions and religious cultures (especially Protestant vs. Catholic cultures), is obviously an oversimplification. But it is only an oversimplification, not a distortion.

have come to call Victorian—was imposed and enforced by women, not men (who stand to gain very little if *all* women are chaste). And women insisted on this code because, while sexually repressive, it was also liberating in all sorts of other ways. Specifically, it liberated women, ideally if not always actually, from their previous condition as sex objects or work objects. To put it another way: All women were now elevated to the aristocratic status of *ladies*, entitled to a formal deference, respect, consideration. (Even today, some of those habits survive, if weakly—taking off one's hat when greeting a female acquaintance, standing up when a woman enters the room, etc.) The "wench," as had been portrayed in Shakespeare's plays, was not dead. She was still very much to be found in the working and lower classes. But her condition was not immutable; she, too, could become a lady—through marriage, education, or sheer force of will.

The price for this remarkable elevation of women's status was sexual self-restraint and self-denial, which made them, in a sense, owners of valuable (if intangible) property. It is reasonable to think that this change in actual sexual mores had something to do with the rise of romanticism, with its strong erotic component, in literature—the return of the repressed, as Freud was later to call it. For most of those who purchased romantic novels, or borrowed them (for a fee) from the newly established circulating libraries, were women. Indeed they still are, even today, two centuries later, though the romantic novel is now an exclusively popular art form, which flourishes outside the world of "serious" writing.

This extraordinary and ironical transformation of the novel from a prosaic art form—a tradition that reached its apogee in Jane Austen—to something radically different was itself a bourgeois accomplishment. It was made possible by the growing affluence of the middle classes that provided not only the purchasing power but also the leisure and the solitude ("a room of one's own"). This last point is worth especial notice.

It is a peculiarity of the novel that, unlike all previous art forms, it gains rather than loses from becoming a private experience. Though novels were still occasionally read aloud all during the romantic era, they need not be and gradually ceased to be. Whereas Shakespeare or Racine is most "enchanting" as part of a public experience—on a stage, in daylight—the novel gains its greatest power over us when we "consume" it (or it consumes us) in silence and privacy. Reading a novel then becomes something like surrendering oneself to an especially powerful daydream. The bourgeois ethos, oriented toward prosaic actualities, strongly disapproves of such daydreaming (which is why, even today, a businessman will prefer not to be known as an avid reader of novels, and few in fact are). But bourgeois women very soon discovered that living simultaneously in the two worlds of nonbourgeois "romance" and bourgeois "reality" was superior to living in either one.

The men and women who wrote such novels (or poems—one thinks of Byron) were not, however, simply responding to a market incentive. Writers and artists may have originally been receptive to a bourgeois society because of the far greater individual freedoms that it offered them; and because, too, they could not help but be exhilarated by the heightened vitality and quickened vivacity of a capitalist order with its emphasis on progress, economic growth, and liberation from age-old constraints. But, very quickly, disillusionment and dissent set in, and the urge to escape became compelling.

From the point of view of artists and of those whom we have come to call "intellectuals"—a category itself created by bourgeois society, which converted philosophers into *philosophes* engaged in the task of critical enlightenment—there were three great flaws in the new order of things.

First of all, it threatened to be very boring. Though the idea of ennui did not become a prominent theme in literature until the nineteenth century, there can be little doubt that the experience is considerably older than its literary expression. One can say this with some confidence because, throughout history, artists and writers have been so candidly contemptuous of commercial activity between consenting adults, regarding it as an activity that tends to coarsen and trivialize the human spirit. And since bourgeois society was above all else a commercial society— the first in all of recorded history in which the commercial ethos was sovereign over all others—their exasperation was bound to be all the more acute. Later on, the term "philistinism" would emerge to encapsulate the object of this sentiment.

Second, though a commercial society may offer artists and writers all sorts of desirable things—freedom of expression especially, popularity and affluence occasionally—it did (and does) deprive them of the status that they naturally feel themselves entitled to. Artists and writers and thinkers always have taken themselves to be Very Important People, and they are outraged by a society that merely tolerates them, no matter how generously. Bertolt Brecht was once asked how he could justify his Communist loyalties when his plays could neither be published nor performed in the USSR, while his royalties in the West made him a wealthy man. His quick rejoinder was: "Well, there at least they take me seriously!" Artists and intellectuals are always more respectful of a regime that takes their work and ideas "seriously." To be placed at a far distance from social and political power is, for such people, a deprivation.

Third, a commercial society, a society whose civilization is shaped by market transactions, is always likely to reflect the appetites and preferences of common men and women. Each may not have much money, but there are so many of them that their tastes are decisive. Artists and intellectuals see this as an inversion of the natural order of things, since it gives "vulgarity" the power to dominate where and when it can. By their very nature "elitists" (as one now says), they believe that a civilization should be shaped by an *aristoi* to which they will be organically attached, no matter how perilously. The consumerist and environmentalist movements of our own day reflect this aristocratic impulse, albeit in a distorted way: Because the democratic idea is the only legitimating political idea of our era, it is claimed that the market does not truly reflect people's preferences, which are deformed by the power of advertising. A minority, however, is presumed to have the education and the will to avoid such deformation. And this minority then claims the paternalist authority to represent "the people" in some more authentic sense. It is this minority which is so appalled by America's "automobile civilization," in which everyone owns a car, while it is not appalled at all by the fact that in the Soviet Union only a privileged few are able to do so.

In sum, intellectuals and artists will be (as they have been) restive in a bourgeois-capitalist society. The popularity of romanticism in the century after 1750 testifies to this fact, as the artists led an "inner emigration" of the spirit—which, however, left the actual world unchanged. But not all such restiveness found refuge in escapism. Rebellion was an alternative route, as the emergence of various socialist philosophies and movements early in the nineteenth century demonstrated.

Socialism (of whatever kind) is a romantic passion that operates within a rationalist framework. It aims to construct a human community in which *everyone* places the common good—as defined, necessarily, by an intellectual and moral elite—before his own individual interests and appetites. The intention was not new—there is not a religion in the world that has failed to preach and expound it. What was new was the belief that such self-denial could be realized, not through a voluntary circumscription of individual appetites (as Rousseau had, for example, argued in his *Social Contract*) but even while the aggregate of human appetites was being increasingly satisfied by ever-growing material prosperity. What Marx called "utopian" socialism was frequently defined by the notion that human appetites were insatiable, and that a self-limitation on such appetites was a precondition for a socialist community. The trouble with this notion, from a political point of view, was that it was not likely to appeal to more than a small minority of men and women at any one time. Marxian "scientific" socialism, in contrast, promised to remove this conflict between actual and potentially ideal human nature by creating an economy of such abundance that appetite as a social force would, as it were, wither away.

Behind this promise, of course, was the profound belief that modern science—including the social sciences, and especially including scientific economics—would gradually but ineluctably provide humanity with modes of control over nature (and human nature, too) that would permit the modern world radically to transcend all those limitations of the human condition previously taken to be "natural." The trouble with implementing this belief, however, was that the majority of men and women were no more capable of comprehending a "science of society," and of developing a "consciousness" appropriate to it, than they were of practicing austere self-denial. A socialist elite, therefore, was indispensable to mobilize the masses for their own ultimate self-transformation. And the techniques of such mobilization would themselves of necessity be scientific—what moralists would call "Machiavellian"—in that they had to treat the masses as objects of manipulation so that eventually they would achieve a condition where they could properly be subjects of their own history making.

Michael Polanyi has described this "dynamic coupling" of a romantic moral passion with a ruthlessly scientific conception of man, his world, and his history as a case of "moral inversion." That is to say, it is the moral passion that legitimates the claims of scientific socialism to absolute truth, while it is the objective necessities that legitimate every possible form of political immorality. Such a dynamic coupling characterized, in the past, only certain religious movements. In the nineteenth and twentieth centuries, it became the property of secular political movements that sought the universal regeneration of mankind in the here and now.

The appeal of any such movement to intellectuals is clear enough. As intellectuals, they are qualified candidates for membership in the elite that leads such movements, and they can thus give free expression to their natural impulse for authority and power. They can do so, moreover, within an ideological context, which reassures them that, any superficial evidence to the contrary notwithstanding, they are disinterestedly serving the "true" interests of the people.

But the reality principle—*la force des choses*—will, in the end, always prevail over utopian passions. The fate of intellectuals under socialism is disillusionment, dissent, exile, silence. In politics, means determine ends, and socialism everywhere finds its incarnation in coercive bureaucracies that are contemptuously dismissive of the ideals that presumably legitimize them, even while establishing these ideals as a petrified orthodoxy. The most interesting fact of contemporary intellectual life is the utter incapacity of so-called socialist countries to produce socialist intellectuals—or even, for that matter, to tolerate socialist intellectuals. If you want to meet active socialist intellectuals, you can go to Oxford or Berkeley or Paris or Rome. There is no point in going to Moscow or Peking or Belgrade or Bucharest or Havana. Socialism today is a dead end for the very intellectuals who have played so significant a role in moving the modern world down that street.

In addition to that romantic-rationalist rebellion we call socialism, there is another mode of "alienation" and rebellion that may be, in the longer run, more important. This is romantic antirationalism, which takes a cultural rather than political form. It is this movement specifically that Trilling had in mind when he referred to the adversary culture.

Taking its inspiration from literary romanticism, this rebellion first created a new kind of "inner emigration"—physical as well as spiritual—in the form of "bohemia." In Paris, in the 1820s and 1830s, there formed enclaves of (mostly) young people who displayed *in nuce* all the symptoms of the counterculture of the 1960s. Drugs, sexual promiscuity, long hair for men and short hair for women, working-class dress (the "jeans" of the day), a high suicide rate—anything and everything that would separate them from the bourgeois order. The one striking difference between this bohemia and its heirs of a century and a quarter later is that to claim membership in bohemia one had to be (or pretend to be) a producer of "art," while in the 1960s to be a consumer was sufficient. For this transition to occur, the attitudes and values of bohemia had to permeate a vast area of bourgeois society itself. The engine and vehicle of this transition was the "modernist" movement in the arts, which in the century after 1850 gradually displaced the traditional, the established, the "academic."

The history and meaning of this movement are amply described and brilliantly analyzed by Daniel Bell in his *The Cultural Contradictions of Capitalism* (1976). Suffice it to say here that modernism in the arts can best be understood as a quasi-religious rebellion against bourgeois sobriety, rather than simply as a series of aesthetic innovations. The very structure of this movement bears a striking resemblance to that of the various gnostic-heretical sects within Judaism and Christianity. There is an "elect"—the artists themselves—who possess the esoteric and redeeming knowledge (*gnosis*); then there are the "critics," whose task it is to convey this gnosis, as a vehicle of conversion, to potential adherents to the movement. And then there is the outer layer of "sympathizers" and "fellow travelers"—mainly bourgeois "consumers" of the modernist arts—who help popularize and legitimate the movement within the wider realms of public opinion.

One can even press the analogy further. It is striking, for instance, that modernist movements in the arts no longer claim to create "beauty" but to reveal the "truth" about humanity in its present condition. Beauty is defined by an aesthetic tradition that finds expression in the public's "taste." But the modern artist rejects the sovereignty of public taste, since truth can never be a matter of taste. This truth always involves an indictment of the existing order of things, while holding out the promise, for those whose sensibilities have been suitably reformed, of a redemption of the spirit (now called "the self"). Moreover, the artist himself now becomes the central figure in the artistic enterprise—he is the hero of his own work, the sacrificial redeemer of us all, the only person capable of that transcendence that gives a liberating meaning to our lives. The artist—painter, poet, novelist, composer—who lives to a ripe old age of contentment with fame and fortune strikes us as having abandoned, if not betrayed, his "mission." We think it more appropriate that artists should die young and tormented. The extraordinarily high suicide rate among modern artists would have baffled our ancestors, who assumed that the artist—like any other *secular* person—aimed to achieve recognition and prosperity in this world.

Our ancestors would have been baffled, too, by the enormous importance of critics and of criticism in modern culture. It is fascinating to pick up a standard anthology in the history of literary criticism and to observe that, prior to 1800, there is very little that we would designate as literary criticism, as distinct from philosophical tracts on aesthetics. Shakespeare had no contemporary critics to explain his plays to the audience; nor did the Greek tragedians, nor Dante, Racine, and so forth. Yet we desperately feel the need of critics to understand, not only the modern artist, but, by retrospective reevaluation, all artists. The reason for this odd state of affairs is that we are looking for something in these artists—a redeeming knowledge of ourselves and our human condition—which in previous eras was felt to lie elsewhere, in religious traditions especially.

The modernist movement in the arts gathered momentum slowly, and the first visible sign of its success was the gradual acceptance of the fact that bourgeois society had within it two cultures: the "avant-garde" culture of modernism, and the "popular culture" of the majority. The self-designation of modernism as avant-garde is itself illuminating. The term is of military origin, and means not, as we are now inclined to think, merely the latest in cultural or intellectual fashion, but the foremost assault troops in a military attack. It was a term popularized by Saint-Simon to describe the role of his utopian-socialist sect vis-à-vis the bourgeois order, and was then taken over by modernist innovators in the arts. The avant-garde is, and always has been, fully self-conscious of its hostile intentions toward the bourgeois world. Until 1914, such hostility was as likely to move intellectuals and artists toward the romantic Right as toward the romantic Left. But Right or Left, the hostility was intransigent. This is, as has been noted, a cultural phenomenon without historical precedent.

And so is the popular culture of the bourgeois era, though here again we are so familiar with the phenomenon that we fail to perceive its originality. It is hard to think of a single historical instance where a society presents us with two cultures, a "high" and a "low," whose values are in opposition to one another. We are certainly familiar with the fact that any culture has its more sophisticated and its more popular aspects, differentiated by the level of education needed to move from the one to the other. But the values embodied in these two aspects were basically homogeneous: The sophisticated expression did not *shock* the popular, nor did the popular incite feelings of revulsion among the sophisticated. Indeed, it was taken as a mark of true artistic greatness for a writer or artist to encompass both aspects of his culture. The Greek tragedies were performed before all the citizens of Athens; Dante's *Divine Comedy* was read aloud in the squares of Florence to a large and motley assemblage; and Shakespeare's plays were enacted before a similarly mixed audience.

The popular culture of the bourgeois era, after 1870 or so, tended to be a culture that educated people despised, or tolerated contemptuously. The age of Richardson, Jane Austen, Walter Scott, and Dickens—an age in which excellence and popularity needed not to contradict one another, in which the distinction between "highbrow" and "lowbrow" made no sense—was over. The spiritual energy that made for artistic excellence was absorbed by the modernist, highbrow movement, while popular culture degenerated into a banal reiteration—almost purely commercial in intent—of "wholesome" bourgeois themes.

In this popular literature of romance and adventure, the "happy ending" not only survived but became a standard cliché. The occasional unhappy ending, involving a sinful action (e.g., adultery) as its effectual cause, always concluded on a note of repentance, and was the occasion for a cathartic "good cry." In "serious" works of literature in the twentieth century, of course, the happy ending is under an almost total prohibition. It is also worth making mention of the fact that popular literature remained very much a commodity consumed by women, whose commitments to the bourgeois order (a "domestic" order, remember) has always been stronger than men's. This is why the women's liberation movement of the past two decades, which is so powerfully moving the female sensibility in an antibourgeois direction, is such a significant cultural event.

In the last century, the modernist movement in the arts made constant progress at the expense of the popular. It was, after all, the only serious art available to young men and women who were inclined to address themselves to solemn questions about the meaning of life (or "the meaning of it all"). The contemporaneous evolution of liberal capitalism itself encouraged modernism in its quest for moral and spiritual hegemony. It did this in three ways.

First, the increasing affluence that capitalism provided to so many individuals made it possible for them (or, more often, for their children) to relax their energetic pursuit of money, and of the goods that money can buy, in favor of an attention to those nonmaterial goods that used to be called "the higher things in life." The antibourgeois arts in the twentieth century soon came to be quite generously financed by restless, uneasy, and vaguely discontented bourgeois money.

Second, that spirit of worldly rationalism so characteristic of a commercial society and its business civilization (and so well described by Max Weber and Joseph Schumpeter) had the effect of delegitimizing all merely traditional beliefs, tasks, and attitudes. The "new," constructed by design or out of the passion of a moment, came to seem inherently superior to the old and established, this latter having emerged "blindly" out of the interaction of generations. This mode of thinking vindicated the socialist ideal of a planned society. But it also vindicated an anarchic, antinomian, "expressionist" impulse in matters cultural and spiritual.

Third, the tremendous expansion—especially after World War II—of postsecondary education provided a powerful institutional milieu for modernist tastes and attitudes among the mass of both teachers and students. Lionel Trilling, in *Beyond Culture*, poignantly describes the spiritual vitality with which this process began in the humanities—the professors were "liberated" to teach the books that most profoundly moved and interested them—and the vulgarized version of modernism that soon became the mass counterculture among their students who, as consumers, converted it into a pseudobohemian lifestyle.

Simultaneously, and more obviously, in the social sciences, the antibourgeois socialist traditions were absorbed as a matter of course, with "the study of society" coming quickly and surely to mean the management of social change by an elite who understood the verities of social structure and social trends. Economics, as the science of making the best choices in a hard world of inevitable scarcity, resisted for a long while; but the Keynesian revolution—with its promise of permanent prosperity through government management of fiscal and monetary policy—eventually brought much of the economics profession in line with the other social sciences.

So utopian rationalism and utopian romanticism have, between them, established their hegemony as adversary cultures over the modern consciousness and the modern sensibility.

But, inevitably, such victories are accompanied by failure and disillusionment. As socialist reality disappoints, socialist thought fragments into heterogeneous conflicting sects, all of them trying to keep the utopian spark alive while devising explanations for the squalid nature of socialist reality. One is reminded of the experience of Christianity in the first and second centuries, but with this crucial difference: Christianity, as a religion of transcendence, of *otherworldly* hope, of faith not belief, was not really utopian, and the Church Fathers were able to transform the Christian rebellion against the ancient world into a new, vital Christian orthodoxy, teaching its adherents how to live virtuously, that is, how to seek human fulfillment in this world even while waiting for their eventual migration into a better one. Socialism, lacking this transcendent dimension, is purely and simply trapped in this world, whose realities are for it nothing more than an endless series of frustrations. It is no accident, as the Marxists would say, that there is no credible doctrine of "socialist virtue"—a doctrine informing individuals how actually to live "in authenticity" as distinct from empty rhetoric about "autonomous self-fulfillment"—in any nation (and there are so many!) now calling itself socialist. It is paradoxically true that otherworldly religions are more capable of providing authoritative guidance for life in this world than are secular religions.

The utopian romanticism that is the impulse behind modernism in the arts is in a not dissimilar situation. It differs in that it seeks transcendence—all of twentieth-century art is such a quest—but it seeks such transcendence within the secular self. This endeavor can generate that peculiar spiritual intensity that characterizes the antibourgeois culture of our bourgeois era, but in the end it is mired in self-contradiction.

The deeper one explores into the self, without any transcendental frame of reference, the clearer it becomes that nothing is there. One can then, of course, try to construct a metaphysics of nothingness as an absolute truth of the human condition. But this, too, is self-contradictory: If nothingness is the ultimate reality, those somethings called books, or poems, or paintings, or music are mere evasions of truth rather than expressions of it. Suicide is the only appropriate response to this vision of reality (as Dostoevski saw long ago) and in the twentieth century it has in fact become the fate of many of our artists: self-sacrificial martyrs to a hopeless metaphysical enterprise. Those who stop short of this ultimate gesture experience that *tedium vitae*, already mentioned, which has made the "boringness" of human life a recurrent theme, since Baudelaire at least, among our artists.

This modern association of culture and culture heroes with self-annihilation and ennui has no parallel in human history. We are so familiar with it that most of us think of it as natural. It is, in truth, unnatural and cannot endure. Philosophy may, with some justice, be regarded as a preparation for dying, as Plato said—but he assumed that there would never be more than a handful of philosophers at any time. The arts, in contrast, have always been life-affirming, even when dealing with the theme of death. It is only when the arts usurp the role of religion, but without the transcendence that assures us of the meaning of apparent meaninglessness, that we reach our present absurd (and *absurdiste*) condition.

Moreover, though utopian rationalism and utopian romanticism are both hostile to bourgeois society, they turn out to be, in the longer run, equally hostile to one another.

In all socialist nations, of whatever kind, modernism in the arts is repressed—for, as we have seen, this modernism breeds a spirit of nihilism and antinomianism that is subversive of *any* established order. But this repression is never entirely effective, because the pseudo-orthodoxies of socialism can offer no satisfying spiritual alternatives. It turns out that a reading of Franz Kafka can alienate from socialist reality just as easily as from bourgeois reality, and there is no socialist Richardson or Fielding or Jane Austen or Dickens to provide an original equipoise. Who are the "classic" socialist authors or artists worthy of the name? There are none. And so young people in socialist lands naturally turn either to the high modernist culture of the twentieth century or to its debased, popularized version in the counterculture. Picasso and Kafka, blue jeans and rock and roll may yet turn out to be the major internal enemies of socialist bureaucracies, uniting intellectuals and the young in an incorrigible hostility to the status quo. Not only do socialism and modernism end up in blind alleys—their blind alleys are pointed in radically different directions.

Meanwhile, liberal capitalism survives and staggers on. It survives because the market economics of capitalism does work—does promote economic growth and permit the individual to better his condition while enjoying an unprecedented degree of individual freedom. But there is something joyless, even somnambulistic, about this survival.

For it was the Judeo-Christian tradition which, as it were, acted as the Old Testament to the new evangel of liberal, individualistic capitalism—which supplied it with a moral code for the individual to live by, and which also enabled the free individual to find a transcendental meaning in life, to cope joyfully or sadly with all the *rites de passage* that define the human condition. Just as a victorious Christianity needed the Old Testament in its canon because the Ten Commandments were there—along with the assurance that God created the world *"and it was good,"* and along, too, with its corollary that it made sense to be fruitful and multiply on this earth—so liberal capitalism needed the Judeo-Christian tradition to inform it authoritatively about the use and abuse of the individual's newly won freedom. But the adversary culture, in both its utopian-rationalist and utopian-romantic aspects, turns this Judeo-Christian tradition into a mere anachronism. And the churches, now themselves a species of voluntary private enterprise, bereft of all public support and sanction, are increasingly ineffectual in coping with its antagonists.

Is it possible to restore the spiritual base of bourgeois society to something approaching a healthy condition?

One is tempted to answer no, it is not possible to turn back the clock of history. But this answer itself derives from the romantic-rationalist conception of history, as elaborated by Saint-Simon and Hegel and Marx. In fact, human history, read in a certain way, can be seen as full of critical moments when human beings deliberately turned the clock back. The Reformation, properly understood, was just such a moment, and so was the codification of the Talmud in postexile Judaism. What we call the "new" in intellectual and spiritual history is often nothing more than a novel way of turning the clock back. The history of science and technology is a cumulative history, in which new ways of seeing and doing effectively displace old ones. But the histories of religion and culture are not at all cumulative in this way, which is why one cannot study religion and culture without studying their histories, while scientists need not study the history of science to understand what they are up to.

So the possibility is open to us—but, for better or worse, it is not the only possibility. All we can say with some certainty, at this time, is that the future of liberal capitalism may be more significantly shaped by the ideas now germinating in the mind of some young, unknown philosopher or theologian than by any vagaries in annual GNP statistics. Those statistics are not unimportant, but to think they are all-important is to indulge in the silly kind of capitalist idolatry that is subversive of capitalism itself. It is the ethos of capitalism that is in gross disrepair, not the economics of capitalism—which is, indeed, its saving grace. But salvation through this grace alone will not suffice.

1979

11

The Cultural Revolution
and the Capitalist Future

It is by now a cliché to say that the most important political event of the twentieth century has been the collapse of the communist regimes and of the socialist idea on which they rested. True, there are still quite a few intellectuals who try to distinguish one from the other, who insist that there is still some life left in the socialist idea, conceived of as a kind of immortal political soul that survives the corruption and decay of its worldly incarnations. But political ideas do not have any such Platonic or otherworldly status. They live and die in history. They are what they become.

It makes no sense to say that a political idea turned out badly because human beings mishandled it or misinterpreted it, or because circumstances conspired against it. If that idea could not withstand human mishandling or unforeseen circumstance, it was a political fantasy rather than a realistic political idea. Political fantasies can only impose themselves on reality by brute coercion. That has been the natural destiny of socialism: a political fantasy incarnated into a reign of terror, a historical nightmare from which humanity has now awakened.

But awakened to what? The implications of the collapse of the socialist idea are still far from obvious. Certainly, the world has been awakened to the merits of a market economy as against a planned economy. But perhaps this is better described as a reawakening. After all, Adam Smith's *Wealth of Nations* was published over two centuries ago; market economies have been the dominant form of economic organization in the United States and most of Western Europe for about seven generations; and all this time, the world could plainly see the benefits that accrued to nations with market economies. Nevertheless, it was during this time and in these very nations that the socialist idea was born, that it flourished and gave rise to the theories from which socialist tyrannies grew and in recent decades threatened to envelop the globe.

How did this happen? What is there about a market economy that, despite the best efforts of our best economists, leads large numbers of people, including a lot of intelligent people, to believe that there is something radically wrong with it? What makes it so vulnerable to erroneous, hostile beliefs?

THE WEAKNESSES OF A MARKET ECONOMY

There are three major weaknesses in a market economy. The first is the self-interested nature of commercial activity. The second is the occasional—relatively rare but traumatic and memorable—malfunctioning of the system. The third is the growing tendency within modern democratic politics to frustrate the system's working by imposing ever-heavier burdens upon it.

Those who have taught elementary economics know how easy it is to teach this subject, how easy it is for students to learn it, and how hard it is for them to remember in practice what they have learned. This is because the fundamental principle of free-market economics—that in a free market, self-interested transactions between consenting adults are mutually advantageous—is so difficult to hang on to when *our own* self-interest is involved. When Adam Smith enunciated this principle, he established for the first time in human history the *moral* legitimacy of a market economy based on self-interested activity. He did so against a hostile, incredulous intellectual tradition that was best summed up in the year 301 A.D. by the Roman Emperor Diocletian: In decreeing wage and price controls throughout the Roman Empire, he declared, "Unregulated economic activity is an offense to the gods." Today, most of us accept the legitimacy of self-interest in general but are nevertheless instinctively suspicious of *other people's* self-interest.

Let me give you an example from my own experience of just how tenacious this suspicion is. In the late 1960s, I lived with my family in an apartment house in New York City that was home to well-educated upper-middle-class types. The landlord decided to make the building a cooperative and offered to sell us our apartments on attractive terms, so attractive that, were we so inclined, we would be able to turn around and sell our apartments for more than double the price that we would pay him. Nevertheless, the offer became very controversial among the tenants, and there were heated meetings, all of which focused on the question, "How much money is the landlord going to make on this deal?" It took some vigorous persuasion over a period of months to move my fellow tenants to do the sensible and profitable thing—profitable for themselves as well as for the landlord.

The inference is clear: A market economy depends on a large degree of economic sophistication among the citizenry, and this level of economic sophistication can only be achieved and sustained by ceaseless economic education of an elementary but fundamental kind. This is hard, uphill work because backsliding is equally ceaseless. Nevertheless, it can be done. One of the reasons Americans are more sensible about economics than are people in other countries is that we have been shaped by an economic education that results from having a Constitution based on sound economic principles, as well as having a judiciary that, until recent decades, insisted on respecting such principles.

But economic education can go only so far if economic realities seem to contradict it—as they have sometimes done. This brings me to the second weakness of a market economy: its tendency to produce what in the nineteenth century were called "gluts" and that we call "depressions." In an urbanized society, these are especially devastating, and in fact it was the emergence of what seemed to be a cruel, uncontrollable "business cycle" in the early nineteenth century that gave rise to socialist critiques of capitalism. To make matters worse, such "gluts" were not supposed to happen, according to prevailing economic doctrine, so the explanations proffered by various socialist critics were all the more credible.

I know exactly how those early socialists reacted to the first capitalist depressions. I remember vividly the flash of insight that turned me into a socialist during my college years. When I was an adolescent in New York City in the 1930s, I saw around me unemployed men eager to work but finding no jobs. I saw well-equipped factories standing idle. I saw a vast wealth of natural resources untapped. I saw a population in dire need of all the things that could be produced. And I said to myself: "Why in hell can't someone put all this together? This situation is not only tragic, it is stupid." Under such circumstances, the notion of an economy planned by governmental authority seemed commonsensical, not ideological.

We are very fortunate in that over these past 50 years we have had only relatively minor and blessedly short breakdowns in our market economy. We seem to be doing something right—but it would be nice to know what. The sad truth is that we have no theory of what we call the business cycle. I will always feel a gnawing uncertainty about the future of our market economy unless our economists reassure me that at least they have got the theory of it right. Then if politics and politicians proceed to mess things up, I'll know whom I can blame.

The third weakness is perhaps the most important of all: Socialism is dead, but versions of the collectivist impulse live on. You don't have to be a socialist to distrust or even destroy a market economy—contemporary liberal politicians can manage that task very well.

John Adams once wrote that he and other members of his generation were compelled by circumstance to devote their lives to war and politics so that their descendants could devote their lives to the study of philosophy and the arts. In our modern democracy, a significant percentage of these descendants, having tasted the fruits of affluence, and having enjoyed the benefits of a superior education, have nevertheless developed a passionate interest in politics—indeed, have come to believe that they are more fit to govern than others less privileged. They have developed a keen and irrepressible desire for political power, firm in the conviction that they are uniquely qualified to exercise this power in the "public interest." These activists are practitioners of what has been called "supply-side politics," in which entrepreneurship creates a market for their programs. Theirs is what Alan Ehrenhalt recently called, quite brilliantly, the "United States of Ambition."

The politics generated by this approach is what we call "contemporary liberalism." Because the intrusion of government involves large numbers of accomplices—sometimes whole professions or institutions—it creates a substantial political base for itself. The consequence is that in all Western democracies with a two-party system, one of those parties has only an expediential, as distinct from principled, commitment to a free-market economy, much preferring an economy in which all businesses and corporations function, or try to function, as regulated public utilities.

For those of us who care about a free-market economy and a free society, this challenge of contemporary liberalism survives the death of socialism. The good news is that this is a challenge we have been confronting for the past half century and that we have gotten better and better at coping with it, more aggressive in criticizing the liberal agenda in intellectually coherent terms. To use a favorite term of the liberal media, we have been able to make the liberal agenda "controversial," whereas only conservative ideas used to be so designated.

The very good news is that although contemporary liberalism has constructed a network of interest groups and media that buttresses much of our welfare state, the American people have nevertheless shown an enduring resistance to it. The average American tends to be unmoved by propaganda to the effect that his life is a bundle of "unmet needs" that government must address. He believes that government can help him best by keeping spending under control and his taxes low. This focus on personal liberty is not uniquely American: People in all the democracies have decided that the market economy is by far the most desirable of all possible alternatives.

CAPITALISM'S CULTURAL CRITICS

It is not, then, the economics of capitalism that is our fundamental, unmanageable problem. That problem today is located in the culture of our society, which is in the process of outflanking our relatively successful economy. While the society is bourgeois, the culture is increasingly, and belligerently, not.

In a bourgeois society, certain virtues are accepted as a matter of course by the majority of the people. These virtues—today we defensively call them "values"—include a willingness to work hard to improve one's condition, a respect for law, an appreciation of the merits of deferred gratification, a deference toward traditional religions, a concern for family and community, and so on. It is a commitment to such beliefs that creates a middle class, which then sustains a market economy.

Today, the old-fashioned animus against a market economy is evolving into an aggressive animus against the bourgeois society that is organically associated with our market economy. If you delegitimate this bourgeois society, the market economy—almost incidentally—is also delegitimated. It is for this reason that radical feminism today is a far more potent enemy of capitalism than radical trade unionism.

In this confrontation, defenders of capitalism are at a great disadvantage. The intense focus on economics and economic growth that is so natural to the heirs of Adam Smith has left them powerless against capitalism's cultural critics, as distinct from its economic critics. Adam Smith himself, though a creative genius in economic thought, was something of a philistine, believing that cultural attitudes and opinions, like religious ones, were matters of personal taste about which reasonable men would not and should not get particularly excited. For two centuries now, Western civilization has been haunted by this stupendous error of judgment, with the result that today, even as a market economy is accepted as superior to any other, at least in principle, the bourgeois society on which the market economy is based is being challenged with unprecedented boldness and success.

This is not a challenge that the defenders of a bourgeois society and its market economy are finding easy to cope with. Bourgeois society is so vulnerable because it is primarily a society oriented toward satisfying the ambitions of ordinary men and women. These are modest ambitions—in the eyes of some, lowly ambitions. They are, in most cases, what earlier eras would have called "domestic" ambitions: bettering the economic conditions of one's family, moving from a "rough" neighborhood to a "nice" neighborhood, and above all, offering one's children the possibility of moving still further ahead in economic and social status. Because bourgeois capitalism has, however irregularly, managed to satisfy these ambitions, it has engendered popular loyalty and kept radical dissatisfaction from achieving a popular base.

But the world is not inhabited by ordinary people alone. From the very beginnings, persons have emerged who found this new order boring and vulgar since it emphasized self-interest as the engine of economic growth and improvement of the common lot as its goal.

These people—we call them intellectuals and artists, and some have indeed been entitled to that label—do not like the marketplace and find the notion of their own participation in it repugnant. They cannot imagine themselves producing commodities for sale or exchange, even if they welcome the profits from such a sale. And whatever they may say about equality, they do not believe that they are merely equal to other people;

they believe that their talents and sensibilities make them superior. The kind of optimistic, rationalistic world view that tends to permeate a bourgeois-society-in-the-making is too "thin," too prosaic for those with an active imagination.

It was in Paris in the 1820s and 1830s that this revolt became an embryonic public counterculture. While those thinkers and groups who were later to be designated "utopian socialists" were constructing schemes for the total transformation of society and the human condition itself—a movement that reached its intellectual climax in Marxism—some hundreds of young people were settling in what was called the Bohemian section of Paris, where they proceeded to dissociate themselves from the society they inhabited by a series of dramatic gestures. Ostensibly committed to the life of the artist, though for most it was more a lifestyle than a productive artistic life, they wore workmen's clothes (the blue jeans of the day), were sexually promiscuous, took drugs (opium then being the drug of choice), committed suicide in alarming numbers, and in general baffled and distressed their elders. From this milieu emerged the vision of a cultural "avant-garde" with a special mission. The term itself, of military origin, referred to the assault troops who led an attack, but it ultimately came to mean a radical cultural critique of bourgeois-capitalist values and the human beings deemed to have been distorted by those values.

In our own time, the concept of an avant-garde has been co-opted by bourgeois-capitalist society to signify merely the latest fashion, the latest trend, in the arts. This absorption of the avant-garde into the fashion market has succeeded in corrupting the artistic enterprise. Unfortunately, it has also been successful in corrupting the co-opters, as the bourgeois world itself has become ever more "trendy."

ROLL OVER, BEETHOVEN

From 1870 to 1950, we witnessed the rise of the "modern" in all of the arts, fueled by bourgeois money seeking status not by buying and living in stately homes but by buying and consuming cultural products. And "modern" art and "modern" literature almost by definition are hostile to bourgeois conventions, morals, and virtues. Sometimes this hostility flows from a reactionary contempt for the present-day world, sometimes from radical fantasies of a more perfect world. In either case, it rejects the rational, secular, technological, progressive society that defined the dominant mode of politics up until World War II.

From these cultural passions evolved such modern phases in painting as Impressionism, Expressionism, Cubism, Futurism, Dadaism, Surrealism, and all those other "isms," swiftly succeeding one another. Each new "ism" invented novel ways of exploring the artist's deepest sensibilities, and these sensibilities, however various, were alike in being incompatible with the everyday world of the average citizen. But it was not until after World War II that our society entered the new era that persists today. Early in this period, the passions of the world of "high" culture began to pervade the universe of popular entertainment—especially among the young—and the result is now solemnly designated "popular culture."

A sign of the troubles ahead was evident in the early 1950s. While parents were watching Milton Berle on their new television sets, their children were listening to Elvis Presley on their old radios. For these adolescents and teenagers, frank sexuality—and what was really new, frank female sexuality—shoved aside the older romantic-erotic appeal of, say, a Frank Sinatra. Rock concerts were soon born, and bourgeois parents were put in the position of encouraging modesty and chastity for their young daughters and then sending them off to Dionysian festivals.

The real breakthrough came with the Beatles. I recall that when this group made their first visit to America, the London Observer asked me to interview Brian Epstein, their manager, and to forecast whether youthful Americans would be as enthusiastic about the Beatles as the British were. I did the interview, shook the hands of those pleasant young Liverpudlians, and published my forecast, to the effect that the Beatles really wouldn't have much appeal over here (not one of my better forecasts . . .).

The significance of the Beatles was twofold. For the first time, young people were producing their own music—actually composing the music and writing the lyrics as well as consuming it. Second, the market for such popular music—a market serviced by the exploding record industry—was taken over by the affluent young. Classical recordings survived, of course, but only as a sideshow. The record industry became an adjunct of a blossoming youth culture, and it was the growing affluence of our society—and of our young, in particular—that made this possible. Ten years later, this same phenomenon was experienced by the movie industry as the baby-boomers took over, consigning their elders to television. Today, it is the affluent young—at least young in their ethos if not in their years—who are reshaping television. Those baby-boomers are now thirty-something or even forty-something. They visit dentists more frequently than discotheques. And—O poetic justice!—they are now trying to raise their children. But we are learning that youthful fantasies can often outlive youth itself, and Hollywood and television are under the dominion of fantasy.

We have, then, been living through a cultural revolution that at one point threatened to become a political revolution—that flash point was experienced during the student revolution of the 1960s—one of those failed revolutions that was nevertheless enormously influential. In the United States, it pretty much forced us to withdraw from Vietnam. It also led quickly and decisively to the capture of the Democratic party by its left wing in 1972, thereby installing a kind of permanent polarization into American politics. And in the cultural world, its energies were channeled into what is now called "postmodernism," whose basic theme was expressed in Paris during the student rebellion of the 1960s by one of the graffiti painted on the walls of the Sorbonne: "All Power to the Imagination." This academic irrationalism is the dominant intellectual mode today not only in the arts but in the study of the humanities in our institutions of higher learning.

From a dissenting culture to a counterculture, we have finally arrived at a nihilistic anticulture. This anticulture permits the postmodernists to abolish the distinction between what used to be called "highbrow" art—it also used to be called "culture," without equivocation—and "popular" culture. The modern movement in the arts, from 1870 to 1950, was distinctly "highbrow." It was "difficult," and it took decades for even our educated classes to feel comfortable with its works in literature and art. A whole new generation had to be trained to understand and appreciate T. S. Eliot, Ezra Pound, and James Joyce in literature, Picasso, Miró, and Klee in painting. Today, in contrast, at some of our best universities you can take a course for credit in the meaning of a popular comic strip, which explores the ways in which American society and Western civilization in general are infested with race, sex, and class antagonism. Indeed, many students in literature, the arts, and the humanities today, in pursuit of self-expression, reveal an extraordinary ignorance of, and lack of interest in, their avant-garde, modernist forebears. So antitraditional are they that they happily dispossess themselves of their formative, antibourgeois traditions. This explains why the mission of an institution such as the National Endowment for the Arts has become a mission impossible. The so-called "arts" it was founded to support have become enmeshed with "arts" that were unimaginable a few decades ago—indeed, that would never have been designated as "arts."

THE REPUDIATION OF RATIONALISM

It is important to understand just how radical this new phase of modern thought is. Whereas modernism had calmly accepted Nietzsche's dictum that "God is dead," it generally interpreted this to mean simply that institutional religion was moribund. But a handful of modernists jumped to the Nietzschean conclusion that if God is dead, everything is now permitted. That was implicit in modernism and more than implicit for those who believed themselves to be the avant-garde of modernism, but only with postmodernism has it become belligerently explicit and a dominant motif in the culture at large.

For centuries, as the focus on religion as a central human experience continued to dim, the intellectual world remained remarkably complacent. The satisfying rituals of religion, it was thought, could be replaced by an esthetic experience of the arts. Indeed, the aura of the sacred has largely been transferred from religion to the arts, so that the burning or even censorship of books is regarded as a greater sacrilege than the vandalization of churches or synagogues. As for the moral code traditionally provided by religion, it was assumed that since modern individuals were rational moral agents, rational philosophy could be relied on to come up with a code that, if not identical with religion's, would be sufficiently congruent with it that the practical moral effect would be the same. From Immanuel Kant to John Dewey, that had been the basic assumption of secular rationalism, and it gave rise to the modern quasi-religion of secular humanism. Such a philosophical enterprise, it was believed, would converge on what John Dewey called "a common faith"—a faith in the ability of reason to solve all of our human problems, including our human need for moral guidance.

But this is a faith that has failed. Secular rationalism has been unable to produce a compelling, self-justifying moral code. Philosophy can analyze moral codes in interesting ways, but it cannot create them. And with this failure, the whole enterprise of secular humanism—the idea that man can define his humanity and shape the human future by reason and will alone—begins to lose its legitimacy. Over the past 30 years, all the major philosophical as well as cultural trends began to repudiate secular rationalism and secular humanism in favor of an intellectual and moral relativism and/or nihilism.

THE ELEVATION OF NIHILISM

Bourgeois capitalism began with a kind of benign toleration of religion but a firm commitment to Judeo-Christian morality. In this respect, Adam Smith and our Founding Fathers were of one mind, one sensibility. Their fundamental error, doubtless attributable to their rationalism, was a complacency about how this morality relates to its religious roots. Having made this error, they compare unfavorably with the Church Fathers of Christianity, who had to confront in the first three centuries A.D. powerful movements to keep the Old Testament out of the Christian Bible. After all, spokesmen for these movements argued, we have a new evangel that transcends the old, so what do we need the old for? The Church Fathers, however, understood that the rather otherworldly New Testament needed to be complemented by the more this-worldly Old Testament if a viable Christian "way of life" was to be propagated. Nor did they make the mistake of scissoring out pieces of the Old Testament—the Ten Commandments, for instance—for incorporation into the New Bible. They understood that in order to establish the absolute legitimacy of those elements in the Old Testament that were lacking in the New, they had to take it all. The Ten Commandments are divine commandments only if the Old Testament itself is of divine status. Without the victory of the Church Fathers in this bitter and prolonged controversy, the Catholic Church could never have created a new and enduring orthodoxy.

The bourgeois capitalist revolution of the eighteenth century was successful precisely because it did incorporate the older Judeo-Christian moral tradition into its basically secular, rationalist outlook. But it erred in cutting this moral tradition away from the religious context that nourished it. And so, in the nineteenth century in all Western nations, we had what was called a "crisis of faith" among writers and philosophers. It was not yet a crisis in moral beliefs. George Eliot wrote that God was "inconceivable," immortality "unbelievable," but Duty nonetheless "peremptory." A few years later, Nietzsche came along to proclaim that Duty was an illusion fostered by the Judeo-Christian "slave morality." Nietzsche was not taken seriously until after World War II—a war that Hitler lost but that German philosophy won.

Today, in our academic and intellectual circles, Nietzsche and his disciple, the Nazi sympathizer Martin Heidegger, are almost unanimously regarded as the two philosophical giants of the modern era. It is important to understand that their teachings are subversive not only of bourgeois society and the Judeo-Christian tradition but also of secular humanism, secular rationalism, bourgeois morality—and, in the end, of Western civilization itself.

ENSURING A CAPITALIST FUTURE

This cultural nihilism will have, in the short term, only a limited political effect—unless we have a massive, enduring economic crisis. The reason cultural nihilism will not prevail—this is still the good news—is that a bourgeois, property-owning democracy tends to breed its own antibodies. These antibodies immunize it, in large degree, against the lunacies of its intellectuals and artists. The common people in such a democracy are not uncommonly wise, but their experience tends to make them uncommonly sensible. They learn their economics by taking out a mortgage, they learn their politics by watching the local school board in action, and they learn the impossibility of "social engineering" by trying to raise their children to be decent human beings. These people are the bedrock of bourgeois capitalism, and it is on this rock that our modern democracies have been built.

But a society needs more than sensible men and women if it is to prosper: It needs the energies of the creative imagination as expressed in religion and the arts. It is crucial to the lives of all our citizens, as it is to all human beings at all times, that they encounter a world that possesses a transcendent meaning, a world in which the human experience makes sense. Nothing is more dehumanizing, more certain to generate a crisis, than to experience one's life as a meaningless event in a meaningless world.

In a sense, it is all Adam Smith's fault. That amiable, decent genius simply could not imagine a world in which traditional moral certainties could be effectively challenged and repudiated. Bourgeois society is his legacy, for good and ill. For good, in that it has produced through the market economy a world prosperous beyond all previous imaginings— even socialist imaginings. For ill, in that this world, with every passing decade, has become ever more spiritually impoverished. That war on poverty is the great unfinished task before us. The collapse of socialism, along with the vindication of a market economy, offers us a wonderful opportunity to think seriously about such an enterprise. Only such an enterprise can ensure a capitalist future.

1992

12

Countercultures

The counterculture that emerged in the United States in the 1960s—
and pretty much simultaneously in all the Western democracies—is certainly one of the most significant events in the last half-century of
Western civilization. It has reshaped our educational systems, our arts,
our forms of entertainment, our sexual conventions, our moral codes.
So it is important that we understand it—more important, indeed, than
that we criticize it.

Perhaps the major difficulty in understanding the counterculture is
that our conventional modes of analysis, whether social-scientific or
journalistic, come up empty. We seek causes, and find none—or we find
so many as to discredit the very enterprise of causal analysis. It is fair to
say that *nothing happened* to provoke this rebellion—there was no visible
crisis, or even any sense of crisis, in the economies, the societies, the
politics of the West. Even America's serious involvement in Vietnam,
which is frequently pointed to as a cause, will not serve, for the emergence of the counterculture antedated it by several years. And anyway,
such a parochial explanation overlooks the international nature of the
movement.

The fact is that the counterculture was not "caused," it was born.
What happened was internal to our culture and society, not external
to it.

The place to begin with any understanding of the counterculture is with its own self-designation *as* a "counterculture." We are dealing here with something that is not just another dissenting movement, not another stylistic revolution accomplished by a new and younger avant-garde, but with a movement that sees itself as *against* culture. It emerged out of an avowed hostility to "culture" itself—and this on the part of intellectuals, professors, and artists. What can that possibly mean?

We can approach its meaning by looking at the idea of "culture" itself—an idea so familiar to us that we tend to think of it as ageless. It is not. It was only in the latter part of the eighteenth century that the modern idea of "culture" was born, referring to a new, autonomous sector of human activity—a sector in which poets, playwrights, novelists, and thinkers offered an intensity of spiritual experience of a kind no longer provided by traditional religion. Goethe's novel *The Sorrows of Young Werther* (1774) supposedly caused dozens of suicides all over Europe. The days of religious turmoil were pretty much over; spiritual turmoil was now a "cultural" event.

At about the same time there was born the modern idea of "art." Previously, of course, the arts had existed in all their variety—ornamental, pedagogic, didactic, entertaining. But just as there was no such comprehensive term as "culture" so there was no such comprehensive term as "art." Both of these concepts came into being in order to designate a new self-consciousness, and a new sense of mission.

That mission was secular, humanistic, and redemptory. All traditional ties with religion were severed, in substance if not in form. The sacred was now to be found in culture and art, where "creative geniuses"—two old terms now endowed with a completely new definition—would give meaning to our lives and sustenance to our spiritual aspirations.

There are intellectual laggards who believe that culture and art are still successfully performing this function today. Susan Sontag, for instance, has written that art is "the nearest thing to a sacramental activity acknowledged by our secular society." But if this was true in the age of T. S. Eliot and James Joyce, and even (perhaps) of Jackson Pollock, it has no relevance to the era of Andy Warhol. Literary critics and art critics used to borrow freely the religious term "epiphany" to describe the intensity of our reactions to the great modernists in literature and painting. The counterculture offers us no such epiphanies, because it is alienated from the modern tradition that created them. The counterculture is "postmodernist."

Both the counterculture and its younger twin, postmodernism, are a rebellion against culture and art seen as autonomous, secular human activities—however infused, as modernism in the arts often was, with a notable spiritual energy. It is now felt, quite correctly, that these activities have been emptied of all their spiritual substance even while continuing to claim a quasi-sacred mission.

Inevitably, the very first target of this rebellion was the modern university, which for the past century or so had established itself as the central institution of secular-humanist orthodoxy. The rebellion was spurred on not only by the mass migration of young people to the university after World War II, but by trends over the past century in the world of modern literature and modern art themselves—a world that originated outside the university and, indeed, in opposition to it. In this world, free of institutional constraints, there had emerged, long before the counterculture, what we now call (following the critic Lionel Trilling) the "adversary culture."

That this modern, adversary culture—spanning the century 1865–1965—was hostile to bourgeois society was obvious enough. That it was also, in a deeper sense, hostile to secular humanism was not so obvious, even to many of those involved in the adversary culture itself. Yet in retrospect it is clear that, with hardly an exception, the leading novelists, poets, and painters—those whom we now call the "moderns" (Eliot, Yeats, Kafka, Proust, Picasso)—could not be enlisted in a secular-humanist canon.

Oddly enough one who saw this early on, and most clearly, was the Marxist critic and philosopher George Lukacs. For Lukacs, the adversary art and literature of the bourgeois West offered a clear sign of an impending cultural crisis that would accompany the general crisis of "capitalism." (What Lukacs did not understand, of course, was that Marxism, precisely because it was so much more radical a version of modern secular humanism, was destined to experience an even more shattering crisis.)

In the 1960s, in any event, the counterculture started to recruit adherents among junior faculty on American campuses. The professors who constituted the senior faculty, although a majority, were the last to understand—most, in truth, still do not understand—what was going on. Together with most commentators in the media, they kept looking for proximate causes of the students' discontents, and persisted in trying to appease those discontents.

Lionel Trilling once referred to "the humanist belief that society can change itself gradually by taking thought and revising sensibility." This is exactly how our professoriat responded, offering all kinds of institutional reforms and procedural concessions, blissfully unaware that it was being attacked for what it was, not for anything in particular that it did. Comfortable in the orthodox humanism incarnated in their institution, the university, these professors could not credit what many of their brightest students believed: namely, that, thanks to secular humanism, the university had become a soulless institution, an institution without any transcendent meaning. Nor did they understand that it is in the nature of things for an institution that has lost its soul to be experienced as "oppressive," even though thoughts of oppression may be the farthest distance from the oppressor's (or professor's) mind.

In their misconception, the professors were aided and abetted by the students themselves, who, grossly undereducated in the American way, and despite the efforts of their mentors among the junior faculty, found it all but impossible to formulate or even to comprehend their own discontents. ("Nietzsche is peachy" is as close as many of them came to articulateness.) One gets a deeper insight by listening to the better educated and intellectually more sophisticated French students who, in 1968, actually came close to making a revolution. They spelled out their message in graffiti on the walls of the Sorbonne: "All power to the imagination," "Real life is elsewhere," "Art is dead, let us create everyday life."

Nevertheless, American students too, just like the French, were undergoing an existential-spiritual crisis, a crisis revealed in their turbulent sexuality, their drug addiction, their desperate efforts to invent new "lifestyles," and their popular music, at once Dionysiac and mournful.

We, in our secular, rationalist world are utterly unprepared for such existential-spiritual spasms. For one thing, we do not study the history of religion in any serious way, even for explanations of religious phenomena. Instead we look for sociological explanations, or economic explanations, or even political explanations, and we do so precisely because we find it almost impossible to posit spiritual appetites and spiritual passions as independent, primary forces in human history.

Yet they are, or they can be. Take the rise of Puritanism in Elizabethan England, Shakespeare's England. At that time the Anglican church was the most tolerant of all national churches. It was a church with a beautiful liturgy and a host of first-rate thinkers. And England itself was the most prosperous and the freest society in the Western world, with a glorious secular culture. So why should people, especially young people among whom were many women, suddenly have decided that they wanted to be, of all things, Puritans?

All one can say is that these things happen, that the spirit bloweth where it listeth, and that sometimes all you need to generate a counterculture is an orthodoxy against which it can rebel. For no orthodoxy can ever fully satisfy our spiritual appetites and our spiritual passions.

The granddaddy of all countercultures, of course, was early Christianity itself. And in a polemic written in the second century by the Greek philosopher Celsus, we have a marvelous document of the bewilderment and incomprehension with which Greco-Roman rationalists of the early Christian era viewed this counterculture. All copies of this polemic were eventually destroyed by the Church, but we have the rebuttal to it, *Contra Celsum*, by the church father Origen. From this rejoinder, the nineteenth-century British historian and rationalist James Anthony Froude wrote an essay reconstructing Celsus's argument.

And what was Celsus saying? He was saying that it was absurd for people to go around believing in miracles, believing that a god-man had been buried and then resurrected, when such things were an affront to reason and utterly impossible. Celsus's baffled critique of Christianity made all the sense in the world, if by sense one means pure rationality. His was philosophy's response to Christian dogma and Christian faith. But philosophy, inherently rationalist, is always disarmed by religion when it is not simply ignored by religion—just as our own academic, rationalist culture is disarmed or ignored by our counterculture.

The countercultural rejoinder to today's rationalist, like the early Christian response to Celsus, is always something like, "You just don't understand." That is not, technically, an argument. But it is a powerful and, for some, a persuasive way of ending the discussion, and ending the discussion is precisely the goal of a counterculture, which always aims to create a new vocabulary, establish new terms, mark new parameters of discourse—in short, to forge a new human and social reality.

It rarely succeeds, however; an orthodoxy has far greater staying power than a counterculture. And even when it does succeed, it creates, willy-nilly, a new orthodoxy of its own.

There have been only two such orthodoxies, enduring orthodoxies, in the history of Western civilization, and both of them began as counter-cultures. They are Christianity and secular, rationalist humanism. Obviously, creating a new orthodoxy is very hard. But even when counter-cultures do not eventuate in a new orthodoxy, they still have an effect, sometimes a lasting effect; the world is never quite the same again when they have done their work, and neither is orthodoxy.

Countercultural challenges to orthodoxy take different forms at differ-ent times, but a common substratum of attitudes and belief is dis-cernible.

To begin with, there is the experience of what we now glibly call alien-ation, and all the forms in which this experience is expressed. Not to feel alienated is, from the point of view of the counterculture, to be "inau-thentic," to be deficient in a fully human sensibility. We have witnessed this phenomenon among the intellectual and artistic classes in the West over the past hundred years, and the notion of the alienated intellectual and artist is, by now, so familiar that we read it backward into history.

This is a misreading, however. It makes no sense to regard Bach and Mozart, Titian and Raphael, Dante and Shakespeare as alienated from the civilization in which they lived. They were, one supposes, discontent-ed often enough, and critical often enough. But mere discontent, and normal criticism of the actual from the viewpoint of the ideal, do not add up to alienation, which is a far more profound experience—the experience of being homeless in a world created by orthodoxy.

Associated with this sense of alienation is a corresponding sense of indignation, even outrage, at the orthodoxy, which is perceived to be the ground of the alienation. It is this indignation at what is felt to be intol-erable that unites people into a countercultural *movement*, as distinct from a collection of tormented individuals, or a mere school of thought. And as all movements, including countercultural ones, seek power, this in turn leads to conflict. It is astonishing how frequently the defenders of orthodoxy fail to see that power is at issue, and deceive themselves into believing that a benign, therapeutic approach can pacify the passions of indignant alienation.

And then there is sex, always sex. "Sexual liberation" is always very near the top of a countercultural agenda—though just what form the liberation takes can and does vary, sometimes quite wildly. Women's liberation, likewise, is another consistent feature of all countercultural movements—liberation from husbands, liberation from children, liberation from family. Indeed, the real object of these various sexual heterodoxies is to disestablish the family as the central institution of human society, the citadel of orthodoxy.

Just how one goes about such disestablishment is of secondary importance, though it is of very keen interest to the participants. Thus, at one end of the spectrum, there have been countercultural movements which promoted sexual promiscuity, on the grounds that the members of the movement are of the "elect," the already redeemed who have recaptured humanity's lost innocence. At the other end of the sexual spectrum there have been countercultural movements that have preached and practiced abstinence. What we call Catholic monasticism was such a movement.

In her wonderful novel *The Abyss*, Marguerite Yourcenar deals with the disastrous Anabaptist rebellion in Germany in the 1520s. The origins of the Anabaptist sect lay in a medieval heretical movement called the Brethren of the Free Spirit (at various times it had other names), which emphasized spiritual Christianity as against organized, institutionalized Christianity, and preached spiritual devotion as against orthodox piety. The Brethren also deplored sex and the family as distractions from the realm of the spirit.

For all these reasons, the Church quite ruthlessly suppressed the Anabaptist movement. But the impulse kept bubbling up for some two centuries, and at one point the movement became sufficiently numerous to gain control of the city of Münster. There, the wheel quickly came full circle, and soon Münster was a city notorious for its uncontrolled licentiousness—after all, there is a very fine line between absolute sexual purity and utter sexual licentiousness, and human beings, especially if they are bereft of institutional guidance and support, can easily lose their balance.

In the end, the German secular authorities laid siege to the city and, after some months, conquered it, slaughtering the inhabitants. In this, the princes had the blessing of Martin Luther, who (like Calvin) was a staunch defender of the family and sought—and achieved—not a liberation from orthodoxy, but a reformation of the prevailing one. Today no one is more emphatic in defense of the family than our own Baptists, who have inherited the anti-institutional animus of their forebears but little else of their counterculture.

Which leads us to another, more recent, attempt to undermine the family.

We have witnessed in our time the extraordinary collapse of Soviet Communism. Most analyses of that collapse have focused on the disaster that inevitably accompanies efforts to create a centralized, planned economy. These analyses are convincing, but I do not think they tell the whole story.

One need not have known a great deal about the theory of free-market economics to have been convinced that Soviet religious doctrine—described, somewhat redundantly but accurately enough, as "godless, atheistic materialism"—could never sink roots among the Russian people. All people, everywhere, at all times, are "theotropic" beings, who cannot long abide the absence of a transcendental dimension to their lives. The collapse of Soviet Communism vindicates this truth.

And there is another point to be made here, which pertains not only to twentieth-century Communism in practice but to socialist doctrine as a whole. This body of thought has always been hostile to the family as an institution, not only because the family is *the* crucial vehicle for the transmission of specific ideas and values, but because it is in the family that the very sense of tradition, the basic human instinct of piety toward an ancestral past, is preserved and conveyed. In seeking to create a brave new world, socialism of necessity subverts tradition and celebrates impiety. It agrees with Tom Paine, a presocialist thinker, that the dead are a "non-entity," that we should "let the dead bury the dead," and that we must resist "the vanity and presumption of governing beyond the grave."

In the early socialist credo, contempt for the family was universal. All the thinkers whom, following Marx's usage, we call "utopian socialists" were agreed on this point, although they approached it from different angles. William Godwin in England professed to despise not only marriage and the family but also sexuality, arguing that the truly rational man would be liberated from such lowly passions. In France, on the other hand, François Fourier insisted that in *his* ideal communities, sex would be absolutely free, and that as a result of such liberation of the passions, men and women would live to 144 years of age, 120 of which would be spent in active lovemaking. A nut, one might say; but Fourier was respected and influential throughout Europe and even among Transcendentalist circles in the United States. When in the grip of a countercultural passion, one can easily lose or repress the ability to distinguish the nutty from the sensible.

When I taught a graduate seminar in social thought, my classes tended to be dominated by young Marxists and quasi-Marxists. We used to read the *Communist Manifesto*, in which Marx launches a vitriolic attack on the bourgeois family as an institution of legalized prostitution for the unfortunate wives. I once asked my students what they thought of these remarks but got no response—it was clear that they preferred not to think about them, though they regarded the *Communist Manifesto* as a kind of scripture. I then asked whether they thought their mothers were prostitutes. An uneasy and baffled silence ensued. What I found and still find fascinating is less the fact that no one had the courage to say "Yes" than the fact that no one had the courage to say "No." Keeping their Marxism intact was obviously more important to them than anything else.

But setting aside the mental contortions of true believers, it remains true that one of the inherent weaknesses of even moderate socialist movements and governments is this ingrained hostility to the family. We are coming to recognize that this hostility, now cloaked as indifference, is a major factor in the political torment of what we still call "liberalism" in the United States. That the hostility is there is revealed by the complaisance of liberalism before the assaults on the family by contemporary radical feminism and the "gay rights" movement. All liberal politicians today feel it necessary to speak highly of the family, but they cannot bring themselves to defend it against its enemies.

And what about our own orthodoxy, the secular, humanist, rationalist orthodoxy against which all the countercultures of the past two centuries—from romanticism through modernism to postmodernism— have rebelled? How has it been coping?

On the whole, it has been coping badly, its survival ensured mainly by its toleration of older religious and moral traditions that still govern, however uncertainly, the lives of most citizens, and by its unqualified faith in progress, material *and* moral—a faith that is grievously wounded but not yet dead.

Because of this faith in progress, our modern orthodoxy has been enabled to ignore the basic principle of any orthodoxy, which is virtue (a principle that all countercultures find intolerable). The word itself has suffered a degradation in our time. As the philosopher Leo Strauss once pointed out, a term that used to refer to the manliness of men came to be limited in its reference to the sexual purity of women—and now even that meaning has, as it were, fallen.

Orthodox virtue is a prescription, whereby people find contentment in their lives by doing the right thing, in the right way, at the right time, and in the right frame of mind. The last qualification is the weakest of the four: All orthodoxies believe that if you do the right thing, in the right way, at the right time, you will probably end up in possession of the right frame of mind. (That is why orthodoxy is always suspicious of those who go around talking enthusiastically about "spirituality.") Orthodoxies have known forever that virtue is a practical, existential discipline, not simply a matter of faith, and definitely not an application of abstract doctrine to behavior.

Beneath the priority that orthodoxy gives to right practice lies a basic, primordial intuition: that the world is meant to be a home for mankind. Leading a life according to virtue is therefore of metaphysical significance. Pursuing the ethical sanctification of the mundane, virtuous practice gains strength by linking the living to the dead and to the unborn. In a traditional orthodox community, both the dead and the unborn have the right to vote.

But *our* orthodoxy is essentially contemptuous of the very idea of tradition; this it has in common with its offshoot, socialism. It also lacks a central principle of virtue. Instead, it proposes a whole set of virtues, the "liberal" virtues—toleration, pluralism, relativism—which, one might say, construct a supermarket of possible good and decent lives. This is a prescription for moral anarchy, which is exactly what we are now experiencing. And there is no way that moral anarchy can pass for moral progress, though there are today, especially in our educational system, a fair number of people who pretend that it can.

And so we come full circle. I began by remarking that today's postmodernist counterculture grew out of trends in modernist culture itself, whose works it disdains but whose work it continues. Essentially, postmodernism's critique of modernism is that it is "academic," seemingly designed from the outset to constitute a "canon." And our current counterculture is opposed to canons, just as it is opposed to Culture (with a capital C) and to Art (with a capital A).

In the poets and painters of the previous adversary culture, there was to be found an intense spiritual energy, an energy derived from their overweening ambition to have art replace religion as that which gives meaning to our lives. The ethos of our current counterculture is, instead, the ethos of a carnival. It is cynical, nihilistic, and exploitative; it is candidly sensationalistic and materialistic.

The energy of the postmodern counterculture goes into self-promotion, public relations, and grant-seeking. In this respect, the counterculture has become an extension of the modern media, favoring exhibitionism in place of intellectual or spiritual ambition. Shopping for, not whoring after, strange gods is the order of day.

Can it last? The original excitement of the counterculture is certainly gone; there is already a sense of tedium about the whole business—too many "lifestyles," too many transient, "protean" selves.

But that does not mean that things will return to "normal." The real danger, it seems to me, is that the collapse of secular humanism signaled by the rise of the counterculture will bring down with it—will discredit—human things that are of permanent importance. A spiritual rebellion against the constrictions of secular humanism could end up—in some way, it has already ended up—in a celebration of irrationalism and a derogation, not simply of an overweening rationalism, but of reason itself. In these circumstances, the idea of an ordered liberty could collapse under pressure from a new spiritual and ideological conformity that rushes in where liberals fear to tread.

Countercultures are dangerous phenomena even as they are inevitable. Their destructive power always far exceeds their constructive power. The delicate task that faces our civilization today is not to reform the secular rationalist orthodoxy, which has passed beyond the point of redemption. Rather, it is to breathe new life into the older, now largely comatose, religious orthodoxies—while resisting the counterculture as best we can, adapting to it and reshaping it where we cannot simply resist.

Resistance is important because it buys time during which the contradictory and self-destructive impulses of the counterculture can work themselves out. (The current conflict between prolesbian feminism and an older "sexual liberation" is a case in point.) At the same time, we have to recognize that some ground may never be recovered. And as for breathing new life into the spirit of older orthodoxies, it must be said that no one can foresee how that would happen, what it would entail, and in what ways a newly inspirited religious orthodoxy would differ from the old.

We have to be prepared for surprises—not all of them, perhaps, to our liking. But, historically, this is the way the clash between orthodoxy and counterculture has always been resolved.

1994

SECTION IV

On Capitalism and the Democratic Idea

13

Machiavelli and the Profanation of Politics

The *Secretum Secretorum* is a brief treatise attributed to Roger Bacon that had great currency during the later Middle Ages, in various "editions" and under various forms of the title *De Regimine Principum* as well as its own. It presents itself as a letter of advice from Aristotle to his student, Alexander of Macedon, who was having trouble ruling the Persians he had just conquered. In the course of this letter, Aristotle says that a king should put God's law before his own; avoid the sin of pride from which all other sins flow; converse with wise men; help the poor and needy; flee from lechery and lust; never break his oath; enjoy music while remaining of grave countenance; and so forth, and so forth. By far the most interesting thing about the *Secretum Secretorum* for the modern reader is its title. What, one wonders, is the secret?

The answer appears to be, quite simply, that there is none. Not really. All the title signifies is that the art of good government is something so rare, something which so few men ever discover, that it can be considered a hidden treasure. I have said "the art of good government"—the art of *self*-government would have been more precise. For the whole vast medieval and early modern literature concerned with *De regimine principum*, *De officio regis*, *De institutione principium*, and so on—Professor Allen Gilbert's *Machiavelli's 'Prince' and its Forerunners* gives us an idea of the number and scope of such works—intends primarily to instruct rulers on how to govern *themselves*. This is, under any conditions and for any

151

man, the most difficult task in the world. It is especially difficult for a man who, like the prince, is surrounded by the temptations that go with wealth, power, and an atmosphere of servile flattery. In most cases, of course, since princes are only human, the effort is bound to fail. Such failures are not described in this highly moralistic literature, in part doubtless for fear of undermining the authority of government itself, but mainly for fear of setting a bad example.

The fact that this political literature was so little "sociological," so blandly mindless of economics, administration, even the military arts, obviously reflects to some extent the simple conditions of medieval life and medieval society. But only to some extent. If it is true that what the king did was less important than what kind of king he was; and if this in turn was less important than the fact that he was, indisputably, the rightful king—nevertheless, he had much to learn about his world that these guides never attempted to teach. Their self-limitation and, to our eyes, curious modesty appears to derive from their assumption that whereas morals, involving as it does a knowledge of the good, may be improved through exhortation and instruction, wise government is a practical activity that cannot be divorced from specific circumstances and which therefore can only be "learned" through the experience of ruling.

"Political science" in the medieval sense meant the description of obligations; it gave no further practical advice for it did not claim any special practical wisdom. It did not deny the existence of such wisdom; it simply denied that philosophers, as against statesmen, possessed it. It is one thing to say a king should be merciful; it is quite another to say that he should spare the life of a particular conspirator—for who can foresee whether such an individual act of mercy might not mean the ruin of the commonwealth and general misery? Providence, of course, knew the answer. But Providence was inscrutable, as much to philosophers as to anyone else. Only prophets could read the future; and all (including the Church) agreed that the age of prophecy was over. For a philosopher to attempt to judge human action by its consequences, instead of its concord with the moral law, was to claim a superhuman ability to foresee the general and ultimate results of specific actions. It was as a denial of this human ability that the Ten Commandments, and the moral code associated with it, were proclaimed as authoritative. And it was because he believed that men did not—and in the nature of things could not—have such power that St. Thomas said flatly: "*Eventus sequens non facit actum malum qui erat bonus, nec bonum qui erat malus.*"*

It is against such a background that one can appreciate the revolution in political theory that Niccolò Machiavelli accomplished. To be sure, the older order of thought did not vanish overnight. The year in which *The Prince* was probably finished was also the year of two such popular works as Erasmus's *Education of a Christian Prince*, an eloquent homily, and Thomas More's *Utopia*. This latter was in the classical rather than in the medieval tradition, but these had more in common with each other than with the modern mode. More's *Utopia* was located, not in the future, but out of time entirely; it posed an ideal and criticized reality in its name—but it did not suggest that reality could be transformed into ideality through political action. It was a purely normative exercise. Within the book itself, More inserts a dialogue on what role philosophers can play in politics (he had just been offered a post by Henry VIII), and concludes that, at best, he can by his counsel prevent some evil from being done. This was hardly what we would today call utopian doctrine. And, in the event, More's own martyrdom was to reveal that even this "at best" was an elusive possibility.

The homiletic tradition, then, continued after Machiavelli. Indeed, one finds innumerable specimens of the genre in the sixteenth and seventeenth centuries. But one also finds that, under the influence of "Machiavellianism," this genre is either being converted into, or tinged with, something new in political philosophy. This "something new" lies not merely in the fact that Machiavelli stands the tradition upon its head. He does do that. Whereas it had claimed moral authority and disclaimed political knowledge, he repudiates the established moral authority and asserts a kind of knowledge that the tradition did not recognize. Yet there had been Christian sects which insisted that the moral law had to be abrogated so as to prepare the way for the Second Coming; and there had been sects, too, which felt that, as a result of some secret communion with either God or the devil, they had been supplied with "the key" to man's temporal destinies. Machiavelli is no Christian heretic; he is the first of the post-Christian philosophers.

---

*A good act cannot be made evil, nor can an evil act be made good, by subsequent events.

Post-Christian, not pre-Christian. Since Machiavelli lived during the Renaissance and, like all Renaissance writers, continually referred to Greek and Roman authors as his authorities, one is inevitably tempted to see in his thought a resurgent paganism. But a careful reading makes it obvious that Machiavelli uses his classical "authorities" in an arbitrary—and often downright cynical—manner. Moreover, the very spirit that pervades Machiavelli is markedly different from that which finds expression in, say, Thucydides or Tacitus. The classical writers, like Machiavelli, had no conception of Providence, believed that men were the toys of chance and necessity, and admitted that the universe was blind to human values—but they also asserted (or, at the very least, implied) that man could be superior to his fate insofar as he faced it with nobility of character, courage, and grace. Their writings breathe a *pietas* before the cosmic condition of the race; whereas Machiavelli writes with the sardonic iciness of inhuman fate itself. He is the first of the nihilists, not the last of the pagans.

This is not to suggest that he was devoid of human feeling. His passionate Italian patriotism was, for instance, doubtless genuine enough. So was the streak of sadism (no other word will do) that runs through his work, from his very first opuscule to his last. But these sentiments, though they have an important effect on the literary quality of his work, and help explain both its popularity in Italy and its notoriety everywhere, are subsidiary to his main purpose. This purpose, as announced in *The Prince*, is to describe "the way things really are" *(la verità effettuale della cosa)* rather than—as the medieval theorists had done—the "imagination" of it. "For many have pictured republics and principalities which in fact have never been known or seen, because how one lives is so far distant from how one ought to live, that he who neglects what is done for what ought to be done, sooner effects his ruin than his preservation."

But what, a modern reader is bound to ask, was so shocking about that? What, moreover, is "nihilistic" about it? Is it not a sensible attitude—indeed a "scientific" attitude?

These questions are best answered by another question: What in our own time is so shocking about de Sade? We know that the kinds of sexual activities he describes do exist and play an important role in men's lives. Lust, adultery, sodomy, pederasty, and all the various sexual aberrations have always been with us; and there is no question that they are necessary to the "happiness" of a large class of people. Yet in no country of the world may de Sade's books circulate freely. Our society seems to believe that unrestricted knowledge of these subjects constitutes pornography. It insists that, if they are to be discussed at all, it must either be in an esoteric manner (in medical textbooks) or within a moral framework that makes it clear one is treating of an evil, not merely a human phenomenon. And, for de Sade, there is no natural and prescriptive moral framework in sex, just as there is none in politics for Machiavelli.

Pornography may be defined as a kind of knowledge which has an inherent tendency to corrupt and deprave our imaginations. The twentieth century formally recognizes that pornography, as such, does exist; but it also feels committed to the contradictory thesis that knowledge per se is good and "enlightening." This is but another way of saying that the twentieth century is experiencing a crisis of values—not simply a conflict between values, but a crisis in the very idea of value. For if one allows that knowledge in and of itself may be the supreme value, one must go on to say that the knowledge of evil is as valuable as the knowledge of good, from which it flows that a man who is engaged in adding to our knowledge of evil is as virtuous as a man engaged in adding to our knowledge of good—in short, that the difference between evil and good is at most a matter of habitual terminology. This is, precisely, nihilism.

One cannot appreciate the new *frisson* that Machiavelli gave to his age without realizing that he appeared to his contemporaries as a kind of political pornographer. "I hold there is no sin but ignorance," Marlowe has him say in one of his plays. The ascription was entirely apt. For the message of Machiavelli was really nothing more than the message of pornographers everywhere and at all times: that there is no such thing as pornography. Nothing that Machiavelli said about affairs of state was really novel to his readers. They knew—everyone had always known— that politics is a dirty business; that a ruler may better secure his power by slaughtering innocents, breaking his solemn oaths, betraying his friends, than by not doing so. But they also knew, or had thought, or had said, that such a ruler would suffer the torments of hell for eternity. Where Machiavelli was original was first, in brazenly announcing these truths, and second, in implying as strongly as he could (he dared not be candid on this subject, for it would have cost him his head) that wicked princes did not rot in hell for the sufficient reason that no such place existed.

These two aspects of Machiavelli's originality were most intimately connected, and necessarily so. Had he accepted Christian morality and the prospect of divine judgment, he would never have wanted to break the traditional silence on the awful things men do in their lust for power; he would have been fearful of depraving the imagination of men, especially of princes, and of incurring responsibility for their damnation. Had he even accepted the moral code of the Graeco-Roman writers (who did not believe in divine judgment either) he would at least have indicated how awful these things were, no matter how inevitable in the course of human affairs. But instead he declared that an honest and enlightened man had no right to regard them as awful at all. They were inherent in the nature of things; and with the nature of things only fools and sentimentalists would quarrel. The classical writers knew that the rule of tyrants was an intrinsic possibility of human politics—one that was bound to find realization under certain circumstances that made tyranny the only alternative to chaos or foreign domination. They might "justify" tyranny; but without ever denying that it was tyranny. Machiavelli, in contrast, wrote a book of advice to aspiring tyrants in which the word "tyranny" simply does not appear.

There is in Machiavelli a deliberate, if sometimes artful, debasement of political virtues. One of the secrets of his sparkling style is the playful way he gravely uses the conventional rhetoric in order to mock its conventional character. Thus, in his eulogy of Castruccio Castracani he writes solemnly: "He was just to his subjects, faithless to foreigners, and he never sought to conquer by force when he could do so by fraud." Such examples can be multiplied a hundredfold. His constant use of the term *virtù* to mean that which characterizes the virtuoso is perhaps his outstanding pun (e.g., Agathocles "accompanied his infamies with so much *virtù* that he rose to be praetor of Syracuse"). In the course of undermining the traditional political virtues, he also takes the opportunity—wherever possible—to show contempt for the established religion. He can do so under the guise of "interpreting" biblical history in his *Discourses*, as when he solemnly praises Moses and King David for their cruelty and ruthlessness; or he can do so more openly in a "technical" work like the *Art of War*, where he blames Christianity for the decline of martial prowess in Italy.

But the most candid statement of "Machiavellianism" is in his *Florentine History*. It is put into the mouth of "one of the boldest and most experienced" of the plebeian leaders during the revolt of 1378; but there can be no doubt that it is Machiavelli himself who is speaking from the heart:

If we had now to decide whether we should take up arms, burn and pillage the houses of the citizens, and rob the churches, I should be the first among you to suggest caution, and perhaps to approve of your preference for humble poverty rather than risking all on the chance of a gain. But as you have already had recourse to arms, and have committed much havoc, it appears to me the point you have now to consider is, not how shall we desist from this destruction, but how we shall commit more in order to secure ourselves. . . . It is necessary to commit new offences by multiplying the plunderings and burnings and redoubling the disturbances . . . because, where small faults are chastised, great crimes are rewarded. . . . It grieves me to hear that some of you repent for consciences' sake of what you have already done and wish to go no further with us. If this be true you are not the sort of men I thought you were, for neither conscience nor shame ought to have any influence upon you. Remember that those men who conquer never incur any reproach. . . . If you watch the ways of men, you will see that those who obtain great wealth and power do so either by force or fraud, and having got them they conceal under some honest name the foulness of their deeds. Whilst those who through lack of wisdom, or from simplicity, do not employ these methods are always stifled in slavery or poverty. Faithful slaves always remain slaves, and good men are always poor men. Men will never escape from slavery unless they are unfaithful and bold, nor from poverty unless they are rapacious and fraudulent, because both God and Nature have placed the fortunes of men in such a position that they are reached rather by robbery than industry, and by evil rather than by honest skill.

This is strong medicine indeed, and it was precisely as a kind of strong medicine that Machiavelli was first apologetically presented to the world. When his *Prince* was posthumously published in 1532, the printer, Bernardo di Giunta, dedicated it to Monsignor Giovanni Gaddi, asking to be protected from those critics "who do not realize that whatever teaches of herbs and medicines, must also teach of poisons—only thus can we know how to identify them." This medical metaphor has been fairly popular with writers on Machiavelli ever since (e.g., Ranke and Macaulay). It testifies to a recognition that Machiavelli *can* be a dangerous teacher; but it also claims that he may be a useful one.

Useful for what? To this question, there have been many answers, and a summary of them would be nothing short of a history of Machiavelli's influence on modern thought—it might be nothing short of a history of modern thought itself. But four of these answers are most prominent and most popular.

1. *The historical-scholarly answer.* The scholarship on Machiavelli and his times has been voluminous, technically superb, and almost invariably misleading. The bulk of this work has been done by Germans and Italians, and in both these countries the growing interest in Machiavelli was concurrent with efforts to form a united nation. For a century and a half after *The Prince* appeared, the commentators on Machiavelli—whether friendly or hostile—paid not the slightest attention to the final chapter, with its exhortation to free Italy from the barbarians. It was Herder who first saw in this the key to Machiavelli's thought, and who set the tone for modern scholarship. The tendency of this scholarship is to admire Machiavelli as one of the ideological founders of the modern national state, and it has seen in his seeming amorality a gesture of desperate patriotism and bitter pathos, suitable to his corrupt epoch. British scholars (usually Italophile) have also been inclined to follow this interpretation. This explains how it is that Macaulay came to say of Machiavelli's *oeuvre* that "we are acquainted with few writings which exhibit so much elevation of sentiment, so pure and warm a zeal for the public good, or so just a view of the duties and rights of citizens," or that in our own day T. S. Eliot could assert, "such a view of life as Machiavelli's implies a state of the soul which may be called a state of innocence."

Now, Machiavelli was certainly an Italian patriot. But (as Professor Leo Strauss has demonstrated, in what is by far the best book on Machiavelli yet written) he was a patriot of a special kind. "I love my country more than my soul," he wrote to Guicciardini; and that he was sincere may be gathered from those scattered remarks in the *Discourses* where he emphasizes that, when a nation's interests are involved, no considerations of justice, legality, or propriety ought to affect our judgment. Whether one finds this laudable or not will, of course, depend on the relative estimates one places upon one's fatherland and one's soul. Very few of the scholars who admire Machiavelli are explicit on this point. A few, following Friederich Meinecke, concede resignedly that it is the ineluctable nature of political life to lead patriotic souls to perdition; though after the German experience of the past thirty years, one may expect to hear less of this. But, in any event, the basic trend of conventional Machiavelli scholarship is to suggest to the student that if a man cares dearly for his country, it does not much matter what else he cares for.

2. *The raison d'état answer.* It is reported that Mussolini kept a copy of *The Prince* on his night table. For all the good it did him, he was following an old tradition that goes back to the sixteenth and seventeenth centuries, when kings and ministers surreptitiously read Machiavelli or pale imitations of him in order to glean the esoteric and dreadful wisdom of *raison d'état.* (After Machiavelli was condemned by the Church, they may have shifted to Tacitus, who during that period was taken to be a proto-Machiavellian.) For with the rise of the absolute monarchies, there was a need for a theory of the state. The previous political theory, not of the state but of society—the theory of the Christian commonwealth, in which kingship was a well-defined office—had been rendered archaic; and into the vacuum thus created there rushed the esoteric doctrine of "reason of state." What this doctrine came down to was that (1) it was perfectly legitimate for a king to extend or secure his power and dominion by any and every means, that is, to act like a tyrant; and (2) his subjects must be left in ignorance of this truth lest it undermine their pious subservience to what passed for "duly constituted" authority—the king had to be hypocritical as well as unscrupulous.

This whole historical episode, during which the fashion of dabbling in *raison d'état* was the rage of courtiers, ministers, confessors, and paramours, has not yet been adequately told. The few ponderous German studies of it, properly humble before something that has the air of *Realpolitik*, completely miss its farcical aspect. For the "rules" of *raison d'état* are very similar to—they are sometimes identical with—the familiar household proverbs that can be quoted to suit any purpose. ("Look before you leap," and "He who hesitates is lost," etc.) Machiavelli is full of general rules and prescriptions—all of which conflict with one another, and some of which, as Professor Butterfield has shown, are patently contradicted by the evidence he marshals for their support. Such a state of affairs is unavoidable, since generalizations of this order have no purchase upon experience. When a king should murder his defeated enemies, and when he should treat them leniently, is not something that can be decided *a priori*—it is difficult enough to decide it *a posteriori*, as historians know. The statesman who tries to substitute abstract deductions for prudent judgment is not long for this world.

In fact, the rulers of the sixteenth and seventeenth centuries managed to survive reasonably well, and the most clever and resourceful of them prospered mightily. This was not because of anything they learned from their readings in the new "philosophy" of politics. They did what they thought was the sensible thing to do under the circumstances; and all that *raison d'état* constituted was the reassurance that whatever they did need not trouble their consciences. This perhaps made them a little more brutal than they might otherwise have been; but one can never be sure. As Machiavelli himself said, rulers had long practiced what he first preached.

3. *The democratic-enlightenment answer.* This has been by far the most influential of all, and it derives directly from the medical metaphor proposed by Bernardo di Giunta. Machiavelli is taken for an acute anatomist and diagnostician of political disorder, who has exposed the unscrupulousness of rulers in order to allow men to recover their political health in pure self-government, that is, popular government.

In its most extreme form, this view regards Machiavelli as a cunning satirist, and his *Prince* as a Swiftian, self-defeating "modest proposal." Though no less an authority on the Renaissance than Garrett Mattingly has recently restated this thesis, it is no more persuasive today than when it was first suggested by Alberico Gentile at the end of the sixteenth century. It involves, to begin with, a reading of the *Discourses* as a "republican" document that expresses Machiavelli's true convictions. Yet, as Macaulay pointed out in rejecting this possibility, all the "Machiavellian" sentiments of *The Prince* are also to be found scattered through the *Discourses*. There is also the fact that when *The Prince* circulated in manuscript before Machiavelli's death in 1527, considerable odium was attached to it by the Florentine republicans, who saw it as a pro-Medici tract. Machiavelli, as we know from his play, *Mandragola*, was capable of first-rate satire; it is implausible that he would have so botched the job in *The Prince* as to make it produce an opposite effect to what was intended.

The main current of thought which takes Machiavelli as a precursor of "enlightenment" is content to see in him merely an honest man who exposed the trickery of princes. Trajano Boccalini, in his *News from Par-*

nassus (1612), recounts a tale in which Machiavelli, having been banished from Parnassus on pain of death, was found hidden in a friend's library. Before the court of Apollo, he enters the following plea in his self-defense:

Lo hear, you Sovereign of Learning, this Nicolas Machiavel, who has been condemned for a seducer and corrupter of mankind, and for a disperser of scandalous political percepts. I intend not to defend my writings, I publicly accuse them, and condemn them as wicked and execrable documents for the government of a State. So if that which I have printed be a doctrine invented by me, or be any new precepts, I desire that the sentence given against me by the judges be put in execution. But if my writings contain nothing but such political precepts, such rules of State, as I have taken out of the actions of Princes, which (if your Majesty gives me leave) I am ready to name, whose lives are nothing but the doing and saying of evil things— then what reason is there that they who have invented the desperate policies described by me should be held for holy, and that I who am only the publisher of them should be esteemed a knave and an atheist? For I see not why an original should be held holy and the copy burnt as execrable. Nor do I see why I should be persecuted if the reading of history (which is not only permitted but is commended by all men) has the special virtue of turning as many as do read with a politic eye into so many Machiavels: for people are not so simple as many believe them to be (and have) the judgment to discover the true causes of all Prince's actions, though they be cleverly concealed.

The judges are so impressed by this logic that they are ready to release him, when the prosecuting attorney reminds them of their responsibility: "For he has been found by night amongst a flock of sheep whom he taught to put wolves' teeth in their mouths, thereby threatening the utter ruin of all shepherds." And for this, Machiavelli is duly burnt on Olympus.

He fared much better, however, down on earth, where shepherds were beginning to lose their good repute, as a preliminary to losing their heads. Harrington saw in Machiavelli the Hippocrates of the body politic; Spinoza praised him by name (a rare honor) as *prudentissimo*; Diderot flattered him in his encyclopedia; while Rousseau eulogized *The Prince* as *"le livre des republicains"* and its author as one who "pretending to give lessons to kings, gave some important ones to the people." Even

John Adams admired him as a republican benefactor.

It is easy to see how Machiavelli's work of "enlightenment" suited the various thinkers of the Enlightenment. Their project was the discrediting of traditional political authority and the revelation to all of the *arcana imperii*, so that the rule of special privilege could be replaced by the sovereignty of the common good.* Machiavelli was all the more attractive in that his writings do contain several laudatory references to popular government, which seemed to give him a "democratic" bias. This was, of course, a misreading. Tyranny and democracy were not, for Machiavelli, exclusive conceptions; and his notion of popular government was sufficiently elastic to include the kind of rule projected by the popular leader of 1378, in the speech already quoted. But the men of the Enlightenment were not much worried about the future of popular morals; they took the moral instinct as natural, unless corrupted by government, and foresaw the progressive accommodation of human government to innate human goodness. The best state was the one that made its own existence as near to superfluous as possible; and any literature which cast obloquy on the medieval idea of the state as a coercive force necessary for man's mundane perfection was welcome.

4. *The "positivist" answer.* Like the nationalist answer, this is of more symbolic than practical significance, since it involves only the corruption of professors. It belongs to the twentieth century and most particularly to America, though it was first stated by Francis Bacon ("We are much beholden to Machiavel and others that wrote what men do, and not what they ought to do"), was revived for our time by Sir Frederic Pollock, and is now being promoted in Europe together with the rest of American "political science." According to this view, Machiavelli was a predecessor to Professor Harold Lasswell in trying to formulate an "objective" set of political generalizations derived from, and to be tested by, experience. His seeming amorality is nothing but the passionless curiosity of the scientific imagination.

It is obvious that this interpretation is incompatible with the medical metaphor, and with the idea that the political thinker is a physician to the state. Medicine, after all, is a normative and practical discipline, in

---

*For the way in which this moral passion was inverted into a set of fanatical ideologies, see Michael Polanyi's Eddington lecture, *Beyond Nihilism* (Cambridge: Cambridge University Press, 1960) (and *Encounter*, March 1960), as well as *The Logic of Personal Knowledge*, chapter 5.

that it has an ideal of bodily health to which its activities are subordinated. Even medicine's allied sciences (anatomy, physiology, etc.) share this character: Structure is studied in terms of function, function in terms of structure, and the whole is related to an ideal human organism— "ideal" in the Aristotelian sense of most appropriately "according to nature." The "positivist" approach—I use quotation marks since the term itself is a source of contention—refers to physics as its model instead of to medicine. It proposes to establish demonstrative "truths" about men in politics that will be available to whatever set of "values" wishes to employ them.

Were this line of thought as fruitful as its proponents think it might be, it would itself pose a major political problem. No government could allow such potent truths to enter freely into political life—any more than it can permit the knowledge of how to make atom bombs to circulate freely. Political scientists who were not content to stick to general theory and academic publications, and who tried to apply their knowledge to specific problems, would have to obtain a security clearance and work under official supervision. Sometimes one gets the impression that the political scientist, in his envy of the intellectual authority of the physical scientist, would not in the least mind such flattering coercion. But, fortunately, the "demonstrable truths" of political science have so far been relatively trivial. And there are even many who think the whole enterprise is misconceived—that it is as senseless for "political scientists" to try to achieve an "objectivity" toward political man as it is for medical science to seek such objectivity toward the human body.

It is interesting, nevertheless, that the assertion should be made—that an influential and reputable group of scholars should insist that it is *right* for political knowledge to be divorced from moral knowledge. This goes a long step beyond the older *raison d'état*, which merely recognized, and took advantage of, their frequent incongruence. Machiavelli would have approved; though he would have been properly skeptical of the willingness of academic persons to carry this assertion through to its boldest implications.

There have been three major figures in the history of Western thought during the last five centuries who have rejected Christianity, not for its failure to live up to its values, but because they repudiated these values themselves. The three are Machiavelli, de Sade, and Nietzsche. A great part of the intellectual history of the modern era can be told in terms of the efforts of a civilization still Christian, to come to terms with Machiavelli in politics, de Sade in sex, Nietzsche in philosophy. These efforts have been ingenious, but hardly successful. The "slave morality" of Christianity is constantly in retreat before the revolt of "the masters," with every new *modus vivendi* an unstable armistice. Heidegger has even gone so far as to say that the struggle is over—that with Nietzsche the Christian epoch draws to a close. If this is so, then it can also be said that Machiavelli marks the beginning of this end.

1961

14

About Equality

There would appear to be little doubt that the matter of equality has become, in these past two decades, a major political and ideological issue. The late Hugh Gaitskell proclaimed flatly that "socialism is about equality," and though this bold redefinition of the purpose of socialism must have caused Karl Marx to spin in his grave—he thought egalitarianism a vulgar, philistine notion and had only contemptuous things to say about it—nevertheless most socialist politicians now echo Mr. Gaitskell in a quite routine way. And not only socialist politicians: In the United States today, one might fairly conclude from the political debates now going on that capitalism, too, is "about equality," and will stand or fall with its success in satisfying the egalitarian impulse. To cap it all, a distinguished Harvard professor, John Rawls, recently published a serious, massive, and widely acclaimed work in political philosophy whose argument is that a social order is just and legitimate *only* to the degree that it is directed to the redress of inequality. To the best of my knowledge, no serious political philosopher ever offered such a proposition before. It is a proposition, after all, that peremptorily casts a pall of illegitimacy over the entire political history of the human race—that implicitly indicts Jerusalem and Athens and Rome and Elizabethan England, all of whom thought inequality was necessary to achieve a particular ideal of human excellence, both individual and collective. Yet most of the controversy about Professor Rawls's extraordinary thesis has revolved around the question of whether he has demonstrated it with sufficient analytical meticulousness. The thesis itself is not considered controversial.

One would think, then, that with so much discussion "about equality," there would be little vagueness as to what equality itself is about—what one means by "equality." Yet this is not at all the case. I think I can best illustrate this point by recounting a couple of my editorial experiences at the *Public Interest*, the journal with which I am associated.

It is clear that some Americans are profoundly and sincerely agitated by the existing distribution of income in this country, and these same Americans—they are mostly professors, of course—are constantly insisting that a more equal distribution of income is a matter of considerable urgency. Having myself no strong prior opinion as to the "proper" shape of an income-distribution curve in such a country as the United States, I have written to several of these professors asking them to compose an article that would describe a proper redistribution of American income. In other words, in the knowledge that they are discontented with our present income distribution, and taking them at their word that when they demand "more equality" they are not talking about an absolute leveling of all incomes, I invited them to give our readers a picture of what a "fair" distribution of income would be like.

I have never been able to get that article, and I have come to the conclusion that I never shall get it. In two cases, I was promised such an analysis, but it was never written. In the other cases, no one was able to find the time to devote to it. Despite all the talk "about equality," no one seems willing to commit himself to a precise definition from which statesmen and social critics can take their bearings.

As with economists, so with sociologists. Here, instead of income distribution, the controversial issue is social stratification, i.e., the "proper" degree of intergenerational social mobility. The majority of American sociologists seem persuaded that American democracy has an insufficient degree of such mobility, and it seemed reasonable to me that some of them—or at least one of them!—could specify what degree would be appropriate. None of them, I am sure, envisages a society that is utterly mobile, in which *all* the sons and daughters of the middle and upper classes end up in the very lowest social stratum, where they can live in anticipation of *their* sons and daughters rising again toward the top, and then of their grandsons and granddaughters moving downward once again! On the other hand, there is much evident dissatisfaction with what social mobility we do have. So why not find out what pattern of social mobility would be "fair" and "just" and "democratic"?

I regret to report that one will not find this out by consulting any issue of *The Public Interest*. I further regret to report that nowhere in our voluminous sociological literature will one find any such depiction of the ideally mobile society. Our liberal sociologists, like our liberal economists, are eloquent indeed in articulating their social discontents, but they are also bewilderingly modest in articulating their social goals.

Now, what is one to infer from this experience? One could, of course, simply dismiss the whole thing as but another instance of the intellectual irresponsibility of our intellectuals. That such irresponsibility exists seems clear enough, but *why* it exists is not clear at all. I do not believe that our intellectuals and scholars are genetically destined to be willfully or mischievously irresponsible. They are, I should say, no more perverse than the rest of mankind, and if they act perversely there must be a reason, even if they themselves cannot offer us a reason.

I, for one, am persuaded that though those people talk most earnestly about equality, it is not really equality that interests them. Indeed, it does not seem to me that equality per se is much of an issue for anyone. Rather, it is a surrogate for all sorts of other issues, some of them of the highest importance; these involve nothing less than our conception of what constitutes a just and legitimate society, a temporal order of things that somehow "makes sense" and seems "right."

A just and legitimate society, according to Aristotle, is one in which inequalities—of property, or station, or power—are generally perceived by the citizenry as necessary for the common good. I do not see that this definition has ever been improved on, though generations of political philosophers have found it unsatisfactory and have offered alternative definitions. In most cases, the source of this dissatisfaction has been what I would call the "liberal" character of the definition: It makes room for many different and even incompatible kinds of just and legitimate societies. In some of these societies, large inequalities are accepted as a necessary evil, whereas in others they are celebrated as the source of positive excellence. The question that this definition leaves open is the relation between a particular just and legitimate society and the "best" society. Aristotle, as we know, had his own view of the "best" society: He called it a "mixed regime," in which the monarchical, aristocratic, and democratic principles were all coherently intermingled. But he recognized that his own view of the "best" regime was of a primarily speculative nature—that is to say, a view always worth holding in mind but usually not relevant to the contingent circumstances (the "historical" circumstances, we should say) within which actual statesmen have to operate.

Later generations found it more difficult to preserve this kind of philosophic detachment from politics. The influence of Christianity, with its messianic promises, made the distinction between "the best" and "the legitimate" ever harder to preserve against those who insisted that *only* the best regime was legitimate. (This, incidentally, is an assumption that Professor Rawls makes as a matter of course.) The Church tried—as an existing and imperfect institution it had to try—to maintain this distinction, but it could only do so by appearing somewhat less Christian than it had promised to be. When the messianic impulse was secularized in early modernity, and science and reason and technology took over the promise of redemptive power—of transforming this dismal world into the wonderful place it "ought" to be—that same difficulty persisted. Like the Church, all the political regimes of modernity have had to preserve their legitimacy either by claiming an ideal character which in obvious truth they did not possess, or by making what were taken to be "damaging admissions" as to their inability to transform the real into the ideal.

The only corrective to this shadow of illegitimacy that has hovered threateningly over the politics of Western civilization for nearly two millennia now was the "common sense" of the majority of the population, which had an intimate and enduring relation to mundane realities that was relatively immune to speculative enthusiasm. This relative immunity was immensely strengthened by the widespread belief in an afterlife, a realm in which, indeed, whatever existed would be utterly perfect. I think it possible to suggest that the decline of the belief in personal immortality has been the most important *political* fact of the last hundred years; nothing else has so profoundly affected the way in which the masses of people experience their worldly condition. But even today, the masses of people tend to be more "reasonable," as I would put it, in their political judgments and political expectations than are our intellectuals. The trouble is that our society is breeding more and more "intellectuals" and fewer common men and women.

I use quotation marks around the term "intellectuals" because this category has, in recent decades, acquired a significantly new complexion. The enormous expansion in higher education, and the enormous increase in the college-educated, means that we now have a large class of people in our Western societies who, though lacking intellectual distinction (and frequently lacking even intellectual competence), nevertheless believe themselves to be intellectuals. A recent poll of American college teachers discovered that no fewer than 50 percent defined themselves as "intellectuals." That gives us a quarter of a million American intellectuals on our college faculties alone; if one adds all those in government and in the professions who would also lay claim to the title, the figure would easily cross the million mark! And if one also adds the relevant numbers of college students, one might pick up another million or so. We are, then, in a country like America today, talking about a mass of several millions of "intellectuals" who are looking at their society in a highly critical way and are quick to adopt an adversary posture toward it.

It is this class of people who are most eloquent in their denunciations of inequality, and who are making such a controversial issue of it. Why? Inequality of income is no greater today than it was twenty years ago, and is certainly less than it was fifty years ago. Inequality of status and opportunity have visibly declined since World War II, as a result of the expansion of free or nearly-free higher education. (The percentage of our leading business executives who come from modest socioeconomic backgrounds is much greater today than in 1910.) Though there has been a mushrooming of polemics against the inequalities of the American condition, most of this socioeconomic literature is shot through with disingenuousness, sophistry, and unscrupulous statistical maneuvering. As Professor Seymour Martin Lipset has demonstrated, by almost any socioeconomic indicator one would select, American society today is— as best we can determine—*more* equal than it was one hundred years ago. Yet, one hundred years ago most Americans were boasting of the historically unprecedented equality that was to be found in their nation, whereas today many seem convinced that inequality is at least a problem and at worst an intolerable scandal.

The explanation, I fear, is almost embarrassingly vulgar in its substance. A crucial clue was provided several years ago by Professor Lewis Feuer, who made a survey of those American members of this "new class" of the college-educated—engineers, scientists, teachers, social scientists, psychologists, etc.—who had visited the Soviet Union in the 1920s and 1930s, and had written admiringly of what they saw. In practically all cases, what they saw was power and status in the possession of their own kinds of people. The educators were enthusiastic about the "freedom" of educators in the USSR to run things as they saw fit. Ditto the engineers, the psychologists, and the rest. Their perceptions were illusory, of course, but this is less significant than the wishful thinking that so evidently lay behind the illusions. The same illusions, and the same wishful thinking, are now to be noticed among our academic tourists to Mao's China.

The simple truth is that the professional classes of our modern bureaucratized societies are engaged in a class struggle with the business community for status and power. Inevitably, this class struggle is conducted under the banner of "equality"—a banner also raised by the bourgeoisie in *its* revolutions. Professors are genuinely indignant at the expense accounts which business executives have and which they do not. They are, in contrast, utterly convinced that *their* privileges are "rights" that are indispensable to the proper workings of a good society. Most academics and professional people are even unaware that they are among the "upper" classes of our society. When one points this out to them, they refuse to believe it.*

The animus toward the business class on the part of members of our "new class" is expressed in large ideological terms. But what it comes down to is that our *nuovi uomini* are persuaded they can do a better job of running our society and feel entitled to have the opportunity. This is what *they* mean by "equality."

Having said this, however, one still has to explain the authentic moral passion that motivates our egalitarians of the "new class." They are not motivated by any pure power-lust; very few people are. They clearly dislike—to put it mildly—our liberal, bourgeois, commercial society, think it unfit to survive, and seek power to reconstruct it in some unspecified but radical way. To explain this, one has to turn to the intellectuals—the real ones—who are the philosophical source of their ideological discontent.

---

*One of the reasons they are so incredulous is that they do not count as "income"—as they should—such benefits as tenure, long vacations, relatively short working hours, and all of their other prerogatives. When a prerogative is construed as a "right," it ceases to be seen as a privilege.

Any political community is based on a shared conception of the common good, and once this conception becomes ambiguous and unstable, then the justice of any social order is called into question. In a democratic civilization, this questioning will always take the form of an accusation of undue privilege. Its true meaning, however, is to be found behind the literal statements of the indictment.

It is interesting to note that, from the very beginnings of modern bourgeois civilization, the class of people we call intellectuals—poets, novelists, painters, men of letters—has never accepted the bourgeois notion of the common good. This notion defines the common good as consisting mainly of personal security under the law, personal liberty under the law, and a steadily increasing material prosperity for those who apply themselves to that end. It is, by the standards of previous civilizations, a "vulgar" conception of the common good: There is no high nobility of purpose, no selfless devotion to transcendental ends, no awe-inspiring heroism. It is, therefore, a conception of the common good that dispossesses the intellectual of his traditional prerogative, which was to celebrate high nobility of purpose, selfless devotion to transcendental ends, and awe-inspiring heroism. In its place, it offered the intellectuals the freedom to write or compose as they pleased and then to sell their wares in the marketplace as best they could. This "freedom" was interpreted by—one can even say experienced by—intellectuals as a base servitude to philistine powers. They did not accept it two hundred years ago; they do not accept it today.

The original contempt of intellectuals for bourgeois civilization was quite explicitly "elitist," as we should now say. It was the spiritual egalitarianism of bourgeois civilization that offended them, not any material inequalities. They anticipated that ordinary men and women would be unhappy in bourgeois civilization precisely because it was a civilization of and for the "common man"—and it was their conviction that common men could only find true happiness when their lives were subordinated to and governed by uncommon ideals, as conceived and articulated by intellectuals. It was, and is, a highly presumptuous and self-serving argument to offer—though I am not so certain that it was or is altogether false. In any case, it was most evidently not an egalitarian argument. It only became so in our own century, when aristocratic traditions had grown so attenuated that the only permissible antibourgeois arguments had to be framed in "democratic" terms. The rise of socialist and communist ideologies made this transition a relatively easy one. A hundred years ago, when an intellectual became "alienated" and "radicalized," he was as likely to move "Right" as "Left." In our own day, his instinctive movement will almost certainly be to the "Left."

With the mass production of "intellectuals" in the course of the twentieth century, traditional intellectual attitudes have come to permeate our college-educated upper-middle classes, and most especially the children of these classes. What has happened to the latter may be put with a simplicity that is still serviceably accurate: They have obtained enough of the comforts of bourgeois civilization, and have a secure enough grip upon them, to permit themselves the luxury of reflecting uneasily upon the inadequacies of their civilization. They then discover that a life that is without a sense of purpose creates an acute experience of anxiety, which in turn transforms the universe into a hostile, repressive place. The spiritual history of mankind is full of such existential moments, which are the seedbeds of gnostic and millenarian movements—movements that aim at both spiritual and material reformations. Radical egalitarianism is, in our day, exactly such a movement.

The demand for greater equality has less to do with any specific inequities of bourgeois society than with the fact that bourgeois society is seen as itself inequitable because it is based on a deficient conception of the common good. The recent history of Sweden is living proof of this proposition. The more egalitarian Sweden becomes—and it is already about as egalitarian as it is ever likely to be—the more enragés are its intellectuals, the more guilt-ridden and uncertain are its upper-middle classes, the more "alienated" are its college-educated youth. Though Swedish politicians and journalists cannot bring themselves to believe it, it should be obvious by now that there are no reforms that are going to placate the egalitarian impulse in Swedish society. Each reform only invigorates this impulse the more, because the impulse is not, in the end, about equality at all but about the quality of life in bourgeois society.

In Sweden, as elsewhere, it is only the common people who remain loyal to the bourgeois ethos. As well they might: It is an ethos devised for their satisfaction. Individual liberty and security—in the older, bourgeois senses of these terms—and increasing material prosperity are still goals that are dear to the hearts of the working classes of the West. They see nothing wrong with a better, bourgeois life: a life without uncommon pretensions, a life to be comfortably lived by common men. This explains two striking oddities of current politics: (1) The working classes have, of all classes, been the most resistant to the spirit of radicalism that has swept the upper levels of bourgeois society; and (2) once a government starts making concessions to this spirit—by announcing its dedication to egalitarian reforms—the working class is rendered insecure and fearful, and so becomes more militant in *its* demands. These demands may be put in terms of greater equality of income and privilege—but, of course, they also and always mean greater inequality vis-à-vis other sections of the working class and those who are outside the labor force.

Anyone who is familiar with the American working class knows—as Senator McGovern discovered—that they are far less consumed with egalitarian bitterness or envy than are college professors or affluent journalists. True, they do believe that in a society where so large a proportion of the national budget is devoted to the common defense, there ought to be some kind of "equality of sacrifice," and they are properly outraged when tax laws seem to offer wealthy people a means of tax avoidance not available to others. But they are even more outraged at the way the welfare state spends the large amounts of tax moneys it does collect. These moneys go in part to the nonworking population and in part to the middle-class professionals who attend to the needs of the nonworking population (teachers, social workers, lawyers, doctors, dieticians, civil servants of all description). The "tax rebellion" of recent years has been provoked mainly by the rapid growth of this welfare state, not by particular inequities in the tax laws—inequities, which, though real enough, would not, if abolished, have any significant impact on the workingman's tax burden. After all, the 20 billion dollars—a highly exaggerated figure, in my opinion—that Senator McGovern might "capture" by tax reforms would just about pay for his day-care center proposals, which the working class has not displayed much interest in.

Still, though ordinary people are not significantly impressed by the assertions and indignations of egalitarian rhetoric, they cannot help but be impressed by the fact that the ideological response to this accusatory rhetoric is so feeble. Somehow, bourgeois society seems incapable of explaining and justifying its inequalities and how they contribute to or are consistent with the common good. This, I would suggest, derives from the growing bureaucratization of the economic order, a process which makes bourgeois society ever more efficient economically, but also ever more defenseless before its ideological critics.

For any citizen to make a claim to an unequal share of income, power, or status, his contribution has to be—and has to be seen to be—a human and personal thing. In no country are the huge salaries earned by film stars or popular singers or professional athletes a source of envy or discontent. More than that: In most countries—and especially in the United States—the individual entrepreneur who builds up his own business and becomes a millionaire is rarely attacked on egalitarian grounds. In contrast, the top executives of our large corporations, most of whom are far less wealthy than Frank Sinatra or Bob Hope or Mick Jagger or Wilt Chamberlain, cannot drink a martini on the expense account without becoming the target of a "populist" politician. These faceless and nameless personages (who is the president of General Electric?) have no clear title to their privileges—and I should say the reason is precisely that they are nameless and faceless. One really has no way of knowing what they are doing "up there," and whether what they are doing is in the public interest or not.

It was not always so. In the nineteenth century, at the apogee of the bourgeois epoch, the perception of unequal contributions was quite vivid indeed. The success of a businessman was taken to be testimony to his personal talents and character—especially character, than which there is nothing more personal. This explains the popularity of biographies of successful entrepreneurs, full of anecdotes about the man and with surprisingly little information about his economic activities. In the twentieth century, "entrepreneurial history," as written in our universities, becomes the history of the firm rather than the biography of a man. To a considerable extent, of course, this reflects the fact that most businessmen today are not "founding fathers" of a firm but temporary executives in a firm: The bureaucratization of modern society empties the category of the bourgeois of its human content. To the best of my knowledge, the only notable biography of a living businessman to have appeared in recent years was that of Alfred P. Sloan, who made his contribution to General Motors a good half century ago.

Nor is it only businessmen who are so affected. As the sociological cast of mind has gradually substituted itself for the older bourgeois moral-individualist cast of mind, military men and statesmen have suffered a fate similar to that of businessmen. Their biographies emphasize the degree to which they shared all our common human failings; their contributions to the common good, when admitted at all, are ascribed to larger historical forces in whose hands they were little more than puppets. They are all taken to be representative men, not exceptional men. But when the unequal contributions of individuals are perceived as nothing but the differential functions of social or economic or political roles, then only those inequalities absolutely needed to perform these functions can be publicly justified. The burden of proof is heavy indeed, as each and every inequality must be scrutinized for its functional purport. True, that particular martini, drunk in that place, in that time, in that company, might contribute to the efficiency and growth of the firm and the economy. But would the contribution really have been less if the executive in question had been drinking water?*

So this, it appears to me, is what the controversy "about equality" is really about. We have an intelligentsia which so despises the ethos of bourgeois society, and which is so guilt-ridden at being implicated in the life of this society, that it is inclined to find even collective suicide preferable to the status quo. (How else can one explain the evident attraction which totalitarian regimes possess for so many of our writers and artists?) We have a "New Class" of self-designated "intellectuals" who share much of this basic attitude—but who, rather than committing suicide, pursue power in the name of equality. (The children of this "New Class," however, seem divided in their yearnings for suicide via drugs, and in their lust for power via "revolution.") And then we have the ordinary people, working-class and lower-middle-class, basically loyal to the bourgeois order but confused and apprehensive at the lack of clear meaning in this order—a lack derived from the increasing bureaucratization (and accompanying impersonalization) of political and economic life. All of these discontents tend to express themselves in terms of "equality"—which is in itself a quintessentially bourgeois ideal and slogan.

It is neither a pretty nor a hopeful picture. None of the factors contributing to this critical situation is going to go away; they are endemic to our twentieth-century liberal-bourgeois society. Still, one of the least appreciated virtues of this society is its natural recuperative powers—its

---

*As Professor Peter Bauer has pointed out, the very term "distribution of income" casts a pall of suspicion over existing inequalities, implying as it does that incomes are not personally *earned* but somehow *received* as the end product of mysterious (and therefore possibly sinister) political-economic machinations.

capacity to change, as we say, but also its capacity to preserve itself, to adapt and survive. The strength of these powers always astonishes us, as we anticipate (even proclaim) an imminent apocalypse that somehow never comes. And, paradoxically enough, this vitality almost surely has something to do with the fact that the bourgeois conception of equality, so vehemently denounced by the egalitarian, is "natural" in a way that other political ideas—egalitarian or antiegalitarian—are not. Not necessarily in all respects superior, but more "natural." Let me explain.

The founding fathers of modern bourgeois society (John Locke, say, or Thomas Jefferson) all assumed that biological inequalities among men—inequalities in intelligence, talent, abilities of all kinds—were not extreme, and therefore did not justify a society of hereditary privilege (of "two races," as it were). This assumption we now know to be true, demonstrably true, as a matter of fact. Human talents and abilities, as measured, do tend to distribute themselves along a bell-shaped curve, with most people clustered around the middle, and with much smaller percentages at the lower and higher ends. That men are "created equal" is not a myth or a mere ideology—unless, of course, one interprets that phrase literally, which would be patently absurd and was never the bourgeois intention. Moreover, it is a demonstrable fact that in all modern, bourgeois societies, the distribution of income is also roughly along a bell-shaped curve, indicating that in such an "open" society the inequalities that do emerge are not inconsistent with the bourgeois notion of equality.

It is because of this "natural tyranny of the bell-shaped curve," in the conditions of a commercial society, that contemporary experiments in egalitarian community-building—the Israeli kibbutz, for instance— only work when they recruit a homogeneous slice of the citizenry, avoiding a cross section of the entire population. It also explains why the aristocratic idea—of a distribution in which the right-hand section of the bell curve is drastically shrunken—is so incongruent with the modern world, so that modern versions of superior government by a tiny elite (which is what the communist regimes are) are always fighting against the economic and social tendencies inherent in their own societies. Purely egalitarian communities are certainly feasible—but only if they are selective in their recruitment and are relatively indifferent to economic growth and change, which encourages differentiation. Aristocratic societies are feasible, too—most of human history consists of them—but only under conditions of relative economic lethargy, so that the distribution of power and wealth is insulated from change. But once you are committed to the vision of a predominantly commercial society, in which flux and change are "normal"—in which men and resources are expected to move to take advantage of new economic opportunities—then you find yourself tending toward the limited inequalities of a bourgeois kind.

This explains one of the most extraordinary (and little-noticed) features of twentieth-century societies: how relatively invulnerable the distribution of income is to the efforts of politicians and ideologues to manipulate it. In all the Western nations—the United States, Sweden, the United Kingdom, France, Germany—despite the varieties of social and economic policies of their governments, the distribution of income is strikingly similar. Not identical; politics is not entirely impotent, and the particular shape of the "bell" can be modified—but only with immense effort, and only slightly, so that to the naked eye of the visitor the effect is barely visible.* Moreover, available statistics suggest that the distribution of income in the communist regimes of Russia and Eastern Europe, despite both their egalitarian economic ideologies and aristocratic political structure, moves closer every year to the Western model, as these regimes seek the kind of economic growth that their "common men" unquestionably desire. And once the economic structure and social structure start assuming the shape of this bell-shaped curve, the political structure—the distribution of political power—follows along the same way, however slowly and reluctantly. The "Maoist" heresy within communism can best be understood as a heroic—but surely futile—rebellion against the gradual submission of communism to the constraints of the bell-shaped curve.

So bourgeois society—using this term in its larger sense, to include such "mixed economies" as prevail in Israel or Sweden or even Yugoslavia—is not nearly so fragile as its enemies think or its friends fear. Only a complete reversal of popular opinion toward the merits of material prosperity and economic growth would destroy it, and despite the fact that some of our citizens seem ready for such a reversal, that is unlikely to occur.

---

*It must be kept in mind, of course, that retaining the shape of the curve is not inconsistent with *everyone* getting richer or poorer. The bell itself then moves toward a new axis.

The concern and distress of our working and lower-middle classes over the bureaucratization of modern life can, I think, be coped with. One can envisage reforms that would encourage their greater "participation" in the corporate structures that dominate our society; or one can envisage reforms that would whittle down the size and power of these structures, returning part way to a more traditional market economy; or one can envisage a peculiar—and, in pure principle, incoherent—combination of both. My own view is that this last alternative, an odd amalgam of the prevailing "Left" and "Right" viewpoints, is the most realistic and the most probable. And I see no reason why it should not work. It will not be the "best" of all possible societies. But the ordinary man, like Aristotle, is no utopian, and he will settle for a "merely satisfactory" set of social arrangements and is prepared to grant them a title of legitimacy.

The real trouble is not sociological or economic at all. It is that the "middling" nature of a bourgeois society falls short of corresponding adequately to the full range of man's spiritual nature, which makes more than middling demands upon the universe, and demands more than middling answers. This weakness of bourgeois society has been highlighted by its intellectual critics from the very beginning. And it is this weakness that generates continual dissatisfaction, especially among those for whom material problems are no longer so urgent. They may speak about "equality"; they may even be obsessed with statistics and pseudo-statistics about equality; but it is a religious vacuum—a lack of meaning in their own lives, and the absence of a sense of larger purpose in their society—that terrifies them and provokes them to "alienation" and unappeasable indignation. It is not too much to say that it is the death of God, not the emergence of any new social or economic trends, that haunts bourgeois society. And this problem is far beyond the competence of politics to cope with.

1972

15

The Frustrations of Affluence

Why, as our industrialized nations get richer and richer, and as the real per capita income moves ever upwards, do so many of our citizens seem to get more querulous about their economic condition? The fact of affluence is indisputable: If you look at the radical economic tracts of the 1930s (by Stuart Chase, Lewis Corey, Norman Thomas, and others), with their glowing statistics on how marvelously well off we would all be under a planned economy, you discover that the economic reality today far surpasses their heady visions. Nevertheless, not many of us *feel* that well off. The instinct for contentment seems to have withered even as our economic condition has radically improved. Why is that?

The most familiar answer is that human beings are insatiably greedy creatures, and that if you give them more, it will only quicken their appetites for still more. We even have fancy sociological terms in which to express this thesis: "relative deprivation," "the revolution of rising expectations," and so on. Now, there is certainly some truth in this explanation, but I cannot accept it as the whole truth, or even the better part of the truth. Indeed, as a general proposition it strikes me as a slander against human nature. We all have our lusts, but not many of us are mere creatures of lust.

For example, there is one of my acquaintances, a distinguished professor of the liberal persuasion who is in favor of radical tax reform and a significant redistribution of wealth and income. Five years ago, he was

179

180 ON CAPITALISM AND THE DEMOCRATIC IDEA

saying that "the rich," with incomes over $30,000 a year, ought to pay a larger share of our taxes. Recently, he mentioned casually that "the rich" getting more than $50,000 a year ought to pay higher taxes. It is likely that, in a few more years, he will see as "rich" those who earn more than $75,000 a year. A cynic would simply assume that his income has moved sharply upwards during these past five years—which it certainly has, and which it will continue to do. But that cynical assumption is not necessarily an adequate explanation of his changing perspective on what it means to be "rich." It could be that he has made some interesting and objectively valid discoveries about the nature of "affluence" in our affluent society. In other words, the change could be an intelligent response to true information, rather than the result of a flawed character. Indeed, since I believe him to be a man of fine character, if erroneous opinions, I think the latter hypothesis is more likely. It is at the very least worth exploring.

It was, I believe, the French social theorist, Bertrand de Jouvenel, who first pointed out the ways in which a dynamic, growing economy may frustrate the *reasonable* expectations which people have of it. This frustration is linked to the two crucial aspects of the affluent society: (1) its dependence on technological innovation, and (2) the effects of mass affluence upon the individual consumer.

Technological innovation is a highly capricious force. It makes many things cheaper and makes some things much, much cheaper. But it also has the unintended consequence of making other things much more expensive. The degree of satisfaction that technological innovation offers you will ultimately depend not on the amount but the *kinds* of things you want.

We can easily discern those commodities and services which technology has made cheaper. Refrigerators, washing machines, freezers, air conditioners, telephones, the automobile, air travel, television, and radio—these are all tangible contributions to our higher standard of living. And they are *real* contributions—despite the existence of so much fashionable antitechnological snobbery, especially among young people who have never lived without these conveniences. One may sneer all one likes at television, but it is an unqualified blessing for old people and has marvelously enriched their daily lives. Similarly, one may think jet airplanes make too much noise, but this is as nothing compared to the way cheap and fast air travel has permitted members of a family to see one another more frequently.

Obviously, the benefits of such technological innovation are most appreciated by those who have had to do without them. That is why the least discontented people in our affluent society are those members of the working class who have moved up from poverty or near-poverty to the kind of "affluence" represented by an ability to enjoy these fruits of modern technology. That explains the so-called "hard-hat" phenomenon of the late 60s, which has so distressed all those who think the working class has some kind of revolutionary mission.

But what if you are not all that interested in having your standard of living raised in this way? Or what if you have already experienced those benefits of an affluent society? You are then in trouble, because the other kinds of benefits you looked forward to, as a result of rising income, turn out to be scarcer and more expensive than they used to be—and sometimes are not available at all. If you thought that, at $25,000 a year, you could go to the theater or opera once a week, you soon learn otherwise. If you really don't care for air travel but have always wanted a sleep-in maid, you are just out of luck. If you had hoped to have your cocktail or dinner parties catered, you find out that, though this was once commonplace at your level of real income, it is now out of the question.

In other words, technological innovation increases one's standard of living in certain, often unpredicted, ways but actually lowers it in other ways. Any images of "gracious living" you may have formed in your childhood or youth turn out to be largely irrelevant. Technology does not necessarily provide you with what you wanted; it offers you what it can, on a like-it-or-lump-it basis. If you are poor, you are certainly delighted to like it. If you are middle-class, or have a vision of the good life based on traditional middle-class experience, you are puzzled and vexed that your affluence, in real income, somehow doesn't translate itself into "affluence" as you always conceived it.

What this comes down to is the fact that human values are inevitably shaped by human memories, whereas the "values" offered by technological innovation are shaped by emerging technological possibilities. There is no fault or blame here—humanity cannot obtain its values, nor can technology achieve its ends, in any other way. But there is enough incompatibility in this partnership to make for a persistent, gnawing frustration.

COMPETING FOR THE "GOOD THINGS"

In addition to this incompatibility there is another: mass affluence. In and by itself it constantly frustrates the perfectly normal and traditional desires of those with above-average incomes. It does so by making marginal benefits extraordinarily expensive. A hundred years ago, it took a relatively small amount of money to make a person much better off. Today, it takes substantial amounts of money to make a person (above the working-class level) only a little better off. The reason is that middle-class people now have to compete with working-class and lower-middle-class people for those "good things in life" they had always aspired to.

When you were twenty-one, and looked forward to making, say, $30,000 a year, you certainly assumed that you would be able to afford more living space. Now that you are fifty-one, and have reached the $30,000 level, you find every extra square foot to be exorbitant in price; the spacious apartment or home of your dreams—and yesteryear's reality—is now beyond your means. The reason, of course, is that the laborer who built your apartment or house used to occupy perhaps one half the space of a well-to-do citizen, whereas now he can afford to occupy two thirds the space. The available space being limited, its price at the margin increases fantastically.

The same holds true in other areas of life. You thought that, as you joined those in the top 15 percent of the income continuum—making $20,000 a year or more—you could eat occasionally in fine restaurants. You now find that fine restaurants these days can only be afforded by those with twice your income. You looked forward to a summer cottage in East Hampton or Martha's Vineyard but you now find these desirable places far beyond your means. You thought of taxiing to work, instead of crowding into the subway, but that, too, is beyond your economic reach. Item after item which used to be available to those who were *relatively* rich (top 15 percent bracket) are now available only to those who are *very* rich (top 5 percent bracket). The increased affluence of your fellow citizens has sent these amenities skyrocketing in price.

It is this state of affairs which accounts for an extraordinary phenomenon of American society today: so many people who are statistically "rich" (in the top 15 percent or 10 percent income segment) but who don't feel "rich," cannot believe they are "rich," and do not have the political or cultural attitudes one associates with "well-to-do" people.

Many of these people, indeed, are all in favor of "taxing the rich" rather than themselves, and it comes as a great shock to them to learn that "taxing the rich" means taxing themselves. At this point, they become the avant-garde of a taxpayer's revolt. The legislator who takes their complaints literally will soon, as Senator McGovern discovered, be caught in a cross fire.

Now, in view of the very real economic problems which nonrich Americans face, it is easy to be supercilious about the kind of discontent I have been describing. These people do not go hungry, they live comfortably enough, and their "deprivations" are not exactly calamitous. True, they definitely need not be objects of our compassion. But I do think they are worthy of our attention. A society which fails to breed contentment among its more successful citizens would seem to have a rather serious problem on its hands. Besides, the numbers in this class are increasing every year. Even now they are not a negligible political quantity and their votes have gradually been shifting away from the traditional conservatism that was associated with high income. If one cannot count on these people to provide political, social, and moral stability—if they do not have a good opinion of our society—how long, one wonders, can that stability and good opinion survive?

1973

16

Utopianism, Ancient and Modern

Men are dreaming animals, and the incapacity to dream makes a man less than human. Indeed, we have no knowledge of any human community where men do fail to dream. Which is to say, we know of no human community whose members do not have a vision of perfection—a vision in which the frustrations inherent in our human condition are annulled and transcended. The existence of such dreaming visions is not, in itself, a problem. They are, on the contrary, a testament to the creativity of man which flows from the fact that he is a creature uniquely endowed with imaginative powers as an essential aspect of his self-consciousness. Only a madman would wish to abolish men's dreams, i.e., to return humanity to a purely animal condition, and we are fortunate in having had—until recently, at any rate—little historical experience of such madness. It is true that, of late, certain writers—notably Norman O. Brown—hold out the promise of such regression as a kind of ultimate redemption. But even their most admiring readers understand that this is largely literary license, rather than a serious political agenda.

On the other hand, and far more common, there are also madmen who find it impossible to disentangle dreams from reality—and of this kind of madness we have had, alas, far too much experience. Indeed, it would not be an exaggeration to say that a good part of modern history takes place under the sign of this second kind of madness, which we familiarly call "utopianism."

I am using the term, "madness," advisedly and not merely to be provocative. The intellectual history of the past four centuries consists of islands of sanity floating in an ocean of "dottiness," as the British call it. We don't see this history in this way, and certainly don't study it in this way, because—I would suggest—we have ourselves been infected by this pervasive "dottiness." Just look at the cautious and respectful way our textbooks treat the French utopian theorists of the nineteenth century: Saint-Simon, Comte, Fourier, and their many loyal disciples. It is no exaggeration to say that all of these men were quite literally "touched in the head" and that their writings can fairly be described as the feverish scribblings of disordered minds. Fourier, for instance, divided humanity into no less than 810 distinct character types and then devised a social order that brought each character type his own special brand of happiness. He also believed that, in the ideal world of the future, the salty oceans would benevolently turn themselves into seas of lemonade, and that men would grow tails with eyes at the tip. Saint-Simon and Comte were somewhat less extreme in their lunacies—but not all that much. To read them, which so few actually do today, is to enter a world of phantasmagoria. Oh yes, one can cull "insights," as we say, from their many thousands of pages. But the inmates of any asylum, given pen and paper, will also produce their share of such "insights"—only it doesn't ordinarily occur to us that this is a good way of going about the collecting of insights. It is only when people write about politics in a large way that we are so indulgent to their madness, so eager to discover inspired prophecy in their fulminations.

It is not too much to say that we are all utopians now, in ways we no longer realize, we are so habituated to them. Further than that: We are even utopian when we think we are being very practical and rational. My own favorite instance of such subterranean utopianism is in an area where one is least likely to look for it. I refer to the area of city planning.

William H. Whyte Jr., in his excellent book, *The Last Landscape*, has pointed out that, if you examine the thousands of plans which now exist for shiny, new, wonderful cities, there is always one thing that is certain to be missing. That one thing is—a cemetery. In a properly planned city, the fact that people die is taken to be such an unwarranted intrusion into an otherwise marvelous equilibrium that city planners simply cannot face up to it. After all, if people die and are replaced by new and different people, then the carefully prescribed "mix" of jobs, of housing, of leisure-time activities—all this is going to be upset. Modern city planning, whether in the form of constructing New Towns or Cities Beautiful, is inherently and radically utopian in that it aims to bring history to a stop at a particular moment of perfection. The two traditions of urban planning I have just mentioned disagree in their attitude toward modern technology and modern industrial society—the one wishing to minimize their influence, the other wanting to exploit their potentialities to the utmost. But both are, as a matter of historical fact, descended from various nineteenth-century utopian-socialist movements, and neither of them can bear to contemplate the fact that men are permanently subject to time and changing circumstances.

That is why city planners are so infuriated when someone like Jane Jacobs comes along and points out that the absence of old buildings in their model cities is a critical flaw because old buildings, with their cheap rents, are needed by the small entrepreneur, the bohemian intellectual, the dilatory graduate student, the amateur scholar, and eccentrics of all kinds. These are the people who give urban life its color, its vitality, its excitement—and who, moreover, play an indispensable role in the dynamics of urban growth and decay. But growth and decay are precisely what most offend the utopian cast of mind, for which time is an enemy to be subdued. And this is why the dimension of time is so rigorously excluded from modern city planning—and from modern architecture too, which derives from the same utopian tradition. Ask a city planner or an architect whether his work will grow old gracefully, and he finds your question incomprehensible. His is the perfection of art, which is immune to time, which does not age or wither or renew itself. That human beings and human societies do age and wither and renew themselves is for him only an immense inconvenience, and he cannot wait until our social sciences shall have resolved that problem.

This utopian cast of mind I have been describing is quite rational, only it has ceased to be reasonable. And this divorce between rationality and reasonableness, which is characteristic of so many forms of madness, is also a crucial feature of modern utopianism.

Rationality has always been taken to be a criterion of utopias. This, in turn, means that utopian dreaming is a very special kind of dreaming. All of us are aware, for instance, that there is a difference between a vision of paradise or heaven on the one hand, and a vision of utopia on the other. The Old and New Testaments—or the Koran, for that matter—

do not present us with utopias. It would be ridiculous to take literally or seriously any specific remarks that are found in these documents concerning the social or economic structure of heaven, or the mode of governance to be found there. Similarly, all depictions of man in his unfallen condition are not meant to be analytically scrutinized. Dreams of this order do tell us something about the nature of man, but only in the most general and allusive way. They are a kind of myth, a kind of poetry, not a kind of political philosophy. And that is why all religions take such a very dim view of those among their adherents who give too much detailed attention to such myths. It is taken as a sign of either mental instability or willful heresy when someone begins speculating in some detail about how things really were in Paradise, or how they are likely to be in Heaven. To ask questions—or worse, to give answers—about, say, the relation between the sexes in Paradise or Heaven is to transgress the boundaries of acceptable discourse. Such speculation is ordinarily forbidden, or at least frowned upon, by religious authorities.

Utopian thinking, in contrast, is a species of philosophical thinking, and arises historically at that moment when philosophy disengages itself from myth and declares its independent status. Which is to say, of course, that it is first observable among the Greeks. Plato's *Republic* is the first utopian discourse we know of, a work of the philosophic imagination. There are myths in *The Republic*, of course, but they are recounted as myths, not as authoritative history. Moreover, *The Republic* is constructed before our eyes, step by step, by dialectical discourse among reasoning men. Though the end result will certainly strike many of us as being quite an absurd picture of an ideal society, there is nothing illogical in it, nothing miraculous, nothing superhuman. It is a possible society, violating none of the laws of nature and inhabited solely by men who are governed by recognizably human motives and passions.

All this is clear, and yet this clarity is but the occasion for a larger mystery which scholars have been exploring for two millennia now. What was Plato's intention? Was he being solemn throughout or playful throughout? How seriously did he mean us to take his ideal society? And if he did mean us to take it seriously, *in what way* did he want us to take it seriously?

These questions continue to be debated today, and will doubtless be debated forever. The view of Plato's utopia which I find most plausible—a view derived from the writings of Professor Leo Strauss—is that it is primarily a pedagogic construction. After all, Plato was neither a fool nor a madman—we could take Aristotle's word for that, even if his other dialogues did not make it evident—and he was not likely to confuse a philosopher's imaginings with the world as it is. Even if he did believe that the society described in *The Republic* would be the best of all possible societies—and we must assume he did believe it, since he says so—he almost surely did *not* believe that it was ever likely to exist. For it to come into existence, as he makes plain, you would need a most improbable conjunction of circumstances: an absolutely wise man given absolute power to construct a new social order—to do it without hindrance or restriction of any kind. This is not a logical impossibility; if it were, there would have been no point at all in writing *The Republic*. On the other hand, it is so unreal a possibility that a reasonable man would not allow it to govern his particular attitude toward any particular society at any particular time. As Professor Strauss puts it, Plato's utopia exists in words, not in deeds. The one existence is as authentically human as the other, but there is a world of difference between them.

This is, I should say, the basic attitude of all classical, premodern utopian thinking. Constructing a utopia was a useful act of the philosophical imagination. Contemplating such a constructed utopia—studying it, analyzing it, arguing over it—was a marvelous exercise in moral and political philosophy. Both the construction and the contemplation were an elevating affair, leading to self-improvement of mind for those talented few who were capable of it. It also provided one with an invaluable perspective on the essential limitations of one's own society—a philosophical wisdom about things political that was superior to the reigning conventional political wisdom. But all of this was, in the highest sense of the term, "academic." Utopias existed to produce better political philosophers, not better politics. True, the existence of better political philosophers *might*, at some point, have a benevolent effect upon the society in which they lived. But the odds were overwhelmingly against it, and in his practical conduct of life the supreme virtue for the philosopher, as for everyone else, was prudence.

All of this is most perfectly and beautifully exemplified in the last of the classical utopias, Sir Thomas More's treatise which introduced the word itself, "utopia," into our Western languages. More's *Utopia* stands as an indictment of the gross imperfections in the social and political orders of his day. It was a most subversive document, but its aim was to subvert only young students of political philosophy, who could read the Latin in which it was written, and who could then be spiritually transported into the "good place" (the literal meaning of the Greek term, *eutopos*), the "no-place" (the literal meaning of *outopos*) which was the philosopher's realm of freedom. More himself, as we know, went into the service of King Henry VIII in order, as he explicitly informs us, to minimize the evils which a ruler may introduce into the world as it is. In loyally serving King Henry, he never repudiated his utopian vision: He never apparently had the sense he was in any way "compromising" it; and he certainly never pretended that he was engaged in "realizing" it. He simply thought that, as a political philosopher with a superior vision of the ideal, he might prudently influence the politics of his time toward somewhat more humane ends. He failed utterly, as we know, and paid for his failure with his life. But he was not at all surprised that he failed, nor was he shocked to discover the price of his failure. A less utopian statesman than the author of *Utopia* is hard to find. And yet there was not an ounce of cynicism in him. His nobility of character consisted precisely in the fact that, even as he could imagine the world as it might be, he could also live and work in the world as it was, trying to edge the latter ever so slightly toward the former, but experiencing no sour disillusionment at his ultimate lack of success. Such a perfect combination of detachment from the world and simultaneous attachment to it is as exemplary as it is rare.

After Sir Thomas More, we are in the modern era, the era of utopian-*ism*. By utopian-*ism* I mean that frame of mind which asserts that utopias are *ideals to be realized*—to be realized in deed and not merely in words, in historical time and not merely in the timelessness of speculative thought. This conception of utopia is so familiar to us, and so congenial to us, that when *we* call someone "utopian" we mean no more than that he is unduly optimistic about the time necessary to achieve the ideal, or perhaps unduly enthusiastic about his particular version of the ideal. The notion that a utopia is an ideal to be realized does not strike us as inherently unreasonable; we ask only that men be not too exigent in demanding their perfect society here and now. *That*, we say, is to be "utopian." In contrast, the ancients tell us that to demand a perfect society in the foreseeable future is to be mad; while to expect a perfect society to exist at all, at any time, is to be utopian. By the standards of the ancients, the modern era and its modern societies are suffused with quite unreasonable expectations, and have therefore an equally unreasonable attitude toward political reality. We confuse words with deeds, philosophical dreams with the substantial actualities of human existence. And, of course, the ancients anticipated that from such a dire confusion only disaster could result.

Just how it happened that the utopian mode of thought emerged so strongly in the sixteenth and seventeenth centuries is something that our historians can only partially explain. Perhaps we ought not to demand more than partial explanations from them; such a mutation of the human spirit is, one might say, as inexplicable as it was unpredictable. Still, it does seem clear that certain identifiable trends of thought, all in their different ways, contributed to the event. These trends can be identified as millenarianism, rationalism, and what Professor Hayek calls "scientism."

Millenarianism is an intrinsic aspect of the Judeo-Christian tradition, and without it there would be no such thing as the *history* of Western civilization, as distinct from the *chronicles* of Western peoples. It is from the millenarian perspective that both Judaism and Christianity derive their very special sense of history as a story with a beginning, a middle, and an end—a conception of historical time that is not to be found in Oriental thought, which seeks and finds ultimate perfection only in a denial of time's meaning, and in a transcendence of time by the contemplative and withdrawn individual. The dynamics of Western civilization are organically linked to this profound belief in "the end of time" as a prospective historical event. This belief always created immense problems for the religious authorities, and Church and synagogue responded with efforts to impose reasonable limitations upon this millennial expectation. In both Judaism and Christianity those who attempted to "hasten the end," whether through magic or politics, were defined as heretics and were expelled from the religious community. This did not prevent such heresies from bubbling up, again and again, but the church did contain them, or even assimilate them (as in the case of the Franciscan movement), for more than a thousand years. In the sixteenth century, however, as religious authority fragmented under the impact of what we call the Reformation, these millennial expectations overflowed, and have never been entirely subdued since. What we now call the "prophetic" element in Judaism and Christianity became the intellectually and even popularly dominant element. Indeed, in the United States today you can claim prophetic status and justify any excess of prophetic fervor on the basis of nothing more than an introductory course in sociology.

What makes modern millenarianism so powerful—one is tempted to say irresistible—is its association with modern scientific rationalism and modern technology. Scientific rationalism also emerges in the sixteenth century, persuading us that reality can be fully comprehended by man's abstract reason, and that therefore whatever exists should be capable of being rationally explained in a clear and consequential way. As applied to all social institutions, this came to mean—it is, indeed, the essential meaning of that period we call the Enlightenment—that existing institutions could be legitimized only by reason: not by tradition, not by custom, not even by the fact that they seemed to be efficacious in permitting men to lead decent lives, but only by reason. It was against this mode of thought, an inherently radical-utopian mode of thought, that Edmund Burke polemicized so magnificently. It was against this radical-utopian temper that modern conservatism emerges. Modern conservatism found it necessary to argue what had always been previously assumed by all reasonable men: that institutions which have existed over a long period of time have a reason and a purpose inherent in them, a collective wisdom incarnate in them, and the fact that we don't perfectly understand or cannot perfectly explain why they "work" is no defect in them but merely a limitation in us. Most ordinary people, most of the time, intuitively feel the force of this conservative argument. But these same ordinary people are defenseless intellectually against the articulated and aggressive rationalism of our intellectual class—and this explains why, when modern men do rebel against the unreasonableness of modern rationalism, they are so likely to take refuge in some form of irrationalism. The 20th-century phenomenon of fascism is an expression of exactly such an exasperated and irrational rebelliousness against the tyranny—actual or prospective—of a radical-utopian rationalism.

But neither millenarianism nor rationalism would, by itself, have been able to sustain the utopian temper had it not been for the advent of modern technology, with its large promise of human control over human destiny. There is nothing dreamlike about technology: It works—and because it works, it gives plausibility to the notion that modern man is uniquely in the position of being able to convert his idealized dreams into tangible reality. It also gives plausibility to the notion that, because the development of technology—of man's control over both nature and man—is progressive, therefore human history itself can be defined as progressive, as leading us from an imperfect human condition to a perfected one. The ancient Hebrews, the Greeks, and the Christians all felt that there was a diabolical aspect to the power of technology; they saw no reason to think that men would always use this power wisely, and thought it quite probable that we would use it for destructive ends. But modern technology, emerging in a context of millenarian aspirations and rationalist metaphysics, was not bothered—at least not until recently—by such doubts. Francis Bacon's New Atlantis is the first truly modern utopia—a society governed by scientists and technologists which, it is clear, Bacon thought could easily exist in fact, and which he proposed as a very possible and completely desirable future.

As one looks back over these past centuries, the wonder is not that there has been so much change and tumult, but rather that there has been so much stability. The main currents of modern thought are all subversive of social stability, and yet the bourgeois-liberal societies of the last two hundred years managed somehow to keep triumphantly afloat. They did this, essentially, by diffusing power—economic power, social power, political power—throughout the body politic, so that the utopian spirit was constantly being moderated by the need to compromise various interests, various enthusiasms, and even various utopian visions. No modern liberal society has failed to express its faith in the potential of science and technology to improve radically the human condition. No modern liberal society has failed to insist that its institutions are created by—and legitimated by—human reason, rather than by mere tradition or custom, and certainly not by divine revelation. And no modern liberal society has ever explicitly rejected the utopian goals and the utopian rhetoric which are spawned by the millenarian spirit. These goals and this rhetoric, indeed, are by now clichés: "a world without war," "a world without poverty," "a world without hate"—in short, a world without any of the radical imperfections that have hitherto characterized every world actually inhabited by man. But what rendered these beliefs less explosive than, in their pure form, they are, was the liberal individualism that bourgeois society insisted they accommodate themselves to. In short, what made bourgeois society so viable was the domestication of modern utopianism by liberal individualism.

It was a viability, however, that was always open to question. The trouble with living in a bourgeois society which has domesticated its utopian spirit is that nothing is permitted to go wrong—at least very wrong, for very long. In all premodern societies, a mood of stoicism permeated the public and private spheres. Life is hard, fortune is fickle, bad luck is more likely than good luck and a better life is more probable after death than before. Such stoicism does not easily cohabit with the progressive spirit, which anticipates that things naturally will and *ought* to get better. When they don't—when you are defeated in a war, or when you experience a major malfunctioning of your economic system—then you are completely disoriented. Bourgeois society is morally and intellectually unprepared for calamity. Calamity, on the other hand, is always ready for bourgeois society—as it has always been ready, or always will be ready, for every other society that has existed or will exist.

When calamity strikes, it is never the utopian temper that is brought into question—that is literally an unimaginable possibility—but rather the liberal individual polity in which this temper has been housed. At such a moment, indeed, the utopian spirit flares up in anger, and declares, in the immortal words of the nineteenth-century French utopian socialist, Etienne Cabet, ". . . Nothing is impossible for a government that *wants* the good of its citizens." This sentiment expresses neatly what might be called the *collectivist imperative* which always haunts bourgeois-liberal society—and which can never be entirely exorcised, since it derives from the utopian worldview that all modern societies share. Once it is assumed that history itself works toward progressive improvement, and that we have the understanding and the power to guide this historical dynamic toward its fruition, it is only a matter of time before the state is held responsible for everything that is unsatisfactory in our condition. There is, after all, nothing else that could be held responsible.

Having made that statement, I must quickly modify it. For more than a century, bourgeois-liberal society *did* have one powerful inner check upon its utopian impulses, and that was the "dismal science" of economic theory. Classical economic theory insisted that, even under the best of circumstances, the mass of the people could expect only small, slow increments of improvement in their condition—and, under the worst of circumstances, could anticipate an actual worsening of their condition. The cornerstone of this theory was the Malthusian hypothesis that the pressure of population among poorer people would tend to wipe out the gains of economic growth. This hypothesis was accepted by most thinking men of the nineteenth century, and helped shape a climate of opinion in which great expectations could not easily flourish, except on the margins of society where all sorts of intellectual eccentricities were naturally to be found. But the discovery by modern economists that technological innovation had rendered Malthusianism false—that increasing productivity could easily cope with population growth—removed this formidable check upon the utopian temper. Indeed, economics itself now became a discipline which constantly challenged the conventional limits of economic possibility. And in this challenge, the role of the state was crucial. Whereas it was once thought that the state had to accommodate itself, like everyone else, to the iron laws of economics, it now became common to think that the state could pretty much write the laws of economics to suit itself. Our liberation from Malthusian economics—one of the truly great intellectual accomplishments of this past century—was quickly perceived by journalists, politicians, and even many among our better-educated people as a liberation from all economic constraint. The result is that the idea that ". . . Nothing is impossible for a government that *wants* the good of its citizens," once a radical proposition, now sounds rather conventional. I don't know that any American politician has actually said it, in so many words. But a great many politicians are strongly implying it—and it is even possible that more than a few of these politicians actually believe it.

The strength of this collectivist imperative is such that it feeds on itself—and most especially (and more significantly) on its own failures. These failures are as immense as they are obvious, and yet it is astonishing how little difference they seem to make. One would have thought that the catastrophic condition of agriculture in the Soviet Union, China, and Cuba would have brought these economies into universal disrepute. Yet no such thing has happened. These regimes are extended infinite moral and intellectual credit for their utopian ideals, and their credit ratings seem little vulnerable to their poor economic performance. Similarly, in the Western democracies, the tremendous expansion of government during these past three decades has not obviously made us a happier and more contented people. On the contrary, there is far more sourness and bitterness in our lives, public and private, than used to be the case; and these very governments, swollen to enormous size, are visibly less stable than they were. Nevertheless, the response to this state of affairs among our educated classes is to demand still more governmental intervention—on the theory that a larger dose of what should be good for us will cure the illness caused by a smaller dose of what should have been good for us. The ordinary people, whose common world always anchors them more firmly in common sense, are skeptical of such a prescription, but they have nothing to offer in its place, and will in the end have to go along with it.

But what about the liberal-individualist ethos? Is that not today, as it was a century ago, an authentic alternative? Some eminent thinkers say it is, and I would like nothing better than to agree with them. But, in truth, I cannot. The liberal-individualist vision of society is not an abstract scheme which can be imposed on any kind of people. For it to work, it needs a certain kind of people, with a certain kind of character, and with a certain cast of mind. Specifically, it needs what David Riesman calls "inner-directed" people—people of firm moral convictions, a people of self-reliance and self-discipline, a people who do not expect the universe to be offering them something for nothing—in short, a people with a nonutopian character even if their language is shot through with utopian clichés. The kind of person I am describing may be called the *bourgeois citizen*. He used to exist in large numbers, but now is on the verge of becoming an extinct species. He has been killed off by bourgeois prosperity, which has corrupted his character from that of a *citizen* to that of a *consumer*. One hears much about the "work ethic" these days, and I certainly appreciate the nostalgic appeal of that phrase. But the next time you hear a banker extolling the "work ethic," just ask him if he favors making installment buying illegal. When I was very young, it was understood that the only people who would buy things on the installment plan were the irresponsibles, the wastrels, those whose characters were too weak to control their appetites. "Save now, buy later," is what the work ethic used to prescribe. To buy now and pay later was the sign of moral corruption—though it is now the accepted practice of our affluent society. A people who have mortgaged themselves to the hilt are a dependent people, and ultimately they will look to the state to save them from bankruptcy. The British have a wonderful colloquial phrase for installment purchasing: They call it buying on "the never-never." The implication is that through this marvelous scheme you enter a fantasy world where nothing is denied you, and where the settling of all accounts is indefinitely postponed. This is a consumer's utopia. And more and more, it is as such a consumer's utopia that our bourgeois society presents itself to its people.

The transformation of the bourgeois citizen into the bourgeois consumer has dissolved that liberal-individualist framework which held the utopian impulses of modern society under control. One used to be encouraged to control one's appetites; now one is encouraged to satisfy them without delay. The inference is that one has a *right* to satisfy one's appetites without delay, and when this "right" is frustrated, as it always is in some way or other, an irritated populace turns to the state to do something about it. All this is but another way of saying that twentieth-century capitalism itself, in its heedless emphasis on economic growth and ever-increasing prosperity, incites ever more unreasonable expectations, in comparison with which the actuality of the real world appears ever more drab and disconcerting. It doesn't matter what economic growth is actually achieved, or what improvements are effected—they are all less than satisfying. Ours is a world of promises, promises—and in such a world everyone, to some degree or another, automatically feels deprived.

Let me give you an illustration that, I think, makes the point nicely. The historic rate of growth of the American economy, over the past century and a half, has averaged about 2.5 percent a year. By historic standards, this is a fantastic and unprecedented achievement; it means that the national income doubles every twenty-eight years. But is this a source of gratification to us? Do we go around complimenting ourselves on doing so well? One can answer these questions by asking another: What if the president of the United States were to declare tomorrow that it was his firm intention to sustain this rate of growth of 2.5 percent a year? What would be the reaction? I think one can safely say that most Americans would think he was being pretty niggardly and mean-spirited. And there would be no shortage of politicians who would point out that 3 percent was really a much nicer number, and 5 percent nicer still. Does anyone doubt that they would be listened to? The proof that they would be is the fact that no president, in our lifetime, is going to mention that 2.5 percent figure. It's too *real* a number, and is therefore offensive to our inflamed political sensibilities.

But one cannot continue in a condition in which reality is always offending our expectations. That is an unnatural condition, and sooner or later people will be seeking relief from it. Oddly enough, even though utopianism gives rise to the collectivist impulse, the collectivist state seems to be one way in which the fires of utopianism are dampened. The institutionalization of utopianism is itself an answer to utopianism. Thus the Christian Church had its origins in a utopian impulse, but the Church then functioned to control and pacify this impulse. The Church solved the problem of the Second Coming by announcing that it had already happened, and that the Church itself was its living testimony. Similarly, in Russia and China today, the regimes of these nations, born out of secular messianism, announce that there is no further need for messianism since their states are its incarnation in the here and now, and there is nothing further to be messianic about. This gives these regimes a double attraction to many people in the West: They affirm utopianism while offering a deliverance from it. This explains what is at first sight a paradox: the fact that so many of our Western intellectuals will simultaneously follow a utopian thinker like Herbert Marcuse in denouncing the bourgeois status quo and at the same time praise Maoist China or Soviet Russia where Marcuse's works are forbidden to be published. Indeed, Marcuse himself is involved in this paradox! The paradox dissolves, however, if one realizes that the utopian impulse, in the end, must actively seek its own liquidation because it is impossible to sustain indefinitely; the psychological costs become too great. Utopianism dreams passionately of a liberation from all existing orthodoxies—religious, social, political—but, sooner or later, it must wearily and gratefully surrender to a new orthodoxy which calms its passions even as it compromises its dreams. The interesting question is whether the various emerging forms of collectivist orthodoxies in our time have the spiritual resources to establish a new order in which men can achieve some kind of human fulfillment. The evidence, so far, is that they do not; they seem to be morally and intellectually bankrupt from the outset. Marxism may be the official religion of Russia and China, but it is a religion without theologians—there isn't a Marxist philosopher worthy of the name in either country—and it is a religion whose holy scriptures, the works of Marx, Engels, and Lenin, are unread by the masses. These orthodoxies are sustained *only* by coercion—which means they are pseudo-orthodoxies, exuding an odor of boredom which is also the odor of decay.

Where does that leave us—we who inhabit the "free world"—the postbourgeois bourgeois world? It leaves us, I should say, with a dilemma—but a dilemma which is also an opportunity. The opportunity is simply the opportunity of taking thought, of reflecting upon our condition, of trying to understand how we got where we are. This does not sound like much—and yet it is much, much more than it sounds. For the real antidote to utopianism is a self-conscious understanding of utopianism. A utopianism which knows itself to be utopian is already on the way to denying itself, because it has already made that first, crucial distinction between dream and reality. And once that distinction is made—as it was made in classical, premodern philosophy—both the legitimacy of the dream and the integrity of reality can be preserved.

The modern world, and the crisis of modernity we are now experiencing, was created by ideas and by the passions which these ideas unleashed. To surmount this crisis, without destroying the modern world itself, will require new ideas—or new versions of old ideas—that will regulate these passions and bring them into a more fruitful and harmonious relation with reality. I know that it will be hard for some to believe that ideas can be so important. This underestimation of ideas is a peculiarly bourgeois fallacy, especially powerful in that most bourgeois of nations, our own United States. For two centuries, the very important people who managed the affairs of this society could not believe in the importance of ideas—until one day they were shocked to discover that their children, having been captured and shaped by certain ideas, were either rebelling against their authority or seceding from their society. The truth is that ideas are *all*-important. The massive and seemingly solid institutions of any society—the economic institutions, the political institutions, the religious institutions—are always at the mercy of the ideas in the heads of the people who populate these institutions. The leverage of ideas is so immense that a slight change in the intellectual climate can and will—perhaps slowly, but nevertheless inexorably—twist a familiar institution into an unrecognizable shape. If one looks at the major institutions of American society today—the schools, the family, the business corporation, the federal government—we can see this process going on before our eyes.

But just as it is ideas that alienate us from our world, so it is ideas which can make us at home in the world—which can permit us to envision the world as a "homely" place, where the practice of ordinary virtues in the course of our ordinary lives can indeed fulfill our potential as human beings. In such a world, dreams complement reality instead of being at war with it. The construction of such a world is the intellectual enterprise that most needs encouragement and support today. It will, on the surface, look like a mere academic enterprise, involving as it does a re-examination and fresh understanding of our intellectual and spiritual history. But such a re-examination and fresh understanding is always the sign that a reformation is beginning to get under way. And a reformation of modern utopianism, I think we will all agree, is what we are most desperately in need of. Only such a reformation can bring us back to that condition of sanity, to that confident acceptance of reality, which found expression in Macaulay's tart rejoinder to Francis Bacon: "An acre in Middlesex is better than a principality in Utopia."

1973

17

Social Reform: Gains and Losses

The 1970s debate over the merits or demerits of the various programs inherited from the Great Society in the 1960s is an important one, but it is in danger of getting lost in a fog of swirling rhetoric. This is perhaps inevitable, but it is also too bad, for it is distracting us from learning the crucial lessons of the Great Society experience, lessons which raise some really interesting questions about social reform itself.

I am thinking of such questions as: How do we know whether or not a social reform has worked? What are the general characteristics of successful as against unsuccessful reforms? Are there any general principles of reform that can guide us toward success and steer us away from failure? After our experience of the past decade, such questions are certainly in order.

This does not mean they are easy to answer. Practically all social reforms "work" in that they do distribute some benefits to the people whom they aim to help. Similarly, no social reform ever works out exactly as its proponents hoped; there are always unanticipated costs and unforeseen consequences. Still, one has to strike a balance. How is that to be done?

Our inclination these days—and this in itself is a "reform" of the 1960s—is to call in a social scientist and ask him to provide us with some kind of cost-benefit analysis. I myself used to believe this was a good idea, but I have been more recently persuaded that it is not.

Today's social scientists, I have come to think, are not a solution but are themselves part of the problem. They are poor guides to social reform because, to the degree that they think economically, they tend to confuse the art of government with the pursuit of particular ideological objectives. It is extremely difficult for social scientists to do what I have previously described as thinking politically. Some do, of course; but they are likely to be regarded within their professions as old-fashioned and unsophisticated. And I should say that a major reason the social reforms of the sixties were so ill-conceived was that they were shaped so powerfully by the thinking of contemporary social scientists.

I can illustrate this point by reference to a social reform that was *not* adopted in the 1960s. Early in that decade, a small group of scholars—Daniel P. Moynihan being prominent among them—proposed that, in order to alleviate poverty in the United States, a system of children's allowances be instituted. This is a simple and feasible program, which has existed in Europe and Canada for decades now, and which is so taken for granted there that no one pays much attention to it anymore. The program, as proposed for this country, had obvious merit. It is a fact that one of the main reasons many families in the United States are poor is because their incomes are too low to support both parents and children—especially when, as is the case, poor families tend to be somewhat larger than average. The children's allowance simply gives every family a very modest sum (say $15 or $20 a month) for each child. To the poor family, this will mean a significant increase in annual income. For the most affluent family, especially if these allowances are classified as taxable income, it means a more or less marginal bonus. Everybody benefits, but the poor benefit far more than the rich. Moreover, the program creates no disincentives: The poor have as much reason as ever to strive to become less poor, since they lose practically nothing by doing so.

Despite the fact that the program seemed to be working well in other countries, the idea of children's allowances never got a favorable hearing in Washington or in reform circles. To some extent, this was because many middle-class liberals, worried about population growth, regarded it as "pronatalist," though the evidence is overwhelming that, in countries that have such a program, people's decisions to have children are unaffected by the prospect of these modest allowances. More important was the fact that the program was bound to be expensive—costing anywhere from $10 billion to $20 billion a year, depending upon the scale of the allowances—and there was no such money in the budget. True, one could have begun the program with very small allowances, increasing them gradually over the years; but this would not have achieved the goal the reformers had their eyes set on, which was to abolish poverty *now*.

Above all, however, the idea of children's allowances did not commend itself to the reform-minded in Washington because it seemed so clearly "uneconomical" and "inequitable." What was the sense, it was asked, of having a universal program which gave money indifferently to everyone, to those who needed it and those who didn't? Why give children's allowances to the middle class and the affluent, who could take care of themselves? Why not give the money *only* to the poor? And so was born the "War on Poverty"—and, I would say, one of the great reform disasters of our age.

The trouble with giving money only to the poor is twofold. First of all, one has to decide who is poor. That decision, it turns out, is inherently arbitrary and controversial. The poor in our society, after all, are not an identifiable class—like the blind or disabled, for instance—set apart from other Americans. They are simply people with incomes below some official figure, and there is no possible consensus as to where the figure should be set. Does it make any sense to say that a family of four with an income of $3,900 is poor and is entitled to various benefits—welfare, Medicaid, housing—while the family next door with an income of $4,200 is not poor and is entitled to no such benefits? It makes no sense at all, as both of those families quickly perceive. The "poor" family feels demeaned at passing this peculiar test, the "nonpoor" family feels cheated at failing it. The upshot is political turmoil and general dissatisfaction. The War on Poverty created divisiveness among the American people, whereas the mark of a successful social reform, I would argue, is to create greater comity among the people.

The second difficulty in giving money only to the poor is that it quickly imprisons them in a "poverty trap." To the extent that they improve their situations and earn more money, they disqualify themselves for all those benefits which the various antipoverty programs reserve for the poor. A huge disincentive is officially established; it becomes positively irrational for a poor family to try to move up a notch or two along the income scale. Having been defined as poor, they are encouraged to remain poor. Ironically, but predictably, the subsequent demoralization of those caught in this "poverty trap" nullifies the supposed ameliorative effects of their benefits. One can see this process only too clearly at work in New York City, where welfare benefits—taken together with Medicaid, food stamps, etc.—bring all the poor above the official poverty line. Statistically, we have abolished poverty in New York City. In actuality, poor people in New York are not at all obviously better off than they were ten years ago. They get more money, better housing, and better medical care but suffer more crime, drug addiction, juvenile delinquency, and all the other varieties of social pathology which dependency creates.

MAKING MATTERS WORSE

In retrospect, the conception of social reform that developed during the 1960s can be seen to have been warped by a misplaced sense of economic efficiency, reinforced by an egalitarian animus against any program which threatened to benefit the nonpoor. The result was a series of "selective" social programs that produced a succession of perverse consequences. Not only did these programs fail to achieve their goals; in many respects they made matters worse.

In contrast, if one looks at the kinds of social reforms which, in historical perspective, may fairly be judged to have been successful, one finds that they were all "universal." The outstanding such reform of this century was, of course, Social Security (and its subsequent corollary, Medicare). Back in the nineteenth century, the most successful social reform was the institution of free public education. No one was excluded from enjoying the fruits of these reforms, which nevertheless were of greater advantage to the poor than to the rich. Everyone benefited from them, since we are all young at some time, all old at another. Both reforms, once established, became noncontroversial. Both contributed to political and social stability by encouraging Americans to have a better opinion of their society—a "good" which the economist is at a loss to measure and which the ideologically oriented sociologist, interested in "social change," is likely to scorn.

To be sure, all such successful, "universal" reforms are extremely expensive. But this represents an insurmountable obstacle only if one insists that such reforms accomplish their ends immediately. Such insistence is itself a recent phenomenon, one of the feverish symptoms of the intemperate '60s. The public school system, at all levels, was the work of over a century; and Social Security was gradually phased into its current state over the course of the last 30 years. Had anyone demanded "public education *now*" or "Social Security *now*," he would have been making an unreasonable and self-defeating demand. Fortunately, very few reformers were then so peremptory, and government was able to institute these reforms in an orderly, gradual, and ultimately successful way.

The reforming spirit of the sixties—and of the seventies too—is less patient, more impassioned. It is bored with the prospect of gradual improvement, and sometimes seems to get a positive satisfaction out of setting American against American—class against class, race against race, ethnic group against ethnic group. This is why I think it fair to say that most of the Great Society programs have failed. They have provoked incessant turbulence within the body politic. A successful reform has just the opposite effect.

One wonders what would happen if all the money spent on Great Society programs had been used to institute, in however modest a way, just two universal reforms: (1) children's allowance, as already described, and (2) some form of national health insurance? My own surmise is that the country would be in much better shape today. We would all—including the poor among us—feel that we were making progress, and making progress together, rather than at the expense of one another.

Yes, such reforms are expensive and technically "wasteful," in that they distribute benefits to all, needy or not. But to stress this aspect of the matter is to miss the point: Social reform is an inherently political activity, and is to be judged by political, not economic or sociological, criteria. When I say social reform is "political," I mean that its purpose is to sustain the polity, to encourage a sense of political community, even of fraternity. To the degree that it succeeds in achieving these ends, a successful social reform—however liberal or radical its original impulse—is conservative in its ultimate effects. Indeed, to take the liberal or radical impulse, which is always with us, and slowly to translate that impulse into enduring institutions which engender larger loyalties is precisely what the art of government, properly understood, is all about.

1973

18

Business and the "New Class"

Everyone wants to be loved, and it always comes as a shock to discover that there are people who dislike you for what you really are rather than for what they mistakenly think you are. Indeed, most of us desperately resist such a conclusion. We keep insisting, to ourselves and others, that those people out there who are saying nasty things about us are merely ill-informed, or misguided, or have been seduced by mischievous propaganda on the part of a handful of irredeemably perverse spirits. And we remain confident, in our heart of hearts, that if they only understood us better, they would certainly dislike us less.

In this respect businessmen are as human—and are as capable of self-deception—as anyone else. On any single day, all over the country, there are gatherings of corporate executives in which bewilderment and vexation are expressed at the climate of hostility toward business to be found in Washington, or in the media, or in academia—or even, incredibly, among their own children. And, quickly enough, the idea is born that something ought to be done to create a better understanding (and, of course, appreciation) of "the free enterprise system." A television series on economics and business for the high schools? Space advertising in the print media? Face-to-face encounters between businessmen and college students? Long and serious luncheons with the editors of major newspapers and newsmagazines? In the end, many of these ideas come to

205

fruition, at substantial costs in money and time—but with depressingly small effect.

Now, I do not wish to seem to be underestimating the degree of ignorance about business and economics which does in fact exist in the United States today. It is indeed amazing that, in a society in which business plays so crucial a role, so many people come to understand so little about it—and, at the same time, to know so much about it which isn't so. We have, for instance, managed to produce a generation of young people who, for all the education lavished on them, know less about the world of work—even the world of their fathers' work—than any previous generation in American history. They fantasize easily, disregard common observation, and appear to be radically deficient in that faculty we call common sense.

Nor, it must be said, are their teachers in a much better condition. The average college professor of history, sociology, literature, political science, sometimes even economics, is just as inclined to prefer fantasy over reality. On every college campus one can hear it said casually by faculty members that the drug companies are busy suppressing cures for cancer or arthritis or whatever; or that multinational corporations "really" make or unmake American foreign policy; or that "big business" actually welcomes a depression because it creates a "reserve army of the unemployed" from which it can recruit more docile workers.

So there is certainly room for all kinds of educational endeavors on the part of the business community, and I do not wish to be interpreted as in any way discouraging them. The fact that they seem so relatively ineffectual is not necessarily an argument against them. Education is at best a slow and tedious process, and that kind of education which tries to counteract a massive, original miseducation is even slower and more tedious. Too many businessmen confuse education with advertising, and almost unconsciously impose the short time horizon of the latter on the former. The unit of time appropriate to the process of education is not a year but a generation.

Having said this, however, I should like to pursue the truly interesting question of *why* so many intelligent people manage to entertain so many absurd ideas about economics in general and business in particular. In truth, one can properly put that question in a much stronger form: Why do so many intelligent people seem *determined* to hold those ideas and to resist any correction of them? Such determination there must be, because mere error and ignorance are not of themselves so obdurate. When they are, it is usually because they also are an integral part of an ideology which serves some deeper passion or interest.

And the more attentively one studies the problem, the clearer it becomes that what is commonly called a "bias" or an "animus" against business is really a by-product of a larger purposiveness. There are people "out there" who find it convenient to believe the worst about business because they have certain adverse intentions toward the business community to begin with. They dislike business for what it is, not for what they mistakenly think it is. In other words, they are members of what we have called "the new class."

This "new class" is not easily defined but may be vaguely described. It consists of a goodly proportion of those college-educated people whose skills and vocations proliferate in a "post-industrial society" (to use Daniel Bell's convenient term). We are talking about scientists, teachers and educational administrators, journalists and others in the communication industries, psychologists, social workers, those lawyers and doctors who make their careers in the expanding public sector, city planners, the staffs of the larger foundations, the upper levels of the government bureaucracy, and so on. It is, by now, a quite numerous class; it is an indispensable class for our kind of society; it is a disproportionately powerful class; it is also an ambitious and frustrated class.

Kevin Phillips calls this class "the mediacracy," in a book of that title. Though the book has many shrewd observations, the term he chooses seems to me to be unfortunate. It helps prolong what might be called the "Agnew illusion," i.e., that many of our troubles derive from the fact that a small and self-selected group, whose opinions are unrepresentative of the American people, have usurped control of our media and use their strategic positions to launch an assault on our traditions and institutions. Such a populist perspective is misleading and ultimately self-defeating. Members of the new class do not "control" the media, they *are* the media—just as they *are* our educational system, our public health and welfare system, and much else. Even if the president of CBS or the publisher of *Time* were to decide tomorrow that George Wallace would be the ideal president, it would have practically no effect on what is broadcast or published. These executives have as much control over "their" bureaucracies as the Secretary of HEW has over his, or as the average college president has over his faculty.

What does this "new class" want and why should it be so hostile to the business community? Well, one should understand that the members of this class are "idealistic," in the 1960s sense of that term, i.e., they are not much interested in money but are keenly interested in power. Power for what? Well, the power to shape our civilization—a power which, in a capitalist system, is supposed to reside in the free market. The "new class" wants to see much of this power redistributed to government, where *they* will then have a major say in how it is exercised.

From the very beginnings of capitalism there has always existed a small group of men and women who disapproved of the pervasive influence of the free market on the civilization in which we live. One used to call this group "the intellectuals," and they are the ancestors of our own "new class," very few of whom are intellectuals but all of whom inherit the attitudes toward capitalism that have flourished among intellectuals for more than a century and a half. This attitude may accurately be called "elitist," though people who are convinced they incarnate "the public interest," as distinct from all the private interests of a free society, are not likely to think of themselves in such a way. The elitist attitude is basically suspicious of, and hostile to, the market precisely because the market is so vulgarly democratic—one dollar, one vote. A civilization shaped by market transactions is a civilization responsive to the common appetites, preferences, and aspirations of common people. The "new class"— intelligent, educated, and energetic—has little respect for such a commonplace civilization. It wishes to see its "ideals" more effectual than the market is likely to permit them to be. And so it tries always to supersede economics by politics—an activity in which *it* is most competent—since it has the talents and the implicit authority to shape public opinion on all larger issues.

ITS OWN GRAVEDIGGER?

So there is a sense in which capitalism may yet turn out to be its own gravedigger, since it is capitalism that creates this "new class"—through economic growth, affluence, mass higher education, the proliferation of new technologies of communication, and in a hundred other ways. Moreover, it must be said that the "idealism" of this "new class," though in all respects self-serving, is not for that reason insincere. It really is true that a civilization shaped predominantly by a free market—by the preferences and appetites of ordinary men and women— has a "quality of life" that is likely to be regarded as less than wholly admirable by the better-educated classes. To be sure, these classes could try to improve things by elevating and refining the preferences of all those ordinary people; that, supposedly, is the liberal and democratic way. But it is so much easier to mobilize the active layers of public opinion behind such issues as environmentalism, ecology, consumer protection, and economic planning, to give the governmental bureaucracy the power to regulate and coerce, and eventually to "politicize" the economic decision-making pro-cess. And this is, of course, exactly what has been happening.

There can be little doubt that if these new imperialistic impulses on the part of "the public sector" (i.e., the political sector) are unrestrained, we shall move toward some version of state capitalism in which the citizen's individual liberty would be rendered ever more insecure. But it is important not to have any illusions about how much can be done to cope with this situation. The "new class" is here, it is firmly established in its own societal sectors, and it is not going to go away. It is idle, therefore, to talk about returning to a "free enterprise" system in which government will play the modest role it used to. The idea of such a counterreformation is utopian. Ronald Reagan was a two-term governor of California, and whatever his accomplishments, the restoration of "free enterprise" was not one of them. Had he become a two-term president, he (and we) would have found that, after the ideological smoke had cleared, not all that much had changed.

Not that the situation is hopeless—it's just that one has to recognize the limited range of the possible. It *is* possible, I think, at least to preserve a substantial and vigorous private sector—not only a business sector, but also a nongovernmental, not-for-profit sector—in the United States. This can happen, not because of the self-evident virtues of business, but because of the profound appeal of individual liberty to all Americans, and because of the equally profound distrust of big government by all Americans. In this appeal and this distrust even members of the "new class" share, to one degree or another. It is our good fortune that they are not doctrinaire socialists, as in Britain, even if they sometimes look and sound like it. They have long wanted their "place in the sun"—they are in the process of seizing and consolidating it—and now they have to be assimilated into the system (even as the system will have to change to assimilate them). It will be a slow and painful business but need not end in calamity.

A good part of this process of assimilation will be the education of this "new class" in the actualities of business and economics—*not* their conversion to "free enterprise"—so that they can exercise their power responsibly. It will be an immense educational task, in which the business community certainly can play an important role. But before it can play this role, business has first to understand the new sociological and political reality within which it is now operating. That, too, is an educational task of no small proportion.

1975

19

Corporate Capitalism in America

The United States is the capitalist nation par excellence. That is to say, it is not merely the case that capitalism has flourished here more vigorously than, for instance, in the nations of Western Europe. The point is, rather, that the Founding Fathers *intended* this nation to be capitalist and regarded it as the *only* set of economic arrangements consistent with the liberal democracy they had established. They did not use the term "capitalism," of course; but, then, neither did Adam Smith, whose *Wealth of Nations* was also published in 1776, and who spoke of "the system of natural liberty." That invidious word, "capitalism," was invented by European socialists about a half-century later—just as our other common expression, "free enterprise," was invented still later by antisocialists who saw no good reason for permitting their enemies to appropriate the vocabulary of public discourse. But words aside, it is a fact that capitalism in this country has a historical legitimacy that it does not possess elsewhere. In other lands, the nation and its fundamental institutions antedate the capitalist era; in the United States, where liberal democracy is not merely a form of government but also a "way of life," capitalism and democracy have been organically linked.

This fact, quite simply accepted until the 1930s—accepted by both radical critics and staunch defenders of the American regime—has been obscured in recent decades by the efforts of liberal scholars to create a respectable pedigree for the emerging "welfare state." The impetus

211

behind this scholarship was justified, to a degree. It is true that the Founding Fathers were not dogmatic laissez-faireists, in a later neo-Darwinian or "libertarian" sense of the term. They were intensely suspicious of governmental power, but they never could have subscribed to the doctrine of "our enemy, the State." They believed there was room for some governmental intervention in economic affairs; and—what is less frequently remarked—they believed most firmly in the propriety of governmental intervention and regulation in the areas of public taste and public morality. But, when one has said this, one must add emphatically that there really is little doubt that the Founders were convinced that economics was the sphere of human activity where government intervention was, as a general rule, least likely to be productive, and that "the system of natural liberty" in economic affairs was the complement to our system of constitutional liberty in political and civil affairs. They surely would have agreed with Hayek that the paternalistic government favored by modern liberalism led down the "road to serfdom."

But one must also concede that both the Founding Fathers and Adam Smith would have been perplexed by the kind of capitalism we have in 1978. They could not have interpreted the domination of economic activity by large corporate bureaucracies as representing, in any sense, the working of a "system of natural liberty." Entrepreneurial capitalism, as they understood it, was mainly an individual—or at most, a family—affair. Such large organizations as might exist—joint stock companies, for example—were limited in purpose (e.g., building a canal or a railroad) and usually in duration as well. The large, publicly owned corporation of today which strives for immortality, which is committed to no line of business but rather (like an investment banker) seeks the best return on investment, which is governed by an anonymous oligarchy, would have troubled and puzzled them, just as it troubles and puzzles us. And they would have asked themselves the same questions we have been asking ourselves for almost a century now: Who "owns" this new leviathan? Who governs it, and by what right, and according to what principles?

THE UNPOPULAR REVOLUTION

To understand the history of corporate capitalism in America, it is important to realize in what sense it may be fairly described as an "accidental institution." Not in the economic sense, of course. In the latter part of the last century, in all industrialized nations, the large corporation was born out of both economic necessity and economic opportunity: the necessity of large pools of capital and of a variety of technical expertise to exploit the emerging technologies, and the opportunity for economies of scale in production, marketing, and service in a rapidly urbanizing society. It all happened so quickly that the term "corporate revolution" is not inappropriate. In 1870, the United States was a land of small family-owned business. By 1905, the large, publicly owned corporation dominated the economic scene.

But the corporate revolution was always, during that period, an unpopular revolution. It was seen by most Americans as an accident of economic circumstance—something that happened to them rather than something they had created. They had not foreseen it; they did not understand it; in no way did it seem to "fit" into the accepted ideology of the American democracy. No other institution in American history—not even slavery—has ever been so consistently unpopular as has the large corporation with the American public. It was controversial from the outset, and it has remained controversial to this day.

This is something the current crop of corporate executives find very difficult to appreciate. Most of them reached maturity during the post-war period, 1945–1960. As it happens, this was—with the possible exception of the 1920s—just about the only period when public opinion was, on the whole, well-disposed to the large corporation. After 15 years of depression and war, the American people wanted houses, consumer goods, and relative security of employment—all the things that the modern corporation is so good at supplying. The typical corporate executive of today, in his fifties or sixties, was led to think that such popular acceptance was "normal," and is therefore inclined to believe that there are novel and specific forces behind the upsurge of anticorporate sentiment in the past decade. As a matter of fact, he is partly right: there *is* something significantly new about the hostility to the large corporation in our day. But there is also something very old, something coeval with the very existence of the large corporation itself. And it is the interaction of the old hostility with the new which has put the modern corporation in the critical condition that we find it in today.

The old hostility is based on what we familiarly call "populism." This is a sentiment basic to any democracy—indispensable to its establishment but also, ironically, inimical to its survival. Populism is the constant fear and suspicion that power and/or authority, whether in government or out, is being used to frustrate "the will of the people." It is a spirit that intimidates authority and provides the popular energy to curb and resist it. The very possibility of a democratic society—as distinct from the forms of representative government, which are its political expression—is derived from, and is constantly renewed by, the populist temper. The Constitution endows the United States with a republican form of government, in which the free and explicit consent of the people must ultimately ratify the actions of those in authority. But the populist spirit, which both antedated and survived the Constitutional Convention, made the United States a democratic nation as well as a republican one, committed to "the democratic way of life" as well as to the proprieties of constitutional government. It is precisely the strength of that commitment which has always made the American democracy somehow different from the democracies of Western Europe—a difference which every European observer has been quick to remark.

But populism is, at the same time, an eternal problem for the American democratic republic. It incarnates an antinomian impulse, a Jacobin contempt for the "mere" forms of law and order and civility. It also engenders an impulse toward a rather infantile political utopianism, on the premise that nothing is too good for "the people." Above all, it is a temper and state of mind which too easily degenerates into political paranoia, with "enemies of the people" being constantly discovered and exorcised and convulsively purged. Populist paranoia is always busy subverting the very institutions and authorities that the democratic republic laboriously creates for the purpose of orderly self-government.

In the case of the large corporation, we see a healthy populism and a feverish paranoia simultaneously being provoked by its sudden and dramatic appearance. The paranoia takes the form of an instinctive readiness to believe anything reprehensible, no matter how incredible, about the machinations of "big business." That species of journalism and scholarship which we call "muckraking" has made this kind of populist paranoia a permanent feature of American intellectual and public life. Though the businessman per se has never been a fictional hero of bourgeois society (as Stendhal observed, a merchant may be honorable but there is nothing heroic about him), it is only after the rise of "big business" that the businessman becomes the natural and predestined villain of the novel, the drama, the cinema, and, more recently, television. By now most Americans are utterly convinced that all "big business" owes its existence to the original depredations of "robber barons"—a myth which never really was plausible, which more recent scholarship by economic historians has thoroughly discredited, but which probably forever will have a secure hold on the American political imagination. Similarly, most Americans are now quick to believe that "big business" conspires secretly but most effectively to manipulate the economic and political system—an enterprise which, in prosaic fact, corporate executives are too distracted and too unimaginative even to contemplate.

Along with this kind of paranoia, however, populist hostility toward the large corporation derives from an authentic bewilderment and concern about the place of this new institution in American life. In its concentration of assets and power—power to make economic decisions affecting the lives of tens of thousands of citizens—it seemed to create a dangerous disharmony between the economic system and the political. In the America of the 1890s, even government did not have, and did not claim, such power (except in wartime). *No one* was supposed to have such power; it was, indeed, a radical diffusion of power that was thought to be an essential characteristic of democratic capitalism. The rebellion of Jacksonian democracy against the Bank of the United States had been directed precisely against such an "improper" concentration of power. A comparable rebellion now took place against "big business."

"BIG BUSINESS" OR CAPITALISM?

It was not, however, a rebellion against capitalism as such. On the contrary, popular hostility to the large corporation reflected the fear that this new institution was subverting capitalism as Americans then understood (and, for the most part, still understand) it. This understanding was phrased in individualistic terms. The entrepreneur was conceived of as a real person, not as a legal fiction. The "firm" was identified with such a real person (or a family of real persons) who took personal risks, reaped personal rewards, and assumed personal responsibility for his actions. One of the consequences of the victorious revolt against the Bank of the United States had been to make the chartering of corporations—legal "persons" with limited liability—under state law a routine and easy thing, the assumption being that this would lead to a proliferation of small corporations, still easily identifiable with the flesh-and-blood entrepreneurs who founded them. The rise of "big business" frustrated such expectations.

Moreover, the large corporation not only seemed to be but actually was a significant deviation from traditional capitalism. One of the features of the large corporation—though more a consequence of its existence than its cause—was its need for, and its ability to create, "orderly markets." What businessmen disparagingly call "cutthroat competition," with its wild swings in price, its large fluctuations in employment, its unpredictable effects upon profits—all this violates the very *raison d'être* of a large corporation, with its need for relative stability so that its long-range investment decisions can be rationally calculated. The modern corporation always looks to the largest and most powerful firm in the industry to establish "market leadership" in price, after which competition will concentrate on quality, service, and the introduction of new products. One should not exaggerate the degree to which the large corporation is successful in these efforts. John Kenneth Galbraith's notion that the large corporation simply manipulates its market through the power of advertising and fixes the price level with sovereign authority is a wild exaggeration. This is what all corporations *try* to do; it is what a few corporations, in some industries, sometimes succeed in doing. Still, there is little doubt that the idea of a "free market," in the era of large corporations, is not quite the original capitalist idea.

The populist response to the transformation of capitalism by the large corporation was, and is: "Break it up!" Antitrust and antimonopoly legislation was the consequence. Such legislation is still enacted and reenacted, and antitrust prosecutions still make headlines. But the effort is by now routine, random, and largely pointless. There may be a few lawyers left in the Justice Department or the Federal Trade Commission who sincerely believe that such laws, if stringently enforced, could restore capitalism to something like its pristine individualist form. But it is much more probable that the lawyers who staff such government agencies launch these intermittent crusades against "monopoly" and "oligopoly"—terms that are distressingly vague and inadequate when applied to the real world—because they prefer such activity to mere idleness, and because they anticipate that a successful prosecution will enhance their professional reputations. No one expects them to be effectual, whether the government wins or loses. Just how much difference, after all, would it make if AT&T were forced to spin off its Western Electric manufacturing subsidiary, or if IBM were divided into three different computer companies? All that would be accomplished is a slight increase in the number of large corporations, with very little consequence for the shape of the economy or the society as a whole.

True, one could imagine, in the abstract, a much more radical effort to break up "big business." But there are good reasons why, though many talk solemnly about this possibility, no one does anything about it. The costs would simply be too high. The economic costs, most obviously: an adverse effect on productivity, on capital investment, on our balance of payments, etc. But the social and political costs would be even more intolerable. Our major trade unions, having after many years succeeded in establishing collective bargaining on a national level with the large corporation, are not about to sit back and watch their power disintegrate for the sake of an ideal such as "decentralization." And the nation's pension funds are not about to permit the assets of the corporations in which they have invested to be dispersed, and the security of their pension payments correspondingly threatened.

One suspects that even popular opinion, receptive in principle to the diminution of "big business," would in actuality find the process too painful to tolerate. For the plain fact is that, despite much academic agitation about the horrors of being an "organization man," a large proportion of those who now work for a living, of whatever class, have learned to prefer the security, the finely calibrated opportunities for advancement, the fringe benefits, and the paternalism of a large corporation to the presumed advantages of employment in smaller firms. It is not only corporate executives who are fearful of "cutthroat competition"; most of us, however firmly we declare our faith in capitalism and "free enterprise," are sufficiently conservative in our instincts to wish to avoid all such capitalist rigors. Even radical professors, who in their books find large bureaucratic corporations "dehumanizing," are notoriously reluctant to give up tenured appointments in large bureaucratic universities for riskier opportunities elsewhere.

So the populist temper and the large corporation coexist uneasily in America today, in what can only be called a marriage of convenience. There is little affection, much nagging and backbiting and whining on all sides, but it endures "for the sake of the children," as it were. Not too long ago, there was reason to hope that, out of the habit of coexistence, there would emerge something like a philosophy of coexistence: a mutual adaptation of the democratic-individualist-capitalist ideal and the bureaucratic-corporate reality, sanctioned by a new revised version of the theory of democracy and capitalism—a new political and social philosophy, in short, which extended the reach of traditional views without repudiating them. But that possibility, if it was ever more than a fancy, has been effectively canceled by the rise, over the past decade, of an anticapitalist ethos which has completely transformed the very definition of the problem.

THE ANTILIBERAL LEFT

This ethos, in its American form, is not *explicitly* anticapitalistic, and this obscures our perception and understanding of it. It has its roots in the tradition of "progressive reform," a tradition which slightly antedated the corporate revolution but which was immensely stimulated by it. In contrast to populism, this was (and is) an upper-middle-class tradition—an "elitist" tradition, as one would now say. Though it absorbed a great many socialist and neosocialist and quasi-socialist ideas, it was too American—too habituated to the rhetoric of individualism, and even in some measure to its reality—to embrace easily a synoptic, collectivist vision of the future as enunciated in socialist dogmas. It was willing to contemplate "public ownership" (i.e., ownership by the political authorities) of *some* of the "means of production," but on the whole it preferred to think in terms of *regulating* the large corporation rather than nationalizing it or breaking it up. It is fair to call it an indigenous and peculiarly American counterpart to European socialism: addressing itself to the same problems defined in much the same way, motivated by the same ideological impulse, but assuming an adversary posture toward "big business" specifically rather than toward capitalism in general.

At least, that is what "progressive reform" used to be. In the past decade, however, it has experienced a transmutation of ideological substance while preserving most of the traditional rhetorical wrappings. That is because it embraced, during these years, a couple of other political traditions, European in origin, so that what we still call "liberalism" in the United States is now something quite different from the liberalism of the older "progressive reform" impulse. It is so different, indeed, as to have created a cleavage between those who think of themselves as "old

liberals"—some of whom are now redesignated as "neoconservatives"—and the new liberals who are in truth men and women of "the
Left," in the European sense of that term. This is an important point,
worthy of some elaboration and clarification, especially since the new
liberalism is not usually very candid about the matter.*

The Left in Europe, whether "totalitarian" or "democratic," has
consistently been antiliberal. That is to say, it vigorously repudiates the
intellectual traditions of liberalism—as expressed, say, by Locke, Montesquieu, Adam Smith, and Tocqueville—and with equal vigor rejects the
key institution of liberalism: the (relatively) free market (which necessarily implies limited government). The Left emerges out of a rebellion
against the "anarchy" and "vulgarity" of a civilization that is shaped by
individuals engaged in market transactions. The "anarchy" to which it
refers is the absence of any transcending goal or purpose which society is
constrained to pursue and which socialists, with their superior understanding of History, feel obligated to prescribe. Such a prescription,
when fulfilled, will supposedly reestablish a humane "order." The "vulgarity" to which it refers is the fact that a free market responds, or tries
to respond, to the appetites and preferences of common men and
women, whose use of their purchasing power determines the shape of
the civilization. Since common men and women are likely to have "common" preferences, tastes, and aspirations, the society they create—the
"consumption society," as it is now called—will be regarded by some
critics as shortsightedly "materialistic." People will seek to acquire what
they want (e.g., automobiles), not what they "need" (e.g., mass transit).
Socialists are persuaded that they have a superior understanding of people's true needs, and that the people will be more truly happy in a society where socialists have the authority to define those needs, officially
and unequivocally.

Obviously, socialism is an "elitist" movement, and in its beginnings—
with Saint-Simon and Auguste Comte—was frankly conceived of as

---

*It must be said, however, that even when it is candid, no one seems to pay attention. John
Kenneth Galbraith has recently publicly defined himself as a "socialist," and asserts that he has
been one—whether wittingly or unwittingly, it is not clear—for many years. But the media still
consistently identify him as a "liberal," and he is so generally regarded. Whether this is mere
habit or instinctive protective coloration—for the media are a crucial wing of the "new liberalism"—it is hard to say.

such. Its appeal has always been to "intellectuals" (who feel dispossessed by and alienated from a society in which they are merely one species of common man) and members of the upper middle class who, having reaped the benefits of capitalism, are now in a position to see its costs. (It must be said that these costs are not imaginary: Socialism would not have such widespread appeal if its critique of liberal capitalism were entirely without substance.) But all social movements in the modern world must define themselves as "democratic," since democratic legitimacy is the only kind of legitimacy we recognize. So "totalitarian" socialism insists that it is a "people's democracy," in which the "will of the people" is mystically incarnated in the ruling party. "Democratic socialism," on the other hand, would like to think that it can "socialize" the economic sector while leaving the rest of society "liberal." As Robert Nozick puts it, democratic socialists want to proscribe only "capitalist transactions between consenting adults."

The trouble with the latter approach is that democratic socialists, when elected to office, discover that to collectivize economic life you have to coerce all sorts of other institutions (e.g., the trade unions, the media, the educational system) and limit individual freedom in all sorts of ways (e.g., freedom to travel, freedom to "drop out" from the world of work, freedom to choose the kind of education one prefers) if a "planned society" is to function efficiently. When "democratic socialist" governments show reluctance to take such actions, they are pushed into doing so by the "left wings" of their "movements," who feel betrayed by the distance that still exists between the reality they experience and the socialist ideal which enchants them. Something like this is now happening in all the European social-democratic parties and in a country like India.

THE "NEW CLASS"

The United States never really had any such movement of the Left, at least not to any significant degree. It was regarded as an "un-American" thing, as indeed it was. True, the movement of "progressive reform" was "elitist" both in its social composition and its social aims: it, too, was distressed by the "anarchy" and "vulgarity" of capitalist civilization. But in the main it accepted as a fact the proposition that capitalism and liberalism were organically connected, and it proposed to itself the goal of "mitigating the evils of capitalism," rather than abolishing liberal capitalism and replacing it with "a new social order" in which a whole new set of human relationships would be established. It was an authentic *reformist* movement. It wanted to regulate the large corporations so that this concentration of private power could not develop into an oligarchical threat to democratic-liberal capitalism. It was ready to interfere with the free market so that the instabilities generated by capitalism—above all, instability of employment—would be less costly in human terms. It was even willing to tamper occasionally with the consumer's freedom of choice where there was a clear consensus that the micro-decisions of the marketplace added up to macro-consequences that were felt to be unacceptable. And it hoped to correct the "vulgarity" of capitalist civilization by educating the people so that their "preference schedules" (as economists would say) would be, in traditional terms, more elevated, more appreciative of "the finer things in life."

Ironically, it was the extraordinary increase in mass higher education after World War II that, perhaps more than anything else, infused the traditional movement for "progressive reform" with various impulses derived from the European Left. The earlier movement had been "elitist" in fact as well as in intention, i.e., it was sufficiently small so that, even while influential, it could hardly contemplate the possibility of actually exercising "power." Mass higher education has converted this movement into something like a mass movement proper, capable of driving a president from office (1968) and nominating its own candidate (1972). The intentions remain "elitist," of course; but the movement now encompasses some millions of people. These are the people whom liberal capitalism had sent to college in order to help manage its affluent, highly technological, mildly paternalistic, "postindustrial" society.

This "new class" consists of scientists, lawyers, city planners, social workers, educators, criminologists, sociologists, public health doctors, etc.—a substantial number of whom find their careers in the expanding public sector rather than the private. The public sector, indeed, is where they prefer to be. They are, as one says, "idealistic," i.e., far less interested in individual financial rewards than in the corporate power of their class. Though they continue to speak the language of "progressive reform," in actuality they are acting upon a hidden agenda: to propel the nation from that modified version of capitalism we call "the welfare state" toward an economic system so stringently regulated in detail as to fulfill many of the traditional anticapitalist aspirations of the Left.

The exact nature of what has been happening is obscured by the fact that this "new class" is not merely liberal but truly "libertarian" in its approach to all areas of life—except economics. It celebrates individual liberty of speech and expression and action to an unprecedented degree, so that at times it seems almost anarchistic in its conception of the good life. But this joyful individualism always stops short of the border where economics—i.e., capitalism—begins. The "new class" is surely sincere in such a contradictory commitment to a maximum of individual freedom in a society where economic life becomes less free with every passing year. But it is instructive to note that these same people, who are irked and inflamed by the slightest noneconomic restriction in the United States, can be admiring of Maoist China and not in the least appalled by the total collectivization of life—and the total destruction of liberty— there. They see this regime as "progressive," not "reactionary." And, in this perception, they unwittingly tell us much about their deepest fantasies and the natural bias of their political imagination.

Meanwhile, the transformation of American capitalism proceeds apace. Under the guise of coping with nasty "externalities"—air pollution, water pollution, noise pollution, traffic pollution, health pollution, or what have you—more and more of the basic economic decisions are being removed from the marketplace and transferred to the "public"— i.e., political—sector, where the "new class," by virtue of its expertise and skills, is so well represented. This movement is naturally applauded by the media, which are also for the most part populated by members of this "new class" who believe—as the Left has always believed—it is government's responsibility to cure all the ills of the human condition, and who ridicule those politicians who deny the possibility (and therefore the propriety) of government doing any such ambitious thing. And, inevitably, more explicitly socialist and neosocialist themes are beginning boldly to emerge from the protective shell of reformist-liberal rhetoric. The need for some kind of "national economic plan" is now being discussed seriously in Congressional circles; the desirability of "public"— i.e., political—appointees to the boards of directors of the largest corporations is becoming more apparent to more politicians and journalists with every passing day; the utter "reasonableness," in principle, of price and wage controls is no longer even a matter for argument, but is subject only to circumstantial and prudential considerations. Gradually, the traditions of the Left are being absorbed into the agenda of "progressive reform," and the structure of American society is being radically, if discreetly, altered.

"THE ENEMY OF BEING IS HAVING"

One of the reasons this process is so powerful, and meets only relatively feeble resistance, is that it has a continuing source of energy within the capitalist system itself. That source is not the "inequalities" or "injustices" of capitalism, as various ideologies of the Left insist. These may represent foci around which dissent is occasionally and skillfully mobilized. But the most striking fact about anticapitalism is the degree to which it is *not* a spontaneous working-class phenomenon. Capitalism, like all economic and social systems, breeds its own peculiar discontents, but the discontents of the working class are, in and of themselves, not one of its major problems. Yes, there is class conflict in capitalism; there is always class conflict, and the very notion of a possible society without class conflict is one of socialism's most bizarre fantasies. (Indeed, it is this fantasy that is socialism's original contribution to modern political theory; the importance of class conflict itself was expounded by Aristotle and was never doubted by anyone who ever bothered to look at the real world.) But there is no case, in any country that can reasonably be called "capitalist," of such class conflict leading to a proletarian revolution. Capitalism, precisely because its aim is the satisfaction of "common" appetites and aspirations, can adequately cope with its own class conflicts, through economic growth primarily and some version of the welfare state secondarily. It can do so, however, only if it is permitted to—a permission which the anticapitalist spirit is loath to concede. This spirit *wants* to see capitalism falter and fail.

The essence of this spirit is to be found, not in *The Communist Manifesto*, but rather in the young Marx who wrote: "*The enemy of being is having.*" This sums up neatly the animus which intellectuals from the beginning, and "the new class" in our own day, have felt toward the system of liberal capitalism. This system is in truth "an acquisitive society," by traditional standards. Not that men and women under capitalism are "greedier" than under feudalism or socialism or whatever. Almost all people, almost all of the time, want more than they have. But capitalism is unique among social and economic systems in being organized for the overriding purpose of giving them more than they have. And here is where it runs into trouble: Those who benefit most from capitalism—and their children, especially—experience a withering away of the acquisitive impulse. Or, to put it more accurately: They cease to think of acquiring money and begin to think of acquiring power so as to improve the "quality of life," and to give *being* priority over *having*. That is the meaning of the well-known statement by a student radical of the 1960s: "You don't know what hell is like unless you were raised in Scarsdale." Since it is the ambition of capitalism to enable everyone to live in Scarsdale or its equivalent, this challenge is far more fundamental than the orthodox Marxist one, which says—against all the evidence—that capitalism will fail because it *cannot* get everyone to live in Scarsdale.

Against this new kind of attack, any version of capitalism would be vulnerable. But the version of corporate capitalism under which we live is not merely vulnerable; it is practically defenseless. It is not really hard to make a decent case, on a pragmatic level, for liberal capitalism today—especially since the anticapitalist societies the 20th century has given birth to are, even by their own standards, monstrous abortions and "betrayals" of their originating ideals. And corporate capitalism does have the great merit of being willing to provide a milieu of comfortable liberty—in universities, for example—for those who prefer *being* to *having*. But the trouble with the large corporation today is that it does not possess a clear theoretical—i.e., ideological—legitimacy within the framework of liberal capitalism itself. Consequently the gradual usurpation of managerial authority by the "new class"—mainly through the transfer of this authority to the new breed of regulatory officials (who are the very prototype of the class)—is almost irresistible.

BUREAUCRATIC ENTERPRISE

So long as business was an activity carried on by real individuals who "owned" the property they managed, the politicians, the courts, and public opinion were all reasonably respectful of the capitalist proprieties. Not only was the businessman no threat to liberal democracy; he was, on the contrary, the very epitome of the bourgeois liberal-democratic ethos—the man who succeeded by diligence, enterprise, sobriety, and all those other virtues that Benjamin Franklin catalogued for us, and which we loosely call "the Protestant ethic."*

On the whole, even today, politicians and public opinion are inclined to look with some benevolence on "small business," and no one seems to be interested in leading a crusade against it. But the professionally managed large corporation is another matter entirely. The top executives of these enormous bureaucratic institutions are utterly sincere when they claim fealty to "free enterprise," and they even have a point: Managing a business corporation, as distinct from a government agency, does require a substantial degree of entrepreneurial risk-taking and entrepreneurial skill. But it is also the case that they are as much functionaries as entrepreneurs, and rather anonymous functionaries at that. Not only don't we know who the chairman of General Motors is; we know so little about the kind of person who holds such a position that we haven't the faintest idea as to whether or not we want our children to grow up like him. Horatio Alger, writing in the era of precorporate capitalism, had no such problems. And there is something decidedly odd about a society in which a whole class of Very Important People is not automatically held up as one possible model of emulation for the young, and cannot be so held up because they are, as persons, close to invisible.

Nor is it at all clear whose interests these entrepreneur-functionaries are serving. In theory, they are elected representatives of the stockholder-"owners." But stockholder elections are almost invariably routine affirmations of management's will, because management will have previously secured the support of the largest stockholders; and for a long while now stockholders have essentially regarded themselves, and are regarded by management, as little more than possessors of a variable-income security. A stock certificate has become a lien against the company's earnings and assets—a subordinated lien, in both law and fact—rather than a charter of "citizenship" within a corporate community. And though management will talk piously, when it serves its purposes, about its obligations to the stockholders, the truth is that it prefers to have as little to do with them as possible, since their immediate demands are only too likely to conflict with management's long-term corporate plans.

It is interesting to note that when such an organization of business executives as the Committee on Economic Development drew up a

---

*I say "loosely call" because, as a Jew, I was raised to think that this was an ancient "Hebrew ethic," and some Chinese scholars I have spoken to feel that it could appropriately be called "The Confucian ethic."

kind of official declaration of the responsibilities of management a few years ago, it conceived of the professional manager as "a trustee balancing the interests of many diverse participants and constituents in the enterprise," and then enumerated these participants and constituents: employees, customers, suppliers, stockholders, government—practically everyone. Such a declaration serves only to ratify an accomplished fact: The large corporation has ceased being a species of private property, and is now a "quasi-public" institution. But if it is a "quasi-public" institution, some novel questions may be properly addressed to it: By what right does the self-perpetuating oligarchy that constitutes "management" exercise its powers? On what principles does it do so? To these essentially political questions management can only respond with the weak economic answer that its legitimacy derives from the superior efficiency with which it responds to signals from the free market. But such an argument from efficiency is not compelling when offered by a "quasi-public" institution. In a democratic republic such as ours, public and quasi-public institutions are not supposed simply to be efficient at responding to people's transient desires, are not supposed to be simply *pandering* institutions, but are rather supposed to help shape the people's wishes, and ultimately, the people's character, according to some version, accepted by the people itself, of the "public good" and "public interest." This latter task the "new class" feels itself supremely qualified to perform, leaving corporate management in the position of arguing that it is improper for this "quasi-public" institution to do more than give the people what they want: a debased version of the democratic idea which has some temporary demagogic appeal but no permanent force.

THE CORPORATION AND LIBERAL DEMOCRACY

Whether for good or evil—and one can leave this for future historians to debate—the large corporation has gone "quasi-public," i.e., it now straddles, uncomfortably and uncertainly, both the private and public sectors of our "mixed economy." In a sense one can say that the modern large corporation stands to the bourgeois-individualist capitalism of yesteryear as the "imperial" American polity stands to the isolated republic from which it emerged. Such a development may or may not represent "progress," but there is no turning back.

The danger which this situation poses for American democracy is not the tantalizing ambiguities inherent in such a condition; it is the genius of a pluralist democracy to convert such ambiguities into possible sources of institutional creativity and to avoid "solving" them, as a Jacobin democracy would, with one swift stroke of the sword. The danger is rather that the large corporation will be thoroughly integrated into the public sector, and lose its private character altogether. The transformation of American capitalism that *this* would represent—a radical departure from the quasi-bourgeois "mixed economy" to a system that could be fairly described as kind of "state capitalism"—does constitute a huge potential threat to the individual liberties Americans have traditionally enjoyed.

One need not, therefore, be an admirer of the large corporation to be concerned about its future. One might even regard its "bureaucratic-acquisitive" ethos, in contrast to the older "bourgeois-moralistic" ethos, as a sign of cultural decadence and still be concerned about its future. In our pluralistic society we frequently find ourselves defending specific concentrations of power, about which we might otherwise have the most mixed feelings, on the grounds that they contribute to a general diffusion of power, a diffusion which creates the "space" in which individual liberty can survive and prosper. This is certainly our experience vis-à-vis certain religious organizations—e.g., the Catholic Church or the Mormons—whose structure and values are, in some respects at least, at variance with our common democratic beliefs, and yet whose existence serves to preserve our democracy as a free and liberal society. The general principle of checks and balances, and of decentralized authority too, is as crucial to the social and economic structures of a liberal democracy as to its political structure.

Nevertheless, it seems clear that the large corporation is not going to be able to withstand those forces pulling and pushing it into the political sector unless it confronts the reality of its predicament and adapts itself to this reality in a self-preserving way. There is bound to be disagreement as to the forms such adaptation should take, some favoring institutional changes that emphasize and clarify the corporation's "public" nature, others insisting that its "private" character must be stressed anew. Probably a mixture of both strategies would be most effective. If large corporations are to avoid having government-appointed directors on their boards, they will have to take the initiative and try to preempt that possibility by

228 ON CAPITALISM AND THE DEMOCRATIC IDEA

themselves appointing distinguished "outside" directors, directors from outside the business community. At the same time, if corporations are going to be able to resist the total usurpation of their decision-making powers by government, they must create a constituency—of their stockholders, above all—which will candidly intervene in the "political game" of interest-group politics, an intervention fully in accord with the principles of our democratic system.

In both cases, the first step will have to be to persuade corporate management that some such change is necessary. This will be difficult: corporate managers are (and enjoy being) essentially economic-decision-making animals, and they are profoundly resentful of the "distractions" which "outside interference" of any kind will impose on them. After all, most chief executives have a tenure of about six years, and they all wish to establish the best possible track record, in terms of "bottom line" results, during that period. Very few are in a position to, and even fewer have an inclination to, take a long and larger view of the corporation and its institutional problems.

At the same time, the crusade against the corporations continues, with the "new class" successfully appealing to populist anxieties, seeking to run the country in the "right" way, and to reshape our civilization along lines superior to those established by the marketplace. Like all crusades, it engenders an enthusiastic paranoia about the nature of the Enemy and the deviousness of His operations. Thus, the *New Yorker*, which has become the liberal-chic organ of the "new class," has discovered the maleficent potential of the multinational corporation at exactly the time when the multinational corporation is in full retreat before the forces of nationalism everywhere. And the fact that American corporations sometimes have to bribe foreign politicians—for whom bribery is a way of life—is inflated into a rabid indictment of the personal morals of corporate executives. (That such bribery is also inherent in government-aid programs to the underdeveloped countries is, on the other hand, *never* taken to reflect on those who institute and run such programs, and is thought to be irrelevant to the desirability or success of the programs themselves.) So far, this crusade has been immensely effective. It will continue to be effective until the corporation has decided what kind of institution it is in today's world, and what kinds of reforms are a necessary precondition to a vigorous defense—not of its every action but of its very survival as a quasi-public institution as distinct from a completely politicized institution.

It is no exaggeration to say that the future of liberal democracy in America is intimately involved with these prospects for survival: the survival of an institution which liberal democracy never envisaged, whose birth and existence have been exceedingly troublesome to it, and whose legitimacy it has always found dubious. One can, if one wishes, call this a paradox. Or one can simply say that everything, including liberal democracy, is what it naturally becomes—is what it naturally evolves into—and our problem derives from a reluctance to revise yesteryear's beliefs in the light of today's realities.

1975

20

On Conservatism and Capitalism

These days, Americans who defend the capitalist system, i.e., an economy and a way of life organized primarily around the free market, are called "conservative." If they are willing to accept a limited degree of government intervention for social purposes, they are likely to be designated as "neoconservative." Under ordinary circumstances these labels would strike me as fair and appropriate. Capitalism, after all, is the traditional American economic and social system; unlike the nations of Europe, we have never known any other. And people who wish to defend and preserve traditional institutions are indeed conservative, in the literal sense of that term.

But the circumstances surrounding the use of such labels today are *not* ordinary; they are almost paradoxical. To begin with, the institutions which conservatives wish to preserve are, and for two centuries were called, *liberal* institutions, i.e., institutions which maximize personal liberty vis-à-vis a state, a church, or an official ideology. On the other hand, the severest critics of these institutions—those who wish to enlarge the scope of governmental authority indefinitely, so as to achieve ever greater equality at the expense of liberty—are today commonly called "liberals." It would certainly help to clarify matters if they were called, with greater propriety and accuracy, "socialists" or "neosocialists." And yet we are oddly reluctant to be so candid.

In part, this lack of candor is simply the consequence of a great many "liberals" being demagogic or hypocritical about their political intentions. It really is absurd that Bella Abzug should call herself a "liberal" when her political views are several shades to the left of Harold Wilson, Helmut Schmidt, Olof Palme, or probably even Indira Gandhi. Obviously, however, she is not about to reject the label, which is so useful to her. Instead, when asked, she may blandly assert that she is truly an enlightened defender of the free enterprise system. One would have to be naive to blame her, and others like her, for saying it; we can only blame ourselves for believing it.

It is clear that, in addition to such routine political deception, there is an enormous amount of a most curious self-deception going on. I find it striking that the media, and members of the business community too, should consistently refer to John Kenneth Galbraith as a "liberal" when he has actually taken the pains to write a book explaining why he is a socialist. And even Michael Harrington, who is the official head of a minuscule socialist party, will often find himself being introduced as "a leading liberal spokesman."

Why does this happen? And why, especially, do conservatives permit it to happen? Why should those who defend liberal institutions have yielded the term "liberal" to those who have no honorable intentions toward these institutions or, indeed, toward liberty itself?

The answer, I think, has to do with the fact that the idea of "liberty" which conservatives wish to defend, and which our liberal institutions are supposed to incarnate, has become exceedingly nebulous in the course of the past century. This puts conservatives in the position of being, or seeming to be, merely mindless defenders of the status quo. Indeed, to many they seem merely intransigent defenders of existing privilege, issuing appeals to "liberty" for such an ulterior purpose alone. This, in turn, has permitted "liberals" to impress their own definition of "liberty" on public opinion.

This "liberal" definition has two parts. First, it entails ever-greater governmental intervention in certain areas—economics, educational administration, the electoral process, etc.—to achieve greater equality, itself now identified with "true liberty." Second, it entails less governmental intervention in those areas—religion, school curricula, culture, entertainment, etc.—which have to do with the formation of character, and in which it is assumed that "the marketplace of ideas" will "naturally" produce ideal results.

The success which this "liberal" redefinition—a combination of moralistic egalitarianism and optimistic "permissiveness"—has achieved means that, in the United States today, the law insists that an 18-year-old girl has the right to public fornication in a pornographic movie—but only if she is paid the minimum wage. Now, you don't have to be the father of a daughter to think that there is something crazy about this situation, and the majority of the American people, if asked, would certainly say so. Nevertheless, conservatives find it very difficult to point out where the craziness lies, and to propose an alternative conception of liberty. As the saying goes, you can't beat a horse with no horse; and right now conservatives are horseless.

Ever since the beginnings of modern capitalism in the eighteenth century, two very different conceptions of liberty have emerged. The first was the "libertarian" idea. It asserted that God and/or nature had so arranged things that, by the operations of an "invisible hand," individual liberty, no matter how self-seeking, could only lead ultimately to humanity's virtuous happiness. "Private vices, public benefits" was its motto—and still is.

The second idea of liberty may be called the "bourgeois" idea. It asserted that liberty implied the right to do bad as well as the right to do good, that liberty could be abused as well as used—in short, that a distinction had to be made between liberty and "license." The making of this distinction was the task of our cultural and religious institutions, especially the latter. It was these institutions which infused the idea of liberty with positive substance, with "values," with an ethos. The basic belief was that a life led according to these values would maximize personal liberty in a context of social and political stability, would ensure—insofar as this is humanly possible—that the exercise of everyone's personal liberty would add up to a decent and good society. The practical virtues implied by the "bourgeois" values were not very exciting: thrift, industry, self-reliance, self-discipline, a moderate degree of public-spiritedness, and so forth. On the other hand, they had the immense advantage of being rather easily attainable by everyone. You didn't have to be a saint or a hero to be a good bourgeois citizen.

It did not take long for the culture emerging out of bourgeois society to become bored with, and hostile to, a life and a social order based on such prosaic bourgeois values. Artists and intellectuals quickly made it apparent that "alienation" was their destiny, and that the mission of this culture was to be antibourgeois. But so long as religion was a powerful force among ordinary men and women, the disaffection of the intellectuals was of only marginal significance. It is the decline in religious belief over the past 50 years—together with the rise of mass higher education, which popularized the culture's animus to bourgeois capitalism—that has been of decisive importance.

ADAM SMITH'S MISTAKE

The defenders of capitalism were, and are, helpless before this challenge. Businessmen, after all, had never taken culture seriously. They have always rather agreed with Adam Smith when he wrote:

> Though you despise that picture, or that poem, or even that system of philosophy which I admire, there is little danger of our quarreling on that account. Neither of us can reasonably be much interested about them.

He could not have been more wrong. What rules the world is ideas, because ideas define the way reality is perceived; and, in the absence of religion, it is out of culture—pictures, poems, songs, philosophy—that these ideas are born.

It is because of their indifference to culture, their placid philistinism, that businessmen today find themselves defending capitalism and personal liberty in purely amoral terms. They are "libertarians"—but without a belief in the providential dispensations of God or nature. Capitalism, they keep insisting, is the most *efficient* economic system. This may be true if you agree with Adam Smith when he said: "What can be added to the happiness of man who is in health, who is out of debt, and has a clear conscience?" But if you believe that a comfortable life is not necessarily the same thing as a good life, or even a meaningful life, then it will occur to you that efficiency is a means, not an end in itself. Capitalist efficiency may then be regarded as a most useful precondition for a good life in a good society. But one has to go beyond Adam Smith, or capitalism itself, to discover the other elements that are wanted.

It was religion and the bourgeois ethos that used to offer this added dimension to capitalism. But religion is now ineffectual, and even businessmen find the bourgeois ethos embarrassingly old-fashioned. This leaves capitalism, and its conservative defenders, helpless before any moralistic assault, however unprincipled. And until conservatism can give its own moral and intellectual substance to its idea of liberty, the "liberal" subversion of our liberal institutions will proceed without hindrance.

1975

21

The American Revolution
as a Successful Revolution

As we approach the bicentennial of the American Revolution, we find ourselves in a paradoxical and embarrassing situation. A celebration of some kind certainly seems to be in order, but the urge to celebrate is not exactly overwhelming. Though many will doubtless ascribe this mood to various dispiriting events of the recent past or to an acute public consciousness of present problems, I think this would be a superficial judgment. The truth is that, for several decades now, there has been a noticeable loss of popular interest in the Revolution, both as a historical event and as a political symbol. The idea and very word, "revolution," are in good repute today; the American Revolution is not. We are willing enough, on occasion, to pick up an isolated phrase from the Declaration of Independence, or a fine declamation from a founding father—Jefferson, usually—and use these to point up the shortcomings of American society as it now exists. Which is to say, we seem to be prompt to declare that the Revolution was a success only when it permits us to assert glibly that we have subsequently failed it. But this easy exercise in self-indictment, though useful in some respects, is on the whole a callow affair. It does not tell us, for instance, whether there is an important connection between that successful Revolution and our subsequent delinquencies. It merely uses the Revolution for rhetorical-political purposes, making no serious effort at either understanding it or understanding ourselves. One even gets the impression that many of us regard ourselves as too sophisticated to take the Revolution seriously—that we see it as one of those naive events of our distant childhood which we have since long outgrown but which we are dutifully reminded of, at certain moments of commemoration, by insistent relatives who are less liberated from the past than we are.

I think I can make this point most emphatically by asking the simple question: What ever happened to George Washington? He used to be a Very Important Person—indeed, *the* most important person in our history. Our history books used to describe him, quite simply, as the "Father of his Country" and in the popular mind he was a larger-than-life figure to whom piety and reverence were naturally due. In the past fifty years, however, this figure has been radically diminished in size and virtually emptied of substance. In part, one supposes, this is because piety is a sentiment we seem less and less capable of, most especially piety toward fathers. We are arrogant and condescending toward all ancestors because we are so convinced we understand them better than they understood themselves—whereas piety assumes that they still understand us better than we understand ourselves. Reverence, too, is a sentiment which we, in our presumption, find somewhat unnatural. Woodrow Wilson, like most Progressives of his time, complained about the "blind worship" of the Constitution by the American people. No such complaint is likely to be heard today. We debate whether or not we should obey the laws of the land, whereas for George Washington—and Lincoln too, who in his lifetime reasserted this point most eloquently—obedience to law was not enough: They thought that Americans, as citizens of a self-governing polity, ought to have *reverence* for their laws. Behind this belief, of course, was the premise that the collective wisdom incarnated in our laws, and especially in the fundamental law of the Constitution, understood us better than any one of us could ever hope to understand it. Having separated ourselves from our historic traditions and no longer recognizing the power inherent in tradition itself, we find this traditional point of view close to incomprehensible.

Equally incomprehensible to us is the idea that George Washington was the central figure in a real, honest-to-God revolution—the first significant revolution of the modern era and one which can lay claim to being the only truly successful revolution, on a large scale, in the past two centuries. In his own lifetime, no one doubted that he was the central figure of that revolution. Subsequent generations did not dispute the fact and our textbooks, until about a quarter of a century ago, took it for granted, albeit in an ever more routine and unconvincing way. We today, in contrast, find it hard to take George Washington seriously as a successful revolutionary. He just does not fit our conception of what a revolutionary leader is supposed to be like. It is a conception that easily encompasses Robespierre, Lenin, Mao Tse-tung, or Fidel Castro—but can one stretch it to include a gentleman (and a gentleman he most certainly was) like George Washington? And so we tend to escape from that dilemma by deciding that what we call the American Revolution was not an authentic revolution at all, but rather some kind of pseudorevolution, which is why it could be led by so unrevolutionary a character as George Washington.

Hannah Arendt, in her very profound book *On Revolution*, to which I am much indebted, has written:

Revolutionary political thought in the nineteenth and twentieth centuries has proceeded as though there never had occurred a revolution in the New World and as though there never had been any American notions and experiences in the realm of politics and government worth thinking about.

It is certainly indisputable that the world, when it contemplates the events of 1776 and after, is inclined to see the American Revolution as a French Revolution that never quite came off, whereas the founding fathers thought they had cause to regard the French Revolution as an American Revolution that had failed. Indeed, the differing estimates of these two revolutions are definitive of one's political philosophy in the modern world: There are two conflicting conceptions of politics, in relation to the human condition, which are symbolized by these two revolutions. There is no question that the French Revolution is, in some crucial sense, the more "modern" of the two. There is a question, however, as to whether this is a good or bad thing.

It is noteworthy that, up until about fifteen years ago, most American historians of this century tended to look at the American Revolution through non-American eyes. They saw it as essentially an abortive and incomplete revolution, in comparison with the French model. But more recently, historians have become much more respectful toward the American Revolution, and the work of Bernard Bailyn, Edmund S. Morgan, Caroline Robbins, Gordon S. Wood, and others is revealing to us once again what the Founding Fathers had, in their day, insisted was the case:

that the American Revolution was an extremely *interesting* event, rich in implication for any serious student of politics. These historians have rediscovered for us the intellectual dimensions of the American Revolution, and it is fair to say that we are now in a position to appreciate just how extraordinarily self-conscious and reflective a revolution it was.

All revolutions unleash tides of passion, and the American Revolution was no exception. But it *was* exceptional in the degree to which it was able to subordinate these passions to serious and nuanced thinking about fundamental problems of political philosophy. The pamphlets, sermons, and newspaper essays of the revolutionary period—only now being reprinted and carefully studied—were extraordinarily "academic," in the best sense of that term. Which is to say, they were learned and thoughtful and generally sober in tone. This was a revolution infused by *mind* to a degree never approximated since, and perhaps never approximated before. By mind, not by dogma. The most fascinating aspect of the American Revolution is the severe way it kept questioning itself about the meaning of what it was doing. Enthusiasm there certainly was—a revolution is impossible without enthusiasm—but this enthusiasm was tempered by doubt, introspection, anxiety, skepticism. This may strike us as a very strange state of mind in which to make a revolution; and yet it is evidently the right state of mind for making a successful revolution. That we should have any difficulty in seeing this tells us something about the immaturity of our own political imagination, an immaturity not at all incompatible with what we take to be sophistication.

Just a few weeks ago, one of our most prominent statesmen remarked to an informal group of political scientists that he had been reading *The Federalist Papers* and he was astonished to see how candidly our founding fathers could talk about the frailties of human nature and the necessity for a political system to take such frailties into account. It was not possible, he went on to observe, for anyone active in American politics today to speak publicly in this way: He would be accused of an imperfect democratic faith in the common man. Well, the founding fathers for the most part, and most of the time, subscribed to such an "imperfect" faith. They understood that republican self-government could not exist if humanity did not possess—at some moments, and to a fair degree—the traditional "republican virtues" of self-control, self-reliance, and a disinterested concern for the public good. They also understood that these virtues did not exist everywhere, at all times, and that there was no guarantee of their "natural" preponderance. James Madison put it this way:

> As there is a degree of depravity in mankind which requires a certain degree of circumspection and distrust; so there are other qualities in human nature which justify a certain portion of esteem and confidence. Republican government presupposes the existence of these qualities in a higher degree than any other form.

Despite the fact that Christian traditions are still strong in this country, it is hard to imagine any public figure casually admitting, as Madison did in his matter-of-fact way, that "there is a degree of depravity in mankind," which statesmen must take into account. We have become unaccustomed to such candid and unflattering talk about ourselves—which is, I suppose, only another way of saying that we now think democratic demagoguery to be the only proper rhetorical mode of address as between government and people in a republic. The idea, so familiar to the Puritans and still very much alive during our revolutionary era, that a community of individual sinners could, under certain special conditions, constitute a good community—just as a congregation of individual sinners could constitute a good church—is no longer entirely comprehensible to us. We are therefore negligent about the complicated ways in which this transformation takes place and uncomprehending as to the constant, rigorous attentiveness necessary for it to take place at all.

The founders thought that self-government was a chancy and demanding enterprise and that successful government in a republic was a most difficult business. We, in contrast, believe that republican self-government is an easy affair, that it need only be instituted for it to work on its own, and that when such government falters it must be as a consequence of personal incompetence or malfeasance by elected officials. Perhaps nothing reveals better than these different perspectives the intellectual distance we have traveled from the era of the Revolution. We like to think we have "progressed" along this distance. The approaching bicentennial is an appropriate occasion for us to contemplate the possibility that such "progress," should it continue, might yet be fatal to the American polity.

In what sense can the American Revolution be called a successful revolution? And if we agree that it was successful, why was it successful? These questions cannot be disentangled, the "that" and the "why" comprising together one's basic (if implicit) explanation of the term, "successful revolution." These questions are also anything but academic. Indeed I believe that, as one explores them, one finds oneself constrained to challenge a great many preconceptions, not only about the nature of revolution but about the nature of politics itself, which most of us today take for granted.

To begin at the beginning: The American Revolution was successful in that those who led it were able, in later years, to look back in tranquillity at what they had wrought and to say that it was good. This was a revolution which, unlike all subsequent revolutions, did not devour its children: The men who made the revolution were the men who went on to create the new political order, who then held the highest elected positions in this order, and who all died in bed. Not very romantic, perhaps. Indeed positively prosaic. But it is this very prosaic quality of the American Revolution that testifies to its success. It is the pathos and poignancy of unsuccessful revolutions which excite the poetic temperament; statesmanship which successfully accomplishes its business is a subject more fit for prose. Alone among the revolutions of modernity, the American Revolution did not give rise to the pathetic and poignant myth of "the revolution betrayed." It spawned no literature of disillusionment; it left behind no grand hopes frustrated, no grand expectations unsatisfied, no grand illusions shattered. Indeed, in one important respect the American Revolution was so successful as to be almost self-defeating: It turned the attention of thinking men away from politics, which now seemed utterly unproblematic, so that political theory lost its vigor, and even the political thought of the founding fathers was not seriously studied. This intellectual sloth, engendered by success, rendered us incompetent to explain this successful revolution to the world, and even to ourselves. The American political tradition became an inarticulate tradition: It worked so well we did not bother to inquire why it worked, and we are therefore intellectually disarmed before those moments when it suddenly seems not to be working so well after all.

The American Revolution was also successful in another important respect: It was a mild and relatively bloodless revolution. A war was fought, to be sure, and soldiers died in that war. But the rules of civilized warfare, as then established, were for the most part quite scrupulously observed by both sides: There was none of the butchery which we have come to accept as a natural concomitant of revolutionary warfare. More important, there was practically none of the off-battlefield savagery which we now assume to be inevitable in revolutions. There were no revolutionary tribunals dispensing "revolutionary justice"; there was no reign of terror; there were no bloodthirsty proclamations by the Continental Congress. Tories were dispossessed of their property, to be sure, and many were rudely hustled off into exile; but so far as I have been able to determine, not a single Tory was executed for harboring counter-revolutionary opinions. Nor, in the years after the Revolution, were Tories persecuted to any significant degree (at least by today's standards) or their children discriminated against at all. As Tocqueville later remarked, with only a little exaggeration, the Revolution "contracted no alliance with the turbulent passions of anarchy, but its course was marked, on the contrary, by a love of order and law."

A law-and-order revolution? What kind of revolution is that, we ask ourselves? To which many will reply that it could not have been much of a revolution after all—at best a shadow of the real thing, which is always turbulent and bloody and shattering of body and soul. Well, the American Revolution was not that kind of revolution at all, and the possibility we have to consider is that it was successful precisely because it was not that kind of revolution—that it is we rather than the American revolutionaries who have an erroneous conception of what a revolution is.

Dr. Arendt makes an important distinction between "rebellion" and "revolution." By her criteria the French and Russian revolutions should more properly be called "rebellions," whereas only the American Revolution is worthy of the name. A rebellion, in her terms, is a metapolitical event, emerging out of a radical dissatisfaction with the human condition as experienced by the mass of the people, demanding instant "liberation" from this condition, an immediate transformation of all social and economic circumstance, a prompt achievement of an altogether "better life" in an altogether "better world." The spirit of rebellion is a spirit of desperation—a desperate rejection of whatever exists, a desperate aspiration toward some kind of utopia. A rebellion is more a sociological event than a political action. It is governed by a blind momentum which sweeps everything before it, and its so-called leaders are in fact its captives, and ultimately its victims. The modern world knows many such rebellions, and all end up as one version or another of "a revolution betrayed." The so-called betrayal is, in fact, nothing but the necessary conclusion of a rebellion. Since its impossible intentions are unrealizable and since its intense desperation will not be satisfied with anything less than impossible intentions, the end result is always a regime which pretends to embody these intentions and which enforces such false pretensions by terror.

A revolution, in contrast, is a political phenomenon. It aims to revise and reorder the political arrangements of a society, and is therefore the work of the political ego rather than of the political id. A revolution is a practical exercise in political philosophy, not an existential spasm of the social organism. It requires an attentive prudence, a careful calculation of means and ends, a spirit of sobriety—the kind of spirit exemplified by that calm, legalistic document, the Declaration of Independence. All this is but another way of saying that a successful revolution cannot be governed by the spirit of the mob. Mobs and mob actions there will always be in a revolution, but if this revolution is not to degenerate into a rebellion, mob actions must be marginal to the central political drama. It may sound paradoxical but it nevertheless seems to be the case that only a self-disciplined people can dare undertake so radical a political enterprise as a revolution. This is almost like saying that a successful revolution must be accomplished by a people who want it but do not desperately need it—which was, indeed, the American condition in 1776. One may even put the case more strongly: A successful revolution is best accomplished by a people who do not really want it at all, but find themselves reluctantly making it. The American Revolution was exactly such a reluctant revolution.

The present-day student of revolutions will look in vain for any familiar kind of "revolutionary situation" in the American colonies prior to 1776. The American people at that moment were the most prosperous in the world and lived under the freest institutions to be found anywhere in the world. They knew this well enough and boasted of it often enough. Their quarrel with the British crown was, in its origins, merely over the scope of colonial self-government, and hardly anyone saw any good reason why this quarrel should erupt into a war of independence. It was only after the war got under way that the American people decided that this was a good opportunity to make a revolution as well—that is, to establish a republican form of government.

Republican and quasi-republican traditions had always been powerful in the colonies, which were populated to such a large degree by religious dissenters who were sympathetic to the ideas incorporated in Cromwell's Commonwealth. Moreover, American political institutions from the very beginning were close to republican in fact, especially those of the Puritan communities of New England. Still, it is instructive to note that the word *republic* does not appear in the Declaration of Independence. Not that there was any real thought of reinstituting a monarchy in the New World: No one took such a prospect seriously. It was simply that, reluctant and cautious revolutionaries as they were, the Founding Fathers saw no need to press matters further than they had to, at that particular moment. To put it bluntly: They did not want events to get out of hand and saw no good reason to provoke more popular turbulence than was absolutely necessary.

One does not want to make the American Revolution an even more prosaic affair than it was. This was a revolution—a real one—and it was infused with a spirit of excitement and innovation. After all, what the American Revolution, once it got under way, was trying to do was no small thing. It was nothing less than the establishment, for the first time since ancient Rome, of a large republican nation, and the idea of reestablishing under modern conditions the glory that had been Rome's could hardly fail to be intoxicating. This Revolution did indeed have grand, even millennial, expectations as to the future role of this new nation in both the political imagination and political history of the human race. But certain things have to be said about these large expectations, if we are to see them in proper perspective.

The main thing to be said is that the millenarian tradition in America long antedates the Revolution and is not intertwined with the idea of revolution itself. It was the pilgrim fathers, not the founding fathers, who first announced that this was God's country, that the American people had a divine mission to accomplish, that this people had been "chosen" to create some kind of model community for the rest of mankind. This belief was already so firmly established by the time of the Revolution that it was part and parcel of our political orthodoxy, serving to legitimate an existing "American way of life" and most of the institutions associated with that way of life. It was a radical belief, in the sense of being bold and challenging and because this new "way of life" was so strikingly different from the lives that common people were then living in Europe. It was *not* a revolutionary belief. Crèvecoeur's famous paean of praise to "this new man, the American," was written well before the

Revolution; and Crèvecoeur, in fact, opposed the American Revolution as foolish and unnecessary.

To this traditional millenarianism, the Revolution added the hope that the establishment of republican institutions would inaugurate a new and happier political era for all mankind. This hope was frequently expressed enthusiastically, in a kind of messianic rhetoric, but the men of the Revolution—most of them, most of the time—did not permit themselves to become bewitched by that rhetoric. Thus, though they certainly saw republic as "the wave of the future," both Jefferson and Adams in the 1780s agreed that the French people were still too "depraved," as they so elegantly put it, to undertake an experiment in self-government. Self-government, as they understood it, presupposed a certain way of life, and this in turn presupposed certain qualities on the part of the citizenry—qualities then designated as "republican virtues"—that would make self-government possible.

Similarly, though one can find a great many publicists during the Revolution who insisted that, with the severance of ties from Britain, the colonies had reverted to a Lockean "state of nature" and were now free to make a new beginning for all mankind and to create a new political order that would mark a new stage in human history—though such assertions were popular enough, it would be a mistake to take them too seriously. The fact is that Americans had encountered their "state of nature" generations earlier and had made their "social compact" at that time. The primordial American social contract was signed and sealed on the *Mayflower*—literally signed and sealed. The subsequent presence of all those signatures appended to the Declaration of Independence, beginning with John Hancock's, are but an echo of the original covenant.

To perceive the true purposes of the American Revolution, it is wise to ignore some of the more grandiloquent declamations of the moment—Tom Paine, an English radical who never really understood America, is especially worth ignoring—and to look at the kinds of political activity the Revolution unleashed. This activity took the form of constitution making, above all. In the months and years immediately following the Declaration of Independence, all of our states drew up constitutions. These constitutions are terribly interesting in three respects. First, they involved relatively few basic changes in existing political institutions and almost no change at all in legal, social, or economic institutions; they were, for the most part, merely revisions of the preexisting charters. Secondly, most of the changes that were instituted had the evident aim of weakening the power of government, especially of the executive; it was these changes—and especially the strict separation of powers—that dismayed Turgot, Condorcet, and the other French *philosophes*, who understood revolution as an expression of the people's will-to-power rather than as an attempt to circumscribe political authority. Thirdly, in no case did any of these state constitutions tamper with the traditional system of local self-government. Indeed they could not, since it was this traditional system of local self-government which created and legitimized the constitutional conventions themselves.

In short, the Revolution reshaped our political institutions in such a way as to make them more responsive to popular opinion and less capable of encroaching upon the personal liberties of the citizen—liberties which long antedated the new constitutions and which in no way could be regarded as the creation or consequence of revolution. Which is to say that the purpose of this Revolution was to bring our political institutions into a more perfect correspondence with an actual American way of life which no one even dreamed of challenging. This "restructuring," as we would now call it—because it put the possibility of republican self-government once again on the political agenda of Western civilization—was terribly exciting to Europeans as well as Americans. But for the Americans involved in this historic task, it was also terribly frightening. It is fair to say that no other revolution in modern history made such relatively modest innovations with such an acute sense of anxiety. The Founding Fathers were well aware that if republicanism over the centuries had become such a rare form of government, there must be good reasons for it. Republican government, they realized, must be an exceedingly difficult regime to maintain—that is, it must have grave inherent problems. And so they were constantly scurrying to their libraries, ransacking classical and contemporary political authors, trying to discover why republics fail, and endeavoring to construct a "new political science" relevant to American conditions which would give this new republic a fair chance of succeeding. That new political science was eventually to be embodied in *The Federalist*—the only original work of political theory ever produced by a revolution and composed by successful revolutionaries. And the fact that very few of us have ever felt the need seriously to study *The Federalist* and that Europeans—or in our own day, Asians and Africans—have barely heard of it tells us how inadequately we understand the American Revolution, and how distant the real American Revolution has become from the idea of revolution by which we moderns are now possessed.

This idea of revolution, as the world understands it today, is what Dr. Arendt calls rebellion. It involves a passionate rejection of the status quo—its institutions and the way of life associated with these institutions. It rejects everything that exists because it wishes to create everything anew—a new social order, a new set of economic arrangements, a new political entity, a new kind of human being. It aims to solve not merely the political problem of the particular political community, at that particular moment, but every other problem that vexes humanity. Its spirit is the spirit of undiluted, enthusiastic, free-floating messianism: It will be satisfied with nothing less than a radical transformation of the human condition. It is an idea and a movement which is both metapolitical and subpolitical—above and below politics—because it finds the political realm itself too confining for its ambitions. Metapolitically, it is essentially a religious phenomenon, seized with the perennial promise of redemption. Subpolitically, it is an expression of the modern technological mentality, confident of its power to control and direct all human processes as we have learned to control and direct the processes of nature. Inevitably, its swollen pride and fanatical temper lead to tragic failure. But precisely because of this pride and this fanaticism, failure leads only to partial and temporary disillusionment. When this kind of revolution is "betrayed"—which is to say, when the consequences of revolution lose all congruence with its original purpose—the true revolutionary believer will still look forward to a second coming of the authentic and unbetrayable revolution.

The French Revolution was the kind of modern revolution I have been describing; the American Revolution was not. It is because of this, one supposes, that the French Revolution has captured the imagination of other peoples—has become indeed the model of "real" revolution—in a way that the American Revolution has not been able to do. The French Revolution promised not only a reformation of France's political institutions, but far more than that. It promised, for instance—as practically all revolutions have promised since—the abolition of poverty. The American Revolution promised no such thing, in part because poverty was not such a troublesome issue in this country, but also—one is certain—because the leaders of this revolution understood what their con-

temporary, Adam Smith, understood and what we today have some difficulty in understanding: namely, that poverty is abolished by economic
growth, not by economic redistribution—there is never enough to distribute—and that rebellions, by creating instability and uncertainty, have
mischievous consequences for economic growth. Similarly, the French
Revolution promised a condition of "happiness" to its citizens under the
new regime, whereas the American Revolution promised merely to permit the individual to engage in the "pursuit of happiness."

It should not be surprising, therefore, that in the war of ideologies
which has engulfed the twentieth century, the United States is at a disadvantage. This disadvantage does not flow from any weakness on our part.
It is not, as some say, because we have forgotten our revolutionary heritage and therefore have nothing to say to a discontented and turbulent
world. We have, indeed, much to say, only it is not what our contemporaries want to hear. It is not even what we ourselves want to hear, and in
that sense it may be correct to claim we have forgotten our revolutionary
heritage. Our revolutionary message—which is a message not of the Revolution itself but of the American political tradition from the *Mayflower* to
the Declaration of Independence to the Constitution—is that a self-
disciplined people *can* create a political community in which an ordered
liberty will promote both economic prosperity and political participation.
To the teeming masses of other nations, the American political tradition
says: To enjoy the fruits of self-government, you must first cease being
"masses" and become a "people," attached to a common way of life,
sharing common values, and existing in a condition of mutual trust and
sympathy as between individuals and even social classes. It is a distinctly
odd kind of "revolutionary" message, by twentieth-century criteria—so
odd that it seems not revolutionary at all, and yet so revolutionary that it
seems utterly utopian. What the twentieth century wants to hear is the
grand things that a new government will do for the people who put their
trust in it. What the American political tradition says is that the major
function of government is, in Professor Oakeshott's phrase, to "tend to
the arrangements of society," and that free people do not make a
covenant or social contract with their government, or with the leaders of
any "movement," but among themselves.

In the end, what informs the American political tradition is a proposition and a premise. The proposition is that the best national government
is, to use a phrase the founding fathers were fond of, "mild government."

The premise is that you can only achieve mild government if you have a solid bedrock of local self-government, so that the responsibilities of national government are limited in scope. And a corollary of this premise is that such a bedrock of local self-government can only be achieved by a people who—through the shaping influence of religion, education, and their own daily experience—are capable of governing themselves in those small and petty matters which are the stuff of local politics.

Does this conception of politics have any relevance to the conditions in which people live today in large areas of the world—the so-called underdeveloped areas, especially? We are inclined, I think, to answer instinctively in the negative, but that answer may itself be a modern ideological prejudice. We take it for granted that if a people live in comparative poverty, they are necessarily incapable of the kind of self-discipline and sobriety that makes for effective self-government in their particular communities. Mind you, I am not talking about starving people, who are in a prepolitical condition and whose problem is to get a strong and effective government of almost any kind. I am talking about *comparatively* poor people. And our current low estimate of the political capabilities of such people is an ideological assumption, not an objective fact. Many of our frontier communities, at the time of the Revolution and for decades afterward, were poor by any standards. Yet this poverty was not, for the most part, inconsistent with active self-government. There have been communities in Europe, too, which were very poor—not actually starving, of course, but simply very poor—yet were authentic political communities. The popular musical *Fiddler on the Roof* gave us a picture of such a community. It is always better not to be so poor, but poverty need not be a pathological condition, and political pathology is not an inevitable consequence of poverty, just as political pathology is not inevitably abolished by prosperity. Poor people can cope with their poverty in many different ways. They are people, not sociological creatures, and in the end they will cope as their moral and political convictions tell them to cope. These convictions, in turn, will be formed by the expectations that their community addresses to them—expectations which they freely convert into obligations.

In *The Brothers Karamazov*, Dostoevski says that the spirit of the Antichrist, in its modern incarnation, will flaunt the banner, "First feed people, and *then* ask of them virtue." This has, in an amended form, indeed become the cardinal and utterly conventional thesis of modern politics.

The amended form reads: "First make people prosperous, and then ask of them virtue." Whatever reservations one might have about Dostoevski's original thesis, this revised version is, in the perspective of the Judeo-Christian tradition, unquestionably a blasphemy. It is also, in the perspective of the American political tradition, a malicious and inherently self-defeating doctrine—self-defeating because those who proclaim it obviously have lost all sense of what virtue, religious or political, means. Nevertheless, practically all of us today find it an inherently plausible doctrine, a staple of our political discourse. This being the case, it is only natural that we ourselves should have such difficulty understanding the American political tradition, and that when we expend it to the world, we distort it in all sorts of ways which will make it more palatable to the prejudices of the modern political mentality.

It would not be fair to conclude that the American political tradition is flawless, and that it is only we, its heirs, who are to blame for the many problems our society is grappling with—and so ineptly. The American Revolution was a successful revolution, but there is no such thing, either in one's personal life or in a nation's history, as unambiguous success. The legacy of the American Revolution and of the entire political tradition associated with it is problematic in all sorts of ways. Strangely enough, we have such an imperfect understanding of this tradition that, even as we vulgarize it or question it or disregard it, we rarely address ourselves to its problematic quality.

The major problematic aspect of this tradition has to do with the relationship of the "citizen" to the "common man." And the difficulties we have in defining this relationship are best illustrated by the fact that, though we have been a representative democracy for two centuries now, we have never developed an adequate theory of representation. More precisely we have developed *two* contradictory theories of representation, both of which can claim legitimacy within the American political tradition and both of which were enunciated, often by the same people, during the Revolution. The one sees the public official as a common man who has a mandate to reflect the opinions of the majority; the other sees the public official as a somewhat uncommon man—a more-than-common man, if you will—who, because of his talents and character, is able to take a larger view of the "public interest" than the voters who elected him or the voters who failed to defeat him. One might say that the first is a "democratic" view of the legislator, the second a "republican" view. The American political tradition has always had a kind of double vision on this whole problem, which in turn makes for a bewildering moral confusion. Half the time we regard our politicians as, in the nature of things, probably corrupt and certainly untrustworthy; the other half of the time, we denounce them for failing to be models of integrity and rectitude. Indeed, we have a profession—journalism—which seems committed to both of these contradictory propositions. But politicians are pretty much like the rest of us and tend to become the kinds of people they are expected to be. The absence of clear and distinct expectations has meant that public morality in this country has never been, and is not, anything we can be proud of.

In a way, the ambiguity in our theory of representation points to a much deeper ambiguity in that system of self-government which emerged from the Revolution and the Constitutional Convention. That system has been perceptively titled, by Professor Martin Diamond, "a democratic republic." Now, we tend to think of these terms as near-synonyms, but in fact they differ significantly in their political connotations. Just how significant the difference is becomes clear if we realize that the America which emerged from the Revolution and the Constitutional Convention was the first democratic republic in history. The political philosophers of that time could study the history of republics and they could study the history of democracies, but there was no opportunity for them to study both together. When the founding fathers declared that they had devised a new kind of political entity based on a new science of politics, they were not vainly boasting or deceiving themselves. It is we, their political descendants, who tend to be unaware of the novelty of the American political enterprise, and of the risks and ambiguities inherent in that novelty. We simplify and vulgarize and distort, because we have lost the sense of how bold and innovative the Founding Fathers were, and of how problematic—necessarily problematic—is the system of government, and the society, which they established. Witness the fact that, incredibly enough, at our major universities it is almost impossible to find a course, graduate or undergraduate, devoted to *The Federalist*.

What is the difference between a democracy and a republic? In a democracy, the will of the people is supreme. In a republic, it is not the will of the people but the rational consensus of the people—a rational consensus which is implicit in the term consent—which governs the people. That is to say, in a democracy, popular passion may rule—*may*, though it need not—but in a republic, popular passion is regarded as unfit to rule, and precautions are taken to see that it is subdued rather than sovereign. In a democracy all politicians are, to some degree, demagogues: They appeal to people's prejudices and passions, they incite their expectations by making reckless promises, they endeavor to ingratiate themselves with the electorate in every possible way. In a republic, there are not supposed to be such politicians, only statesmen—sober, unglamorous, thoughtful men who are engaged in a kind of perpetual conversation with the citizenry. In a republic, a fair degree of equality and prosperity are important goals, but it is liberty that is given priority as the proper end of government. In a democracy, these priorities are reversed: The status of men and women as consumers of economic goods is taken to be more significant than their status as participants in the creation of political goods. A republic is what we would call "moralistic" in its approach to both public and private affairs; a democracy is more easygoing, more "permissive" as we now say, even more cynical.

The Founding Fathers perceived that their new nation was too large, too heterogeneous, too dynamic, too mobile for it to govern itself successfully along strict republican principles. And they had no desire at all to see it governed along strict democratic principles, since they did not have that much faith in the kinds of common men likely to be produced by such a nation. So they created a new form of "popular government," to use one of their favorite terms, that incorporated both republican and democratic principles, in a complicated and ingenious way. This system has lasted for two centuries, which means it has worked very well indeed. But in the course of that time, we have progressively forgotten what kind of system it is and *why* it works as well as it does. Every now and then, for instance, we furiously debate the question of whether or not the Supreme Court is meeting its obligations as a democratic institution. The question reveals a startling ignorance of our political tradition. The Supreme Court is not—and was never supposed to be—a democratic institution; it is a republican institution which counterbalances the activities of our various democratic institutions. Yet I have discovered that when you say this to college students, they do not understand the distinction and even have difficulty thinking about it.

So it would seem that today, two hundred years after the American Revolution, we are in a sense victims of its success. The political tradition out of which it issued and the political order it helped to create are imperfectly comprehended by us. What is worse, we are not fully aware of this imperfect comprehension and are frequently smug in our convenient misunderstandings. The American Revolution certainly merits celebration. But it would be reassuring if a part of that celebration were to consist, not merely of pious clichés, but of a serious and sustained effort to achieve a deeper and more widespread understanding of just what it is we are celebrating.

1976

22

What Is "Social Justice"?

I recently received a letter from a magazine which is preparing a special issue on the distribution of income in the United States. The letter asked for my thoughts on such questions as: "How should a society determine wages and salaries? Does our society do a fair job of distributing income?" And so on.

The issue to which these questions are addressed is certainly a crucial one. It is nothing less than the issue of "social justice"—or what used to be known, among political philosophers, as "distributive justice." The change in terminology, as it happens, has its own significance; in politics, the language we use to ask questions is always more important than any particular answer. "Distributive justice" is a neutral phrase; it points to a problem without suggesting any particular solution. "Social justice," however, is a loaded phrase: It blithely suggests that "society" ought to determine the distribution of income. This assumption is now so common that few people realize how controversial its implications are.

The social order we call "capitalism," constructed on the basis of a market economy, does *not* believe that "society" ought to prescribe a "fair" distribution of income. "Society," in this context, means government; "society" is voiceless until the political authorities speak. And the kind of liberal society historically associated with capitalism was, from its very beginnings, hostile to any political or "social" definition of distributive justice.

253

It is the basic premise of a liberal-capitalist society that a "fair" distribution of income is determined by the productive input—"productive" as determined by the market—of individuals into the economy. Such productivity is determined by specific talents, general traits of character, and just plain luck (being at the right place at the right time). This market-based distribution of income will create economic incentives and thereby encourage economic growth. As a result of such economic growth, everyone will be better off (though not necessarily equally better off). The economic growth that ensues may itself shape society in ways not everyone might like. But a liberal-capitalist order does not—except in extraordinary circumstances—concede to any authority the right to overrule the aggregate of individual preferences on this matter.

In contrast, noncapitalist societies—whether precapitalist or postcapitalist—have a very different conception of "fairness," based on one's contribution *to the society*, not merely to the economy. In such noncapitalist societies, economic rewards are "socially" justified, as distinct from being economically justified. Thus, in the Middle Ages it was thought to be fair to compel ordinary people to support the church and the clergy, whose activities were deemed to be of major social significance and social value. Similarly, in the Soviet Union today, the Communist party does not have to defend its budget on any economic grounds: The value of its contribution to the polity as a whole is put beyond question. Such societies, of course, place no high valuation on individual liberty.

NO "PURE" TYPES OF SOCIETY

Obviously, there is no such pure type as "a capitalist society" or "a noncapitalist society." All noncapitalist societies recognize, to one degree or another, the importance of economic activity and material welfare. They therefore will allow differential rewards—again, to one degree or another—based on one's skill at such activity.

Similarly, all capitalist societies recognize, to one degree or another, that there is more to life than economic growth or material welfare, and they therefore make some provision for differential rewards based on one's skill at literary criticism, music, and philosophy. Ohio State University, for example, is exactly such a provision.

Still, though "pure" types may not exist, the types themselves do, in however impure a form. And there are three important points to be made about these different conceptions of a good society and the principles of "fairness" in income distribution by which they operate.

1. There is no rational method which permits us to determine, *in the abstract*, which principle of distribution is superior. It is absurd to claim that capitalism, anywhere, at any time, is superior to noncapitalism, or vice versa. Any such judgment is bound to be contingent, i.e., based on the particular society's history and traditions, on the attitudes and social habits of its citizenry, and the like. There is no point in arguing that a particular society "ought" to be capitalist or socialist if the overwhelming majority of the people are not of a mind to be bound by the different kinds of self-discipline that these different political philosophies require, if they are to work. And this, of course, holds true for all large political ideals. Which is why Jefferson, living in Paris before the French Revolution, could write—in all good republican conscience—that the French people were not "ready" for republican self-government, and that it would be a mistake for them to try to establish it immediately.

2. A distribution of income according to one's contribution to the society—to the "common good"—requires that this society have a powerful consensus as to what the "common good" is, and that it also have institutions with the authority to give specific meaning and application to this consensus on all occasions. Now, when you have such a consensus, and such authoritative institutions, you do not have—cannot have—a liberal society as we understand it. It can certainly be a good society (if the values behind the consensus are good); but it will not be a liberal society. The authorities which represent the "common good," and which distribute income in accordance with their conception of the common good, will—with a clear conscience—surely discriminate against those who are subversive of this "common good." They may, if they are broad-minded, tolerate dissidents, but they will never concede to them equal rights—even if equality is a prime social value. The dissidents, after all, may be those who believe in inequality.

3. A liberal society is one that is based on a *weak* consensus. There is nothing like near-unanimity on what the "common good" is, who contributes to it, or how. There is not utter disagreement, of course; a liberal

society is not—no society can be—in a condition of perpetual moral and political chaos. But the liberty of a liberal society derives from a prevalent skepticism as to anyone's ability to know the "common good" with certainty, and from the conviction that the authorities should not try to define this "common good" in any but a minimal way. That minimal definition, in a liberal society, will naturally tend to emphasize the improvement of the material conditions of life—something that very few people are actually against. A liberal society, therefore, will be very tolerant of capitalist transactions between consenting adults because such transactions are for mutual advantage, and the sum of such transactions is to everyone's material advantage. And, consequently, a liberal society will think it reasonable and "fair" that income should, on the whole, be distributed according to one's productive input into the economy, as this is measured by the marketplace and the transactions which occur there.

LIBERTY AS A VALUE

In sum, the distribution of income under liberal capitalism is "fair" if, and only if, you think that liberty is, or ought to be, the most important political value. If not, then not. This distribution of income under capitalism is an expression of the general belief that it is better for society to be shaped by the interplay of people's free opinions and free preferences than by the enforcement of any one set of values by government.

But there have always been many people in this world who do not believe that liberty is the most important political value. These people are sincere dogmatists. They believe they know *the* truth about a good society; they believe they possess *the* true definition of distributive justice; and they inevitably wish to see society shaped in the image of these true beliefs. Sometimes they have prized religious truth more than liberty; sometimes they have prized philosophic truth more than liberty (e.g., the Marxist philosophy); and sometimes they have prized equality more than liberty. It is this last point of view that is especially popular in some circles—mainly academic circles—in the United States today.

Thus Professor Ronald Dworkin, one of our most distinguished liberal legal philosophers, has recently written that "*a more equal society is a better society even if its citizens prefer inequality.*" (Italics mine.) From which it follows that "social justice" may require a people, whose preferences are corrupt (in that they prefer liberty to equality), to be coerced into equality. It is precisely because they define "social justice" and "fairness" in terms of equality that so many liberal thinkers find it so difficult genuinely to detest left-wing (i.e., egalitarian) authoritarian or totalitarian regimes. And, similarly, it is precisely because they are true believers in justice-as-equality that they dislike a free society, with all its inevitable inequalities.

As one who does like a free society, I have to concede to these people the right to hold and freely express such opinions. But I do find it ironical that their conception of "social justice" should be generally designated as the "liberal" one. Whatever its other merits, an authentic attachment to liberty is not one of them.

1976

23

Adam Smith and the Spirit of Capitalism

The founding text of modern capitalism, Adam Smith's *An Inquiry into the Nature and Causes of the Wealth of Nations*, was published in 1776, the same year that the Declaration of Independence founded the modern world's capitalist nation par excellence. This is one of those nice historical coincidences that seems to have a touch of the providential about it, especially since Adam Smith turned out to be sympathetic to the cause of the rebellious American colonies, while the Founding Fathers turned out to be followers of Adam Smith *avant la lettre*—that is, they subscribed to his doctrines before they had ever been promulgated. What Madison called the new "science of politics," as later enunciated in *The Federalist Papers* and as incarnated in the Constitution, is incomprehensible without an understanding of that new science of society which is animated by the spirit of modern capitalism and whose economic aspects are delineated in *The Wealth of Nations*. Not many of the Founding Fathers actually read the entire book, but they certainly read summaries of it, knew about it, and—most important—"understood" it thoroughly (in their bones, as it were) without having to read it. It is fair to say that the American democracy was born as a capitalist democracy, that the spirit of capitalism infuses our institutions and what has come to be known as the "American way of life," and that the destiny of this democracy as it enters its third century of existence is profoundly intertwined with the fate of modern capitalism.

Both this destiny and this fate seem, at the moment, to be highly dubious, and it is not an exaggeration to apply the term "crisis" to the events of recent decades. In such times of crisis, it is natural for all political communities to turn their attention back to their origins—perhaps in anticipation of finding grounds for hopeful reaffirmation, perhaps (and more probably) out of an acute need to answer the question "Where did we go wrong?" It turns out to be a fiendishly difficult question to answer, mainly because people who have been formed by a particular civilization—in this case a democratic-capitalist civilization—are least likely to have a true understanding of that civilization. Time breeds a kind of amnesia, so that one simply forgets, not the answers, but the original questions which gave birth to those answers. One takes things for granted which, at the beginnings, could not be and were not taken for granted. One has only the dimmest sense of the alternatives which were possible but which were rejected. One finds it very hard, above all, to keep vividly in mind the *problematics* of one's own civilization—the recurring costs which make all benefits possible and which, at the same time, make all benefits ambiguous. We are likely to think either that the benefits are intrinsic to "the system," whereas the costs are malevolently and contingently imposed from without, or that the founders, being circumscribed by the "climate of opinion" of their times, never really understood the implications of their ideas and intentions.

As concerns capitalism and democracy, we would be wrong on both counts. The founders understood reasonably well what they were doing—including the ultimate limitations of their accomplishments. They understood the alternatives at hand, because these were authentic alternatives, not academic ones. They were not prisoners of the "climate of opinion" prevailing in their era; on the contrary, it is we who are prisoners of the climate of opinion which they created for us to live in. In a sense, it is accurate to say that they understand us better than we understand them. Our task, therefore, is not to attempt a peremptory judgment upon them but rather to try to understand them as they understood themselves. If and when we have done that—assuming we ever do—we shall then be in a better position to understand ourselves and our predicaments.

In the case of the Founding Fathers, such an exploration into our origins is now well under way—though one must add that it still lacks much of the necessary philosophic rigor. The reason for this can be quite simply stated: The Founding Fathers understood that democracy is an inherently problematic regime—more problematic, indeed, than any other. They learned this from their reading of classical (i.e., premodern) political thought as well as from a casual glance at history, which revealed democratic regimes to be turbulent, short-lived, and generally less than admirable. *Our* difficulty is that we tend to regard democracy as the most "natural" as well as the best of all possible regimes, so that even our most critical scholars find it almost impossible to achieve a critical detachment from the democratic idea itself. Among our major historians, only Henry Adams was able to manage this—more than half a century ago.

In the case of capitalism, the situation is almost the reverse. We have become so acutely aware of the problematics of this economic and social system, so critically detached from it, that we find it difficult to perceive the *intentions* of this system—and, in the light of these intentions, its accomplishments. Even those who defend the intentions and the accomplishments usually misunderstand both. We overwhelm all discussions of capitalism with accusations of abstract possibilities unrealized—possibilities that the founders of capitalist thought specifically excluded from their perspective, as having "costs" that were unacceptable. Or else we constrict our discussions of capitalism by apologias that the founders would have found to be only marginally relevant—sometimes even directly contrary—to their purposes. Before one can address oneself to the question "Does capitalism work?" one must have a clear sense of what *working* means in this context. That is to say, one must have a sense of what kind of society capitalism is supposed to create. To learn that, there is no better way than to turn back to the writings of Adam Smith.

One cannot understand Adam Smith without knowing something about the intellectual movement out of which he emerged, and of which he may be said to be the culminating figure. That movement, the Anglo-Scottish Enlightenment, has remained in relative obscurity. It has received a fair degree of scholarly attention, to be sure, but usually in terms of one particular aspect or another—its relationship to the history of economic thought, to eighteenth-century English literature, or to modern British philosophy. It is rarely considered on its own as a major intellectual movement that had a decisive influence in shaping the world we live in, and also in shaping our ways of thinking about this world.

When university students today take a course on "the Enlighten-ment," their attention is almost invariably focused on the French

Enlightenment. They are likely to be asked to read selections from Rousseau, or Voltaire, or Diderot, or Condorcet—or even from such relatively minor figures as d'Holbach or La Mettrie. They are less likely to be asked to read Locke, Hume, or Adam Smith as Enlightenment thinkers and will surely complete their course without ever having heard of Shaftesbury or Adam Ferguson. This posthumous victory of the French over the Anglo-Scottish Enlightenment is itself a major event in the intellectual history of the West—indeed, of the modern world—during the past two hundred years.

There is, of course, no denying the intellectual and literary brilliance of the major French thinkers of the eighteenth century. But this "brilliance" is not an independent or accidental factor. It is intimately connected with the *intentions* of the French Enlightenment. To say that these intentions were ambitious would be grossly to understate the case. They were nothing less than grand, even grandiose. The goal of the French Enlightenment was the "universal regeneration of mankind," to use a phrase that was commonplace among both the thinkers of the French Enlightenment and their nineteenth-century heirs. This grand and inspiriting and extreme intention gave rise to a grand and inspiriting and extreme event: the French Revolution, which has established itself for modernity as *the* paradigm of what a revolution is supposed to be like, and, above all, what it is supposed to aim at. We all today find it quite natural to think of Robespierre, Saint-Just, and Marat as prototypical "revolutionary heroes." We certainly do not perceive George Washington as a prototypical revolutionary hero. Earlier generations of Americans were able to do so—but that was before the intellectual currents of modernity washed over traditional American pieties.

In comparison with the French Revolution, the American Revolution has come to seem a parochial and rather dull event. This, despite the fact that the American Revolution was successful—realizing the purposes of the revolutionaries and establishing a durable political regime—while the French Revolution was a resounding failure, devouring its own children and leading to an imperial despotism followed by an eventual restoration of the monarchy. The explanation for this apparent paradox lies in the intellectual sources of the two revolutions and in the subsequent fate of those intellectual traditions.

Though the American Revolution was inspired by a rather casual intermingling of the two Enlightenments, it was the Anglo-Scottish

Enlightenment that was, in the end, decisive. It was this heritage of the Anglo-Scottish Enlightenment that enabled the American Revolution to achieve its climax, not in a reign of terror, but in the Constitutional Convention. And it was this same heritage that made a George Washington, rather than a Robespierre or a Saint-Just, into the national revolutionary hero. For those who hold grand and utopian expectations of politics transforming the human condition, George Washington is a comparatively "dull" figure and the American Revolution a comparatively "dull" event. Such grand and utopian expectations were at the very heart of the French Revolution and have become exceedingly common in the course of the past two hundred years—with the consequence that the intellectual traditions of the Anglo-Scottish Enlightenment now fail to appease the feverish yearnings of an inflamed political imagination.

These traditions are melioristic rather than eschatological in intention: They aim at a gradual improvement of the human condition—a process, moreover, in which each individual bears his share of responsibility for a successful outcome, rather than salvation being provided "from above" by a ruling party or class. These same traditions are also skeptical in temper, hostile to all forms of enthusiasm (political, or religious, or whatever), disbelieving of all dogmatic certainties about human nature and the "meaning of history," and suspicious of either the ability or desire (or both) of those who wield political power to do good rather than harm. In short, these traditions place an immense burden on the individual for the achievement of personal happiness and social contentment, while in return promising (1) a gradual—that is, slow but, over the longer term, steady—improvement in his material conditions, and (2) a degree of individual liberty without precedent in the history of nations. That the terms of this transaction should appear unexciting today ought not to blind us to the fact that there was a time when they seemed positively exhilarating, and to the further fact that, out of the traditions of the Anglo-Scottish Enlightenment there merged a sociopolitical order that defines an important epoch in human history: the "bourgeois" epoch, in which we Americans, at any rate, still live, though with increasing unease.

The Anglo-Scottish Enlightenment was a kind of response—the French Enlightenment being another—to the historical experience of Europe in the previous centuries. Two aspects of this experience were decisive: the wars of religion and the economic consequences of mercantilism.

Modern bourgeois society has, as its original traumatic memory, the successive spasms of butchery, persecution, and international turmoil experienced by Europe in the two centuries following the Reformation. These had the effect of bringing discredit upon traditional religious dogmas as well as upon the religious institutions that so stubbornly proclaimed them. A powerful yearning for a predominantly *civil* society developed, a society in which citizens, as individuals or as national collectivities, could live at peace with one another—or, at the very least, *not* battle over controversial questions of theology whose adjudication by force of arms was inherently absurd.

Both the French and Anglo-Scottish Enlightenments shared this aspiration toward a civil society, but there was a significant difference in emphasis between them. The French Enlightenment was shot through with romantic visions of a new political community in which all previous religions would be replaced by a new civic religion: the religion of rationalist humanism, in which the civic bonds themselves would constitute a kind of religious association. This vision was subsequently incorporated into the Socialist and Communist movements, becoming, as it were, their dogma, and at its extreme producing in our time the odd phenomenon of vast polities whose official religion is atheism.

The Anglo-Scottish Enlightenment dreamed more prosaic visions. It had no ambition to create a new religion of any kind. Instead, it aimed at the establishment of religious toleration, and its method of achieving this was to convert religion into a "private affair," the individual's "own business" (itself a revealing phrase), and thereby to absorb religion *into* civil society. In this view, a church becomes one form of private association among many, immune (under ordinary circumstances) to governmental interference. The government itself would be secular, but not at all hostile to the religions of its citizens. On the contrary: Though most thinkers of the Anglo-Scottish Enlightenment tended to be religious skeptics, and were at most vague deists, they conceded that organized religion was, for the average person, a necessary and desirable form of human association. It served the very important purposes of inculcating moral habits and, above all, of providing consolation and hope to those whose earthly lives were less than satisfying. Government, therefore, would be benevolently respectful of all religions, even helpful to all religions—but partial toward none. This was the original notion of the "separation of church and state" as inscribed, for instance, in the American Constitution.

It is important to note the kind of society in which this vision could be realized. To begin with, it was a society in which government was *limited*, in both authority and power, in regard to what was then thought of as the most critical social fact: the religious beliefs of the citizenry. And it was a society in which the individual was free of religious authority as well—*free* to choose those religious beliefs and those religious associations which suited him best, a freedom that had never before been legitimated in the entire history of Western civilization. These notions, of *limited government* and *individual liberty*, were radically innovative and were bound to have an impact on all spheres of life. One such sphere was the economic.

The dominant economic philosophy against which the Enlightenment pitted itself was mercantilism. This economic philosophy was never vigorously articulated, and its meanings are still being debated by scholars. In large measure this was because it was never a "proper" economic philosophy at all, but rather an ideological offshoot of the political system of absolute monarchy, which, by 1700, was the norm for most of Europe (though, after 1688, not for Britain). As the late Professor Jacob Viner put it:

> What we call "mercantilism" consisted primarily of a body of doctrine expounding and of practice employing ways and means whereby government could make private interest, when subjected to taxes, import and export duties and prohibitions, subsidies, and other regulatory and coercive measures, operate to augment national wealth and national power.*

In its crudest form, mercantilist doctrine demanded that a nation seek to have a perpetually favorable balance of trade, with the "surplus" (in the form of gold) being available for purposes (usually military) of statecraft. From the point of view of modern economics this doctrine makes no sense: Since every seller must have a buyer, and vice versa, a perpetual imbalance in the terms of international trade will merely lead to a col-

---

*Jacob Viner, "The Intellectual History of Laissez-Faire," *Journal of Law and Economics* 3 (October 1960): 45–69.

lapse of the international market and a crisis in international trade itself. But mercantilism did not look at things in terms of modern economics. It was much more a political doctrine than an economic one and was therefore ready to regard commerce as an *exploitative* affair, in which there is a loser for every winner—not, as in later capitalist economics, an arrangement for mutual profit. Mercantilism was not interested in increasing the permanent wealth of the people, which was (and is) the goal of capitalist economics, but rather in increasing the temporary wealth of the state, a wealth that could then be translated into international power.*

From the point of view of subsequent developments, there are two other noteworthy aspects of the mercantilist mode of thinking. First, it tended to regard man—most especially the man engaged in commerce—as a creature of avarice, little more than a self-seeking and self-regarding animal whose selfish energies and purposes had to be directed toward the achievement of a larger national purpose. We usually associate this conception of man with the spirit of capitalism—but, as we shall soon see, that spirit was far more complex and ambiguous. The theory of capitalism, as adumbrated by Adam Smith and his circle, certainly was indebted to mercantilism for "clearing the ground," as it were, of classical-medieval political moralism, which insisted that an individual could be virtuous only to the degree that he renounced his selfish qualities and aimed directly at the common good. But the capitalist idea can be best understood as a reaction against *both* that classical-medieval moralism and the gross indifference of mercantilism to individual motives at all.

Second, mercantilism was in principle also indifferent to the condition of the laboring classes, and it was commonly argued that the majority of the people had to be kept poor so that the price of exports could be kept low and the nation (i.e., the government) thereby become rich. It was also generally agreed that just as merchants were naturally avaricious, so working people were naturally lazy and could be brought to labor only when they faced actual starvation as an alternative.

The developing spirit of capitalism, as finally embodied in *The Wealth of Nations*, flatly rejected both of these ideas. Indeed, the reason capital-

---

*Those who, having taken a course in modern economic theory, still find this concept "irrational" and therefore incomprehensible might examine with profit the approach to foreign trade of the Soviet Union and Communist China.

ism commended itself to the most generous and compassionate men of the eighteenth century, of whom Adam Smith was one, was precisely because it offered a cheerful alternative to the bleak mercantilist assumptions. It is true that nineteenth-century economic theory tended to return to those assumptions, but this fact ought to warn us not to identify the original spirit of capitalism with its later transmogrifications.

When one speaks of the "spirit of capitalism," one is bound to have in mind the Anglo-Scottish Enlightenment rather than the French. It is true that there was considerable mutual influence and that both joined in rejecting classical mercantilism. But the French reaction to mercantilism, as represented by the Physiocrats, was doomed to ineffectuality. While the Physiocrats formulated the slogan "laissez-faire, laissez-passer" in opposition to the mercantilist ethos, they were not much less hostile to the emerging commercial ethos. "Real" wealth, they insisted, derived from agricultural productivity, and *only* from agricultural activity. When, after the Revolution, French thinkers and economists turned their attention to the new socioeconomic order that had replaced the ancien régime, it was Adam Smith they looked to for instruction, not to their Physiocratic predecessors. To be sure, they did not always understand Adam Smith as he might have wished to be understood, but this was equally true in Britain as well—and is largely true, everywhere, even today.

The Anglo-Scottish Enlightenment was a revolutionary movement, and like all successful revolutions it did not try to impose a set of preconceived ideals on a recalcitrant reality. Again, like all successful revolutions, it did not merely destroy an old order but created a new and viable one. And it was able to do this because it responded to the "intimations" (to use Michael Oakeshott's marvelous term) of the new order that were massively present in the old. It would be an exaggeration to say that it ratified changes in the polity that had largely already happened but which had not achieved lucid and widespread self-consciousness. It would be an exaggeration—but not much of one.

The Anglo-Scottish Enlightenment, therefore, was an authentic response to the emergence of a bourgeois-capitalist Britain as well as the indispensable intellectual agent of this process. The ideas of the Anglo-Scottish Enlightenment not only were thinkable but were actually acceptable to significant portions of public opinion, because Britain was the kind of liberal (by the standards of its day) constitutional monarchy that it was, because the British aristocracy (unlike the French) was much more interested in money than in the purity of its bloodlines, and because the agricultural revolutions of the preceding two centuries (1550–1750) had so increased productivity as to disarm what later came to be known as the "Malthusian scissors." But if these were necessary conditions for the development of a capitalist Britain, they were not sufficient conditions. We have in our own time seen more than one instance of a nation which, according to the conventional socioeconomic indicators, "ought" to have followed the British precedent, ought to have "taken off" into capitalist growth, but did not—simply because the dominant ideas, the "culture," as we now say, of that nation inhibited or frustrated such a process. Ideas, if they are to be influential, need to be born into a certain kind of world, but any kind of world will always be susceptible to diverse intellectual influences, and, in the end, it is the various fates of these ideas that will decide the destiny of the world. In Britain it was the Anglo-Scottish Enlightenment, offering a coherent, persuasive, and intellectually powerful statement of what might be called the "bourgeois persuasion," that ultimately prevailed.

At the heart of this bourgeois persuasion there is a shift of focus from the community to the individual as the proper subject of moral and philosophical inquiry.* The classical-medieval world took as primary the question "What virtues does the individual have to possess in order for him to be a member of a good community in which he can lead a good life?" This question itself assumed that the proper subject of moral and philosophical inquiry was a "polity," not a "society." Society, as the classical-medieval world saw it, came into existence out of the self-preserving needs of the individual in a "state of nature." "Polity" or "community" emerged because man has a "higher" yet equally "natural" need, not merely to survive, and not even merely to survive prosperously, but to lead a good life that fulfills his true "nature" (defined metaphysically or religiously). For such a good life to exist, a good community must make it possible for it to exist. Obviously, there are very different versions of "the good community," depending on the variety of circumstances which humanity encounters. And it is also true that, for a tiny minority of "the best"—that is, philosophers and saints—the meaning of the appropriate

---

*Alasdair MacIntyre's *A Short History of Ethics* (New York: Macmillan, 1966) has an excellent discussion of this topic.

"virtues" will not be quite the same as for the average person. But it is precisely questions such as these which engaged the moral and political philosopher, who regarded society—the aggregation of individuals for the purpose of self-preservation—as a prephilosophical subject, as it is a prepolitical condition.

The modern tradition of political thought, as established by the bourgeois persuasion, abolishes the distinction between polity and society and takes the individual in his state of nature as the proper point of departure for political speculation. It is this individual who then asks the new political question: "What must I do to survive—and, after survival is assured, what must I do to survive most comfortably and happily?" It is reasonable to assume that the eventual popularity of putting *the* political question in this way owes much to the fact that Protestantism had reformulated *the* religious question as "What should *I* do to be saved?" as well as to the revival of Stoic and Epicurean modes of thought in the Renaissance, with its own question: "How do I live nobly in an ignoble world?" But this should not detract in any way from the bold originality of modern political philosophy. For, quietly and ruthlessly, it dismissed as "scholastic nonsense" all notions of man as having "higher" needs— needs that, if frustrated, cast him into misery. With this dimension of humanity denied, political philosophy could become "political science" or, better yet, "social science," an objective, value-free discipline dealing with a human animal who, for all his extraordinary differences from other animals, remains fundamentally of their kind: a creature of prescribed needs, desires, and appetites whose activities are directed to their appeasement.

This abstract, schematic description of the "modernist revolution" of the sixteenth to eighteenth centuries is true only abstractly and schematically. In the real and historical world, as distinct from the universe of pure ideas, the relation of modern thought to modern actuality was far more complex (and, one may venture to say, more interesting). Though the entire structure of classical political thought was dismissed as an irrelevant confusion between the way things are and the way things ought to be, the "ought" turned out to be not so easily severed from the "is." Men, when they contemplated their condition and their destiny in the light of the bourgeois persuasion, generally seemed to end up by thinking themselves out of this perspective—generally seemed to find that the idea of "happiness" was not self-sufficient but rather had to be compounded with some idea of "virtue" to become viable. Similarly, the primordial individualism of modern political and social thought generally culminated in some vision of a good community. How one got from the one to the other was, of course, an intellectual and practical problem of the utmost difficulty, and it is not much of an exaggeration to say that the better part of the intellectual and political history of the past two centuries consists of contentious solutions to this problem. Such solutions are various, but they basically fall into two categories.

The first, the eighteenth-century "French" solution (later incorporated into Marxist and other totalitarian solutions), was to preserve in its harsh purity the modern idea of man as a creature of appetite and circumstance, but then to reply upon the redeeming activism of a "virtuous" elite to manipulate men and circumstance in such a way as to create a good community. One may fairly call this the "managerial" solution. It did not assume that men had to become virtuous (in whatever sense) for a virtuous community to exist. Rather, it assumed that if a virtuous elite created—by coercion, if necessary—the circumstantial preconditions of a good community, men would then "naturally" adapt to virtue as they had previously adapted to vice. One may also fairly call this the "utopian" as well as the managerial solution: Beginning with what is (by classical standards) a "low" conception of the nature of man, it ends with an effort to realize, in the here and now, a universal regeneration of humanity.

The second, the "bourgeois" solution to the problem posed by the bourgeois persuasion, is associated with the Anglo-Scottish Enlightenment and especially with Adam Smith (once that thinker is properly understood). This solution involved a modification of the modern idea of man so as to place an inclination toward virtue somewhere within him. It then sought to create a decent society which would have some of the aspects of a virtuous community but would make no serious attempt to realize any such ideal. In short, the bourgeois solution elevated (though only to a moderate degree) the "low" conception of human nature so characteristic of modern thought and limited its aspirations to a vision of society which, for all its merits, fell far short of anything one might wish to call an ideal and virtuous community. In only one respect was this bourgeois society deemed to be markedly superior to all ideal communities, past or future: This was the degree of individual liberty it ascribed to the average citizen. If one wishes to use modern economic jargon, one can say that the Anglo-Scottish solution "traded off" virtue for the sake of liberty, whereas the French solution did exactly the opposite.

It is worth lingering a bit on these two modes of thought, if only because the differences between them are crucial to an understanding of the ideological turmoil of the twentieth century. It is interesting to note, for instance, that one readily calls the thinkers of the French Enlightenment—such as Voltaire, Diderot, d'Alembert, Condorcet—"intellectuals," whereas one does not think to apply that term to the likes of Locke, Hume, Ferguson, and Smith. Similarly, one would find it unexceptionable to refer to these French writers as "brilliant," a word that does not come to mind as appropriate to the Anglo-Scottish, who impress us with their "sobriety." These differences are of great importance. They reflect, above all, the marginal situation of the French men of letters, at home in the Parisian salons but not in the society as a whole, whereas the Anglo-Scottish thinkers were respectable and respected members of the community, frequently holding high academic positions and at ease in the company of worldly men (whether it was the world of politics or commerce). The French intellectuals were an "alienated" class (as we would now say), with all the wit, verve, boldness of imagination, and blithe irresponsibility that such a class will often display. The Anglo-Scottish philosophers were a more mundane lot, both sociologically and intellectually; they were in a position where they might anticipate that their ideas could be effectual, would be taken seriously by those who exercised power and authority. Being more or less "at home" in their world, they were content with melioristic ambitions, whereas the French intellectuals were inclined to rage against things as they were in the name of what they might ideally be.

Nowhere is the difference between these two intellectual currents, both children of the Age of Reason, more striking than in what they made of the idea of progress, in which they shared a common belief. For the French intellectuals, a realization of all the promises of progress became a mission, and peculiarly *their* mission, to be achieved against the massive resistance of tradition, custom, habit, and all the institutions of the ancien régime. French rationalism thereby identified the condition of being progressive with the condition of being rebellious, for the spirit of progress demanded the rational reconstruction of the social order if it was to fulfill itself. It did not take long for this French idea of progress to become wedded to a rationalist political messianism that has, ever since, been a dominant characteristic of continental "progressive" thought (and has, in our own time, been taken to be the only legitimate form of progressive thought by most of the world). The Anglo-Scottish Enlightenment was no less rationalist than the French, but it found its appropriate expression in a calm historical sociology rather than in a fervent political messianism. These thinkers were convinced that a great deal of progress had already taken place, that the inhabitants of the British Isles were already the happy beneficiaries of it, and that it required but some amendment of contemporary practices for it to continue on its incremental and inexorable way. Above all, they did not share the French "voluntaristic" notion that the idea of progress was a truth possessed by an enlightened elite who had to impress this truth on a recalcitrant reality. On the contrary: The Anglo-Scottish philosophers conceived of social progress—the rise of commerce, the gradual "refinement" of manners and morals, the increase in knowledge—as something that happened to men as they strove to "improve their condition," a striving they took to be utterly natural. Implicit in this perspective is the notion of a "hidden hand," but it is a sociological rather than a quasi-theological (or providential) notion. That the human race as a whole, or any single nation, should be creative in a way beyond the intentions or prevision of any single individual or class of individuals they took to be inevitable. As Adam Ferguson (who was Adam Smith's teacher) put it:

> Every step and every movement of the multitude, even in what are termed enlightened ages, are made with equal blindness to the future; and nations stumble upon establishments, which are indeed the result of human action but not the execution of human design.*

This almost proto-Darwinian conception of social evolution has a crucial corollary: For such progress to occur, a maximum of human liberty is necessary, because it is only through the exercise of such liberty that the serendipitous effects of social evolution can emerge. The Anglo-Scottish Enlightenment, therefore, is emphatic in the value it places on individual freedom and a more "liberal" society. The French Enlightenment, in contrast, ends up emphasizing the importance of power rather

---

*Gladys Bryson, *Man and Society: The Scottish Inquiry of the Eighteenth Century* (Princeton: Princeton University Press, 1945), p. 49.

than liberty: The rational understanding of progress is the intellectual property of an elite which, furthermore, acquires the talent of prevision through the exercise of such understanding—and given such foreknowledge of the future, human freedom becomes otiose or destructive. Anglo-Scottish rationalism asserts that the past can be understood only in retrospect, that the present can be understood as the product of its past, and that the future cannot be understood at all since it will be unwittingly created; it will be the consequence of human actions but not of any clear human intention. French rationalism claims to "understand" progress in a far more comprehensive way—claims for the mind of an "enlightened" man the ability to make congruent human intention and the consequences of human action; a society which can explain itself rationally only by way of recounting its history, rather than by its approximation to a prescribed design, is in its eyes an irrational society.

It is not unexpected, then, that French rationalism proved to be so contemptuous of traditional French institutions, whereas Anglo-Scottish rationalism was so respectful of traditional British institutions. This also explains what, to the modern eye, seems to be a riddle of intellectual history: that Adam Smith, the father of nineteenth-century liberalism, and Edmund Burke, the father of nineteenth-century conservatism, should have shared a mutual affection and admiration. Both of these thinkers saw no intrinsic difficulty in reconciling the commercial spirit, with its emphasis on individual liberty, to the prescriptive claims of traditional institutions and traditional modes of individual behavior. The reason we find this perplexing is that we have become, in the twentieth century, more the heirs to the French Enlightenment than to the Anglo-Scottish.

But if the Anglo-Scottish Enlightenment appears, when counterposed to the French, so homogeneous, there is nevertheless a significant heterogeneity within it. More than heterogeneity: There is contradiction. For while the bourgeois persuasion was unanimous in its belief that modern man had to be (and was in fact) animated by "a spirit of avarice and industry" (Hume), and that it was foolish to rely upon his direct, personal concern for the public good,* there was a sharp division of opinion over just how radically this proposition was to be interpreted. At

---

*David Hume, *A Treatise of Human Nature*, Book 2.

the root of this quarrel within the bourgeois persuasion was a disagreement over the nature of human nature.

One school of thought, represented by Thomas Hobbes and Bernard de Mandeville, considered man to be by nature an antisocial animal, ruled exclusively by self-concern and self-interest. The question then became "How does one create a decent polity if it is to be inhabited by such creatures?" Hobbes's answer was the sovereignty of Leviathan, the relinquishment of all human rights to the guardian-state, which, while interfering as little as possible in the "private" (i.e., nonpolitical) affairs of the citizenry, would ensure the most important right of all: self-preservation. Though this political solution was discredited by the Glorious Revolution of 1688, its mode of thought was partially preserved in mercantilist economic philosophy, in which the "liberated" selfishness and avarice of the individual—as exemplified in his "microeconomic" activity—was "managed" at a distance by the state to achieve the "macroeconomic" goal of national wealth as well as such political aims as power and glory.

The most provocative statement of this point of view is to be found in Bernard de Mandeville's *Fable of the Bees* (1714), a work so frank and bold and even cheerful in its inversion of traditional (i.e., classical and Christian) moral values that scholars have ever since wondered to what degree its intention was satirical and to what degree its author literally meant what he said. This scholarly controversy need not detain us. Mandeville's contemporaries certainly took him at his word and were, for the most part, duly shocked. More important, his ideas took on a life of their own and gradually infused the political and economic philosophies even of those who, when put to the question, would have denounced him as perverse to the point of wickedness. Among these latter were the authors of *The Federalist* and the American Constitution, and Adam Smith—who explicitly rejected Mandeville's teachings but nevertheless did not escape their influence.

Mandeville's views were crisply summed up in the subtitle to his work: *Private Vices, Publick Benefits*. He blandly accepted—or seemed to accept—the traditional distinctions between vice and virtue, right and wrong, but then proceeded to declare them to be utopian and utterly useless as a guide to the real world. Men can never govern themselves, can never attain virtue by aiming directly at it, by the practice of self-denial, for example. Their selfish instincts are simply too strong for any such program to succeed in the large: The history of human affairs, as distinct from the history of human philosophy, testifies to the truth of this proposition. But, Mandeville went on to say, "Private vices by the dextrous Management of a skilful Politician may be turned into Publick Benefits." One must not understand this as asserting merely that, in this imperfect world, political philosophers should not conceive of a good society that is too demanding of human nature. Mandeville went further, to argue that without those human vices a good society could not possibly exist:

> I flatter myself to have demonstrated that, neither the Friendly Qualities and kind Affections that are natural to Man, nor the real Virtues he is capable of acquiring by Reason and Self-Denial, are the Foundation of Society; but that what we call Evil in this World, Moral as well as Natural, is the grand Principle that makes us sociable Creatures, the solid Basis, the Life and Support of all Trades and Employments without Exception: That there we must look for the true Origin of all Arts and Sciences, and that the Moment Evil ceases, the Society must be spoiled, if not totally dissolved.

One can appreciate the revulsion such a teaching would arouse among Mandeville's contemporaries, most of whom conceived of themselves as being good Christians, and all of whom thought that, though Christian dogmas may not be beyond disputation, Christian morality most certainly was. Even those who agreed with his critique of premodern political thought were alarmed that Mandeville had gone too far in his positive praise of what were still universally deemed to be symptoms of human wickedness. Nevertheless, the Mandeville credo served the purpose of those who, while criticizing its "extremism," wished to see modern society arranged on a principle of official *indifference* to the moral qualities of the individual. Its success in helping to "liberate" economic and political thought from moral philosophy can be seen by the fact that Immanuel Kant, justly famed as a moral philosopher, could later state, in all equanimity: "Harsh as it might sound, the problem of establishing the just state is soluble even for a nation of devils, if they have sense." And this conception of the inevitable relation between a good society and the average, unreformed individual profoundly shaped both capitalist and anticapitalist thought in the nineteenth and twentieth centuries.

Traces of what seem to be Mandeville-ism also appear intermittently in Adam Smith's *Wealth of Nations*. But one has to approach them, and interpret them, with caution. For Adam Smith was a violent critic of both Hobbes and Mandeville and claimed as his heritage a quite contrary current of thought within the Scottish Enlightenment: the so-called Sentimental School of eighteenth-century philosophy. This school of thought, associated with the names of Lord Shaftesbury and Francis Hutcheson, was launched as a rejoinder to Hobbes, and it was against the teachings of this school that Mandeville had directed his own writings.

The Sentimental School, vaguely deist in theology but still Christian in morality, also placed great emphasis on the self-regarding desires and ambitions of men as the rock on which a better society could be built. In this sense, it too was distinctively "modern" and antitraditional. It was this school which ultimately, in the work of Adam Smith, laid the basis for modern economics by freeing it from the sovereignty of moral philosophy. But that freedom was not total and unlimited, nor was moral philosophy dismissed as irrelevant to the possibility of a good life in a good society.

Adam Smith certainly subscribed to what has become, perhaps, the most fundamental axiom of modern economics, that is, that human behavior can in large measure be explained as the rational pursuit of self-interest. But it is worth noting that he did *not* say, as a Mandevillean would have, that a rational person must always seek to *maximize* such behavior. For the Sentimental School assumed and asserted that there were natural and self-correcting limits to the pursuit of self-interest. Their "liberal" society was not liberated from the traditional moral virtues but was, in its own way, still rooted in them. As one scholar wrote half a century ago:

It is true that seventeenth- and eighteenth-century liberals accorded to the self-regarding desires and ambitions of individual men a measure of moral approval which medieval Christians had denied to them. But it does not follow that they wished to discard all moral restraints that might protect the community against the overweening greed of individuals. The new leniency toward individual desires was closely connected with a new faith in the moral faculties of individuals, and in the goodness of normal human nature. Self-centered desires were trusted to promote the general welfare, because reason and the moral sense were trusted to restrain them wherever their indulgence would be inconsistent with that welfare.*

The existence of such a "moral sense," as an integral and ineradicable part of human nature, had been posited by John Locke, who further argued that moral certainties could be deduced from the axioms revealed to this moral sense. The Sentimental School—encouraged by the decline of the doctrine of original sin in the seventeenth century, and its gradual replacement by a belief (widespread even among Protestant divines) in the original goodness of human nature—proceeded to put this thesis to work and came up with an elaborate set of "benevolent affections" which were as natural to man as his self-centered appetites. This philosophical psychology has little academic standing today, at a time when psychology strives to be as "scientific" as possible. But if we merely dismiss it as a fashionable intellectual eccentricity of the eighteenth century, as most textbooks do, we shall miss its real significance. For it was this philosophical psychology that lay behind Adam Smith's version of capitalism—though to what degree is a matter of dispute—and it was Adam Smith who, in his *Theory of Moral Sentiments*, following the line of thought traced by Locke, Shaftesbury, and (to a lesser degree) Hume, provided that theory of human nature with its most extensive and persuasive rationale. The exact relationship between the earlier *Theory of Moral Sentiments* (1759) and the later *Wealth of Nations* (1776) is a subject of scholarly controversy and constitutes what the Germans have portentously called *Das Adam-Smith Probleme*. But if the controversy is academic, its significance is not, for what is involved is nothing less than the meaning of "capitalism" as Adam Smith understood it, and whether modern conceptions of capitalism are simply an elaboration of his teachings or rather a perversion of them.

For an understanding of the teachings of Adam Smith, a knowledge of his life and a study of his personality are singularly unhelpful. Though some enthusiastic (or desperate) "psychohistorian" will surely, one of these days, "explain" his thinking by reference to his father's death before Adam was born, his bachelor condition, his attachment to his mother, the sexual inhibitions in the Scottish Presbyterian milieu in

---

*Overton H. Taylor, "Tawney's Religion and Capitalism, and Eighteenth-Century Liberalism," *Quarterly Journal of Economics* 41, no. 4 (August 1927): 718–31.

which he was raised, or whatever, the plain fact is that he was a familiar type: a distinguished, absentminded scholar, unprepossessing, with a mumbling manner of speech, amiable but often sharp-tongued, easy to get along with but difficult to get close to, a respected teacher, a pleasant dinner guest, a good citizen of Glasgow. In short, he was a man whose habits and demeanor were utterly conventional and whose thinking achieved its influence by synthesizing current intellectual opinion rather than by confronting it. He was born into modest circumstances, won scholarships, became an impecunious professor, then a more affluent tutor in a noble household, finally obtained a sinecure in a civil service—a fairly common version of the Scottish success story. The only untoward event in his life was his being kidnapped, at the age of four, by a band of passing gypsies, who soon abandoned him by the woodside. They must have realized what an improbable recruit he would make.*

But if there is little that is enigmatic about Adam Smith as a person, there is much that is puzzling about Adam Smith as the author of *The Wealth of Nations*. True, the argument itself is clear enough. It is a sustained brief for the "system of natural liberty," and the logic of this brief has been admirably summed up by Professor William Letwin:

The proof proceeds in stately steps. In order to establish that the free private market gives good results, Smith showed first that it tends naturally to set the prices of goods at their proper levels (Book I), and to steer capital into the uses that are most beneficial to society (Book II). He then demonstrates that efforts of government to improve on the workings of the free market are injurious, whether they aim to stimulate commerce or manufacture or agriculture (Books III and IV). Then, as Natural Liberty is not to be equated with anarchy, he explains what things government must do because they must be done in a civilised community and cannot be done reliably by private persons responding to private incentives (Book V).†

This argument, extending over half a million words, constitutes the structure of *The Wealth of Nations*. It is a clean, coherent, and remarkably

---

*An excellent short portrait of Adam Smith is to be found in Robert Heilbroner's *The Worldly Philosophers*, chap. 3, "The Wonderful World of Adam Smith" (New York: Simon and Schuster, 1972). See also Walter Bagehot's essay, "Adam Smith as a Person," in his *Biographical Studies*, ed. Richard Holt Hutton (1881; reprint, New York: AMS Press, 1970).

†William Letwin, "Adam Smith: Re-reading the 'Wealth of Nations,'" *Encounter* (March 1976).

persuasive structure—but it is less than the whole book, when that book is closely read. For the texture of Smith's thinking is not entirely congruent with this structure, and this is where problems of interpretation arise.

The Wealth of Nations, though infinitely more readable than Karl Marx's Capital, has experienced a not dissimilar fate. Not many people read it carefully or even at all, but practically everyone seems to think he knows what it "essentially" says. Scholars, on the other hand, who study both of these texts, end up in a state of bafflement and disagreement among themselves. And just as the major topic of controversy among the students of Marx is the relation of the earlier neo-Hegelian Marx to the later "scientific" Marx, so students of Adam Smith are divided on the issue of the relation of the earlier Smith, author of the "sentimental" Theory of Moral Sentiments, to the later author of the "tough-minded" Wealth of Nations. Moreover, there is a sense in which the "Adam Smith problem" is more perplexing than the "Karl Marx problem." The later Marx did, after all, repudiate his earlier writings, so one has to argue for a connection in the face of Marx's own opinion. Adam Smith, however, never suggested or hinted that his two major works were in any way incongruent with one another. On the contrary, after publishing The Wealth of Nations he carefully "revised" The Theory of Moral Sentiments, but the new edition shows little significant change from the earlier one. So Adam Smith himself seems not to have perceived any contradiction between his two major works. Yet practically everyone else sees, if not an outright contradiction, at least a decided difference in tone, emphasis, and perspective. And this difference is not an illusion.

In tone, The Theory of Moral Sentiments is cheerful and benign; it is even in some ways an inspirational book. The Wealth of Nations, in contrast, tends to be more objective in its rhetorical mode and is not infrequently dour and acerbic—almost Veblenesque—in its judgments on all classes of humanity. To some extent, which we can only guess at, this may have something to do with changes in Smith's attitude toward religion over the years. Though he was never an orthodox Christian and made no secret of the fact that he had no high personal regard for organized religion in general—a contemporary quotes him as saying, "God made heaven and earth but man made Holland"—in his earlier book he is very much a conventional deist, after the fashion of his teachers. That is to say, he asserts (or assumes) a minimal theology, to the effect that there is a benevolent deity about whom we know, if we know nothing else, that he is the author and guide of nature. On these terms, the world is a place mankind can feel at home in, a place in which its ideals and finer feelings have an inner compatibility with the nature of things. In *The Wealth of Nations*, however, the world is a much bleaker place: That benevolent deity seems to have become a *deus absconditus*—he is barely mentioned— and there is a persistent undercurrent of doubt and anxiety about the possibility of human happiness, regardless of the material prosperity that a correct economic philosophy would provide.

It might be said—it has been said by some scholars—that one ought not to take this change in tone too seriously, that one should not expect too much continuity between a book on moral philosophy and a book on economics, and that since Adam Smith exhibited no unease or concern about the matter, neither should we. But against this argument is the fact that there is an obvious intellectual difference between the two works, a difference in their conception of human nature and of the principle that shapes human behavior.*

The Theory of Moral Sentiments sees as the mainspring of human motivation what Arthur O. Lovejoy calls "approbativeness."† Smith expresses that principle in these terms:

> What are the advantages of that great purpose of human life which we call bettering our condition? To be observed, to be attended, to be taken notice of with sympathy, complacency, and approbation, are all the advantages we can propose to derive from it. [Pt. 1, sec. 2, chap. 2]

But, Smith says, in addition to being so attentive to the expressed opinion of the community, all human ambition and striving operates under a kind of "inner check" as well. This takes the form of an ideal "impartial spectator" who resides within each of us, and who internalizes the community's approbation and disapprobation. The impartial spectator— who very much resembles Freud's "superego" and is also a kind of vulgarized version of the Protestant idea of conscience—does his work in this way:

---

*These differences are nicely explored in Jacob Viner's essay "Adam Smith and Laissez-Faire," in *Adam Smith, 1776–1926* (Chicago: University of Chicago Press, 1928).

†Arthur O. Lovejoy, *Reflections on Human Nature* (Baltimore: Johns Hopkins Press, 1961).

We can never survey our own sentiments and motives, we can never form any judgment concerning them, unless we remove ourselves, as it were, from our natural station, and endeavor to view them as at a certain distance from us. But we can do this in no other way than by endeavoring to view them with the eyes of other people, or as other people are likely to view them. Whatever judgment we can form concerning them, accordingly, must always bear some secret reference, either to what are, or to what, upon a certain condition would be, or what we imagine ought to be, the judgment of others. We endeavor to examine our own conduct as we imagine any other fair and impartial spectator would view it. [Pt. 3, chap. 1]

From all of this it follows that, "to feel much for others, and little for ourselves, that to restrain our selfish, and to indulge our benevolent affections, constitutes the perfection of human nature."

Now, this last sentence is not the kind of thought we ordinarily associate with the founding father of capitalism—even though it is, in this same *Theory of Moral Sentiments*, carefully connected with "that great purpose of human life which we call bettering our condition," a purpose that is also central to *The Wealth of Nations*. The earlier Adam Smith seems to have had a keen sense of the importance of moral and political community, and of the need for each striving and achieving individual, as he "betters his condition," to affirm and strengthen the bonds of community. The individualism of *The Theory of Moral Sentiments* is distinctly "bourgeois," in that it has as its goal, not merely the happiness of the individual, but the creation of a more humane and elevated bourgeois community, one with powerful feelings of fraternity and fellowship. It is explicitly anti-Mandevillean, envisioning a society in which individual liberty is perfectly reconciled with the conventional bourgeois—Christian—virtues, and in which this reconciliation is a source of profound satisfaction to all.

It is perhaps worth remarking that the Adam Smith of *The Theory of Moral Sentiments* was a professor of moral philosophy. Economics, as an independent intellectual discipline, did not yet exist, while its immediate progenitor, the discipline of "political economy," was only just emerging. "Moral philosophy," as then conceived, comprehended all of the social sciences, as we now term them—plus psychology, which had the crucial role of replacing metaphysics and theology as the ultimate basis of morality. (Psychology fulfilled this role by discovering those qualities

common to everyone—sensations and sentiments—which could serve
as the foundation for a more "realistic" definition of the good life and a
more "realistic" foundation for a good society.) *The Theory of Moral Sentiments*, despite its immense and radical revision of the classical-Christian
tradition, was still linked to this tradition by its inability or unwillingness
to "think economically," to regard the economic sphere of men's activity
as autonomous.* It was with *The Wealth of Nations* that such a mode of
thinking was introduced to the world.

Whether it was Adam Smith's intention to accomplish this is, as has
been indicated, a question that evades an authoritative answer. It is not
difficult to show the many continuities between *The Theory of Moral Sentiments* and *The Wealth of Nations*, and a determined, ingenious reading of
both texts can even come up with a final and utter reconciliation of the
two. The most powerful argument along these lines has been constructed
by Joseph Cropsey in his *Polity and Economy: An Interpretation of the Principles
of Adam Smith*. Professor Cropsey insists that Adam Smith's writings do
constitute a whole, that they proposed a "system of natural liberty" (to use
Smith's term) which was quite different from later conceptions of "capitalism" (a term not yet invented). As Cropsey puts it: "Smith advocated
capitalism because it makes freedom possible—not because it *is* freedom."† Which is to say: Smith was not a "libertarian" who saw the chief
blessing of liberal capitalism as leaving everyone free to become prosperous as he saw fit, but rather defined freedom in a way that retained a firm
connection with an idea of virtue to which the free individual submitted.
The individual, free to "better his condition," was freed *from* various traditional tyrannies, large and petty, and was free *to* participate in a bourgeois
way of life whose ethos and institutions were taken for granted.

It is always dangerous to disagree with Professor Cropsey, and his analysis is both detailed and powerful. Still, his argument convinces only during
the reading of it, and when one turns back to the two texts themselves, one
is struck by the differences as much as by the connections between them.
The mainspring of human action in *The Wealth of Nations* is simply the "self-

---

*The attitude of the premodern world toward economics and economic thinking is delineated
in M. I. Finley's *The Ancient Economy* (Berkeley: University of California Press, 1973).

†Joseph Cropsey, *Polity and Economy: An Interpretation of the Principles of Adam Smith* (The Hague:
M. Nijhoff, 1957), p. x.

interest" of the individual, and a market economy is a "natural" way of serving the self-interestedness of individuals because there is "a certain propensity in human nature" to "truck, barter, and exchange one thing for another." True, there is mention of an "invisible hand," which ultimately reconciles the multiplicity of self-interests—but this famous phrase appears only once in *The Wealth of Nations*, and then in the hypothetical mood. And almost nothing is said, anywhere in the book, to suggest that there is such a thing as the "perfection of human nature," much less that such perfection is achieved through the flowering of our "benevolent affections." The tenor of *The Wealth of Nations* is such as to suggest that human beings are, by nature, little more than self-seeking, acquisitive creatures, but that it is nevertheless possible through statecraft—the creation of a market economy—to construct a humane and prosperous society. There is not the faintest suggestion that any kind of human "perfection" is likely to emerge through the workings of the market.

Yet Smith would hardly have recommended his "system of natural liberty" if he did not believe that humanity would be the better for it (not merely better *off*). One may surmise an assumption on his part that the incessant mutuality and interdependency of commercial transactions would themselves constantly refine and enlarge the individual's sense of his own self-interest, so that in the end the kind of commercial society that was envisaged would be a relatively decent community. Such self-interest "rightly understood" (to use Tocqueville's famous formulation) might even approximate, in its consequences, the results to be expected from the operation within each individual of a principle of benevolence.

In *The Wealth of Nations* Smith still firmly rejects the tradition of Calvin, Hobbes, and Mandeville. Man's "natural" instincts and man's reason, if given their freedom, will in the end lead to decent rather than to vicious behavior. In this sense, *The Wealth of Nations* is decidedly an "optimistic" book and was interpreted by Smith's contemporaries in this light. But such decent behavior, apparently, is something that appears *in the end*, not at the beginning—it is something man inevitably learns through the discipline of freedom in a free economy. Man could not learn it if his nature were such as to make such learning impossible. Smith never succumbs to the paradox of "private vices, public benefits," even though isolated sentences in *The Wealth of Nations*, quoted out of context, can make it seem as if he did. He expects men, in a free market society, to improve their spiritual as well as their material condition—to better themselves entirely. Only he does not expect them to become *much* better, and he does not think their betterment will occur automatically and easily. Though *The Wealth of Nations* is pungent and pointed in its criticisms of almost all interference with the workings of the free market, it is remarkably lacking in unconstrained enthusiasm for the world that the free market will create, or in joyful admiration for the kinds of people who will inhabit it.

One class of people for whom almost no enthusiasm of any kind, and almost no respect, is expressed is the businessman. He is presented as a scheming, conniving, self-seeking, soulless person, always looking for ways to conspire with other businessmen to defeat the workings of the free market and thereby to make illegitimate profits. In many references (which critics of capitalism are fond of quoting), the businessman is casually described as an incipient profiteer, that is, someone who, dissatisfied with the mutual, and inevitably limited, benefits that arise from the exchange of goods and services, seeks to achieve a one-sided advantage by "rigging" the market. (And joint-stock companies, the forerunners of the modern corporation, are even more harshly judged.) Almost nowhere in *The Wealth of Nations* does the upright, honest, public-spirited bourgeois businessman make an appearance. And yet, oddly enough, the contemporary readers of *The Wealth of Nations* seemed not to notice this fact and took it as a vindication of that very same bourgeois entrepreneur. Did they understand Smith better than we do? Did they read *The Wealth of Nations* in a larger context—of Smith's other writings, of his known opinions, of the shared assumptions of the time—that it is difficult for us, who read it as an isolated work in "economics," to discern? That is a possible explanation, in some ways a plausible one, but one cannot claim it is immediately convincing. Like all great books, *The Wealth of Nations* does not yield up its deepest meanings easily and unequivocally; that is why, again like all great books, it needs to be reread as much as read. What is fairly clear, however, is that the idea of business as a morally indifferent activity, an idea utterly alien to *The Theory of Moral Sentiments* but seemingly insinuated in *The Wealth of Nations*, was to have a profound and enduring influence on later economic thought.

There is another class of people who, in *The Wealth of Nations*, do not appear to good advantage: the factory workers. This is the result of the division of labor, about which the book is surprisingly ambivalent. For Smith the division of labor is practically identical with capitalism itself, and the absolute precondition of progress—economic progress, to begin with. It is the division of labor which makes possible the increase in productivity which, in turn, makes it possible for *everyone* in a capitalist society gradually to better his condition. As Smith puts it in Book I of *The Wealth of Nations*: "It is the great multiplication of the productions of all the different arts, in consequence of the division of labour, which occasions, in a well-governed society, that universal opulence which extends itself to the lowest ranks of the people." Moreover, it is this same division of labor which, by reason of the increase it engenders in the material well-being of all, is a necessary condition for the "refinement of manners" and general cultural elevation which make a free commercial society more "progressive" and more "civilized" than its predecessors, and which consequently make *all* of its citizens more fully "human" (as well as humane) than was ever the case previously.

So *The Wealth of Nations* has, unsurprisingly, many commendatory statements about the division of labor and its consequences. The economically progressive commercial society is described by Smith as "the cheerful and the hearty state to all the different orders of the society" (Bk. I). Yet in Book V there appears a now-famous passage which presents the division of labor in quite a different light.

In the progress of the division of labour, the employment of the far greater part of those who live by labour, that is, of the great body of the people, comes to be confined to a few very simple operations, frequently to one or two. But the understandings of the greater part of men are necessarily formed by their ordinary employments. The man whose whole life is spent in performing a few simple operations, of which the effects are perhaps always the same, or very nearly the same, has no occasion to exert his understanding or to exercise his invention in finding out expedients for removing difficulties which never occur. He naturally loses, therefore, the habit of such exertion, and generally becomes as stupid and ignorant as it is possible for a human creature to become. The torpor of his mind renders him not only incapable of relishing or bearing a part in any rational conversation, but of conceiving any generous, noble, or tender sentiment, and consequently of forming any just judgment concerning many even of the ordinary duties of private life.

This has come to be known as the notorious "alienation" passage,* since many scholars read it as an anticipation of Karl Marx's indictment of capitalism in *Capital*. It is a passage that does indeed consort oddly with the generally laudatory observations on the division of labor that Smith makes elsewhere. True, one of the original features of *The Wealth of Nations* is its emphasis on the importance of education for all citizens, and it is not unreasonable to understand him as saying that the stultifying effects of the division of labor can be overcome by education, which both prepares the worker for upward mobility toward less monotonous work and provides him with the inner resources necessary to prevent that monotony from dehumanizing him. It is also true that such a critical attitude toward the division of labor in the factory was fairly widespread among Smith's contemporaries, even those who were all in favor of capitalist economic development, and may be viewed simply as a species of "cultural lag." This state of mind, moreover, would have been encouraged by the wave of romanticism then beginning to pervade all of society, a kind of bourgeois nostalgia for aspects of prebourgeois life that were perceptibly vanishing from the world.†

But whatever the explanation, the fact remains that there are in *The Wealth of Nations* all kinds of crosscurrents and even countercurrents to the dominant flow of the argument.†† Adam Smith as a moral philosopher and Adam Smith as the father of modern economic analysis are not easily reconciled to one another, though the ultimate possibility of such reconciliation must never be excluded if only because Adam Smith himself seemed to take that possibility for granted. These crosscurrents and countercurrents within *The Wealth of Nations*, together with the strikingly

---

*For an excellent discussion of this topic, see E. G. West, "The Political Economy of Alienation: Karl Marx and Adam Smith," in *Oxford Economic Papers* (March 1969).

†A rather ingenious explanation of Smith's attitude toward the division of labor, to the effect that he saw it as elevating the level of civilization of society as a whole, while excluding the lowest class of industrial worker—a minority in Smith's time, it must be remembered—from participating in that general improvement, is to be found in Nathan Rosenberg, "Adam Smith on the Division of Labour: Two Views or One?" *Economics* 32 (May 1965): 127–39.

††A provocative discussion of other such "contradictions" in *The Wealth of Nations* may be found in Robert Heilbroner, "The Paradox of Progress: Decline and Decay in *The Wealth of Nations*," *Journal of the History of Ideas* 34, no. 2 (April–June, 1973). Mr. Heilbroner sees the ideal world of Adam Smith as having implicit in it, not only moral decay, but eventual economic stagnation.

different conceptions of human motivation in *The Theory of Moral Sentiments* (with its emphasis on a benevolence derived from an innate conscience) and in *The Wealth of Nations* (with its emphasis on the bourgeois individual as a self-interested and self-seeking creature), ensure that the task of understanding Adam Smith will occupy scholars for a long time to come.

Still, when all is said and done, one has to return to the dominant meanings of *The Wealth of Nations* as these were perceived by Smith's contemporaries, on whom the book had such an immense influence. And there is no doubt whatsoever that the book was read, or was interpreted without having been read, as containing an essentially optimistic message about the human condition and the future of humanity under capitalism. A clear distinction was seen between bourgeois "acquisitiveness" and prebourgeois "avarice," the latter representing a sterile hoarding of wealth, the former contributing to the general welfare by the reinvestment of accumulated capital. Commercial exchange in a bourgeois society, precisely because it was so common—with so many people competitively involved in it, and with all the information necessary for rational decisions easily available to all—would be exchange for mutual benefit. Both buyer and seller would profit, and the more nearly perfect the competition and the more comprehensive the marketplace, the greater would be the probability of both profiting equally. Profits in a bourgeois-commercial society, therefore, would be something qualitatively different from profits in a society where commerce was only a marginal activity, involving only a tiny minority of the population. In that prebourgeois state profits were not easily distinguishable from the fruits of profiteering, that is, an unequal transaction in which one party was at a clear advantage over the other and used this advantage to exploit the other. It was an indispensable premise of Adam Smith's espousal of capitalism that it of necessity created conditions in which such profiteering and exploitation would become ever more difficult.

Bourgeois acquisitiveness, therefore, was both natural and good, arising not from the desire to gain at someone else's loss but from "the desire of bettering our condition"—a desire that is universal—and in fact contributing to the improvement of *everyone's* condition. That this process of improvement might not lead to a greater overall equality of wealth was not taken to be a fact of much significance. What *was* significant was the fact that a general improvement in everyone's standard of living would inevitably lead to a greater equality in the *necessities of life*—

food, shelter, clothing—since any rich person could consume only so much of these necessities and would then spend his money on "super-fluities" (i.e., luxuries) or would simply reinvest it. As a Scotsman, Adam Smith had a scarcely concealed contempt for such superfluities and did not see why their unequal distribution should be a matter of concern to a thoughtful and reasonable man.

And, perhaps most important of all, *The Wealth of Nations* promised an economic system that not only made possible political and religious lib-erty for the individual; it made a fair degree of such liberty practically inevitable. An individual who possesses property, and has the right to augment this property as best he can, has the basic means to withstand the pressures of even the most autocratic government. If such property is divided very unequally, then it is only a relatively small proportion of the population that can set limits to the power of government. But these limits are nonetheless real, and if they benefit immediately only the small class of property owners, they offer a kind of protective umbrella under which everyone can, in an emergency, find protection. Moreover, if the free market operates as it is supposed to, with everyone gradually better-ing his condition, an ever-larger percentage of the population will come to own property of one kind or another. This, in turn, will represent an immense diffusion of economic power that will make tyrannical govern-ment more difficult.

It used to be said in the Middle Ages that "city air makes men free." What generated this relatively free atmosphere was the fact that cities were centers of commercial activity, populated by bourgeoisie who had earned their wealth and property in the marketplace rather than holding it on the sufferance of lords or kings or churchmen. Modern capitalism universalizes this phenomenon; it urbanizes the world, both in fact and in principle. This is not to assert that a capitalist society is incompatible with, say, racial or religious discrimination, or even oppression. The his-tory of Negro slavery in the United States shows otherwise. But it is instructive to note that, to achieve this effect, bourgeois society has to violate its own principles, that is, prohibit Negroes from owning and acquiring property, from becoming bourgeois, in other words. It also is possible that bourgeois society might discriminate against some of its own bourgeois citizens—blacks, or Jews, or Orientals. But so long as this discrimination only hinders their ability to better their condition, with-out stifling it completely, such disadvantaged groups can create their own "space" in which they live as free individuals. And in the end, all the inequalities of bourgeois society must yield to the great dissolvent, money, which knows nothing of race or religion or ideology.

The Wealth of Nations, and the spirit of capitalism which found such full-bodied expression in it, was not at all naive about the propensity of men to mistreat one another for ideological reasons. Memories of the bloody religious conflicts of the sixteenth and seventeenth centuries were still fresh in everyone's minds. What made capitalism so attractive was not merely its promise of gradually achieving "opulence" for all. Even more important was the hope it offered of "de-ideologizing" human relationships by emphasizing their purely economic aspect. Later generations were to see in this transformation a source of "alienation" of man from man, and of all men from their political or ideological community. (Adam Smith's near-contemporary, Jean-Jacques Rousseau, who anchored modern radicalism in a nostalgia for precapitalist modes of human association, perceived this process of alienation clearly enough. So, indeed, did the Catholic Church.) The accusation is not without substance: Bourgeois society does tend to make all human relations "thinner" and more abstract than is the case with a noncapitalist order. But what the objection failed to take into account—still fails to take into account—is the fact that this condition is merely the obverse of a society that permits greater individual liberty than history has ever known. There are no benefits without costs in human affairs (though there are frequently costs without benefits). Capitalism has its costs, but to hope to eliminate all of these costs while preserving all its benefits is surely a utopian fantasy. It was, however, precisely this utopian fantasy which was to enchant socialist thinkers in the nineteenth century.

Not only is there is an organic connection—a connection in both theory and fact—between modern capitalism and liberal society; such a connection is also to be found between modern capitalism and modern democracy, especially American democracy. For the American system of government is based on the same premises as Adam Smith's vision of capitalism, and, not accidentally, it reveals the same tensions and ambivalences. Though, in the abstract, capitalism may be regarded as one thing and democracy as another, modern democracy—a democracy in which the individual is actually encouraged to satisfy his desires and appetites, even as he multiplies them—is incomprehensible without its capitalist underpinnings.

One says *modern* democracy, with such emphasis, because it is a special and historically unique version of the idea of popular self-government. That idea, in premodern times, would have been called the "republican" idea, since the term "democracy" then meant no more than the rule of the majority (i.e., of the poor), which could easily be tyrannical. A "republic," on the other hand, was the political system appropriate to self-government by a citizenry. It envisaged a small, self-governing community, bound together by a powerful and automatically coercive consensus on religious and moral and political values—such a consensus being necessary to ensure that each individual, as he participated in the tasks of self-government, would place the interests of the community before his own. It was, by our lights, an "elitist" idea, available only to some fortunate people at some lucky historical moment. It is the kind of community envisaged by Rousseau in *The Social Contract*—a community so "virtuous" that the love of self need never be sacrificed to the "general will" since there is simply no disjunction between the two. The Greek city-states, at their peaks of excellence, were thought to represent this classical idea of democracy. In our own time, we can best get a sense of it by looking at the Israeli kibbutz: a voluntary "commune" that is a stable and enduring self-governing polity. Or one can see a grotesque parody of it in the theory and practice of "people's democracy" in Communist countries, where perpetual terror strives to achieve the pretense of such a voluntary and "virtuous" community. Indeed, the world today, as capitalism comes more and more to be regarded as a retrograde system of human relations, is constantly spawning farcical and vicious simulacra of the premodern democratic idea—"reigns of virtue" which are in actuality secular pseudotheocracies, but which claim nevertheless to be democratic in some abstruse metaphysical sense.

Modern democracy, as it emerges from the thinking of such men as Locke, Montesquieu, Adam Smith, and the Founding Fathers, is a popular government made safe for a liberal and commercial world. It does assume a moral-religious-political consensus, of course—there is no political community without consensus—but it is a "weak" consensus, extending not to the definition of happiness but rather to the means whereby government makes it possible for individuals to *seek* their happiness. A modern democracy, in their conception of it, can therefore be a heterogeneous society, a tolerant society, in short a liberal society—a government of laws, not of virtue. It is also inevitably a commercial society, since individuals in pursuit of happiness will surely seek to better their condition by engaging in commercial transactions with one another. Virtue, like religion, now becomes a private affair, to be achieved through institutions in the private sector—churches, the family, all kinds of voluntary associations. As concerns the public sector, the only virtue needed is a minimum of public-spiritedness, and this, fortunately, is provided by human nature itself. That minimum of public-spiritedness was thought to be sufficient to sustain the minimal government that was envisaged.

To twentieth-century eyes, the founders may seem to have had too low an appreciation of men's capacity to behave decently in government, and too high an estimate of the likelihood of their behaving well in what we now call the "private sector." Whether they were right or wrong about government is one of those questions of political philosophy which will doubtless be debated forever, with recurrent alternating cycles of faith in, and skepticism about, politics as a means to a better life. (In this respect, the future of political philosophy will be a recapitulation of its past.) But as to the private sector, it must be remembered that the Founding Fathers and Adam Smith were able to take certain important things for granted, and did take them for granted, in a way that we are not able to do. Above all, they were able to take for granted a *coherence* in the private sector achieved through the influence of organized religion, traditional moral values, and the family. To put it another way: Their confidence in the ability of men and women to live together socially and civilly under capitalism was not a fantasy; it was based on a realistic enough vision of the real world, as it then existed. But that was before the modern world was touched by the breezes of nineteenth-century rationalist doctrine, and devastated by the hurricanes of twentieth-century nihilism. If we today have less confidence in "natural" human sociableness, it is not because we see things as they are, while the founders were utopian, but rather because the preconditions of social life, which they imagined to be immutable, have turned out to be fragile. The climate of opinion has changed with the changes which have occurred in the capitalist world itself since their time.

From the point of view of *The Wealth of Nations*, the most relevant and significant of these changes involve capitalism's own conception of itself. Since the history of economic thought in the nineteenth and twentieth centuries is invariably written by scholars who are much interested in economics but little concerned with problems of political philosophy, this history is generally recounted as the "progress" (irregular, but inexorable) of man's ability to think "scientifically" about economic matters. The immense increase in that ability is indisputable. Whether it is such a pure gain, however, is not. Adam Smith, for one, while he would certainly have been appreciative of the technical virtuosity of later economic thought, would also have been perplexed by its moral implications. He would have been most perplexed by the blithe disregard by modern economics, in its eagerness to become a rigorous science, of the fact that any system of economic theory *must* have moral implications—must have, at its base, moral presuppositions and therefore must be a kind of moral philosophy as well as a purely economic one. The bland disregard of such presuppositions might well tempt one to describe the history of modern economics as chapters in the "degradation of the capitalist dogma."

The first great alteration in capitalist economic thought began shortly after Adam Smith's death, with the publication of Malthus's *An Essay on the Principle of Population* (1798). This inaugurated the era, which would last for more than a century, in which economics became the "dismal science." That conception of economics was so overwhelmingly popular among bourgeois theorists that one is likely to forget (as they did, for the most part) that in the founding text of capitalist economics, *The Wealth of Nations*, economics is not really a dismal science at all. True, it has its dismal aspects, in that it is alert to the human costs of a liberal capitalist society as well as to its economic benefits. But *The Wealth of Nations* was, overall, an optimistic book in that it expected those benefits to be substantial. Smith believed, as did the Founding Fathers, that in a liberal capitalist society *everyone* would gradually improve his condition. It was precisely this optimistic and reassuring message that permitted the proponents of capitalism in his time to advocate its cause in good conscience and in a cheerful spirit.

After Malthus, all this changed. Malthus proposed the thesis that, even though society as a whole would increase its wealth under capitalism, the laboring classes would not participate in this increase since, with the slightest improvement in their condition, their rate of population growth would quickly absorb and then outstrip the income available to them. In short, capitalism was an economic system in which the bourgeois minority would become ever more affluent while the laboring classes, the bulk of the population, were doomed to perpetual misery. A dismal teaching indeed! And a most curious one: It is difficult to think of a comparable social doctrine ever having achieved such widespread acceptance, a doctrine whose "iron laws" of wages and population doomed most of mankind to a living hell, without any credible promise of redemption in this world or the next. Presumably mankind was supposed to accept this doctrine in a spirit of resignation, simply because the authority of economic "science" said it had to. To the degree that capitalism in the nineteenth century acquired an ever more tarnished reputation, this new and revised vision of capitalist economic theory bore much of the responsibility.*

The oddity of this whole phenomenon has not been sufficiently explored by intellectual or social historians. Not merely the strangeness of defending an economic system with an argument from misery, but the paradox of learned men proposing such an argument in the face of overwhelming and obvious contrary evidence is extraordinary. The original edition of Malthus's work was published at a time when it was generally believed that Britain's population was declining, not rising, a belief Malthus himself did not challenge. Later editions, it is true, added more and more "empirical" material, but as often as not the empirical data worked against his thesis rather than for it.† Nevertheless, Malthus's work made an immediate and profound impression upon his contemporaries, and his thesis became the "conventional wisdom" of economic science for later generations. Indeed, these generations continued to subscribe to Malthusian doctrine in face of the fact that the condition of the laboring classes in the nineteenth century continued to improve, as

---

*It is true that Malthus later did suggest that, if the masses exercised rigorous sexual self-restraint, their condition was not utterly hopeless. The masses refused to get excited by such glad tidings.

†For a penetrating analysis of Malthus's weakness as an economic demographer, and his importance as an ideologist, see Gertrude Himmelfarb's essay in *Victorian Minds* (New York: Alfred A. Knopf, 1968).

Adam Smith had predicted. This improvement was irregular—in cyclical spurts, as it were—but obvious enough. Nevertheless, even in the United States, which Malthus had conceded might be an exceptional case, where the possibility of bettering one's condition was indubitably real, and where popular opinion reflected this reality, learned men continued to pay their respects (if less dogmatically than elsewhere) to Malthus's teaching.

It is a most curious episode in intellectual history, this sovereignty of the dismal science during the heyday of capitalist growth and expansion. In the end, of course, ideology caught up with reality, and economics became less ideologically pessimistic, more scientifically optimistic. But, as we shall see, the versions of this new optimism were associated with profound problems of their own. And in the meantime, the prevalence of Malthusianism left the intellectual and emotional arena open for a utopian philosophy of hope, that is, socialism.

As the popularity of Malthusianism gradually waned, it was replaced (or supplemented) by a new doctrine which, while not disputing the Malthusian essentials, nevertheless absorbed them into a more "affirmative" vision. One has to use quotation marks in this case because the affirmation was of a very peculiar kind indeed. Basing itself on the Darwinian conception of the survival of the fittest, it conceived of capitalism as the economic and social system that gave most perfect expression to the constant "war of all against all," which was presumably the foundation of all human societies. It was during this period—approximately 1880–1914, and most especially in the United States—that the idea of capitalism as a system of "free enterprise" was born, the term itself having a connotation of successful aggression on the part of those who aspired to the rank of the fittest to survive.

This conception of capitalism went back beyond Mandeville to Hobbes. Mandeville, after all, with his formula of "private vices, public benefits," did maintain a traditional moral distinction (however sophistical) between vice and virtue. Social Darwinism, resting itself squarely on a mechanistic rather than a teleological biology, dispensed with the moral dimension entirely. Society was merely the arena in which men exercised their "natural right" to self-preservation and survival. This was exactly Hobbes's idea, of course, but Hobbes understood that a society so conceived needed a powerful sovereign ("Leviathan") to keep the struggle among men within bounds, to prevent society from being permanently involved in civil strife and self-destruction. The Social Darwinists, in contrast, were individualists *à outrance*, believed in only a minimal state, and were utterly confident that they could persuade their fellow citizens, regardless of their degree of "fitness," to accept the "natural law" of Social Darwinism in the same calm way they accepted the law of gravitation. The smug arrogance behind this belief was of near-pathological dimensions, encouraging otherwise intelligent and worldly men to believe what a momentary accession of common sense would have shown to be absurd. In the event, of course, the majority who were "unfit" began to have an adverse opinion of capitalism, to see it as a "dog-eat-dog" system in which a few canines devoured all the rest.

And so, for more than a century after Adam Smith, the prevailing ideologies of capitalism were of a kind to be offensive and repugnant to the overwhelming majority of the citizenry of a capitalist society. Indeed, they affronted that basic human impulse which Smith saw as the cornerstone of his "system of natural liberty," namely, the desire of every man to better his condition, in terms of both material comfort and social esteem. Such a situation could not last: Whatever the "contradictions" of capitalism posited by socialists, they were of little weight when compared with *this* contradiction which capitalist ideologists imposed upon the system they were presumably defending. And it did not last. In the twentieth century there developed a new conception of capitalism which represented, in good part, a return to Adam Smith. It is this conception that is at the root of the modern science of economics, and it has become the "conventional wisdom" with which capitalism is defended today.

This new-old idea of capitalism, flowing from the development of marginal utility analysis in the last decades of the nineteenth century, once again sees the free market as a creative and benign institution. Through it, individuals may engage in transactions as a result of which *everyone* is better off than was previously the case. The free market, therefore, not only is a wealth-creating mechanism; it is also a wealth-distributing mechanism. The pattern of distribution might be unequal—a fact which provokes socialists to indignation—but that is regarded as less important than the fact that (1) everyone does benefit, even if unequally, and (2) inequalities are likely to be temporary, in the sense that different people, at different times, will be the beneficiaries of such inequality. This last point is of crucial significance. It means that capitalism, through the dynamics of a free market, does not give birth to any kind of permanent oligarchy which would subvert that "free society" which it is capitalism's ultimate purpose to create and sustain. The rich will always be with us, but in the course of several generations the old rich will gradually be superseded by the new rich, since the ability to respond to market opportunities is not—nor has anyone ever claimed it to be—an inherited human characteristic.

This conception of capitalism is today incorporated in the science of economics to such a degree that most economists cannot even see that it is there. The image of man—an isolated individual with a set of "preference schedules," a creature of appetite and of self-defined "wants"—seems so "natural" as also to appear self-evidently valid. And, indeed, there is a considerable degree of truth in it; otherwise, economic theory would not have the kind of explanatory and (to a lesser degree) predictive power which it unquestionably does have. Man in modern economic theory is congruent with man in modern capitalist society, an ultimate atom with measurable desires. The interaction of these desires in the marketplace can be given expression in sophisticated mathematical formulas, and criteria of economic efficiency can be devised to analyze whether or not the "system is working." The most popular of such criteria is the "Pareto maximization rule," which defines an efficient transaction as one in which someone is made better off without anyone else's being made worse off. The very idea behind such a criterion—that it is possible for people to better their condition without this being disadvantageous to others—certainly represents a reversion to the original optimistic Smithian notion of capitalism, after a century of neo-Malthusian and neo-Darwinian heterodoxy.

But it is a reversion that is a vulgarization, despite—or perhaps because of—the mathematical power which modern economic theory unquestionably possesses. The "economic man" of modern economics is not quite the same creature as the "bourgeois man" of *The Theory of Moral Sentiments* or even *The Wealth of Nations*. They do overlap, to be sure, but less than completely. Smith never did reduce man, as modern economic thought does, to the status of a naked individual who was the sum of his individual appetites. *That* kind of reductionism is necessary if one aims at the kind of mathematical precision and rigor which is the mark (and, in all fairness, the glory) of modern economics. But Smith's economic abstractions were of a more homely, less ambitious kind. In all of his writings, the human beings who are also economic men remain recognizably human and therefore remain recognizably social and political and moral beings as well. Economics, for Smith, was not a substitute for moral and political philosophy.

Because of this, Smith was able to speak to a central economic question about which modern economic theory is so strikingly impotent, that is, the *causes* of the "wealth of nations." He was able to address himself to this question for the same reason that modern economics cannot: The causes of economic prosperity are not themselves economic phenomena. They are rather "cultural" in the largest sense of that term, involving a sense of self, and of the relation between oneself and others, which in turn generates attitudes and practices that are favorable or inimical to economic growth. For the past twenty-five years economists have been trying to explain "economic development" in purely economic terms, for example, in terms of the intensity of capital investment or as a function of international economic relations. The results have been so pitiful, in their lack of explanatory power, that economists have been forced to conscript some noneconomic factors and try to convert them into economic quantities, for example, "human capital" defined in terms of the average years of schooling in the population. This has not helped much; the perspective is still too limited. Everyone, whether economist or not, is quite certain that if India or Peru were inhabited by Swiss and Dutchmen, they would be fairly prosperous countries, not poor ones. But this knowledge cannot be reduced to terms that fit into modern economic theory.

Adam Smith would not have been so baffled. His conception of economic theory was still sufficiently close to commonsense observations, and sufficiently distant from the often misplaced precision of modern economics, to take account of factors that were real enough even if difficult to define and quantify. He understood that men were not just producers and consumers, and that their religious and political traditions were bound to affect, in a powerful and pervasive way, their economic performance. This is not to say that religious or political traditions are necessarily to be judged by their economic consequences; such a judgment has to be philosophical, not economic. But it does mean that economic development—either of a nation, or a particular class of citizens within the nation—is to be understood within the perspective of a broad historical sociology, a humanistic historical sociology, rather than a narrow economic theory. In short, the "causes" of both prosperity and poverty are to be understood in terms of the consequences for economics of noneconomic behavior by individuals or their institutions, including the institution of government.

But even more important than an understanding of the causes of economic prosperity is an understanding of its *consequences*. Or, to put it in terms that would have been more congenial to Adam Smith, of its *purposes*. For Smith did not think it possible to talk about the best economy without reference to the character of the people who were the end result of the economic process. As Joseph Cropsey has written: "When authors like Adam Smith advocated policies and institutions that promoted production and accumulation, they did so because the wealth-giving institutions had salutary noneconomic consequences of the highest importance." And Professor Cropsey goes on to complain that "in one way or another contemporary welfare economics has substituted the economy for the polity."*

The complaint is worth paying close attention to. It directs itself to one of the most puzzling features of the modern world, the fact that as societies become more affluent as a result of adhering to Smithian economics, they seem to breed all sorts of new social pathologies and discontents, so that the Smithian conception of the best economy no longer seems to have any connection, in the minds of the citizenry, with a best polity. Crime and all kinds of delinquency increase with increasing prosperity. Alcoholism and drug addiction also increase. Civic-mindedness and public-spiritedness are corroded by cynicism. The pursuit of happiness no longer is organically related to the instinct to better one's condition by diligent application. And, ironically, it is among the children of the affluent especially that these two activities now are seen to be in radical opposition to one another.

In a bourgeois, affluent society, happiness comes to mean little more than the sovereignty of self-centered hedonism. The emphasis is on the pleasures of consumption rather than on the virtues of work. The ability to defer gratification, which is a prerequisite for a gradual bettering of

---

*Joseph Cropsey, "What Is Welfare Economics?" *Ethics* 65, no. 2 (January 1955): 122.

ON CAPITALISM AND THE DEMOCRATIC IDEA

one's condition, is scorned; "fly now, pay later" becomes, not merely an advertising slogan, but also a popular philosophy of life.* And in the realm of politics, a similar kind of debasement—as Adam Smith would certainly have termed it—takes place. The purpose of politics becomes the maximum gratification of desires and appetites, and the successful politician is one who panders most skillfully to this "revolution of rising expectations," a revolution which affluent capitalism itself generates and before which the politics of bourgeois democracy prostrates itself. Inevitably, the democratic state becomes ever more powerful, and more willing to supersede the processes of the free market, as it strives to satisfy these inflated demands of both the economy and the polity. Equally inevitably, since the demands *are* inflated, the democratic state fails in this effort, and it becomes possible for a great many people to think that a nondemocratic state might do better. It will not, of course; unreasonable demands are by definition insatiable. But it is true that the nondemocratic state will have the power to curb and repress these demands, where it cannot satisfy them, whereas the bourgeois-democratic state can rely only on the self-discipline of the individual, which affluent capitalism itself subverts.

Adam Smith did not foresee this situation. In part, this was because his conception of the nature of human nature, as expressed in *The Theory of Moral Sentiments*, reassured him that the bonds of social solidarity in a bourgeois community were too strong to be disrupted by the acquisitive instincts. In part, too, it was because, as a Scotsman in the last half of the eighteenth century, he took for granted the restraining influence of a set of institutions—organized religions, the family, the educational system— which did not otherwise much interest him. In this respect, he was of one mind with the Founding Fathers, who also took the "wholesome" influence of these institutions for granted, without devoting much thought to them. But what they took for granted has, in the twentieth century, become unsettled, controversial, ineffectual. Bourgeois affluence has "liberated" men (and women) from these wholesome influences and has thereby reopened all the large questions of moral and political philosophy that Adam Smith and the Founding Fathers thought had been definitively answered by "modernity" itself. Which is not to exclude the possibility

*See Daniel Bell, *The Cultural Contradictions of Capitalism* (New York: Basic Books, 1976).

that we may yet conclude that their vision of the best society and polity is, indeed, the best available one. Only we can no longer support this conclusion by a mere recapitulation of their reasoning.

To put it another way: Though Adam Smith and the Founding Fathers might well have the right answers, more or less—and the history of the twentieth century does not suggest that other, better answers are close at hand—it could be that they did not, from our point of view, ask the right questions. After two hundred years, their "system of natural liberty" has, by its very success, reopened fundamental questions as to the good life and the good society, and the meaning of life itself, which they felt no need to address themselves to. We, who are the beneficiaries of their vision, are also in a better position to appreciate the limits of their vision. But first we must understand that vision, fairly and comprehensively, that is, as they understood it. Then, and only then, will be truly free to modify or supplement it. And we ought always to remember what it is so very easy to forget: This very freedom of ours is a legacy from them.

1976

24

Socialism: An Obituary for an Idea

The most important political event of the twentieth century is not the crisis of capitalism but the death of socialism. It is an event of immense significance. For with the passing of the socialist ideal there is removed from the political horizon the one alternative to capitalism that was rooted in the Judeo-Christian tradition and in the Western civilization which emerged from that tradition. Now, to ever-greater degree, anticapitalism is becoming synonymous with one form or another of barbarism and tyranny. And since capitalism, after two hundred or so years, is bound to endure crisis and breed disaffection, it is nothing short of a tragedy that anticapitalist dissent should now be liberated from a socialist tradition which—one sees it clearly in perspective—had the function of civilizing dissent, a function it was able to perform because it implicitly shared so many crucial values with the liberal capitalism it opposed.

Today, we live in a world with an ever-increasing number of people who call themselves socialists, an ever-increasing number of political regimes that call themselves socialist, but where the socialist ideal itself has been voided of all meaning, and frequently of all humane substance as well. It must be emphasized that this is not a question of the institutional reality diverging markedly from the original, inspiring ideal—as the Christian Church, let us say, diverged from the original vision of the Gospels. That kind of wayward development is natural and inevitable, if always dismaying—ideals pay a large price for their incarnation. In the case of contemporary socialism, however, the ideal itself has ceased to be of any interest to anyone—it has not been adapted to reality but contemptuously repudiated by it.

True, there is a dwindling band of socialist fideists who keep insisting that we must not judge socialism by any of its works. The Soviet Union, they tell us, is not "socialist" at all; nor is China, or Yugoslavia, or Cuba, or Hungary, or all those other "people's democracies." Neither, of course, are such regimes as exist in Peru or Syria or Zaire, whose claims to socialist legitimacy are not to be taken seriously. As for Western countries with social-democratic governments, such as Britain or Sweden—well, they get a passing grade for "effort" but it seems that they are insufficiently resolute or intelligent to bring "true" socialism about.

This is all quite ridiculous, of course. Socialism is what socialism does. The plaintive lament of the purist that socialism (or capitalism, or Christianity) has "never really been tried" is simply the expression of petulance and obstinacy on the part of ideologues who, convinced that they have a more profound understanding than anyone else of the world and its history, now find that they have been living a huge self-deception. People who persist in calling themselves socialist, while decrying the three quarters of the world that has proclaimed itself socialist, and who can find a socialist country nowhere but in their imaginings—such people are anachronisms. As such they do serve a purpose: They help the historian and scholar understand what socialists used to think socialism was all about. One could discover that from reading books, to be sure, but it is sometimes enlightening to interview an actual survivor.

The absolute contradiction between the socialist reality today and the original socialist ideal is most perfectly revealed by the utter refusal of socialist collectivities even to think seriously about that ideal. Perhaps the most extraordinary fact of twentieth-century intellectual history is that all thinking about socialism takes place in nonsocialist countries. In this respect, one can again see the fallacy in the analogy—so frequently and glibly made—between contemporary socialism and early Christianity. The Church certainly did deviate from the original teachings of Jesus and his apostles, and did transform these teachings into a theology suitable for an institutional religion. But these deviations and transformations, this development of Christian doctrine, were the work of the Church Fathers, whose powerful minds can fascinate us even today. In the case of contemporary socialism, there are no Church Fathers—only heretics, outside the reach of established orthodoxies, developing doctrines for which socialist authority has no use at all. Not a single interesting work on Marxism—not even an authoritative biography of Karl Marx!—has issued from the Soviet Union in its sixty years of existence. If you want to study Marxism, with Marxist intellectuals, you go to Paris, or Rome, or London, or some American university campus. There are no intellectual hegiras to Moscow, Peking, or Havana. Moreover, the works of Western Marxist thinkers—and some are indeed impressive—are suppressed in socialist lands. Sartre's Marxist writings have never been published in Russia, just as Brecht's plays have never been produced there, and just as Picasso's paintings have never been exhibited there. Socialism, apparently, is one of those ideals which, when breathed upon by reality, suffers immediate petrifaction. Which is why all those who remain loyal to this ideal will always end up bewailing another "revolution betrayed."

The inevitable question is: What was the weakness at the heart of this ideal that made it so vulnerable to reality? But in an obituary, it is indelicate to begin with the deceased's flaws of mind and character. It is more appropriate to take cognizance of, and pay one's respects to, his positive qualities. And the socialist ideal was, in many respects, an admirable one. More than that: It was a *necessary* ideal, offering elements that were wanting in capitalist society—elements indispensable for the preservation, not to say perfection, of our humanity.

The basic defects of a liberal-capitalist society have been obscured from us by the socialist critique itself—or, to be more precise, by the versions of this critique which ultimately became the intellectual orthodoxy of the socialist movements. The original sources of socialist dissent are best discovered by going back to the original socialists: the so-called utopian socialists, as distinguished from the later "scientific" socialists. Reading them, one finds that socialism derives its spiritual energy from a profound dissatisfaction, not with one or another aspect of liberal modernity, but with that modernity itself. Indeed, the original socialist criticism of the bourgeois world is, to a remarkable degree, a secular version of the indictment which the "reactionary" Catholic Church was then continually making, though to a world increasingly deaf to Christian tonalities.

The essential point of this indictment was that *liberty was not enough*. A society founded solely on "individual rights" was a society that ultimately

deprived men of those virtues which could only exist in a *political community* which is something other than a "society." Among these virtues are a
sense of distributive justice, a fund of shared moral values, and a common vision of the good life sufficiently attractive and powerful to transcend the knowledge that each individual's life ends only in death.
Capitalist society itself—as projected, say, in the writings of John Locke
and Adam Smith—was negligent of such virtues. It did not reject them
and in no way scorned them, but simply assumed that the individual
would be able to cope with this matter as he did with his other "private"
affairs. This assumption, in turn, was possible only because the founders
of capitalism took it for granted that the moral and spiritual heritage of
Judaism and Christianity was unassailable, and that the new individualism of bourgeois society would not "liberate" the individual from this
tradition. It might free him from a particular theology, or a particular
church; but he would "naturally" rediscover for himself, within himself,
those values previously associated with that theology or church. This was
very much a Protestant conception of the relation between men and the
values by which they lived and died. It survived so long as traditional religious habits of mind survived in the individualist, secularized society of
bourgeois capitalism. Which is to say, for many generations capitalism
was able to live off the accumulated moral and spiritual capital of the
past. But with each generation that capital stock was noticeably depleted,
had to be stretched ever thinner to meet the exigencies of life. Bankruptcy was inevitable, and we have seen it come in our own time, as a
spirit of nihilism has dismissed not only the answers derived from tradition but the very meaningfulness of the questions to which tradition provided the answers. A "good life" has thus come to signify a satisfactory
"lifestyle"—just another commodity that capitalism, in its affluence and
generosity, makes available in a thousand assorted varieties, to suit a
thousand tastes.

Socialism can be seen, in retrospect, to have been a kind of rebellion
against the possibilities of nihilism inherent in the bourgeois Protestant
principle—an effort, within the framework of modernity, to reconstruct
a political community that would withstand the corruptions of modernity
itself. To call it a "secular religion" is not far off the mark, and most of the
original "utopian" socialists would have found nothing arguable in this
ascription. The Saint-Simonians, as we know, very consciously set out to
establish a post-Christian religion that preserved the best of Christianity

as they understood it. All the utopian-socialist communities had a religious core—at the very least a "religion of humanity" into whose values young people were indoctrinated. To challenge or criticize those values, and the way of life associated with them, was to risk immediate expulsion. In our own time, the Israeli kibbutz can remind us of what a socialist community, in the original sense, was supposed to be like.

This utopian socialism was not really utopian at all. Indeed, it is the only kind of socialism that has ever worked. The trouble is that it can only work under certain very restricted conditions. (1) The people who set out to create a socialist community must sincerely subscribe to socialist beliefs. (2) They must be satisfied with a *small* community—otherwise there will be division of labor, bureaucracy, social classes, in short a "society" rather than a community. And (3) they must be fairly indifferent to material goods, so that a *voluntary* equality will easily prevail. In circumstances such as these, socialist communities "work," in the sense of continuing to exist and continuing to hold on to the loyalties of a new generation as well as those of the founding members. They work most effectively, as historians of socialism are fond of pointing out, when the religious core is strongest, because then the shared values are most successfully affirmed and reaffirmed. It is no accident, after all, that the Greek *polis*—the model of political community—neither believed in nor practiced religious toleration, to say nothing of religious pluralism.

But this kind of socialism has always been marginal to socialist history, which had much larger ambitions. The "scientific socialism" of Marx and his followers—whether they defined themselves as "orthodox" Marxists, "neo"-Marxists, "revisionist" Marxists, or whatever—aimed to transform all of society, and quickly. It derided the idea of slowly converting people to a belief in socialism, until these people formed a majority. Similarly, it contemptuously rejected the notion of creating model socialist communities within the womb of capitalist society—as, say, the early Christians created their own exemplary communities throughout the Roman empire. Though the moral and spiritual impetus toward socialism may have been derived—and is still largely derived—from a profound sense of the inadequacy of modernity to satisfy the yearnings for political community, postutopian socialism itself has become a modernist political doctrine. This is true of both the Communist and social-democratic versions of scientific socialism, each of which, in its own way, takes a "managerial" and manipulative approach to politics, and tries to create a new political community through the actions of government upon an unenlightened and recalcitrant populace.

The crucial difference between scientific socialism and utopian socialism lay in the attitude toward economic growth and material prosperity. The utopians were not much interested in affluence, as we have come to understand that term—that is, an ever-increasing amount and variety of consumers' goods made available to an ever-increasing proportion of the population. They were by no means Spartan in their conception of a good community. They *did* expect to abolish poverty and to achieve a decent degree of material comfort, which would be equally shared. But their conception of a "decent" standard of living was, by twentieth-century standards, quite modest. This modesty was a matter of principle: Being community-oriented rather than individual-oriented, utopian socialism saw no merit in the constant excitation of individual appetites, which would inevitably place severe strains on the bonds of community. The main function of the socialist community, as they conceived it, was to produce a socialist type of individual—a person who had transcended the vulgar, materialistic, and divisive acquisitiveness that characterized the capitalist type of individual. Here again, the Israeli kibbutz gives us an insight into the utopian intention. The kibbutz aims to satisfy all the basic economic needs of the community, and even to achieve a pleasing level of comfort for its membership. But "affluence," in the sense of widespread individual possession of such "luxuries" as automobiles, television sets, hi-fi radios and record players, freezers and refrigerators, travel abroad, and so forth, is solemnly regarded as a political threat, to be coped with cautiously and prudently.

Scientific socialism, in contrast, denounced capitalism for failing to produce the society of abundance made possible by modern technology, and mocked at utopian socialism for wishing to curb "needs" rather than satisfying them copiously. This approach made it possible for scientific socialism to become the basis of a mass movement, since it pandered so explicitly to the mass appetites excited—but also, to some degree, at any particular moment, frustrated—by capitalism. The political mass movements that had socialist goals then divided into two kinds: those which thought a liberal parliamentary democracy should be preserved within a socialist community, and those which thought this both unrealistic and undesirable. In the twentieth century, both these movements succeeded in establishing themselves as the governments of major nations. And in all such instances the end result has been frustration and disillusionment.

In the case of totalitarian socialism—that current of socialist thought for which Lenin stands to Marx as St. Paul did to Jesus—the frustration has been absolute and definitive. Central economic planning of a rigorous kind has demonstrated a radical incapacity to cope with a complex industrialized economy and urbanized society. Obviously, the central planners can do certain things—that is, build steel mills or dams or armament factories. But the Pharaohs of ancient Egypt could boast of comparable achievements—there is nothing socialist about the ability of an all-powerful state to get certain things done. What the central planners of the Soviet Union clearly cannot do is to create an "affluent" society in which its citizens would have a standard of living on the level of that of Western Europe and America. The immense bureaucracy involved in such planning simply cannot compete with the free market as an efficient mechanism for allocating resources, nor is bureaucratic caution able to substitute for entrepreneurial risk-taking as a mechanism of innovation and economic growth.

Yet a Western standard of affluence is precisely what the Soviet citizens want. These citizens were never socialists in any meaningful sense of that term, nor have sixty years of Communist rule succeeded in making them such. In the earlier decades of the Soviet regime there was a lot of windy talk about "the new Soviet man" who would emerge from "the Soviet experiment." One hears little such prattle today, even from official Soviet sources. Soviet Communism is a pseudoreligion, and the Soviet government is a pseudotheocracy, which, even after decades of coercion and terror, has been pitifully unable to effect any kind of mass conversion to socialist beliefs. As has been noted, there are no socialist intellectuals in the Soviet Union—only an increasing number of antisocialist intellectuals. The effort to create a socialist society that would be more prosperous, more "affluent," than a capitalist one, while creating a socialist citizenry through unremitting *force majeure*, has been a disastrous failure. "Managerial" socialism has turned out to be far more utopian than utopian socialism.

The same destiny has awaited the non-Leninist, social-democratic version of managerial socialism. Where one can claim success for it, it is a success that is a kind of failure in socialist terms. Such is the case of

Sweden, after decades of social-democratic government. It has been a prosperous country, with a healthy economy and a stable society—but its economy and society can be fairly described as "mixed," that is, half private capitalism, half state capitalism. Those Swedes who still think of themselves as socialists are intensely dissatisfied with this state of affairs, and are constantly urging the government toward greater state control and a more egalitarian distribution of income. Since the Swedish Social Democrats are still officially committed to the socialist ideal, they find it impossible to resist this ideological pressure. The drift is unremittingly toward the Left, and will remain so, as long as the Social Democrats are in office. The consequences for the Swedish economy are entirely pre-dictable: slower economic growth, higher inflation, lower productivity—all amidst increasing popular discontent. That discontent will not be calmed by a more punitive and egalitarian tax system. Egalitarianism, in Sweden, does not reflect any sincere personal commitment on the part of the Swedish people to the ideal of equality. It is, rather, a strategy whereby organized labor on the one hand and the state bureaucracy on the other receive an ever-increasing share of the national income and of political power. This appetite will not be appeased by a more equal dis-tribution of income or wealth. The demand for "more"—not for "more equal" but for "more"—will feed upon itself, until an economic, and eventually political, crisis will either create an authoritarian regime that copes with discontent by repressing it or provokes a reversion to a more liberal-capitalist economic order.

In a sense, Great Britain represents Sweden's socialist future. Though Britain's movement toward socialism came much later than Sweden's, and though some of the more conservative British socialists still talk as if a Swedish condition were the ultimate ideal they are striving for, the British impulse has been more powerful, less controllable, less deferen-tial toward economic realities. There has been more nationalization of industry in Britain, the trade unions are far more belligerent, the Left socialists—the ideological fanatics who redouble their socialist efforts as the socialist ends fade into unreality—are more influential. The conse-quences for the British economy have been disastrous—Britain now vies with Italy for the title "the sick man of Europe"—and there have been no discernible compensating improvements in the British social and political order. No one even seriously claims that the British people are in any sense "happier" as a result of their socialist experiences. Indeed,

all the objective indices of social pathology—crime, juvenile delinquency, corruption, ethnic dissent, emigration, and so forth—show steady
increases.

It is hard to believe that Britain will simply continue on this downward course. The British love of liberty is still strong, the British liberal
political tradition still possesses a large degree of popular acceptance, the
British people as a whole are still more reliant on common sense than
they are enamored of political fantasies. It is reasonable to expect that
the Labour government will be succeeded by a Conservative government, and the British experience with socialism will be followed by a
"reactionary" affirmation of the principles of liberal capitalism. But then
the issue will be posed anew: What can a liberal-capitalist society do to
inoculate itself against a resurgence of anticapitalist dissent?

We now know part of that answer. One of the things that can be done
is to design all measures of "social welfare" so as to maintain the largest
degree of individual choice. The demand for a "welfare state" is, on the
part of the majority of the people, a demand for a greater minimum of
political community, for more "social justice" (i.e., distributive justice),
than capitalism, in its pristine, individualistic form, can provide. It is not
at all a demand for socialism or anything like it. Nor is it really a demand
for intrusive government by a powerful and ubiquitous bureaucracy—
though that is how socialists and neosocialists prefer to interpret it.
Practically all of the truly popular and widespread support for a welfare
state would be satisfied by a mixture of voluntary and compulsory insurance schemes—old-age insurance, disability insurance, unemployment
insurance, medical insurance—that are reasonably (if not perfectly)
compatible with a liberal-capitalist society. Over the past quarter century, a host of conservative and neoconservative economists and social
critics have showed us how such mechanisms could and would work,
and their intellectual victory over earlier "Fabian" conceptions of social
reform has been decisive. The problem, at the moment, is to persuade
the business community and the conservative (i.e., antisocialist) political
parties of their practicality. Not an easy mission, but not in principle an
intractable one.

Other problems indigenous to a liberal-capitalist society are still virgin
territory so far as constructive theory is concerned. What, for instance,
shall we do about the government of those most peculiar capitalist institutions, the large corporations—bureaucratic (and, in a sense, "collec-

tivist") versions of capitalist enterprise that Adam Smith would surely have detested? And, even more important, what can a liberal-capitalist society do about the decline of religious beliefs and traditional values—a decline organically rooted in liberal capitalism's conception of this realm as an essentially "private affair" neither needing nor meriting public sanction? These and other questions will continue to make any "counterreformation" on the part of liberal capitalism an exceedingly fragile enterprise. But they will have to be answered if the death of socialism is not simply to mean a general disintegration into political pseudosocialist forms whose only common element is a repudiation, in the name of "equality," of individual liberty as a prime political value.

As Cardinal Newman once observed, it is not too hard to show the flaws in any system of thought, religious or political, but an erroneous idea can be expelled from the mind only by the active presence of another idea. The dead idea of socialism is now putrifying both the world's mind and the world's body. It has to be removed and buried—with appropriate honors if that will help. Ironically, only liberal capitalism can perform that funereal task.

1976

SECTION V

The Conservative Prospect

25

American Historians
and the Democratic Idea

Although it is hardly a secret, I had better affirm it explicitly right at the outset: I am no kind of historian. I am a journalist, at best a man of letters, and I am keenly aware that, as Voltaire observed, a man of letters resembles a flying fish: "If he raises himself up a little, the birds devour him; if he dives, the fish eat him up." I take this to mean that insofar as I refer to general ideas, I shall be devoured by the scholarly eagles, and that insofar as I refer to particular details, I shall be eaten alive by the scholarly sharks. On the other hand, it is in the nature of a flying fish that he cannot for too long skim nervously along the surface. That suits neither his instincts nor his appetite. So, in what follows, I shall be at the historian's mercy, without really expecting any from him.

As a matter of fact the only reason I feel justified in proposing these thoughts to a scholarly public is that some years ago I set out to write a book. The book was supposed to deal with the present state of the democratic idea in America and with the way in which the ambiguities surrounding this idea have been the cause of many of our contemporary social and political problems. For obvious reasons, some background reading in American history seemed like a useful preparatory exercise. Well, that exercise turned out to be more strenuous and less satisfying than I anticipated. To my dismay, I discovered that, far from providing me with any convenient, ready-made historical perspective on the fate of the democratic idea in America, most American historians simply

313

offered me further and quite unwelcome evidence of, first, how confused this idea has been during most of America's history and, second, how confused American historians themselves have been about this idea. It is not that American historians are notably reticent about what has happened to democracy in America. They obviously have a great deal to say. But they appear to have given so very little thought to the various meanings that the idea of democracy might have. Perhaps it ought not to have surprised me that American historians, like other Americans, have so little aptitude for, or interest in, what is essentially a problem of political philosophy. But I confess that it did.

Let me give a couple of examples of what I have in mind. If one were to ask, "What is the most effectively conservative piece of legislation passed by the federal government in this century?" the answer, I submit, is both obvious and incontestable. It is the Nineteenth Amendment, extending the suffrage to women. The voting habits of the American population are something we know a great deal about, and there is just no question but that women, to the extent that they do more than duplicate their husbands' votes, are to be found disproportionately in the conservative wing of the electorate. Yet in all our history books the Nineteenth Amendment is regarded as a progressive and liberal action, not at all as a conservative one. This strikes me as being a curious state of affairs and suggests that there is something odd about the way in which Americans go about writing their history.

Another example. If one were to ask, "What is the most effectively conservative piece of legislation passed by state legislatures in this century?" the answer—which I again submit is both obvious and incontestable—is the popular referendum. There must be hundreds of American historians alive today who, in their respective localities, have seen some of their most cherished and most liberal ideas—school integration, for instance, or less restrictive zoning laws—buried in a referendum. Yet when they enter their classrooms, or write their books, all this is forgotten or ignored. Almost invariably they regard the advent of the popular referendum as a victory for both democracy and liberalism. They are very upset when you point out that this seems not to be the case. And they get utterly bewildered if you dare to suggest that based on certain other conceptions of democracy or liberty one need not regard it as a victory for either.

It is clear that something is at work here that is not to be explained by the ordinary canons of historical scholarship. What is involved, it seems to me, is an ideology so powerful as to represent a kind of religious faith. Indeed, we can fairly call this ideology "the democratic faith," since this term is frequently and approvingly used by members of the congregation themselves. Because it is an authentic faith, it is a very complicated and conglomerate affair. But I believe one can say two truthful and simple things about it.

First of all, it evidently cares much more about ascertaining the source and origin of political power than it does about analyzing the existential consequences of this power. Which is to say, like all faiths it places much more emphasis on men's "good" intentions—in this case, men's democratic intentions—than on whatever may follow from these intentions. And, of course, like all faiths it ends up grappling with the problem of evil—with the existence of disorder, and decay, and injustice, which ought not to exist in a society constructed on democratic principles, but which patently do. This problem itself is usually resolved in the traditional religious way—that is, by assuming that it flows from the conspiracy of wicked demiurges ("vested interests," in American jargon) or the undue influence of "alien" ideas that frustrate the perfection we are entitled to.

Second, and this is but a corollary of my first point, what we are dealing with is obviously *not* a political philosophy. The only reason I go to the trouble of pointing this out is that once upon a time, in this country, the question of democracy *was* a matter for political philosophy, rather than for faith. And the way in which a democratic political philosophy was gradually and inexorably transformed into a democratic faith seems to me to be perhaps the most important problem in American intellectual—and ultimately political—history. In this transformation, American historians have played a significant role—although, being themselves for the most part men of good democratic faith, they have been so busy playing this role that they have rarely got around to explaining it to us, or to themselves.

The difference between a democratic faith and a democratic political philosophy is basically this: Whereas a faith may be attentive to the *problems* of democracy, it has great difficulty perceiving or thinking about the *problematics* of democracy. By "problematics" I mean those kinds of problems that flow from, that are inherent in, that are generated by democracy itself. These problematics change their hue with time and circumstance: The Founding Fathers would have been as bewildered by the current status of the popular referendum as are our progressive historians. But what makes them problematics rather than problems is that they are organically connected with the political system of democracy itself rather than with any external or adventitious factors.

It really is quite extraordinary how the majority of American historians have, until quite recently, determinedly refused to pay attention to any thinker, or any book, that treated democracy as problematic. Although our historians frequently quote from this source, and much effort has been made to determine who wrote which paper, it is a fact that no American historian has ever written a book on The Federalist Papers. (As a further matter of fact, no one in America—historian, political scientist, jurist, or whatever—ever published a book on The Federalist until a few years ago, when a Swiss immigrant scholar rather clumsily broke the ice.) Men like E. L. Godkin, Herbert Croly, Paul Elmer More, even Tocqueville, have interested American historians mainly as "source material"—hardly anyone goes to them to learn anything about American democracy. And it is certainly no accident that our very greatest historian, Henry Adams, who did indeed understand the problematics of democracy, is a "loner," with no historical school or even a noteworthy disciple to carry on in his tradition. As Richard Hofstadter pointed out, there are plenty of Turnerites and Beardites and, of course, Marxists among American historians, but there are no Adamsites or Tocquevillians.

In this respect, the contrast between American historians and the men who created this democracy is a striking one. Although none of the Founding Fathers can be called a political philosopher, most of them were widely read in political philosophy and had given serious thought to the traditional problems of political philosophy. One of these traditional problems was the problematic character of democracies. The Founding Fathers were aware that, in centuries past, democracy—in the sense of the unfettered rule of the demos, of the majority—had been one of the least stable and not always the most admirable of political regimes. And this awareness—shared by practically all educated men of the time— caused them to devise a system that was more democratic than the "mixed regimes" that most political philosophers approved of, yet that also possessed at least some of the virtues thought to be associated with a mixed regime. Such virtues pertained not to the origins of government but to its *ends*. In short, the Founding Fathers sought to establish a "popular government" that could be stable, just, free; where there was security of person and property; and whose public leaders would claim legitimacy not only because they were elected officials but also because their character and behavior approximated some accepted models of excellence. The fact that they used the term "popular government" rather than "democracy" is an accident of historical semantics. They were partisans of self-government—of government by the people—who deliberately and with a bold, creative genius "rigged" the machinery of the system so that this government would be one of which they, as thoughtful and civilized men, could be proud.

In establishing such a popular government, the Founding Fathers were certainly under the impression that they were expressing a faith in the common man. But they were sober and worldly men, and they were not about to hand out blank checks to anyone, even if he was a common man. They thought that political institutions had something to do with the shaping of common men, and they took the question, *"What kind of common man does our popular government produce?"* to be as crucial a consideration as any other. They took it for granted that democracy was capable of bringing evil into the world, and they wanted a system of government that made this as unlikely as possible, and that was provided with as strong an inclination toward self-correction as was possible. And I should guess that they would have regarded as a fair test of their labors the degree to which common men in America could rise to the prospect of choosing uncommon men, speaking for uncommon ideals, as worthy of exercising authority over them.

The Founding Fathers, then, established what they thought to be— and what the world then unanimously thought to be—a democratic process for the American people. But they looked beyond this democratic process to the spirit—the ideal intent—that might animate it. This conception is very nicely expressed in words that Matthew Arnold a century later directed toward his American audiences:

The difficulty for democracy is, how to find and keep high ideals. The individuals who compose it are, the bulk of them, persons who need to follow an ideal, not to set one; and one ideal of goodness, high feeling, and fine culture, which an aristocracy once supplied to them, they lose by the very fact of ceasing to be a lower order and becoming a democracy. Nations are not truly great solely because the individuals composing them are numerous, free, and active; but they are great when these numbers, this freedom, and this activity are employed in the service of an ideal higher than that of an ordinary man, taken by himself.

These words doubtless sound anachronistic to the ears of those who have in their lifetime heard a president of the United States declare that he would disarm the ideological opponents of democracy by distributing the Sears, Roebuck catalog among them. But such words would not have sounded strange to the Founding Fathers, many of whom had occasion to say much the same thing. Between the political philosophy of the Founding Fathers and the ideology of the Sears, Roebuck catalog, there stretches the fascinating—and still largely untold—story of what happened to the democratic idea in America.

In the writing of our first major historian, George Bancroft, one can already see a clear premonition of things to come. His was a muted and rather covert operation: The Jacksonians, of whom Bancroft was one, were not eager to emphasize any ideological or philosophical differences they might have had with the Founding Fathers, whose memory was still revered among the electorate. Nevertheless, what was involved in Bancroft's work was a giant step toward the redefinition of the democratic idea. It is striking that in his voluminous writings Bancroft paid hardly any attention—gave only passing notice—to *The Federalist*. Indeed, in his *History of the Formation of the Constitution* he pretty much denied that the Founding Fathers had any serious political ideas in their heads at all. "The men who framed it [the Constitution] followed the lead of no theoretical writer of their own or preceding times. . . . They wrought from the elements which were at hand, and shaped them to meet the new experiences which had arisen." It was important for Bancroft to assert this, because he did not want to seem to be taking issue with the Founding Fathers in articulating his belief that "the common judgment in taste, politics, and religion is the highest authority on earth, and the nearest possible approach to an infallible decision." Bancroft's strategy was to defend Jacksonian democracy as a restoration of the original republic in the face of an "aristocratic" conspiracy. It was only if, as Bancroft claimed, the Founding Fathers had no political ideas that his own political ideas could be represented as the natural extension of their work. In fact, and of course, Bancroft's notion of popular infallibility was utterly alien to the Founding Fathers, and had been explicitly rejected by them.

It was, then, within less than half a century of the founding of the republic that this major revolution in American thought took place, that an original political *philosophy* of democracy was replaced with a religious *faith* in democracy. The sources of this revolution—in theology, in literature, and in politics itself—are not at all mysterious, although they have usually been studied in quite other connections. And the impact of this revolution on American politics and American thought is no mystery, either. Still, the men who were involved in it were usually careful to play down its revolutionary character, and preferred to say—some in all sincerity, others with a seeming sincerity that I find suspect—that all they were doing was to draw some natural inferences from the heritage bequeathed to them by the Founding Fathers.

The nature of this new democratic faith was perhaps most candidly expressed, in political terms, by George Sidney Camp in his book *Democracy* (1841). Camp claimed that his book was the first defense of democracy as the best form of government for all people, in all places, at all times, ever to be written in the United States. So far as I know, he is absolutely justified in this claim. No man who ever studied political philosophy, and seriously contemplated the problems of governing men, had ever said such a thing; certainly none among the Founding Fathers ever did. But Camp could and did say it because he and his contemporaries had abolished political philosophy, to all intents and purposes, and replaced it with a transcendental faith in the common man. The quality of this transcendental faith can be exemplified by quotations from dozens of writers of the time, of which the following—from the senior Henry James, in 1852—is not untypical:

> Democracy is not so much a new form of political life as a dissolution and disorganization of old forms. It is simply a resolution of government into the hands of the people, a taking down of that which has before existed, and a recommitment of it to its original sources.

In this mass endeavor at redefining the democratic idea, historians after Bancroft were much less involved than poets, publicists, and men of letters. On the contrary: American historians of the nineteenth century were distinctly more Whiggish and neo-Federalist in their ideological complexion than other classes of writers. Most of them were born in

Whiggish households, were engaged in such Whiggish occupations as university education and the law, and had connections with the genteel Brahmin culture of New England and New York. One can understand, therefore, why they were not easy converts to the new transcendental faith of democracy. What is less easy to understand is how most of them—always excepting Adams—managed to dodge any kind of direct confrontation with the transformation of American democracy that was occurring before their very eyes. Perhaps they were intimidated by popular opinion; perhaps, as patriotic Americans, they were reluctant to look too hard and too closely at this matter; perhaps they really did believe that, although the democratic faith clearly represented a departure from the political philosophy of the Founding Fathers, nevertheless this was a temporary phenomenon, and that ultimately there would be an amiable convergence. Whatever the explanation, however, it is the case that the bulk of nineteenth-century American historiography has about it a curious evasiveness, what one may even call a lack of relevance. (In the case of someone like Parkman, who was perhaps the most gifted of his generation, it is not too harsh to use the term "escapism.") That this is more than a personal impression on my part is indicated by the fact that American historians of today have little occasion to refer back to these predecessors—and, indeed, most of their writings are out of print.

Such was the situation until the advent of Turner and Beard—at which point, of course, everything changed. Now, for the first time, the historical profession—the official guardians of our civic traditions—made explicit to the American mind what had conveniently been hitherto implicit in American life: the repudiation of the political philosophy of the Founding Fathers. The shock of recognition that this effected upon the American public was profound and unwelcome.

In browsing through the literature generated by "the Turner thesis" and "the Beard thesis," I am impressed by the way in which most twentieth-century historians have managed to convert an important ideological debate into a matter of academic opinion. Much of this literature centers around the question of whether Turner and Beard were right or wrong in the inferences they drew from their evidence. Only rarely will a historian poke around the premises on which Turner and Beard established their historical writings. Yet it is these premises that are the most interesting and important aspects of their work.

In Turner's writings, the various things he has to say about the frontier are of no great significance compared with the way he uses the term "democracy." After all, no one has ever doubted that the frontier experience had an impact on the American character, that this impact was in the direction of egalitarianism, and that this egalitarianism in turn has had repercussions in all areas of American life. The exact degree of the egalitarian tilt that the frontier, as compared with other influences, did exercise is an issue that may be—and has been—debated. But Turner would hardly have created such a fuss, he would hardly be the major historian he is, if all he had done was to call attention in a somewhat exaggerated fashion to the influence of the frontier. To appreciate Turner's importance, I would argue, one has to see him not so much as a historian as an ideologue; and to understand his work fully, one should regard it as being primarily an ideological enterprise.

The point of this enterprise is indeed to be found in Turner's famous dictum that American democracy was born on the frontier—but that point is not to be found where we have customarily looked at it. Turner was not saying anything terribly novel about the frontier, but he *was* saying something new and important about the way we should use the term "democracy." In effect, he was redefining the democratic idea for the historical profession along lines that had already become familiar outside this profession. He was saying that by democracy we ought to mean the Jacksonian-egalitarian-populist transcendental faith in the common man, and he was further explicitly stating that this was something different from, and antithetical to, the kind of democratic political philosophy that the Founding Fathers believed in. Turner made Americans aware that the conventional republican pieties, which used the word "democracy" as little more than a synonym for "American," were, to say the least, ambiguous. And he offered to young historians the exciting prospect of rewriting American history in the light of a democratic faith.

To get a clear notion of what Turner really did, it is useful to turn to an earlier essay on the relation of the frontier to American democracy. I refer to the essay by E. L. Godkin entitled "Aristocratic Opinions of Democracy," which was published in 1865. The fact that this essay is not much read, and only infrequently referred to, even by historians of American democracy, indicates with what success Turner achieved his true intention—which was, precisely, to make essays like Godkin's as unread and unremembered as possible, even by historians of American democracy.

Godkin's essay is a thoughtful rejoinder to what he took to be Tocqueville's excessively pessimistic views of the prospects for American democracy. Whether or not Godkin was correct in his interpretation of Tocqueville is here beside the point. In any case, Godkin—who regarded himself as a perfectly good American democrat—was dismayed by what he took to be Tocqueville's assertion that the many virtues of American democracy were incompatible with a high degree of civilization, an elevated culture, and a noble conception of public life. He conceded that these were not yet to be found in America, but attributed their absence to the special material circumstances of American history—*and especially to the continual, pervasive influence of the frontier*. Although Godkin had many kind words for the frontier, he did allow that it was the aggressive, self-seeking individualism, the public disorderliness, the philistine materialism of the American frontier that prevented American democracy from achieving a more splendid destiny. And he held out the hope that, as the influence of the frontier inevitably declined, the quality of American civilization and of American public life would markedly improve.

Now, it is clear that Godkin's idea of democracy was not Turner's—was, indeed, very much at odds with Turner's. It was what we would today designate as a neo-Federalist idea, which regarded egalitarianism as not only an attribute of democracy but also a problem for it, which was very much concerned with seeing to it that the American democracy was deferential to certain high republican ideals—and, of course, to those republican institutions and those "best men" that represented these ideals. Turner never refuted Godkin; Turner—even in his later years, when his feelings about the frontier were mixed—never really tried to come to terms with Godkin; he never really argued, in a serious way, with anyone whose conception of democracy differed from his own. He simply did what all successful ideologues do when they establish a new orthodoxy; he ignored, and persuaded everyone else to ignore, the very existence of these different views—and where this was impossible, he blandly excluded these views from the spectrum of democratic opinion, relocating them on another spectrum vaguely called "aristocratic."

I shall not discuss Charles A. Beard in any detail, since his originality, like Turner's, lay in persuading the historical profession to accept the new ideological redefinition of the democratic idea. Aside from imputing crudely self-interested motives to the founders—a bit of malice that was not really crucial to his argument—Beard, so far as I can see, ended up with the aggressive assertion that the Founding Fathers were not Jack-sonian democrats and were men of only partial democratic faith. He was right, of course. The really interesting question is *why* they were not, and whether perhaps they might have had good reason for being what they were. It was not until the end of his life that Beard addressed himself to this question, and in the course of answering it he tacitly abandoned his original thesis. But, by this time, American historians had naturally ceased being interested in Beard.

Nor shall I say anything more about the "progressive" school of histor-ical scholarship that has been the dominant orthodoxy of these past six decades. I am sure I have made it sufficiently clear that, whatever the merits—and they are often considerable—of particular progressive his-torians, their work seems to me crucially deficient by virtue of their *simpliste* conception of democracy. I find too much theodicy in their writings, and too little political philosophy. I have learned much from them—but only rarely have I learned what they set out to teach me.

As one might expect, I am far more sympathetic to the work of the so-called revisionists—such men as Richard Hofstadter, Marvin Meyers, Stanley Elkins, and others—who have perceived that the democratic faith of progressive historiography does not really square with the facts of our democratic history. These are the historians of my lifetime whom I find most instructive and most "relevant." And yet in the end I have to con-clude that even they are curiously unsatisfying. They trouble me because they are, precisely, revisionists in their attitude and perspective. That is to say, they are excellent in pointing out the shortcomings of the standard, progressive account of such historical phenomena as Jacksonianism, abo-litionism, populism. But it is never clear to me what they would put in its place—or whether, indeed, they really want to go so far as to put anything new in its place. They seem to see their task as primarily corrective, and while their corrections strike me as persuasive and pertinent, such revi-sionism leaves me with the feeling that many important things—perhaps even the most important things—remain to be said.

It is true that a few scholars, sometimes counted very loosely among the revisionists, *have* offered such a perspective and general statement. But this only reinforces my uneasiness. Thus, in reacting against the notion that American history can be seen as one long conflict between those of true democratic faith and an ever-incipient "aristocratic" reac-tion, Daniel Boorstin has emphasized—quite correctly, in my view—the "consensus" in political attitudes that most Americans have, throughout their history, subscribed to. For him, the relative immunity of our society to ideological speculation is a fortunate circumstance, and he quotes with approval Edmund Burke: "The bulk of mankind on their part are not excessively curious concerning any theories, whilst they are really happy; and one sure symptom of an ill-conducted state is the propensity of the people to resort to them." Now I happen to agree with both Burke and Boorstin on the truth of this proposition. I dislike ideologically turbulent societies because they have a tendency to barbarize men who may previously have been at least modestly civilized, and to primitivize ideas that may previously have been at least modestly fine and complex. But I would go on to note that Boorstin is reading Burke carelessly, and that Burke does not mean what Boorstin seems to think he does. Burke, in this quotation, was talking about "the bulk of mankind" and "the people." He was *not* talking about political philosophers or historians or scholars—he was, after all, one himself. Burke thought it was a disaster when political philosophies became popular ideologies. But he never meant to suggest that truly thoughtful men should not engage in political philosophy, and one can hardly doubt that he valued political philosophy and political philosophers very highly. Burke could not have had a high regard for a society where *no one* was engaging in the serious study of politics—a study that was, for him, one of the noblest of human enterprises. In short, I do not think Burke, were he alive today, would regard the history of American democracy with quite the same satisfaction that Boorstin does. He might even be somewhat appalled at the enduring *mindlessness* of this democracy.

Professor Louis Hartz has also a new and general interpretation of American history. But there is an interesting difference between Hartz and Boorstin. Where Boorstin emphasizes the *non*-ideological character of American democracy, Hartz emphasizes its *uni*-ideological character. He, too, stresses the extent to which American political opinion has represented an enduring consensus, but this time it is around an idea, and does not merely reflect, as in Boorstin, a "pragmatic" adaptation to life on the American continent. The idea—the American liberal-democratic idea—is compounded of a few Lockean dogmas. And the history of American thought is little more than the changes rung—the permutations and combinations—within this idea.

Anyone who is even reasonably familiar with European history over these past two centuries cannot doubt the validity of this thesis—cannot doubt that, in comparison with Europe, America has had a remarkable homogeneity of ideology. But what is truly astonishing is that Hartz, after demonstrating the dominion of Lockean ideology, proceeds to insist that ideology itself is of no importance anyway. "The system of democracy," he tells us, "works by virtue of certain processes which its theory never describes, to which, indeed, its theory is actually hostile." This process involves "group coercion, crowd psychology, and economic power"; out of the push and pull of conflicting interests, there emerges an equilibrium that represents a kind of gross public interest. If and when we examine the ideology of this democratic process, and find it faulty or deficient, this is a crisis of democracy's image, not of its reality—a mere "agony of the mind rather than of the real world."

I must say that I was taken aback when Hartz, who is an intellectual historian of considerable talent and insight, led me to this conclusion. Only in America, I thought, could a historian of ideas—whose major work reveals the very great influence that a particular version of the democratic idea has had upon our history—end up with the assertion that political mind has no dominion over political matter. That the statement is false on the basis of Hartz's own work bothers me less than the fact that it is false in general—I honestly do not see how any intelligent man with even the slightest bit of worldly experience could entertain this belief. The political ideas that men have *always* help to shape the political reality they live in—and this is so whether these be habitual opinions, tacit convictions, or explicit ideologies. It is ideas that establish and define in men's minds the categories of the politically possible and the politically impossible, the desirable and the undesirable, the tolerable and the intolerable. And what is more ultimately real, politically, than the structure of man's political imagination? Hartz's own book reveals that there is nothing more real; and his book will survive the rather bewildering lessons he has managed to learn from it.

Reading Boorstin and Hartz, one comes away with the strong impression that America has been a very lucky country. I do not doubt this for a moment. But unless one is willing to claim that this luck is a sign of an enduring Divine benevolence—unless one believes that Americans are indeed sons of the Covenant, a chosen people—it is very difficult to argue from the fact of luck to the notion that democracy in America is a *good* form of government, or that we have more than an expediential commitment to this form of government. And while, as I have said, I recognize America's good luck, I really cannot believe that Americans are a historically unique and chosen people. I am myself a Jew and an American, and with all due respect to the Deity, I think the odds are prohibitive that He would have gone out of His way to choose me twice over.

Lucky we have been, but perhaps our luck is beginning to run out. I believe that all of us are well aware that the areas of American life that are becoming unstable and problematic are increasing in numbers and size every day. Yet our initial response—and it usually remains our final response—is to echo Al Smith: "All the ills of democracy can be cured by more democracy." But is this really true? Is it true of our mass media, of our political party system, of our foreign policy, of our crisis in race relations? Is it not possible that many of the ills of our democracy can be traced to this democracy itself—or, more exactly, to this democracy's conception of itself? And how are we even to contemplate this possibility if our historians seem so unaware of it?

It appears to me that there is a great deal of work still to be done in American history. To begin with, one would like to know *why* the political philosophy of the Founding Fathers was so ruthlessly unmanned by American history. Was it the result of inherent flaws in that political philosophy itself? Was it a failure of statesmanship? Was it a consequence of external developments that were unpredictable and uncontrollable? These questions have hardly been asked, let alone answered. And the reason they have not been asked is, first of all, the dominance of the progressive historian, who sees American history in terms of an ineluctable and providential "Rise of the Common Man," and, second, that even the revisionists shy away from raising the basic issues of political philosophy that are involved.

I should like to think that I am as good a democrat as the average historian, with as genuine an affection for the common man. But unlike the "consensus historians," I do not see that the condition of American democracy is such as automatically to call forth my love and honor, although I respect it enough to offer it my obedience. And unlike the so-called "conflict historians," I get no relief in discovering as many instances as possible of civil strife and mob disorder. Both of these schools of thought, it seems to me, perceive the common man—the one in his potential for merely self-centered activity, the other in his exclusive potential for resisting authority—in terms that remind me of Ortega's definition of the "mass man": the individual who is not capable of assuming responsibility for self-limitation, for a kind of self-definition that is both generous and self-respecting. Interestingly enough, Ortega's definition of the mass man is identical with Plato's definition of the tyrant. Which in turn suggests that the idea of the tyranny of the majority—whether it be an essentially mindless, self-seeking majority or a simply rancorous one—is capable of more general application than has hitherto been thought to be the case. And this, in its turn, leads me to wonder whether American historians themselves have not too frequently, and all too willingly, fallen victim to what is ultimately a tyrannical vulgarization of the democratic idea.

1970

26

Urban Civilization and Its Discontents

It is in the nature of democratic countries that, sooner or later, all serious controversy—whether it be political, social, or economic—will involve an appeal to the democratic principle as the supreme arbiter of the rights and the wrongs of the affair. One might begin by invoking the idea of justice, or liberty, or equity, or natural rights; but in the end what is unjust or illiberal or unnatural—or even what is simply "un-American"—will be defined in terms of what is most properly democratic. It follows, therefore, that to the extent to which our idea of democracy is vague or unrealistic or self-contradictory, we shall be less able to resolve the issues that divide us.

I do not mean, of course, that a neat and precise and generally accepted definition of democracy will in and of itself automatically pacify the body politic and avoid bitter conflicts of interests and values. There is no magic in ideas, even when we superstitiously attribute a quasi-divine authority to them. But ideas do give shape to our sentiments, our consciences, and our moral energies. And a muddled idea can, in time, give birth to some fairly grotesque political realities. One has only to recall that, for nearly a century after the formation of the American republic, it was widely accepted that our idea of democracy for all was compatible with a condition of slavery for some, to realize that this is no mere abstract possibility. And the fact that it required a bloody civil war to establish what the authentic intentions of our democracy were would indicate that—as in

328

certain older theological controversies that disrupted the real world of Christendom—the precise meaning of the democratic dogma can have the most material bearing upon the kind of society we live in and the ways in which we live in it.

At the moment, for example, we are all of us much exercised about the quality of life in our American urban civilization. I have no intention, at this time, of analyzing the numerous problems which make up what we familiarly call the "crisis of our cities." Instead, I should like to focus on the apparent incapacity of our democratic and urban civilization to come to grips with these problems. In other words, if it is proper to say that we experience the crisis of our cities, it is equally proper to say that we *are* the urban crisis. And what I want to suggest further is that one of the main reasons we are so problematic to ourselves is the fact that we are creating a democratic, urban civilization while stubbornly refusing to think clearly about the relation of urbanity to democracy.

In this respect, we are far removed indeed from the Founding Fathers of this republic, who thought deeply about this relationship—but in a way so uncongenial to us that we find it most difficult to take their thinking seriously. We even find it difficult to study their thinking fairly. Thus, in the many books that have appeared in recent years surveying the history of the American city and of American attitudes toward the city, we usually find a discussion of the "agrarian bias" of the Founding Fathers. More often than not, this is taken quite simply to mean that their opinions were an unreflective expression of their rural condition: a provincial prejudice, familiar enough—the antagonism of country to town is no new thing—and understandable enough in human terms, but now to be regarded as rather quaint and entirely unilluminating. I think that this approach is not only an obstacle to our understanding the American past; it also represents a lost opportunity for us to take our bearings in the present.

To take such a bearing, we ought to begin with an appreciation of the fact that the ideas of the Founding Fathers did not, in their sum, amount to an agrarian *bias* so much as an antiurban *philosophy*; which is to say, the Founding Fathers had reasons for thinking as they did, and until we consider these reasons and come to terms with them, we are more likely to be living testimony to the validity of their apprehensions than to the presumed anachronistic character of these apprehensions.

The Founding Fathers saw democracy in America as resting upon two major pillars. The first, whose principles and rationale are so superbly set forth in *The Federalist Papers*, was the "new science of government" which made popular government possible in a large and heterogeneous republic. This new science designed a machinery of self-government that has to be considered as one of the most remarkable political inventions of Western man. The machinery is by now familiar to us; representative and limited government, separation of powers; majority rule but refined so that it had to express the will of various majorities elected in various ways; a diffusion of political and economic power which would thwart the intentions of any single-minded faction no matter how large and influential, and so on and so forth. The basic idea behind all these arrangements was that the pursuit of self-interest was the most reliable of human motivations on which to build a political system—but this pursuit had to be, to use one of their favorite phrases, the pursuit of self-interest "rightly understood," and such right understanding needed the benevolent, corrective checks and balances of the new political machinery to achieve decent self-definition—that is, to converge at a point of commonweal.

The second pillar envisaged by the Founding Fathers was of a spiritual order—and the fact that most of us today prefer to call it "psychological" rather than spiritual would have been taken by them as itself a clear sign of urban decadence. To designate this pillar they used such phrases as "republican morality" or "civic virtue," but what they had constantly in mind was the willingness of the good democratic citizen, on critical occasions, to transcend the habitual pursuit of self-interest and devote himself directly and disinterestedly to the common good. In times of war, of course, republican morality took the form of patriotism—no one, after all, has ever been able to demonstrate that it is to a man's self-interest to die for his country. In times of peace, republican morality might take the form of agreeing to hold public office; since the Founding Fathers assumed that the holders of such office would be men of property, to whom the pleasures of private life were readily available, and since they further thought of political ambition as a form of human distemper, they could candidly look upon public service as a burden as well as an honor. But whatever the occasion, such a capacity for disinterested action seemed to them—as even today, it still seems to some—a necessary complement to the pursuit of self-interest rightly understood.

Now, given these ideas on how popular government in America could survive and prosper, it is only natural that the Founding Fathers should have taken a suspicious view of big cities and should have wondered whether, in the end, they could be compatible with a free and popular government. In this suspicion and wonder they were anything but original. The entire literature of classical political philosophy—from Plato, Aristotle, and Cicero on to Montesquieu—exhibits a similar skepticism, to put it mildly, concerning the quality of life that people lead in big cities, and expresses doubt whether the habits of mind generated there—what we might call the urban mentality: irreverent, speculative, pleasure-loving, self-serving, belligerent toward all conventional pieties—are compatible with republican survival. Nor, it should be observed, did the real, historical world present much reassurance, by way of contrary evidence. The big cities that the Founding Fathers knew or read about all displayed in luxuriant abundance the very vices they wished above all to avoid in the new nation they were constructing. From imperial Rome to imperial London and Paris, the big city was the locus of powerful, illiberal, and undemocratic government, inhabited by people who were either too wretched and depraved to be free, democratic citizens, or by ambitious, self-seeking men to whom the ideals of popular government were utterly alien and even repugnant.

That *small* cities could be soberly and democratically governed, the Founding Fathers understood well enough—Geneva and Athens and the towns of New England testified to that. That medium-sized cities could sustain a modified and partial form of popular government, based on a deferential citizenry and a patrician elite, they also knew—the histories of republican Rome and Venice were very familiar to them, and their own Boston or Philadelphia offered them living instances of this general truth. But the wisdom of the ages had reached an unequivocal conclusion, in which they concurred, about large, populous, cosmopolitan cities: The anonymous creatures massed in such a place, clawing one another in a sordid scramble for survival, advantage, or specious distinction, their frantic lives reflecting no piety toward nature, God, or the political order—such people were not of the stuff of which a free-standing, self-governing republic could be created. Or, to put this point in a more philosophical way, which would have been immediately comprehensible to our ancestors even if it sounds a little strange to us: If self-government, as an ideal to be respected, means the willingness of people to permit their baser selves to be directed by their better selves, then this precondition of self-government is least likely to be discovered among the turbulent and impassioned masses of big cities.

Today, in the second half of the twentieth century, this theory of the Founding Fathers is being put to the test, and I do not see how anyone can be blithely sanguine about the ultimate conclusions that will be drawn. Our most obvious difficulty is that we have so many big cities and seem so persistently inept in devising a satisfactory machinery of self-government in them—swinging wildly from the corrupt rule of political machines to abortive experiments in decentralized, direct democracy, with a slovenly bureaucracy providing the barest minimum of stability in between. This is indeed a sore perplexity to us; and no clear solution seems visible even to the most thoughtful among us—witness the uncertainty among our political scientists whether our major cities should evolve into supercities, almost little 'states, or whether they would be better off dissolving into mini-cities, almost small towns. Twenty years ago the first prospect seemed the more enchanting; today it is the second; tomorrow the winds of doctrine might once again suddenly reverse themselves. Our ideas about our cities are as unsettled and as uneasy as the cities themselves.

But this obvious difficulty is only the smaller part of the challenge posed us. Though we are indeed becoming ever more "a nation of cities," we are *not*—despite a contrary impression created by the news media—on our way to becoming a nation of very big cities. The proportion of our population in cities of over one million has been drifting downward for several decades now, and this proportion is, in the decades ahead, more likely to decline further than it is to increase. Many of the traditional functions of the great metropolis are being radically decentralized, both by technological and by sociological innovation. Air travel has already robbed the metropolis of its role as a transportation hub for people; air freight is gradually doing the same thing for goods. And just think of the extraordinary way in which our cultural community—our writers and artists and sculptors and musicians and dramatists—has, with recent years, been dispersed among the university campuses of the nation. A city like New York is more and more becoming a showplace for the work of creative artists, rather than a milieu in which they live. Even bohemia, that most urban of cultural phenomena, has been transplanted to and around the university campus.

It is conceivable, therefore, that, though our major cities keep floundering in a sea of troubles, the nation as a whole will not be profoundly affected. And what so many people now proclaim to be an imminent apocalypse may yet turn out to be not much more than—though it is also not much less than—a change of life for our older cities. Even the most critical problem which today confronts these cities—the problem of black Americans living in the squalid isolation of their ghettos—may yet reveal to posterity a very different meaning from the despairing significance we ascribe to it today. For these are the citizens who, if we are lucky, might infuse these cities with a new vigor and a new purpose. It is hard to see who else can accomplish this—it is hard even to see who else would care enough to try. As a white New Yorker, born and bred, I am bound to have confused feelings about such a course of events. But I should like to think I am a sufficiently objective student of the city not to see as a crisis what may merely be a personal problem of adaptation to historical change.

But I digress: Because I am a man who has lived all his life in big, old cities, I am inevitably more keenly interested in them than, as a student of the contemporary city, I perhaps ought to be. The overwhelming majority of my fellow Americans clearly prefer to live elsewhere, and this preference is by now an established feature of American life, for better or worse. If we are a nation of cities, we are also becoming to an ever greater degree a nation of relatively small and middle-sized cities. These are the growing centers of American life—especially if we count as "small cities," as we should, those scattered university campuses which support populations of 30,000 or more. It is quite true that these new cities are not spread uniformly over the land but tend to cluster in what we call "metropolitan areas." This fact has led some observers to conclude hastily that such settlements have only a transient, juridical existence—that they ought properly to be regarded as part of an incipient "megalopolis," in the process of coalescing. This is almost surely an illusion—or, if one prefers, a nightmare. Though a great many urban sociologists and urban journalists seem to be convinced that Americans in large numbers would really prefer to live in the central city and are being forced out of their cities by one external cause or another, the evidence is quite plainly to the contrary. People leave the big cities, or refuse to come to them, because they positively prefer the kinds of lives they can lead in smaller suburban townships or cities of modest size; and these people are not going to become citizens of any kind of megalopolis.

Indeed, though most central cities are now aware of their ghetto populations only as a source of trouble and calamity, one can predict with considerable confidence that ten years from now these same central cities
will be fighting tooth-and-nail to hold on to these populations, as they
too begin to experience the attractions of urban life outside our major
urban centers.

And here, I think, we have at last come to what I would consider the
heart of the matter. For the overwhelming fact of American life today,
whether this life be lived in a central city or a suburb or a small city—or
even in those rural areas where something like a third of our population
still resides—is that it is *life in an urban civilization*. In terms of the *quality*
of American life, the United States is now one vast metropolis. Cities are
nothing new; the problems of cities are nothing new; but an urban civilization is very new indeed, and the problems of an urban civilization are
without precedent in human history.

When I say that our urban civilization is something radically new, I am
obviously not unmindful of the historical fact that, in a profound sense,
just about every civilization we have known has been urban in origin and
character. Civilization, both the high and the low of it, is something that
has always been bred in cities—which is why all romantic rebels against
civilization, in the past as in our own time, so vehemently repudiate the
"artificiality" and "superficiality" and "inhumanity" of city life. But the
city and its civilization have always been one thing, while the rest of the
nation and its way of life have been another. Between these two things
there has always existed a high degree of tension—on the whole a creative tension, though it has sometimes found release in exceedingly ugly
moments. Between urban life in the city and provincial life outside the
city there has always been a gulf of mistrust, suspicion, and contempt.
Yet it is not too far-fetched to say that each was an indispensable antibody for the other's healthy existence. Life in the city could, for example, be careless of conventional morality, and even have an experimental
attitude toward all moral rules, precisely because of the reassuring certainty that, throughout the rest of the nation, there prevailed a heavy
dullness and conformity. This dullness and conformity reassured the city
man, even as he mocked it, that his moral experiments were in the
nature of singular explorations with no necessary collective consequences. Similarly, the sovereignty of conventional morality outside the

city was sustained by reason of the fact that those who would rebel against it simply emigrated to the urban center. In addition, the rigid character of this traditional morality was made more tolerable to the provincial citizenry because of the known and inevitable fact that, in most cases, urban experiments in freedom were not equally or altogether successful for the individual who was presumptuous enough to engage in them. And when they did succeed—when they resulted in artistic creativity or political distinction—the provincial nation participated, at no cost to itself, in the glory.

Now, this provincial nation has been liquidated. To anyone like myself who watches old movies on television—and by old movies I mean no more than fifteen or twenty years old—the most striking impression is of a world that belongs to another era. These movies have farmers' daughters—honest-to-goodness farmers' daughters, with all that this implies for the sophisticated urban imagination; they have happy, neighborly suburban families who smugly and snugly pass the evening watching themselves on television; they have prim schoolmarms and prissy schoolmistresses; they have absentminded professors who do not know the difference between a foundation garment and a foundation grant; they have hicks who run gas stations and cops who drop in for apple pie; they have children who address their fathers as "sir"; they have virginal college maidens and hardly any graduate students at all; they have wildly efficient and fanatically loyal secretaries—in short, they have a race of people who only yesterday were the average and the typical, and who have so suddenly become, in their laughable unreality, a species of "camp."

What has happened, clearly, is that provincial America—that America which at least paid lip service to, if it did not live by, the traditional republican morality; that America which, whether on the farm or in suburb or small town, thought it important to preserve the appearance of a life lived according to the prescriptions of an older agrarian virtue and piety; that America which was calmly philistine and so very, very solid in its certainties—that America is now part and parcel of urban civilization. The causes of this transformation are so obvious as to need no elaboration; one can simply refer in passing to the advent of the mass media and of mass higher education, and there is not much more that needs to be said. The ultimate consequences of this transformation, however, are anything but obvious. We know what happens—both for good and bad;

and it is ineluctably for both good and bad—when an urban center liberates the energies—both for creation and destruction; and it is ineluctably for both—of provincial émigrés; what happens constitutes the history of urban civilization. But we do not know what happens, for the sufficient reason that it has never happened before, when an urban civilization becomes a mass phenomenon, when the culture of the city becomes everyman's culture, and when urban habits of mind and modes of living become the common mentality and way of life for everyone.

If the Founding Fathers were worried about the effects of a few large cities upon the American capacity of self-government, what—one wonders—would they make of our new condition? One is reasonably certain they would regard it as an utterly impossible state of affairs. And whether they would be correct in this regard is something that it will be up to us to determine. Certainly the history of American cities, during this past century and a half, does not permit us to dismiss their fears as either irrational or anachronistic. Though these cities have made America great, and though a city like New York can be said—especially in these last years, when it has become a world cultural capital—to have made America glorious, it does not follow, as we so naturally might think, that they have strengthened the fundaments of American democracy. Greatness and glory are things the human race has always prized highly, but we ought not to forget that the political philosophers of democracy have always looked upon them with distrust, as virtues appropriate to empires rather than to self-governing republics, and have emphasized moral earnestness and intellectual sobriety as elements that are most wanted in a democracy.

We can, perhaps, have a better appreciation of the problem we have created for ourselves if we start from the proposition—which sounds like a tautology but has far-reaching implications—that in a democracy the people are the ruling class. This does not mean, of course, that the people as a whole run the affairs of state or that the people's will finds prompt expression in the decisions of government. Even in a society which is officially an aristocracy, the ruling class never has that kind of instant power and instant authority. Indeed, one suspects that a government which was *so* responsible would barely have the capacity to govern at all—and one knows for certain that, were such a government to exist, it could be manned only by servile mediocrities who set no value upon their own opinions or judgment. No, when one says that in a democracy the people are the ruling class, one means that the character of the government and the destiny of the nation are in the longer run determined by the character of the people rather than of any particular class of people.

I know that we are today unaccustomed to thinking in terms such as these, and that the very phrase "the character of the people" has an odd ring to it. In part, this is because American political theory, as it has evolved into American political science, has tended to conceive of democracy exclusively in terms of procedural and mechanical arrangements—in terms of self-interested individuals who rightly understand that it is to their own interest to follow the "rules of the game." This idea goes back to the Founding Fathers, as has been said—but taken by itself, and divorced from the idea of republican morality, it leads to a self-destructive paradox, as some political scientists have recently come to realize. For when everyone follows the rules of the game, it can then be demonstrated—with all the rigor of a mathematical theorem—that it is to the self-interest of individuals or of organized factions *not* to follow the rules of the game, but simply to take advantage of the fact that the others do. That there are such individuals and factions, only too willing to draw this logical inference, and to act upon it, current American events vividly remind us. And political science, being "value-free," as they say, cannot come up with any persuasive arguments as to why they should not act this way.

Another reason why we cannot seriously contemplate this question of "the character of the people" is that, in the generations which succeeded that of the Founding Fathers, it came to be believed that this character was not something formed by individual efforts at moral self-definition, but rather that the popular character was inherently good enough—not perfect perhaps, but good enough—so as not to require self-scrutiny. What we may call the transcendental-populist religion of democracy superseded an original political philosophy of democracy. This religion has now so strong a hold that the mention of the very idea of a "corrupt people," a common idea in classical political philosophy, is taken as evidence of a nasty antidemocratic bias upon the part of the thinker who would dare entertain it. If things go wrong in our democracy, the persons we are least likely to blame are ourselves. Instead, we seek out the influence of wicked "vested interests," malign "outside agitators," or arrogant "Establishments."

I am not asserting that the American people, at this moment, are a corrupt people—though it worries me that they are so blandly free from self-doubt about this possibility. What I am saying is that they are more and more behaving in a way that would have alarmed the Founding Fathers even as it would have astonished them. To put it bluntly, they are more and more behaving like a collection of mobs.

The term "mob" entered the language in the latter part of the eighteenth century and was used to describe the new population of the new industrial cities that were then emerging. This population was not only a population uprooted from its villages; it was also déraciné with regard to traditional pieties, whether religious, moral, or political. It was a population which felt itself—as in truth it largely was—the victim of external forces, in no way responsible for its own fate, and therefore indifferent to its own character. It was a population which, in its political dependency, could be exploited by unscrupulous profiteers; it was a population which, in its political isolation, could be exploited by zealous demagogues; it was a population which, in its moral bewilderment, could be exploited by wild mystagogues; it was a population whose potential did not go much beyond riotous destructiveness.

It was because the Founding Fathers did not see how such a population could be capable of self-government that they took so dim a view of large cities. The mob, as it was then to be seen in London and Paris, and even incipiently in New York or Boston, seemed to them the very antithesis of a democratic citizenry: a citizenry self-reliant, self-determining, and at least firmly touched by, if not thoroughly infused with, republican morality. It takes a transcendental-populist faith of truly enormous dimensions to find in this attitude a mere agrarian bias. The Founding Fathers were philosophic men, of no such populist faith, and they had no qualms about insisting that popular government was sustained by "a people" as distinct from a mob.

The history of all modern industrial societies is the story of the gradual transformation of original urban mobs into a people, even as their numbers increased manyfold. The secret behind this transformation was not faith but economics—and especially the economics of technological innovation. If it did not occur to the Founding Fathers that such a transformation was likely or even possible, this was because they could have no intimation of the fantastic economic growth that the coming century and a half would experience. It was not, indeed, until the turn of this century that thinking men began to be shaken loose from their Malthusian spectacles and to be able to see things as they really were. Even so intelligent and liberal a thinker as E. L. Godkin, in several decades of writing for the *Nation*, could not disabuse himself of the notion that the lower urban classes were doomed to exist as something like a permanent mob by the iron laws of Malthusian doctrine. The politics of such a mob, obviously, could only be the politics of expropriation as against the bourgeois politics of participation.

Well, it worked out differently and better. As productivity increased, the urban mob became an urban citizenry—and, more recently, a suburban citizenry, mimicking in an urban context various aspects of that agrarian lifestyle which was once thought to be of such political significance. The "bourgeoisification" of society was *the* great event of modern history. Where once we had the bourgeois confronting the masses, we now have bourgeois masses—a fact which has been a source of concern to revolutionary romantics and romantic revolutionaries, both of whom have expectations for the masses which far outrun the bourgeois condition. Even many cautious liberals have been taken aback at the ease with which this society was breeding bourgeois men and women, and a small library of literature was published between 1945 and 1965 that complained of the "homogenization" of American society, of its passionless and conformist quality, of the oppressive weight of consensus, and of the disinclination to conflict and dissent.

That library is now gathering dust, along with the voluminous literature on the iron law of wages. For something very odd and unexpected has, in the past decade, been happening to the bourgeois masses who inhabit our new urban civilization. Though bourgeois in condition and lifestyle, they have become less bourgeois in ethos, and strikingly more moblike in action. Perhaps this has something to do with a change in the economic character of our bourgeois civilization. Many critics have noted the shift from a producer's ethic (the so-called Protestant ethic) to a consumer's ethic, and go on to affirm that a bourgeois society of widespread affluence is in its essence radically different from a bourgeois society where scarcity automatically imposes a rigorous discipline of its own. This explanation is all the more plausible in that it echoes, in an academic way, the wisdom of the ages as to the corrupting effects of material prosperity upon the social order. The fact that these consequences come as so great a surprise to us—that, having created the kind of affluent society we deliberately aimed at, and having constructed the kind of "progressive" urban civilization we always wanted, that, having done all this, we have also created an unanticipated problem for ourselves—this fact is but a sign of our impoverished political imagination.

The ways in which various strata of our citizenry—from the relatively poor to the relatively affluent—are beginning to behave like a bourgeois urban mob are familiar to anyone who reads his newspaper, and I do not propose to elaborate upon them. The interesting consideration is the extent to which a mob is not simply a physical presence but also, and above everything else, a state of mind. It is, to be precise, that state of mind which lacks all those qualities that, in the opinion of the Founding Fathers, added up to republican morality: steadiness of character, deliberativeness of mind, and a mild predisposition to subordinate one's own special interests to the public interest. Since the Founding Fathers could not envisage a nation of bourgeois—a nation of urbanized, prosperous, and strongly acquisitive citizens—they located republican morality in the agrarian sector of American life. We, in this century, have relocated it in the suburban and small-city sector of American life—our contemporary version of America's "grass roots." And it now appears that our anticipations may be treated as roughly by history as were those of the Founding Fathers.

The causes for this dismaying reversal of expectations are only now being explored by our social critics. Lionel Trilling, especially, has pointed out how the avant-garde, antibourgeois, elite culture—what he calls "the adversary culture"—of our bourgeois society has been gradually incorporated into our conventional school curriculum and, with the spread of mass higher education, has begun to shape the popular culture of our urbanized masses. This is an ambiguous process toward which one can only have ambiguous feelings. No one, after all, can sincerely mourn the passing of the *Saturday Evening Post* and of that superficial, provincial, and, above all, philistine popular culture it so smugly affirmed. This culture may have contributed to political stability, but it also represented a spiritual torpor that, in the end, could only be self-defeating because it was so thin in its sense of humanity. On the other hand, there is something positively absurd in the spectacle of prosperous suburban fathers flocking to see—and evidently enjoying—*The Graduate*, or of prosperous, chic, suburban mothers unconcernedly humming "Mrs. Robinson" to themselves as they cheerfully drive off to do their duties as den mothers. This peculiar schizophrenia, suffusing itself through the bourgeois masses of our urban society, may be fun while it lasts; but one may reasonably suppose that, sooner or later, people will decide they would rather not die laughing at themselves, and that some violent convulsions will ensue.

Why the very best art of bourgeois society—the work of our most gifted poets, painters, novelists, and dramatists—should have, and should have had from the very first days of the romantic movement, such an animus against its own bourgeois world is a question one can only speculate on. Presumably it has something to do with the diminished role that disinterested social values, or transcendent religious values, play in a society governed by the principle of self-interest, even perhaps self-interest rightly understood, but most especially self-interest that makes no effort at self-understanding or self-discipline. But if one can only speculate about the deeper causes of our present disorders, no subtle speculation is needed to see that a democratic-urban civilization which is empty of democratic-urban values is almost surely a civilization in trouble. The symptoms of this trouble plague us every day and in just about every way. If I dwell upon one such symptom, it is only because this one in particular strikes me as so perfectly signifying our inability—it may even be our unwillingness—to comprehend the role of republican morality in a democratic-urban civilization. I refer to the problems of drugs.

Now, I have no interest in venturing into the swamp of controversy that surrounds this topic in the conventional terms in which it is publicly discussed. I do not think it so important to ascertain which drugs are medically bad for you, or just how bad each one is. I think the problem of drugs would be just as serious even if it were determined that marijuana, or amphetamines, or LSD were medically harmless; or if some biochemist were to come up with a way to make these drugs—or even a drug like heroin—medically harmless. What makes a drug a truly serious problem is less its medical aspect than its social purpose. Cigarettes are bad for you, but cigarette smoking poses no kind of threat to our society or to our civilization. Alcohol is likely to cause more harm than good to the average person, but the cocktail party is no threat to our society or our civilization. On the other hand, it is well to recollect that a century ago all social critics agreed that alcohol was such a threat, because it was being consumed by the new urban working class in such a way—not only to such a degree, but in such a way—as to demoralize this class and prevent its assimilation into bourgeois, democratic society.

And here we have arrived at the nub of the question as I see it. What counts is *why* drugs or intoxicants are taken, not whether they are. What counts is the meaning and moral status of the action, not its physiological dimensions. Alcohol ceased to be a public issue in this country when social drinking, for purposes of conviviality, succeeded gin-swilling, whose aim was to get out of this world as rapidly as possible. With drugs, the reverse process has taken place. Drug addiction is not itself a new thing; the doctor who would take an occasional shot of morphine so as to be able to keep functioning, the elderly lady who relied upon an opium-laced patent medicine to keep her on her rounds of civic and familial activities—these are familiar enough figures in our past. But today drug taking has become a mass habit—among our young masses especially—whose purpose is to secede from our society and our civilization; and such a declaration requires a moral answer, not a medical one.

Though the prohibition movement is now very censoriously treated by our American historians, one thing must be said for it: It not only knew the gin mills were medically bad—anyone could see that—it also knew *why* it was bad for a citizen to destroy himself in this way. It had *reasons* to offer, reasons that had to do with the importance of republican morality for those citizens of a self-governing nation—which is to say: The movement for prohibition had a good conscience, both social and moral. Today, in dismal contrast, even those, and they are certainly an overwhelming majority, who believe that the drug habit is bad seem incapable of giving the reasons why. I mean the real reasons why, which have to do with the reasons why it is desirable to function as an autonomous and self-reliant citizen in our urban, democratic society, rather than to drift through life in a pleasant but enervating haze. The moral code for all civilizations must, at one time or another, be prepared to face the ultimate subversive question: "Why not?" Our civilization is now facing that very question in the form of the drug problem, and, apparently, it can only respond with tedious, and in the end ineffectual, medical reports.

It is this startling absence of values that represents the authentic urban crisis of our democratic, urban nation. The fact that the word "urbanity" applies both to a condition of urban things and a state of urban mind may be an accident of philology, but if so it is a happy accident, for it reminds us of the interdependence of mind and thing. That same interdependence is to be found in the word "democracy," referring as it does simultaneously to a political system and to the spirit—the idea—that animates this system. The challenge to our urban democracy is to evolve a set of values and a conception of democracy that can function as the equivalent of the republican morality of yesteryear. This is our fundamental urban problem. Or, in the immortal words of Pogo: "I have seen the enemy and they is us."

1970

27

The Republican Future

Every political party has its roots in some vision of an ideal nation. Left-wing parties are usually quite precise in defining this ideal—they are fond of "blueprints for the future"—and try to be equally precise in prescribing the means for achieving the ideal (redistribution of income, nationalization of industry, new governmental "initiatives," etc.). It is because this work of definition is an intellectual task that left-wing parties are always so interested in recruiting intellectuals. And it is because they are assigned so crucial a political function that intellectuals tend to find left-wing parties so congenial.

But the dilemma of left-wing parties is that their ideals are invariably utopian to begin with, and all that passionate precision turns out to be self-defeating. The trouble with an exact route to nowhere—and "nowhere" is the original, literal meaning of "utopia"—is that it doesn't get you any closer to home, no matter how long you travel. So left-wing politics has within it the seeds of its own frustration. And this frustration always takes the form of denouncing the party leadership for lacking sufficient devotion to the party's ideals and sufficient determination to realize them. This is what is happening in the Labor party in Britain today, and in the Social-Democratic party in Germany. We have also seen it happen in our own Democratic party.

Something similar happens to conservative parties—but, in their case, because they tend to have only a blurred vision of a vague ideal.

344

They are the party of "practical" men, uninterested in large ideas or in a precise elaboration of the relation of means to ends. Being so excessively "practical," they soon find themselves the prisoners of circumstances; they become political managers entirely, with no sense of political entrepreneurship. The problem of a conservative party in a democracy is not its inability to get elected. It usually does get elected, once the left has made a mess of things (as it inevitably will). But the victory turns out to be a hollow one. The clock is neither set back, nor is it pushed forward according to some new mode of political reckoning. All that happens is that the machinery is tinkered with so as to make it workable once again.

This situation, as it pertains to the American scene, was neatly summed up by the British journalist, Henry Fairlie, in an article in *The New Republic*. Since the end of World War II, Mr. Fairlie said, the Republican party and the Democratic party have occupied the White House for the same number of years, but no one thinks of these as Republican years. . . . The conservatives and the Republican party just do not seem to be part of the history of this century in the way in which the Democratic party so clearly has been.

To this, Republican leaders might defensively reply that those Republican presidents usually had to coexist with Democratic Congresses, and therefore had little power to accomplish their objectives. But this rejoinder doesn't dispose of the question, it merely reformulates it. *Why* do the American people seem willing to elect Republican presidents but not Republican Congresses? The answer, I would suggest, is that they will not return the Republican party to power because they do not have clear and reassuring ideas as to (a) what the Republican vision of the American future is, and (b) how it will go about shaping that future.

And so we get conservative frustration, and rebellions against the party leadership, the most obvious recent case being the Reagan rebellion, which may well have cost the Republicans an election they might otherwise have won. But if Mr. Ford had been elected, would that have meant anything more than a slight pause in our march into a Democratic future? And if Mr. Reagan himself had been elected president, how much difference would even that have made? Would he have been able to create a conservative America, any more than he created a conservative California? That's the real trouble with the Republican party: it loses even when it wins.

Whereas the Democratic left is frustrated because its ideals are inherently unrealizable, Republican conservatives are frustrated because their party has not been able, over these past decades, to articulate any coherent set of ideals and to suggest a strategy for achieving them. The Republican party has functioned primarily as a critic of Democratic efforts to shape the American future. The criticisms have often been cogent. But finding fault with someone else's program is no substitute for a program of your own.

Why hasn't the Republican party been able to construct a program of its own, in which the American people can have confidence? I would suggest two reasons. First, the party has never fully reconciled itself to the welfare state, and therefore has never given comprehensive thought to the question of what a *conservative welfare state* would look like. Second, because of their close historic association with the business community, Republican leaders tend to think like businessmen rather than like statesmen, and therefore bumble their way through their terms in office. Let me elaborate.

The idea of a welfare state is in itself perfectly consistent with a conservative political philosophy—as Bismarck knew, a hundred years ago. In our urbanized, industrialized, highly mobile society, people need governmental action of some kind if they are to cope with many of their problems: old age, illness, unemployment, etc. They need such assistance; they demand it; they will get it. The only interesting political question is: *How* will they get it?

This is not a question the Republican party has faced up to, because it still feels, deep down, that a welfare state is inconsistent with such traditional American virtues as self-reliance and individual liberty. Those virtues are real enough, and are a proper conservative concern. But the task is to create the kind of welfare state which is consistent, to the largest possible degree, with such virtues.

That is not an impossible task, though it would be foolish to pretend it is an easy one. It is a matter of relating means to ends. But before one can do that, one has to take the ends seriously. One has to believe that the American people really need some sort of medical insurance program, or old age assistance program. Because the Republican party has never been able to make up its mind about this, it has left the initiative to liberal Democrats. It then finds itself in the position, when in office, of having to administer Democratic programs in the least extravagant way. That's no way for a party to govern.

The basic principle behind a conservative welfare state ought to be a simple one: Wherever possible, people should be allowed to keep their own money—rather than having it transferred (via taxes) to the state—on condition that they put it to certain defined uses. Thus, the Republican party should be demanding that the individual's medical insurance premiums be made tax-deductible. It should be insisting that individuals ought to be free to make additional contributions to their Social Security or pension funds, that all such contributions should be tax-deductible. (One would then, of course, tax all retirement income, but this would be no great hardship.) It should be demanding that life insurance premiums be made tax-deductible, at least up to a specific point. Policies such as these have the obvious advantage of reconciling the purposes of the welfare state with the maximum degree of individual independence and the least bureaucratic coercion. They would also have the advantage of being quite popular.

So why hasn't the Republican party been proposing them? The answer has to do with the businessman's mentality that prevails in the party.

I say "businessman's mentality," but a more accurate description would be "accountant's mentality." All of the reforms suggested above would cost the Treasury a lot of money. And all Republican administrations will be quick to explain that, desirable as such reforms might be, they are not feasible "at this time" because they would dangerously unbalance the budget. It is the way they look at the budget that hypnotizes Republican administrations into impotence.

Democrats are more interested in the shape of the budget than its size. Republicans are more interested in its size than its shape. One result of this situation is that Democrats care far less about fiscal integrity and fiscal responsibility than they ought; this is their weakness, for which they are intermittently chided by the electorate. The other result is that Republicans care more about balancing the books than about *what* is being balanced. And this is a far more serious weakness. Indeed, it is a fatal flaw. For it means that the Republican party spends practically all of its time and energy trying to bring a Democratic budget into balance.

It is the Democratic party that shapes the nation's future by shaping the federal budget. The self-assigned mission of the Republican party is to administer this budget so that the nation doesn't go bankrupt. To perform this task, it is intermittently put in office by the electorate. No wonder conservatives become restless and rebellious under such an arrangement!

If the Republican party were capable of thinking politically—i.e., thinking in terms of shaping the future—it would realize that its first priority is to shape the budget, not to balance it. Then it could go to the electorate with the proper political questions: How do you want the budget balanced? By more taxes for more governmental services? Or by lower taxes, lower governmental expenditures, and incentives for the citizen to provide for his own welfare?

Obviously, there is some risk in such a bold approach. The budget, for a while, would indeed be in a perilous condition if some such Republican programs were passed while Democratic programs were not cut back. But that is the only way to permit the American people to choose their future—by making the choice, not only a clear-cut one, but a necessary one.

Unless and until the Republican party is willing to overcome its bookkeeping inhibitions and become a truly political party, it will be of only marginal significance which faction is in control, or which candidate it proposes.

1976

28

"The Stupid Party"

John Stuart Mill once remarked, from the vantage point of his own liberalism, that a conservative party always tends to be "the stupid party." But such a judgment need not be invidious or censorious. Conservative "stupidity," properly understood, is intimately connected with sentiments that are at the root of conservative virtues: a dogged loyalty to a traditional way of life; an instinctive aversion to innovation based on mere theoretical speculation; and a sense of having a fiduciary relation to the whole nation—past, present, and future.

There is always a kind of immunity to fashionable political ideas which is associated with conservatism, and a country that does not have a goodly portion of it is incapable of stable and orderly government. No political or social system can endure without engendering, in a perfectly organic way, this kind of conservative "stupidity." It is the antibody of the body politic.

But there will always come periods in the life of a nation when "stupidity" is not enough. At such times, fundamental questions of political philosophy emerge into the public forum and demand consideration. The life of politics then becomes enmeshed with the life of the mind, for better or worse. Venerable clichés, long regarded as self-evident truths, lose their moral standing as well as all power to persuade. Intellectuals, who are marginal to a healthy society, suddenly become important political spokesmen. Everything becomes controversial, and political argument between partisan theorists replaces customary political debate between politicians. Obviously, when this happens, "the stupid party"—which is always the less articulate party—finds itself at an immense disadvantage. And that, it seems to me, is the situation of the Republican party in the United States today.

Indeed, this has been the situation of the Republican party for more than half a century now, which helps explain why it is today such a minority party. True, the Republican party has won its share of elections during this period, but these successes masked an ever-increasing weakness. In almost every case, a Republican victory has been the consequence of a Democratic default—of Democratic mismanagement, of Democratic corruption, of Democratic factionalism. Through it all, the Democratic party has more surely secured its position as the majority party and the "natural" governing party. Each Republican administration is marked at birth as an interregnum, which is what it invariably grows up to be.

A 20TH-CENTURY TRANSFORMATION

This is not a purely American affair, as developments in Britain testify. It has to do with the transformation of democratic politics in the twentieth century. This politics has become, at one and the same time, a more naked expression of group interests and a more ideological expression of political ideals. This may seem paradoxical, but it is not. It is in the very nature of ideological politics in a democracy to anchor itself in specific interests, to draw sustenance from these interests, to mobilize these interests into a party, and in the end to "use" them for its creative purposes.

The politics of "conservative stupidity," however, is uncomfortable with blunt appeals to interest groups, which it feels to be "divisive." True, when it is out of power the Republican party can benefit, in a general way, from the dissatisfaction various interests may have with an incumbent administration. But it rarely feels the need to link itself firmly to any of them, to establish itself as their "natural" representative. And when in office, it rarely pays much attention to these interests, preferring to imagine itself as a "national" party whose responsibility is to be "fair" to all citizens.

Similarly, the Republican party is made uneasy by too close an association with political ideas. In a better world, this would be a desirable, even admirable, trait. But in such a world, the conservative party would indeed be the "natural" governing party—losing an occasional election, to be sure, but then patiently waiting for the "common sense" of the citizenry to reassert itself. That is not the kind of world we live in, and a conservative party which tranquilly watches itself become the party of a minority of registered voters has carried "conservative stupidity" beyond the limits of political reason. Today, a conservative party has to "stand for" a perceived vision of a decent society; it has to be able to articulate the elements and rationale of this vision; and, when it has been in office, one should be able to say what it "stood for," win or lose. Republican administrations since World War II have been sadly lacking in this quality.

It really is ironic that the Democratic party should have been able to persuade an apparent majority of the American people that it represents the "public interest," whereas the Republican party is the party of "vested interests." It has been successful in this strategy precisely because it can incorporate its interest-group appeals into a large ideological perspective. But one has only to compare the Democratic and Republican platforms to see which party is more seriously engaged in interest-group politics. And one has only to observe the behavior of Republicans in office to see how negligent they are of their constituencies, actual or possible.

Take the case of old people, for instance. Old people tend naturally to be conservative. They have lived long enough to be skeptical of politicians' easy promises about "creating a better world" today or tomorrow. And they have experienced enough fiscal adversity in the course of their own lives to appreciate the importance of fiscal integrity; they "know the value of a dollar," as one says. They ought, therefore, to be voting overwhelmingly for Republican candidates. But they do not, and the reason is simple: Republican administrations never show any particular concern for old people. Ever since its idiotic hostility to the original Social Security legislation, the Republican party in office has never, on its own initiative, gone out of its way to do anything striking for the benefit of the elderly. On the contrary: It always ends up in the position of trying to pare existing benefits for these people.

When one inquires in Washington why this is the case, the answer is always in terms of "fiscal integrity." Programs for the elderly are very expensive; the budget is out of balance; economies must be made. But this is to substitute a narrow accounting perspective on reality for a truly political one, i.e., a comprehensive one. To begin with, the money saved by a Republican administration will promptly be spent by a Democratic Congress or a subsequent Democratic administration, to whom will accrue all the political credit. But more important, one cannot achieve fiscal integrity in government until one has a strong constituency in favor of it; and old people must be part of any such constituency. Spending money on old people may be bad for the budget in the short run, but it is a step toward eventual fiscal sobriety. If our senior citizens are not given any stake in the success of a conservative party, but on the contrary are constantly being alarmed and menaced by this party, where shall a conservative politics sink its roots?

THE "REAL" BUSINESS COMMUNITY

Or take the case of "the business community," with which the Republican party is supposed to have an intimate association. In fact, that intimacy is mainly with the executives of a few hundred large corporations, not with the several million small businesses, which Republican administrations tend to ignore. Such intimacy, in turn, is largely the result of substituting a narrow economic perspective on reality for a comprehensive political one. Our large corporations are crucial economic institutions, and their condition is of great significance for the kind of macroeconomic thinking that goes on in the Council of Economic Advisers, the Treasury, and the Office of Management and Budget. But they have, if anything, a negative value as a political constituency. They suggest a combination of privilege and power which a democracy will always be suspicious of, and they can offer precious few votes. Meanwhile, the real business community (real in political terms), made up of smaller business proprietors, benefits hardly at all from a conservative administration and is given little stake in conservative successes. Just contrast the consideration with which the Democrats treat trade unions to the petty, grudging concessions which the Republicans make to small business, and the point is only too obvious.

Much the same point can be made about other elements that might add up to a conservative constituency: farmers, homeowners (actual or prospective), and others. There is a possible conservative majority out there—unless a nation is in the process of disintegration—but it has to be welded together out of disparate parts; it has to be created, not just assumed. And it can only be created through the unifying power of political ideas.

There are many conservative thinkers in this country now trying to provide such ideas. I happen to have grave reservations about many of those ideas. Too often they are engaged in futile protest against the principles of the welfare state, instead of trying to construct a conservative welfare state. But such disagreement is less important than the fact that all such ideas float around the periphery of the Republican party. No one seems to take them seriously.

The world would doubtless be a nicer and healthier place if large ideas were kept at a distant remove from political power. The close conjunction is a dangerous one. But the world is what it is. It is a world of media, a world where habit and custom are weak before the forces of communication. It is, therefore, a world where ideas and their articulation are indispensable to effective conservative government, because it is only such ideas that can provide definition and coherence to the conservative constituency. "Political stupidity," alas, will no longer suffice.

1976

29

The Emergence of Two Republican Parties

Since the 1980 election we have witnessed many thoughtful discussions of whether it was a "critical" election—that is, whether it represented one of those basic party realignments, the dethronement of an established majority party by its opposition, which appear to occur about every thirty years. Interesting as these discussions have been, they miss an important point: The really basic political changes in a modern democracy invariably involve changes within parties which, over the longer term, alter the very meaning of a party alignment.

It is often said that the election of Franklin D. Roosevelt and his first steps toward the welfare state assured the hegemony of the Democratic party in the decades to follow. This is true in a sense, but it overlooks the fact that the Democrats in those decades energetically evolved into a very different party from the one that elected Roosevelt. Had there not been such an evolution, it is doubtful there would have been electoral hegemony.

The Democratic party of 1932–36, like all modern political parties, had its "liberal" and "conservative" wings, represented respectively by the Northern urban "machines" and the Southern agrarian populists. The tension between these wings was such that the party could be described as an uneasy and unstable coalition that could hardly look forward to being a relatively secure majority. Nevertheless, that is what it became. How did it happen?

354

The usual explanation is that various economic, demographic, and cultural changes gradually ensured the dominance of the liberal Northern wing over the conservative South. But this ignores the fact that the liberalism that eventually conquered the party was not at all the liberalism of the Northern, urban machines, but rather a liberalism that destroyed those machines in the very process of coming to power.

It was a liberalism that provided a whole new army of party activists, recruited new constituencies, produced new leadership at all levels, created whole new agendas for public attention and concern. During 1936–72, this new liberalism "tore the party apart" with factional strife, as the party establishment kept complaining. But it was a creative factionalism, for it also infused the party with new political and intellectual energy, and it did this by making the Democratic party *interesting*, the place where the action was. It is not surprising, then, that U.S. political history since the New Deal is mainly the history of the Democratic party, with the Republicans providing a series of running footnotes.

Since 1972, however, this new wave *is* the establishment, and signs of inertia and decay are visible. The younger leaders of the Democrats are mere replicas of yesteryear's leaders, and the party has become largely reactive, promising simply a restoration to the better times of an earlier era. In short, it is becoming boring—as boring as the Republican party has been for more than half a century.

The question is whether the Republicans, after the election of 1980, are on the move, whether there are new creative energies at work. It is a most difficult question. The major difficulty centers on Ronald Reagan. Does he really *want* to move the party forward, even at the cost of intraparty tension, or even dissension? Above all, is he a political leader or merely another conventional Republican president?

Not since Theodore Roosevelt has the Republican party shown the faintest comprehension of the nature of presidential leadership in a modern democracy. It has failed to understand that the idea of limited government is not contradictory to the idea of energetic government or (what comes to the same thing) responsive government.

Theodore Roosevelt correctly perceived that the sudden emergence of giant corporations ("the trusts") ran against the American grain of his day, for such concentrations of private power seemed to most Americans incongruent with the individualistic version of "free enterprise" so long familiar to them. He acted with dispatch and vigor—not always wisely, but he did act.

In contrast, the Republican party ever since World War I has been ignoring its constituencies, actual or potential, and narrowing its vision. It has won elections, but often only in reaction to Democratic incompetence or outright misgovernment. Each victorious election since 1932 has been a mere interregnum, a holding pattern of activity. Presidents Eisenhower, Nixon (in his first term, that is), and Ford were good presidents by conventional standards, and historians are already beginning to speak more benignly about them. But they did nothing to rejuvenate or even strengthen their party, or to alter the drift of politics. It is no wonder that Democrats have come to regard themselves as the natural, preordained, governing party, and behave with such irresponsible, petulant fury when in opposition.

The Republican party as we know it came into being in the 1920s. It was then that the GOP defined itself proudly as the "businesslike" party—expressing the ethos of the business community, especially the corporate community. In that decade a best-selling book by a Republican advertising executive explains that Jesus Christ could be best understood and appreciated as the greatest salesman ever. Political leadership came to be wholly equated with prudent, astute management of the affairs of state. So-called country-club Republicans—at the highest level Bohemia Grove Republicans—became a dominant element.

Fortunately, party loyalties die hard in a democracy, and the Republican party did retain enough strength in white Anglo-Saxon Protestant rural and small-town communities, and among small businessmen, to be viable. It was a gradually dwindling strength, however, as many in these areas found Democratic energy more attractive than Republican inertia. Meanwhile, Catholics, Jews, "ethnics" of all kinds, blacks and the rapidly increasing (in both numbers and influence) academic-intellectual-media communities took up residence in the Democratic party.

The election of 1980, for the first time, provided signs that a new Republican party might be emerging. Ronald Reagan was anything but a typical Republican candidate, and never earned the favor of the Republican establishment—not even of the corporate community, which definitely preferred a John Connolly or a George Bush. He came "out of the West," riding a horse, not a golf cart, speaking in the kind of nationalist-populist tonalities not heard since Teddy Roosevelt, appealing to large sections of the working class, to the increasingly numerous religious fundamentalists, and even to the growing if still small number of conservative and neoconservative intellectuals. His posture was forward-looking, his accent was on economic growth rather than on economic sobriety. All those Republicans with the hearts and souls of accountants—the traditional ideological core of the party—were nervous, even dismayed.

They need not have been. There are, it turns out—perhaps there always have been—two Ronald Reagans. The presidential Ronald Reagan is quite different from the campaigning Ronald Reagan. Not altogether different, it must be said in all fairness, but disquietingly different to an unexpected degree. Only at the United Nations, with Jeane Kirkpatrick, does one see the kind of spiritedness one had hoped for in the administration as a whole; as a result, she is easily the most popular figure in the cabinet. David Stockman, who promised to be another untypical Republican, has been inexplicably transformed into a conventional guardian of the federal budget—an important job, but one others could have performed as well. Most of the rest of the high officials in this administration would have felt perfectly at home working for Nixon and Ford, as many in fact did.

Mr. Reagan himself seems content, most of the time, to assume the role of chief executive officer, the topmost manager of a managerial-Republican administration. Every now and then he shows a flash of the Ronald Reagan that might have been but these intermittent flashes are quickly dimmed. The influence of conservative Republican economists—talented men who equate the political imagination with a dangerous concupiscence—remains strong. So does the influence of the established Republican leaders in the Senate, for whom aversion to risk is the cardinal rule of conservative politics. So the administration bumbles along in foreign policy, in social policy, in economic policy, resembling more and more the caricature of Republicans in liberal cartoons.

It is not that mistakes, as some complain, are made too often. An administration that provides energetic leadership will always make its fair share of mistakes—but will leave those mistakes behind it, to be contemplated by historians. On the other hand, an administration that lies dead in the water will accumulate its errors like barnacles.

So was the critical election of 1980 merely a mirage? One would have to concede the likelihood of this were it not for the presence in the House of several dozen new, younger congressmen, and in the Senate of a handful of new Republican senators, who are becoming increasingly frustrated, increasingly restive, increasingly active. They are post–New Deal Republicans who have far less regard for Herbert Hoover than for Teddy Roosevelt.

One might recall that in 1933 the Democratic House and Senate had no greater number of such representatives who turned out to be architects of the party's future. They prevailed in the end by being determined, factional, and "divisive." The Republican party has always regarded with horror such unmannerly conduct from its members. It is just possible, however, that the new "model" Republicanism these younger Republicans represent will, in the years ahead, break the Republican mold. If they do, 1980 will in truth have been a critical election.

1983

30

The New Populism: Not to Worry

My friend the late Martin Diamond, one of the most thoughtful of political scientists, used to say that the American democracy is based on one key assumption: that the people are usually sensible, but rarely wise. The function of our complex constitutional structure is to extract what wisdom is available in the people, at any moment in time, and give it a role in government. Our system of representation (as distinct from direct, participatory democracy) is supposed to play this role, as do the bicameral Congress, the separation of powers, our federal arrangements, and the Constitution itself with its careful delineation of rights and prerogatives. Ultimately, of course, the popular will cannot be denied in a democracy. But only "ultimately." Short of the ultimate, the Founders thought it appropriate that popular sentiments should be delayed in their course, refracted in their expression, revised in their enactment, so that a more deliberate public opinion could prevail over a transient popular opinion.

From the beginning, there were those who argued that this approach was repugnant to the true spirit of democracy, and that it was based on a fear of popular government, real self-government. The Founders replied that popular government—a term they placidly accepted—had its own problems, and that what they had discovered, their boldest innovation, was "a republican remedy for the diseases of republican government." In short, a principle of self-correction had been incorporated into the democratic body politic. The opposing point of view the Founders would have called "populism," had the term then been in use.

FUTILE OR DAMAGING

Ever since, "populism" has not had a good name among American political scientists, jurists, and social critics. It has been taken to signify a movement of popular passions to overwhelm the political and legal process by which our democracy has traditionally operated. We have had quite a few such movements in American history, and the consensus among our historians is that, though they may have been an understandable reaction to real problems and real abuses, they were on the whole either futile or damaging to our social and political fabric. Populism, it is generally agreed, is democracy at its least rational, its least sensible.

It is something of a shock, therefore, to observe that so many of our political leaders, at all levels of government, and whether they are conservative, liberal, or radical, today go about proudly claiming to be "populist." Indeed, it is quite impossible to find any political leader who will say that he is not a populist. But these are the very people who are, after all, our government! Are they launching a popular crusade against themselves? What on earth is going on?

Well, what is going on is something very strange and without precedent. To put it simply: The common sense—not the passion, but the common sense—of the American people has been outraged, over the past 20 years, by the persistent un-wisdom of their elected and appointed officials. To the degree that we are witnessing a crisis in our democratic institutions, it is a crisis of our disoriented elites, not of a blindly impassioned populace. If you are going to have a crisis, this may be the better kind to have—but it is still a crisis.

The crisis began with the conduct of the Vietnam War, when the "best and the brightest" pursued a strategy that led us to an unmitigated disaster. Liberal and left-wing politicians promptly seized the issue and interpreted popular discontent as a vindication of their view that the war was inherently immoral, or even that our society was so immoral that it could not righteously intervene, anywhere, anytime, in support of our national interests. The shock of Vietnam has largely worn off among the people—one even gets the sense, from the immense popularity of a movie like "Rambo," that perhaps they wouldn't mind doing it again, only this time doing it right, i.e., winning. But in Washington the shock has been very slow to wear off, and those involved in making foreign policy, whether in Congress or the White House or the State Department or the Pentagon, are either still living in the 1960s or are filled with anxiety and uncertainty as they fumble issue after issue.

I recently attended a couple of private dinners in Washington with foreign-policy experts, both in the administration and out. These were all more or less conservatives—no "doves"—and I was shocked to hear every discussion of policy turn around such questions as: "Dare we propose such a course of action to the American people?" "What will they think?" "How will they respond?" Constant reference was made to opinion polls as indicating how difficult the making of foreign policy now is. But surely it is evident that, on matters of foreign policy, opinion polls are not worth the paper they are written on.

The American people know—their common sense tells them—that this is a subject (economic policy is another) about which they know little, and that their opinions are not reasoned opinions, only shallow attitudes that are waiting to be shaped or reshaped into firm opinion. That shaping is the task of political leadership, which has to lead—to make decisions and then be judged by the results. The kind of timid deference to supposed popular opinion now visible in Washington's elites only serves to diminish popular confidence in their wisdom and their competence.

But it is mainly in the area of domestic social policy that the gulf between the common sense of the American people and the un-wisdom of its governing elites—whether elected, appointed, or (as with the media) self-appointed—has become so vast as to provoke a new kind of populism. We have, since the 1960s, witnessed a veritable revolution in social policy in this country, a revolution-from-above, a revolution imposed on the people. That this imposition has largely been the work of a nonelected judiciary is especially exasperating, but this judiciary could not wield such power without the consent, overt or tacit, of our elected representatives. It is common for many of these representatives to talk out of both sides of their mouths—to indicate dissent from judicial or administrative decisions while obstructing any legislative effort to reverse or limit them. Such hypocrisy is most common among liberal politicians—they made this revolution, after all, or at least did not oppose it—and helps explain the conservative drift of popular opinion.

And the seeming impotence of our elected officials on this matter ensures that this conservative drift—the new populism—will accelerate. The issues of education and crime clearly illustrate why this new populism exists and flourishes. That two such simple, fundamental issues should, for the first time in American history, have become so controversial is an unambiguous signal something has gone very wrong.

The American people have always had perfectly reasonable expectations about our educational system. Professional educationists may have had grandiose ambitions, and certainly always have had a grandiose rhetoric, but American parents are of a more modest cast of mind. They do not think that the school experience can transfigure their children in some remarkable, wonderful way. They do want schools to improve their children—to make them literate, to instill good study habits, to acquaint them with the importance of discipline, self-discipline, and deference toward authority. They do not want our schools to debase their children—to instill them with bad habits, bad manners, and an undisciplined disposition.

The controversy over prayer in the schools plays a symbolic role in this set of expectations. Most parents do not really care whether their children pray in school. For two centuries, most parents didn't even know whether such prayer existed. If our educationists, our courts and our legislators had not been bereft of all common sense about education, if they had not succumbed to trendy fantasies, there would be very little fuss about the matter. But when parents see a prescribed curriculum on "sex education" that seems to encourage (or at least not discourage) teenage promiscuity, and are then told it is illegal to post the Ten Commandments in a classroom, they are bound to become very upset. School prayer then appears to offer an antidote to the corruption of our educational ethos. The un-wisdom of our elites is what accounts for the populist rebellion against our current educational practices—a rebellion whose demands are basically commonsensical, not at all extreme.

The same thing holds true for crime. The main purpose of a sensible criminal-justice system—its first priority—is to punish the guilty. It is *not* to ensure that no innocent person is ever unfairly convicted. That is a second priority—important, but second. Over these past two decades, our unwise elites—in the law schools, in the courts, in our legislatures—have got these priorities reversed. The consequence is a criminal-justice system that seems, to the average person, ineffectual, and often positively uninterested, in either punishing or deterring crime.

NO BLIND REBELLION

It is interesting to watch the slippery way that our liberal elites respond to the populist anger provoked by this situation. Rather than address the problem, they have declared war on *white-collar* crime, trying to make this the focus of attention. They become indignant at crimes against property committed by the relatively affluent, rather than crimes against the person committed by the relatively poor. But it is murder and robbery and rape that the average American is today most concerned about, not financial fraud. And his common sense tells him that our unwise elites do not share his concern.

There are other issues as well that are feeding the new populism. The important point to emphasize, however, is that this new populism is no kind of blind rebellion against good constitutional government. It is rather an effort to bring our governing elites to their senses. That is why so many people—and I include myself among them—who would ordinarily worry about a populist upsurge find themselves so sympathetic to this new populism.

1985

31

The Coming "Conservative Century"

The beginning of political wisdom in the 1990s is the recognition that liberalism today is at the end of its intellectual tether. The fact that it can win elections is irrelevant. Conservatives continued to win elections during "the liberal century" (1870–1970); but, once in office, they revealed themselves to be impotent to enact a sustained conservative agenda. The tide of public opinion was too strong against them.

That tide has now turned. It is liberal administrations today, in all the Western democracies, that find themselves relatively impotent when in office. Just as conservative administrations used to nibble away at liberal reforms previously enacted, so liberals in office today do their share of nibbling at the occasional conservative reform that has taken root. More often, they find themselves nibbling away at the liberal reforms of their predecessors, reforms that threaten fiscal insolvency as well as political fragmentation.

THE STERILITY OF "SECULAR HUMANISM"

The liberal consensus, as expressed in the media, is that, with the election of Bill Clinton, conservatism in America is in disarray, is groping for some center of equilibrium, and that only a "moderate" Republican coalition, one that disengages itself from the religious right, can create an

American majority. This may be true in the shorter term, as defined by the next presidential election or two, but in the longer term that consensus is false. The religious conservatives are already too numerous to be shunted aside, and their numbers are growing, as is their influence. They are going to be the very core of an emerging American conservatism.

For the past century the rise of liberalism has been wedded to the rise of secularism in all areas of American life. In the decades ahead, the decline of secularism will signify the decline of liberalism as well. Already on the far-left fringes of liberalism itself, artists and philosophers are welcoming the collapse of a "secular humanism" that they find sterile and oppressive. They can offer nothing with which to replace this liberal-secular humanism. But others can, and will. Today, it is the religious who have a sense that the tide has turned and that the wave of the future is moving in their direction.

The three pillars of modern conservatism are religion, nationalism and economic growth. Of these, religion is easily the most important because it is the only power that, in the longer term, can shape people's characters and regulate their motivation. In economics, secular incentives (i.e., materialist incentives) can be effective. But in the really troubled areas of modern life, where social policy is at work, the welfare state has given birth to a long train of calamities. Perverse economic incentives can encourage a corrupting dependency, and liberalism has, in the name of compassion, created a network of such perverse incentives. But it does not follow that modifying such incentives will have a dramatic effect.

The reason is simple: It is not possible to motivate people to do the right thing, and avoid doing the wrong thing, unless people are told, from childhood on, what the right things and the wrong things are. This explains why so many of our newer immigrants, from traditional families, ignore these tempting, corrupting incentives and instead move on to productive law-abiding lives. Even then, some do not pay heed. But most do, most of the time.

The most extraordinary social phenomenon of the liberal century has been the totally unexpected increase in criminality. The first obligation of government always has been to ensure the security of the person. Liberalism does not believe this—it represents "too punitive" a conception of the governmental mission. Instead, liberalism believes that if you diminish income inequalities and provide cradle-to-birth income security, criminality will wither away. In the face of increasing criminality, therefore, liberalism responds with ever more fanciful and ever more desperate "therapeutic" programs, all of which are ineffectual.

As with crime, so with all the other social pathologies that now infest our liberal society and its welfare state. The "joy of sex" has been compromised by an infusion of sexual anxiety, as venereal diseases ranging from the fatal to the noxious proliferate. It has also produced a large and growing population of unwed mothers and their babies. The liberal answer to this human disaster is either to deny that it is any kind of disaster—"just a new kind of family," the social workers chirp—or to create more programs of "sex education." But it is such secular, nonjudgmental education—an education bereft of moral guidance—that has helped create this problem in the first place.

Back in 1897, John Dewey defined the essence of the liberal credo: "The practical problem of modern society is the maintenance of the spiritual values of civilization, through the medium of the insight and decision of the individual."

A noble idea but ultimately a self-contradictory one. You do not preserve spiritual values by turning them over to a rampant spiritual individualism. That experiment has been tried, and it has failed—though any admission of failure is not something we can expect.

On the contrary: What we are witnessing and living through is a prolonged spasm of liberal fanaticism—a redoubling of liberal effort as liberal program after liberal program fails. With each failure, the credibility of government is diminished and cynicism about politics increases. Does anyone really believe that the Clinton administration will significantly reduce, or that a Bush administration would have significantly reduced, the budget deficit?

The plain truth is that if we are ever going to cope with the deficit, and the social programs that inflate it, we are going to have to begin with a very different view of human nature and human responsibility in relation to such issues as criminality, sexuality, welfare dependency, even medical insurance. Only to the degree that such a new—actually very old—way of looking at ourselves and our fellow citizens emerges can a public opinion be shaped that will candidly confront the fiscal crisis of the welfare state. Presidential calls for "sacrifice," meaning a willingness to pay higher taxes, are a liberal cop-out. Why don't we hear something about self-control and self-reliance? It's the traditional spiritual values that we as individuals need, not newly invented, trendy ones.

We hear it said constantly and with pseudo-solemnity that this fiscal crisis results from the people demanding benefits that they are then unwilling to pay for. Were this so, the inference would be that such a corrupt people are incapable of democratic self-government and are in need of an elite to do the job for them. Liberals, despite their populist rhetoric, have been discreetly drawing this inference for many years now. Much of our overblown welfare state was created by liberal political entrepreneurs, not in response to an evident popular demand. Liberals may scornfully dismiss "supply-side" economics, but they are profoundly committed to "supply-side" politics—the politics of "unmet needs," a category that is constantly expanding. Also expanding, of course, are the official bureaucracies and those "helping" professions that cope with those "needs."

To counter the crisis that liberalism is provoking in our society, conservatism has to rediscover and reaffirm its attachment to its three traditional pillars. A reaffirmation of the goal of economic growth should not be difficult. It is becoming even more widely appreciated that economic growth is crucially dependent on the ability of "economic activists" to invest and innovate. Just as political activists, spurred by political ambition, are at the heart of liberal public policy, so economic activists, spurred by economic ambition, are at the heart of conservative economic policy. It is they who promote the growth that pacifies egalitarian and redistributional appetites. There is still an influential segment of "old conservatives" who do not understand that a pro-entrepreneurial emphasis in economic policy is not simply a "pro-business" policy. But they are gradually fading away.

Similarly, an affirmation of the national spirit is practically inevitable, as the liberal internationalism that has defined American foreign policy since the days of Woodrow Wilson continues to unravel. The U.S. will surely want to, and will need to, remain an active world power, but this activity will not be within the confines prescribed by the United Nations or NATO or whatever. In this post-Cold War era, those organizations are on their way to becoming moribund. Nor are we about to engage in some kind of benign humanitarian imperialism—except in very special circumstances, decided case by case. A renascent nationalism will be accompanied by a renascent neo-realism in foreign policy. This is something that most conservatives have long wished for.

EMBRACING THE RELIGIOUS

Coping with a religious revival, however, is something that conservatives and the Republican party are not yet prepared to do. Religious people always create problems since their ardor tends to outrun the limits of politics in a constitutional democracy. But if the Republican party is to survive, it must work at accommodating these people. In a sense, the influx of the religious into American politics is analogous to the influx of European immigrants into our urban centers between 1870 and 1914. They created many problems, but the Democrats welcomed them while the Republicans shunned them. That was the origin of the "natural" Democratic majority.

The Democrats are never going to be able to welcome the religious, but if the Republicans keep them at arm's length instead of embracing them, and shaping their political thinking, a third party and a restructuring of American politics are certain. One way or another, in the decades ahead they will not be denied.

1993

32

The New Face of American Politics

A struggle for both the soul and body of American conservatism is taking place before our eyes, but because of the intervention of the liberal media our vision of it is cloudy and confused. The two poles of this struggle are best expressed by quotations from two conservative thinkers.

The first is from the interesting new book by David Frum, *Dead Right* (New Republic/Basic Books). Mr. Frum writes from the point of view of an economic conservative for whom Big Government is the central political problem of our era:

"Social conservatism is potentially more popular than economic conservatism. But . . . the force driving the social trends that offend conservatives . . . is the welfare function of modern government. Attempting to solve these social problems while government continues to exacerbate them is like coping with a sewer main explosion by bolting all the manhole covers to the pavement."

The second is from social conservative Paul Weyrich in a letter in the August issue of *Commentary* magazine. Posing the question, "Which comes first, a government that subsidizes immorality or a culture that tolerates it?" he answers it from the point of view of a social-cultural conservative:

"Single young women do not have babies in increasing numbers just because it pays. In fact, the welfare state notwithstanding, single motherhood is an almost certain road to lifelong poverty. [But] these young women . . . have absorbed a culture of instant gratification, and they have sex because they feel like it. . . . The welfare state encourages them, certainly, but it is not the driving factor. Cultural collapse is the driving factor."

EMPHASIS AND PRIORITIES

The polarization of these two views is less extreme than it seems from these two quotations. One can safely assume that Mr. Frum is unhappy that 30 percent of babies born in the U.S. today are born to single mothers. And one knows that Mr. Weyrich, a veteran conservative activist, is highly critical of our overblown welfare state, what Mr. Frum calls "Big Government." The issue is one of emphasis and priorities. But emphasis and priorities are closer to the heart of electoral politics than abstract political principles. That is why the Republican party is now under such stress as economic conservatives and social conservatives strive for dominance in state after state, in primary after primary.

It is interesting to note that the Democratic party seems not to be involved in any such conflict. The explanation is simple enough: The cultural left, over the past twenty years, has been so totally absorbed into the party that its priorities are fully respected. Some observers have been mystified by the fact that President Clinton's first initiative was to raise the controversial issue of gays in the military. Why didn't he insist on an increase in the minimum wage instead? That would have been more in accord with the party's traditional orientation.

But the Democratic party of today is not the Democratic party of yesteryear. Its trade-union base has not only shrunk as union membership in general has declined, but the nature of this membership has radically changed. Most of the union activists in the Democratic party today come from the so-called helping professions—teachers, social workers, nutritionists, psychologists, etc.—most of whom work for the various levels of government itself.

Not only are these professions economically dependent on the welfare state, but they are completely dominated by the cultural left. (There is even a sense in which, along with professors and those in the arts world, it can be said they are now the cultural left.) It certainly wasn't the old-line unions of the AFL-CIO that defined the Democratic party's position on abortion or on the distribution of condoms in high schools.

This does leave the Democratic party with the problem of the traditional working class, union or nonunion, that has habitually voted Democratic, if less reliably so in recent years. The Clinton administration has been careful to offer the labor movement a bill that prohibited corporations from replacing striking workers. But it couldn't get enough Democratic votes to pass it—and, in truth, it didn't try all that hard. There are Republicans who see this Democratic problem as an opportunity—but these are almost entirely social conservatives, whose popular base is the working class, the lower-middle class, and the self-employed middle class. Economic conservatives speak to this dispossessed class in a language that does not appeal to human sensibilities.

There really is a class war, of a sort, in the U.S. today. President Clinton keeps trying to invoke older class-war slogans, when attacking the wealthy "vested interests." But he is having only minimal success. The reason is that the real class war in this country today is between the cultural conservatives, otherwise known as social conservatives, mainly in the working and lower-middle classes, and the cultural left in the higher-paid and more economically secure professions. And the Republican party is being drawn into this class war, willy-nilly.

It is impossible to overestimate the dismay and confusion that this is causing within the Republican party. All the potential candidates for the presidency in 1996 are self-consciously walking a very fine line between the economic conservatives, whose traditional constituency is business, and the new, populist social conservatism that, as Mr. Frum admits, is potentially more popular. There is much angst within the party, much hedging and double-talk. Every one of these candidates knows that he cannot get the nomination, and even more certainly cannot win the election, without the support of the social conservatives. Why can't the Republicans do what the Democrats have done with their cultural left and simply, in a matter-of-fact way, embrace them?

The reason is religion. The social-cultural conservatives are also, in the main, religious conservatives, and this is something new in American politics. The Republican party doesn't quite know what to do about it. The party is certainly not antireligious, but it is secular, as our political parties have always been. In addition, there is the fact that the top executives of our larger corporations, who have a privileged position in the party, have views on social issues that are molded by economics, not religion or morality. Their idea of reforming welfare is to revise the system so as to make it more efficient and less costly. The notion of reforming the people on welfare is foreign to them.

Why this religious-political upsurge? Wouldn't it be better if both our parties remained secular? It probably would be, but that option has been foreclosed by the fact that the Democratic party has itself ceased being secular and has become secularist. (Since the media themselves are secularist, the transformation has gone unnoticed.)

SECULAR VS. SECULARIST

A secular political party, in the traditional sense, has been neutral as between religions—at least insofar as they represent different versions of traditional morality. A secularist political party is neutral as between religion and irreligion: It believes that moral issues "have no place in politics," and replaces such issues with the idea of "fair and equal" treatment of all "lifestyles," all beliefs about what is permissible and what is not. This is accompanied by a powerful animus against the dominant traditional beliefs, especially religious beliefs. The American Civil Liberties Union and the National Education Association faithfully represent this ideology, which explains why they are comfortable banning the Ten Commandments from the classroom but don't mind feminist or homosexual art.

So, in addition to differences in economic policy and social policy, there is emerging a profound religious difference between the two parties—a difference that, in turn, shapes modes of thinking about economic and social issues. The Republican party, always slow to change, is reluctant to recognize this new reality, and many in the party are resisting it. But such resistance will surely crumble in the years ahead, and the party alignments will be novel and different in important respects. A new era in American politics has already begun.

1994

33

America's "Exceptional" Conservatism

I remember the day very well, back in 1956, when I arrived at my office at *Encounter*—of which I was then coeditor—and found on my desk an unsolicited manuscript by Michael Oakeshott which he was submitting for publication. This, I thought, is the way every editor's day should begin, with an over-the-transom arrival of an essay by one of the finest living political thinkers and certainly the finest stylist. The manuscript was called "On Being Conservative" and I read it with pleasure and appreciation. It was beautifully written, subtle in its argument, delicate in its perceptions, and full of sentences and paragraphs that merit the attention of anthologists for decades, perhaps even centuries, to come. Fortunately, this essay is to be found in his book, *Rationalism in Politics*. I say "fortunately" because, after loving every line of this essay, I sat down and wrote to Michael, as I was then privileged to call him, rejecting it.

I forget what disingenuous circumlocutions I invented for that letter—probably something about its being both too "abstract" and too specifically British in its frame of reference for our journal. But the truth is that, while I admired the essay immensely, I didn't really like it. Which is but another way of saying that I disagreed with it. At that time, I wasn't sure why I disagreed with it. Today, looking back over the past forty years, I can see why. I was American, Michael was English. And I was then in the earliest stages of intellectual pregnancy with those attitudes and dispositions that later emerged as "neoconservatism." And American neoconservatism is very different from the kind of ideal English conservatism that Oakeshott was celebrating so brilliantly. It is also different from the much less ideal conservatism that still dominates the Conservative party today. Indeed, I think it fair to say that it is different from whatever passes for conservatism in all the democracies of Western Europe today. Which doesn't necessarily mean that it is irrelevant to the politics of these nations. It does mean, however, that conservatism in America today is on a different track from that of Britain and Western Europe—I insist on the distinction—and that it is reasonable to think that one of us may be on the better track.

Oakeshott's essay focuses on what he calls "the conservative disposition." Let him describe that disposition in his own lovely language:

> To be conservative is to be disposed to think and behave in certain manners; it is to prefer certain kinds of conduct and certain conditions of human circumstances to others. . . . The general characteristics of this disposition . . . centre upon a propensity to use and enjoy what is available rather than what was or what may be. . . . What is esteemed is the present; and it is esteemed not on account of its connections with a remote antiquity, nor because it is recognized to be more admirable than any possible alternative, but on account of its familiarity. . . . To be conservative, then, is to prefer the familiar to the unknown, to prefer the tried to the untried, fact to mystery, the actual to the possible, the limited to the unbounded, the near to the distant . . . the convenient to the perfect, present laughter to utopian bliss.

These eloquent words are bound to strike a chord in the soul of any reader, since all of us, in varying degrees, participate in such a disposition. What we call civilization is itself based on the power of this disposition. But even as I respond to Oakeshott's ideal conservatism, I know—as I knew back in 1956—that it is not for me. And this for two reasons:

First, it is irredeemably secular, as I—being a Jewish conservative—am not. Were I a Christian conservative, my reaction would be the same. For it is impossible for any religious person to have the kinds of attitudes toward the past and the future that Oakeshott's conservative disposition celebrates. Our Scriptures and our daily prayer book link us to the past and to the future with an intensity lacking in Oakeshott's vision. Not that this religious dimension of our humanity in any way necessarily denigrates the present, in all its fullness. Judaism especially, being a more this-worldly religion than Christianity, moves us to sanctify the present in our daily lives—but always reminding us that we are capable of doing so only through God's grace to our distant forefathers. Similarly, it is incumbent upon us to link our children and grandchildren to this "great chain of being," however suitable or unsuitable *their* present might be to our conservative disposition. And, of course, the whole purpose of sanctifying the present is to prepare humanity for a redemptive future.

In short, Oakeshott's ideal conservative society is a society without religion, since all religions bind us as securely to past and future as to the present. The conservative disposition is real enough; but without the religious dimension, it is thin gruel. The conservative disposition can have no singular, unmediated existence because it is never the only disposition in anyone's character. In addition to the conservative disposition, there is what might be called the "theotropic" disposition. Just as, in all societies known to us, Oakeshott's conservative disposition is plainly visible, so is the religious disposition. In the concluding sentence of his inaugural lecture at the London School of Economics, Oakeshott made that magnificent declaration to the effect that this is the best of all possible worlds and everything in it is a necessary evil. That is more a Biblical assertion than a philosophical one. In any case, his conservative disposition offers us no guidance in coping with all those necessary evils, which can tear our lives apart and destroy whatever philosophical equanimity we have achieved as a result of reading the writers of philosophy.

Secondly, Oakeshott's conservative disposition runs squarely against the American grain. Oh, Americans possess such a disposition all right. Despite all one reads about the frustrations of American life, it is the rare American who dreams of moving to another land, and hardly any do. We are, in some respects, a very conservative people—but not quite in the Oakeshottian sense.

To begin with, we have a most emphatic and explicit relation to our past—an "ideological" relation some would say. In the United States today, all schoolchildren, in all fifty states, begin their day with a recitation of the Pledge of Allegiance to the flag and to the Constitution of the United States of America. There is no national legislation to this effect; it is entirely up to the states. Despite some efforts by radical educators, no state has removed this prescription.

In addition, there is the extraordinary fact that at the opening of every high school, college, and professional sporting event—and high school and college sports are major foci of attention for Americans—players and spectators rise to their feet and sing the national anthem. And it is not a good idea to fail to do so, if you wish to avoid hostile encounters with your fellow countrymen. It is easy to say, without fear of contradiction, that the United States today is the most vibrantly patriotic of all the Western democracies. Some might say—a sophisticated European would surely be tempted to say—that this merely demonstrates that the United States is, in some crucial respects, a premodern country. Perhaps so. Or perhaps we are a postmodern country—one should not blandly exclude that possibility.

Behind this ideological patriotism is the fact, noted by all historians and observers, that the United States is a "creedal" nation. Being American has nothing to do with ethnicity, or blood ties of any kind, or lineage, or length of residence even. What we scornfully call "nativism" in the United States is what passes for authentic patriotism among many Germans and Frenchmen. None of this is surprising if one recalls that the United States is literally a nation of immigrants, and in the course of time has developed astonishing powers of assimilation. What is surprising is the intensity of patriotism generated by this fact—no one ever really expected that. One might easily have expected the opposite. Ironically, that opposite reaction is now being sponsored by the Left in the guise of "multiculturalism," which has practically nothing to do with culture and everything to do with politics. So far, at any rate, the impact on American patriotism has been minimal, being limited to a fraction of the educated elite.

This "creed" and this ideological fervor are suffused with a kind of religious sensibility. Indeed, American patriotism was born out of, and was sustained for our first two centuries by, the sensibility of Protestant dissent. In the last two centuries, our increasingly secular outlook has tempered this sensibility, so that sociologists now blandly refer to an American "civic religion" that unites the community with secular ties. The concept of a "civic religion" has its validity, up to a point. We are no longer the "nation under God," a providential nation, as we once casually defined ourselves. But that reservoir of religiosity, though now diminished, is still there, and these still waters run deep. Most Americans thought Soviet Communism to be an awful idea, and a terrible reality, simply because it was "atheistic and godless," and therefore doomed. And they didn't have to read Hayek to come to this conclusion. Scholars may debate the reasons for the collapse of Soviet Communism, which surprised so many of them. The ordinary American was less astonished.

There are tensions between American religiosity and the more secular "civic religion," but they coexist because they also have much in common. They subscribe equally to a somewhat less rigorous version of the Judeo-Christian moral tradition. Both are individualistic when it comes to economic matters, wedding the Protestant ethic (at least in Max Weber's version) to the philosophy of Adam Smith. Both approve of economic growth, as a character-building exercise and as a way of improving the human condition. And both are, in general, future-oriented and "progressive" in their political vision. When Americans deplore the present, and even when they do so in comparison with the past, they always assume that ameliorative possibilities are available. American politics is about those ameliorative possibilities and the controversial choices they entail. And today there is so much to deplore in this American present that Oakeshott's paean to present-mindedness is singularly inapt.

All of this is by way of a background explanation of my own problem with Oakeshott's writings and to the fact that these writings do not have and will not have any large appeal to Americans. I can speak from bitter experience here. When I was an editor with the publishing house Basic Books, I published the American edition of *Rationalism in Politics*. It sold 600 copies.

But it is also by way of a background explanation of what I see as a major divergence between today's American conservatism and British as well as European conservatism. It is a divergence with significant implications for the future of the Western democracies. The difference between the American and the British (or European) view can be summed up this way: Conservatism in America is a *movement*, a popular movement, not a faction within any political party. Though, inevitably, most conservatives vote Republican, they are not party loyalists and the party has to woo them to win their votes. This movement is issue oriented: It will happily meld with the Republican party if the party is "right" on the issues; if not, it will walk away. This troubled relationship between the conservative movement and the Republican party is a key to the understanding of American politics today. The conservative movement has become a powerful force within the party, but it does not dominate the party. And there is no possibility of the party ever dominating the movement.

Post-World War II American conservatism begins to take shape with the American publication of Hayek's *The Road to Serfdom* and the founding some years later of William F. Buckley's *National Review*. Previously, there had been a small circle who were admirers of the Jeffersonian, quasi-anarchist teachings of the likes of Albert Jay Nock, but no one paid much attention to them. Hayek's polemic against socialism did strike a chord, however, especially among members of the business community as well as existing conservative groups. There may have been people converted from "statism" to "antistatism" by that book, but my impression is that most admirers of the book were already antistatist and pro-free market. What Hayek did was to mobilize them intellectually, and to make their views more respectable. I have to confess that I still haven't got around to reading *The Road to Serfdom*, though I am a great admirer of Hayek's later writings in intellectual history and political philosophy. The reason was, and is, that not for a moment did I believe that the United States was (or is) on any kind of road to serfdom. Socialism has never had much of a presence in America and, besides, having gone through a brief Trotskyist phase in my college days, I needed no instruction on socialist illusions or the evils of Soviet Communism.

Still, it is fair to say that an antisocialist, anti-Communist, antistatist perspective dominated the thinking and politically active part of American conservatism from the end of World War II to the Goldwater campaign of 1964. William F. Buckley's *National Review* faithfully represented this point of view and it gradually recruited enough younger political activists to become a force within the Republican party. But the Goldwater debacle revealed how limited a force it was. And the Nixon elections of 1968 and 1972 revealed that, even when winning elections—largely through Democratic default—the basic principles of postwar conservatism had little relevance to American realities and had to be admixed with a large portion of fumbling opportunism to gain currency. And yet, from the ashes of the Goldwater and Nixon debacles there arose Ronald Reagan, to become a two-term President only a few years later. What happened?

What happened, I would say, were two things. First in time, though certainly not in order of political significance, was the emergence of an intellectual trend that later came to be called "neoconservatism." This current of thought, in which I was deeply involved, differed in one crucial respect from its conservative predecessors: Its chosen enemy was contemporary liberalism, not socialism or statism in the abstract. (About communism—as distinct, say, from Soviet foreign policy—we had almost nothing to say, we were so utterly hostile to it.) The dozen or so academics and intellectuals who formed the original core of neoconservatism, located at the *Public Interest*, a journal Daniel Bell and I founded in 1965, were all disillusioned liberals—disillusioned with the newest twists and turns of that liberalism, but also (in varying degrees) with their past liberalism whose inherent flaws now rose to visibility. We were, most of us, social scientists, but there were no economists in the group—they came later, along with the cultural critics.

In a way, the symbol of the influence of neoconservative thinking on the Republican party was the fact that Ronald Reagan could praise Franklin D. Roosevelt as a great American president—praise echoed by Newt Gingrich a dozen years later, when it is no longer so surprising. The message was clear: The Republican party was no longer interested in destroying the welfare state, in the name of "antistatism," but intended rather to reconstruct it along more economical and more humane lines. The emphasis on "more humane" is another sign of neoconservative influence. Whereas traditional conservatism had tried to focus attention on welfare cheating, the writings of various neoconservatives over the years has emphasized the terrible, demoralizing effects of our welfare system on the recipients of welfare themselves. It is now no longer a matter of simply saving the budget from welfare expenditures but of redeeming the welfare population from the kind of "exploitation" involved in a system that created and encouraged dependency. The new message—that dependency corrupts and that absolute dependency tends to corrupt absolutely—has given a moral dimension to welfare reform that it had lacked. And in the United States there can be no successful reform movement without such a moral dimension.

To the surprise of most observers, the critique of liberalism by neoconservative intellectuals, scholars, and publicists was far more effective than the older attack on "statism." Paradoxically, precisely because there was no socialist movement—no ideological "statist" movement—in the United States, the neoconservative critique went deeper, and was more radical, than conservative critiques in Britain or Western Europe.

Oakeshott has evoked little active response—as distinct from passive admiration—in the United States, but the writings of Leo Strauss have been extraordinarily influential. Strauss's analysis of the destructive elements within modern liberalism, an analysis that was popularized by his students and his students' students, has altered the very tone of public discourse in the United States. Who would have thought it possible, thirty years ago, that in 1995 one third of the American public would designate itself as conservative while only 17 percent designated itself as liberal—with the rest claiming the label of "moderate." To bring contemporary liberalism into disrepute—its simplistic views of human nature, its utopian social philosophy, its secularist animus against religion—is no small achievement.

The second and most spectacular thing that happened was the emergence of religious conservatives, especially Protestant evangelical conservatives, as a force to be reckoned with. This has no parallel in any of the other Western democracies, where secularist habits of thought still rule supreme. It has been estimated that something like one third of the American electorate are (or claim to be) regular churchgoers. Not all of them are conservative, of course, but the overwhelming majority are. And it is important to emphasize that, insofar as they are antistatist, as most are, it is not only on economic grounds, or even on Jeffersonian-individualist grounds. These religious conservatives see, quite clearly and correctly, that statism in America is organically linked with secular liberalism—that many of the programs and activities of the welfare state have a powerful antireligious animus. School prayer is a very live issue among religious conservatives, not because public schools are especially suitable places for young people to pray in, but because our educational system, dominated by the teachers' unions, the schools of education, and the liberal politicians who count on their active electoral support, is biased in an antireligious way. And because this religious conservatism is not only antistatist but antiliberal on philosophical grounds (however "unsophisticated" those philosophical grounds are), the role of neoconservative intellectuals has become especially important.

Conservative politicians woo the religious conservatives, but only neoconservatives can really speak to them. The intellectual class in the United States is so violently opposed to religious conservatism that the presence of even a relatively small number of friendly neoconservatives makes a difference. Many of these neoconservatives are not themselves religiously observant in their private lives—though more and more are coming to be. This leads to accusations by liberal intellectuals of hypocrisy or cold-blooded political instrumentalism. But such accusations miss the point. All political philosophers prior to the twentieth century, regardless of their personal piety or lack thereof, understood the importance of religion in the life of the political community. Neoconservatives, because of their interest in and attachment to classical (as distinct from contemporary) political philosophy, share this understanding. Just as there is a difference between being pious and being observant, so there is a difference between being observant and being religious. As it happens, a disproportionate number of neoconservatives are Jewish, and within the Jewish community such distinctions have always been blurred. In any case, more and more Christians and Jews these days who themselves have a secular lifestyle are seeing to it that their children are raised within a religious tradition. Modern secularism has such affinities to moral nihilism that even those who wish simply to affirm or reaffirm moral values have little choice but to seek a grounding for such values in a religious tradition.

Most foreign journalists, like their American counterparts, tend to be secularist in outlook and therefore have difficulty in understanding what is happening within American politics. One has only to read the American reporting in such a distinguished journal as *The Economist* to experience this difficulty—to read reporting that is sophisticated, blandly superficial, and misleading. But it is not only the issue of religion that creates this difficulty. There is also the equally significant issue of populism.

American democracy regularly witnesses populist upsurges. European and British observers, along with most American scholars, tend to describe them as "spasms," or even "paroxysms." But they are nothing of the sort. They are built into the very structure of American politics in a way that is alien to British or European politics, where "politics" is what the government says or does. In a sense, it is fair to say that contemporary political journalism as well as most political scholarship is "statist" in its preconceptions and vision. Whenever a populist upsurge occurs, as is happening today, national politics in the United States trails behind local politics, and to focus one's attention on Washington is to misdirect it.

In the United States, most school boards are locally elected, and school board politics is the way most adult Americans begin their political education. If you are looking for some of the reasons for the strength of American conservatism today, watching local school board politics is a good, though difficult place to begin—difficult because there are so many such school boards, and the issues that cause contention vary from place to place. Still, had one been paying attention to them, one would be better prepared to appreciate the anxieties and frustrations of so many American parents with the educational establishment. It is not simply that their children do not often get a decent education in the basics of reading, writing, arithmetic, history, and geography, but that the "youth culture" and "counterculture" born after World War II have captured the school system itself, and have been codified in the leading schools of education. Parents are loath to argue with educators, who are presumed to be the experts, and when they do argue they are sufficiently confused and intimidated to argue badly. But anxiety about what happens to their children—a diffuse terror, even, about what kinds of mature young people they will grow up to be—is widespread in the United States today. Sooner or later, politicians emerge to tap this view of anxiety. That is why the so-called "social issues," more accurately described as moral issues, are so powerful today. The Clinton Administration, convinced (as most liberals are) that economic issues are at the center of politics, finds itself bewildered and impotent when confronted by such issues. Economic frustration liberals are sensitive to, but moral frustration is incomprehensible to them. The major reason for this incomprehension, of course, is that it is the doctrines of modern liberalism itself that have given rise to this frustration.

In Washington, D.C., the most liberal and "statist" city in the nation, school board politics across the country is unworthy of the attention of the national media, as is state and local politics for the most part. Indeed, our liberal media really detests our entire federal system, which complicates their journalistic mission. They don't mind presidential primaries or primaries for governorships, which fit into their framework of politics-as-a-horse-race. But they hate primaries for lower offices— that's "local news" and unworthy of their attention. Referenda—a legacy of the Progressive movement that is institutionalized in many of our states—are now equally despised because they introduce a "wild card" into the established political "game," and because these days they are more successfully used by conservative activists. The secular liberals are horrified by politicians who mix religion with politics, since their media are convinced that religion is, at best, a private affair and has no place at all in the public square. A politician who so much as mentions Jesus Christ alarms them.

Ironically, Washington and the liberal media are least prepared for conservative changes within the media itself. These changes have come from an unexpected source—from yesteryear's technology, not today's. There is a comfortable symbiosis between our national newsmagazines, our half-dozen or so newspapers that claim national attention, and our national television networks. They are all liberal, more or less, and feel that they share the journalistic mission of "enlightening" (as well as entertaining) the American public. They have tried, somewhat less than halfheartedly, to give "representation" to the conservative viewpoint whenever they sense that this viewpoint has become popular. But they were utterly unprepared for the sudden emergence and swift rise of radio "talk shows," which now rival TV's daytime soap operas in popularity. These talk shows are overwhelmingly conservative in their politics and populist in their rhetoric—which is another way of saying that they are, more often than not, stridently conservative, vulgarly conservative, and not at all urbane or sophisticated.

All of this happened without anyone planning it, or directing it, or even anticipating it. It was made possible by the federal structure of our polity and by the fact that there are well over a thousand local radio stations. Once a local program—that of Rush Limbaugh, for instance—becomes popular, other local stations, always eager for listeners, will rush to broadcast him. And if, for competitive reasons, they cannot do so, they will try hard to invent their own popular conservative talk shows. The owners of these stations are interested primarily in making some money, not in spreading any kind of liberal "enlightenment." And, given the near-absence of government regulation, the market works.

In the United States, there is always a latent populist potential simply because the structure of our polity and of our economy makes it possible for the *vox populi* to find expression. There are obstacles to overcome, of course, but not too many and not too large. This populist potential disturbs political theorists, even conservative ones who fear that populist dissatisfaction is likely to have an anticapitalist thrust. In fact, this has rarely been the case in the United States. Even the original populist movement at the beginning of this century, generally identified as belonging to the left, was not really so. It was hostile to big business, not to the free market, and the big business it opposed were the "trusts," the emerging monopolies and quasi-monopolies that then were becoming dominant economic institutions. The populist response was to "break them up," so as to reestablish free enterprise and a competitive market-place. The idea of nationalizing large corporations is almost never on the populist agenda, and the idea of governments regulating them rather than disassembling them was very grudgingly accepted as a second best. It is interesting to note that today populist opinion—as every poll shows—is more concerned about cutting the federal deficit than about lowering taxes, which has come as a great surprise to many conserva-tives, who learned in their "political science" courses in college that "the people" always want to be pandered to. It is also worth noting that the current Republican Congress is turning a cold shoulder to the lobbyists of the major corporations while exuding friendliness to those organiza-tions that represent smaller businesses. This upsets many conservative economists, who point to macrostatistics that show the economic importance of multinational corporations. Which only shows that the macrostatistics of economists, along with the microstatistics of the pub-lic opinion polls, are best ignored by a conservative government that is interested not merely in being reelected but in creating an enduring, national conservative majority. Economists are always complaining that politicians are usually too shortsighted, thereby revealing themselves to be too often myopic.

As concerns foreign policy, too, the new conservative populism is playing a crucial—though as yet ambiguous—role in an interesting political realignment that is occurring. The liberal Democrats, ever since the 1930s, have generally been interventionist and multilateralist in for-eign policy. The conservative Republicans have tended to be nationalist and isolationist. This situation is changing. Liberal Democrats are now well on their way to being economic protectionists and are much less interested than formerly in seeing the United States play a major role in world affairs. In contrast, Republicans now favor international free trade and, while still nationalist, are no longer isolationist. Just how those trends, still embryonic, will develop in the future is unknowable. The Republicans have a special problem in defining a nationalist foreign poli-cy in a post-Cold War world. But one thing is clear: Multilateralism is dead so far as *both* parties are concerned. This is something our European allies seem not to understand. It isn't that American opinion has turned hostile to the United Nations and NATO. Rather, there isn't even enough interest in such organizations to breed hostility.

The populist conservatism that is the major trend in American conservatism also has its own internal problems. There are still a lot of traditional conservatives who are suspicious of populism. Many of them are still in the Senate, which is elected for longer terms and in staggered stages. But even in the House of Representatives there is internal dissension. Those in the "right-to-life" movement, like the abolitionists of a century-and-a-half ago, are fanatically determined to make the best the enemy of the good. Partial victories they tend to regard as a distraction from the total victory they seek. And then there are all those newly-elected Republican governors, critical of the welfare state but reluctant to give up federal funds that help them cope with their own budgetary shortfalls. In short, all talk about an abrupt "conservative revolution" is dangerous hyperbole, even if it does inspire the troops. There will surely be defeats ahead, some of them self-inflicted.

The United States today shares all of the evils, all of problems, to be found among the Western democracies—and sometimes in an exaggerated form. But it is also the case that the United States today is the only Western democracy that is witnessing a serious conservative revival that is an active response to these evils and problems. The further fact that it is a populist conservatism dismays the conservative elites of Britain and Western Europe, who prefer a more orderly and dignified kind of conservatism—which, in actuality, always turns out to be a defensive and therefore enfeebled conservatism. It is certainly true that any kind of populism can be a danger to our democratic orders. But it is also true that populism can be a corrective to the defects of democratic orders—defects often arising from the intellectual influence, and the skillful entrepreneurial politics, of our democratic elites. Classical political thought was wary of democracy because it saw the people as fickle, envious, and inherently turbulent. Those thinkers had no knowledge of democracies where the people were conservative and the educated elites that governed them were ideological elites, always busy provoking disorder and discontent so as to achieve some utopian goal. Populist conservatism is a distinctly modern phenomenon, and conservative political thinking has not yet caught up with it. That is why the "exceptional" kind of conservative politics we are now witnessing in the United States is so important, and is to be looked at seriously. It could turn out to represent the "last, best hope" of contemporary conservatism.

What would Michael Oakeshott have made of this populist conservatism? I don't for a moment think he would have admired it. But Michael was a very wise man, and I believe he might very well consider it as one of those "necessary evils" in this "best of all possible worlds." I would like to think so, anyhow.

1995

SECTION VI

On Jews

34

God and the Psychoanalysts

*My courage fails me, therefore, at the thought of rising up as a prophet before my
fellow-men, and I bow to the reproach that I have no consolation to offer them;
for at bottom that is what they all demand—the frenzied revolutionary as passionately as the most pious believer.*

—SIGMUND FREUD

Psychoanalysis was from its very beginnings disrespectful, when not positively hostile, toward all existing religious creeds and institutions. Naturally, the religious rhetoricians replied with heat, though, it must be said,
with unequal light. The contest was not exactly an exciting one, if only
because few people could get enthusiastic about God, one way or the
other. The psychoanalysts found it sufficient to explain with supreme
objectivity just how it was that this mountain of nonsense and error
came to rest on human shoulders. The preachers retorted with anathe-
mas or plaints of misrepresentation. The general conviction of the century was that the analysts were going to unnecessary extremes of detail
to dissect a patient ripe for the grave, and that the patient was showing a
lack of taste in hanging on so grimly to a life that held no future for him.

But then the contest was transplanted to the melting pot of America,
with astonishing consequences. In America all races and creeds live and
work peacefully side by side—why should not ideas do likewise? For the
ancient habit of supposing that an idea was true or false, there was sub-

389

stituted the more "democratic" way of regarding all ideas as aspects of a universal Truth which, if all of it were known, would offend no one and satisfy all. It is under such favorable circumstances, and in such a benign climate of opinion, that the current love affair between psychoanalysis and religion has been, time and again, consummated. There have been bickerings and quarrels, of course, and the Catholic Church has shown itself to be a rather frigid partner. But, all in all, things have gone well, and the occasional Catholic reserve has been more than made up for by Protestant acquiescence and Jewish ardor.

Where once a Judaism liberated from the ghetto fled into the arms of a universal Pure Reason (which did, after all, proclaim honorable intentions), now a Judaism liberated from just about everything religious embraces psychoanalysis without a first thought as to the propriety of the liaison. So we read of a speech by the dean of Hebrew Union College, calling for a reexamination of religious teachings to determine whether "they strengthen or weaken the mental and emotional health of the common man"—the assumption obviously being that God is a fiction anyhow and He may as well make Himself useful. Another distinguished professor at Hebrew Union College is on record with this "tip" for alert investors: "The person who will contribute money for religio-psychoanalytic inquiry will have entered upon the way of all ways in which religion can be furthered by money." And two bright young rabbis have proposed to a conference of Jewish chaplains that the prayer books for hospitalized Jewish veterans be "screened" by psychiatrists to eliminate "any mystic elements from religion." Everyone knows how toxic mysticism is.

The monument to this tendency is, of course, the late Joshua Loth Liebman's *Peace of Mind*. This book informs us quite simply that "psychological discoveries about conduct and motive are really the most recent syllables of the divine"; that "men who are inwardly tormented and emotionally unhappy can never be good partners of God"; that the Decalogue was, for its time, rather sensible: "In the stages of human development from infancy to adolescence, it is quite proper to present rules of moral behavior as categorical commandments"; that atheism is the result of a child's being rejected by its parents; that "businessmen attacking the administration, grumbling about taxes, or worrying about our relations with Russia" ignore the fact that "the true root of their anxiety lies deep within themselves"; that "a wise religion" [no mention is made of a true one] "is indispensable to peace of mind"; that self-confident Americans who regard themselves as "responsible co-workers with God" can have no use for all those religious notions which arose out of the "helpless, poverty-stricken, powerless motifs in European culture." The book closes with a list of "commandments of a new morality," the first of which is: "Thou shalt not be afraid of thy hidden impulses."

In an attempt to dispel the impression that *Peace of Mind* made upon many—that today no one is so sick as our spiritual healers—Fulton J. Sheen has written a Catholic *Peace of Soul*. Monsignor Sheen makes it clear that it is only with the greatest of distaste that he has written this book, and that it is to be taken as a concession to modern man's moral disorder. He is repelled by the "scum and sediment" of the unconscious and feels sure that ecclesiastical dogma would prefer that the unconscious not exist. But since it reputedly does, Monsignor Sheen sets out to purge psychoanalysis of its impurities, absorb it into the Catholic intellectual hierarchy, and leave it to perish there of boredom. These impurities are attributed to a misemphasis on "sex analysis" (Freudianism), which Monsignor Sheen accuses of undermining the moral order and defying the prerogatives of religion and church. Specifically, he dislikes the fact that psychoanalytical patients spend so much time on their backs, a posture which invites the devil; he wishes to save "sin" as a reality born of a defective will and not let it be dismissed as a neurotic fancy; and he would like to mark out the boundaries between the confessional and psychoanalysis, leaving for the latter only those situations where the emotional derangement could have had no moral (or immoral) antecedents—which would leave it with very little at all. He is especially friendly to self-analysis because the intimacy between patient and analysis is a sore temptation as well as a trespass on the clerical province.

All this indicates that Monsignor Sheen is considerably more zealous than was Rabbi Liebman in asserting the priority of morality and the Church over psychoanalysis. Yet they have more in common than would appear at first sight, even more than their literary ties to the fraternity of vulgar journalism (Monsignor Sheen writes: "Nine months later the Eternal established its beachhead in Bethlehem."). Both would like to be of assistance to those modern psychoanalysts who would "revise" or emasculate Freud to make him palatable, or even useful, to the *ecclesia*. Though Monsignor Sheen, unlike Rabbi Liebman, gives a positive religious status to anxiety—as a necessary quality of man who is a fallen creature, and as a spur to seeking God—he is just as eager for this anxiety not to be taken too much to heart: Monsignor Sheen promises peace of soul inside the Catholic Church as glibly as Rabbi Liebman promises peace of mind outside it. Where for Rabbi Liebman an excess of anxiety is "unhealthy," for Monsignor Sheen it is—unless it is quickly dissolved into Catholic "peace of soul"—a possible prelude to heresy and a certain sign of deficient faith. For neither of these two clerics is the existence of God, and man's relation with Him, a problem which should worry men to morbid excess. And both join their voices in eagerly quoting from psychiatrists' testimonials concerning the beneficent influence of religion on mental health.

But, most of all, what Monsignor Sheen and Rabbi Liebman and their numerous Protestant counterparts share is a disinclination, or inability, to take Freud seriously, to take his challenge to religion seriously, and in the end, to take religion itself seriously.

What is remarkable in all current demonstrations of how well religion and psychoanalysis supplement each other is that the question of truth—whether we live under God or entirely in the realm of nature—is ignored. Most clerics and analysts blithely agree that religion and psychoanalysis have at heart the same intention: to help men "adjust," to cure them of their vexatious and wasteful psychic habits (lasting despair and anxiety), to make them happy or virtuous or productive. Insofar as religion and psychoanalysis succeed in this aim, they are "true." But against this stands the overwhelming objection of Nietzsche: "Nobody will very readily regard a doctrine as true merely because it makes people happy or virtuous. . . . A thing could be *true*, although it were in the highest degree injurious and dangerous; indeed the fundamental constitution of existence might be such that one succumbed by a full knowledge of it."

And Moses and Freud are in agreement with at least the first part of Nietzsche's statement; they came to speak the truth about the fundamental constitution of existence and not to sow propaganda which would lead men to feel themselves happy or virtuous. Moses did not promise the Jews "happiness," nor did he say they should walk in the path of the Law because he thought it a virtuous law. The Law was true because it was divine—it was God's Law, a revelation of man's place in the fundamental constitution of existence. Though men suffer and die in the following of it, yet it is the truth, and men's true happiness and virtue are in adhering to this truth—because it is true; any other kind of pretended happiness is but mere euphoria. Freud, in turn, did not assert that religion made men "unhappy,"* but that it was based on an illusion about the fundamental constitution of existence. Freud, like Moses, could not conceive of authentic happiness as something separate from truth. In his eyes, religion was a mass obsessional neurosis, and all attempts to enlist psychoanalysis in its support were dementedly clever stratagems whereby the neurotic incorporated a new experience into a larger obsessional pattern. Even if it could be proved that men could not live without religion, that "they succumbed by a full knowledge" of reality, this showed only that man was a creature who could not live in the truth.

The truths of religion and psychoanalysis, it should be clear, lay mutually exclusive claims upon the individual; their understanding of "the fundamental constitution of existence" is antithetical.

For religion, we live under the jurisdiction of the past. The truth is in the revelation on Sinai, and in Scripture, which fully comprehends us while we are powerless to fully comprehend it. God's word, spoken in the remote past and now hardly audible, is ever more true than the persistent chatter of men. Religion informs us that our ancestors were wiser and holier than we; that they were therefore more normal because they lived by divine Law, while our laws are driftwood in the stream of time; that no matter how mightily we strive we shall probably never see with their clarity into the fundamental constitution of existence and shall always be of little worth compared with them; and that, indeed, the virtue we inherit by reason of being descendants of Abraham, Isaac, and Jacob is far greater than any we can hope to claim to have merited. "What are we? What is our life? What is our piety? . . . Nevertheless we are Thy people, the children of Thy covenant, the children of Abraham."

Psychoanalysis, on the other hand, must repeat Freud's words: "But these ancestors of ours were far more ignorant than we." Psychoanalysis insists that it understands the past better than the past understood itself. Since all men have been driven by unconscious motivations which only we

---

*That religion could claim a "therapeutic" value, Freud understood very well in his own way: "The true believer is in a high degree protected against the danger of certain neurotic afflictions; by accepting the universal neurosis he is spared the task of forming a personal neurosis"; and further: "At such a cost—by the forcible imposition of mental infantilism and inducing a mass delusion—religion succeeds in saving many people from individual neuroses."

moderns really understand, and of which past generations were for the most part ignorant, a Freud of the twentieth century, or, presumably, one of his competent pupils, equipped with the tools of psychoanalysis, can know Moses, Da Vinci, Michelangelo, and Dostoevski better than they knew themselves. At most we can say of certain great minds of the past that they had an intuitive and premature inkling of the true constitution of human nature and existence which is now known (or will soon be known) in its fullness. The history of the human race is a tale of growth from primitive times—when men were as children—to the present age of adulthood, when man finally understands himself and his history.

There is a crucial disagreement here, which can never be mediated, as to what is the true and the real. Psychoanalysis explains religion; it describes how and why religion came into being, how and why what we clearly see to be irrational was accepted as superrationally true, and how and why that which we know to be a product of the human fancy came to be regarded as an existing, supernatural being.* To this, religion answers that the understanding of psychoanalysis is only a dismal, sophisticated misunderstanding, that human reason is inferior to divine reason, that the very existence of psychoanalysis is a symptom of gross spiritual distress, and that religion understands the psychoanalyst better than the psychoanalyst understands himself.

In this dialogue between psychoanalysis and religion, it is to be expected that psychoanalysis would try to establish its position behind the starched apron of science. What is surprising is that the religionists should be so eager to assist it—until we remember that in the long, grueling warfare between science and organized religion, the latter received valuable instruction in tactics. Abandoning the frontal attack, the pastors were successfully able to persuade the scientists that science was not at all atheistic, as some brash people claimed, but that its sphere of activity was quite a different one from that of religion, that it dealt with an "abstract" reality and not the "real" reality, that its arid language was inadequate to religious statement, that it operated on another "level of meaning," and so on. In the same way today, pacific priests and analysts

---

*The psychoanalytical theories of Jung which accept the subjective religious experience as something ultimate, are an interesting deviation from this line. But Jung never commits himself as to whether God *is*, and therefore cannot genuinely decide whether the religious experience is normal or abnormal.

are eager that psychoanalysis should renounce its wild and Freudian past and become a medical science; for the more medicinal it is, the smaller is the danger that it will seem to say anything about the fundamental constitution of existence, the less does it encroach upon religion, and the greater is the mutual security of religious and psychoanalytic institutions; psychoanalysis would deal only with "health" and never with "truth." The result is a revision and "correction" of Freud—especially in America—which tends to make of psychoanalysts mental counselors, in no necessary conflict with religion, "adjusting" patients to their infirmities, their limitations of talent, their jobs (or else the analyst serves as a vocational guide), their bad luck, their wives, their children, and, in the armed forces, to their officers. Some analysts even send their patients to church, as a therapy.

Psychoanalysis, then, would seem to be on its way to becoming simply the medical treatment of the psyche, cohabiting with religion in all amiability. But on this way it stumbles and falls. For if psychoanalysis is disloyal to the implications of its method—to what this method assumes as the fundamental constitution of existence, as enunciated by Freud—it sinks into a realm of relativism in which the human intellect circles upon itself like a dog chasing its tail.

Psychoanalysis is unlike traditional medicine in that nature does not so readily supply us with a working definition of the psychically "normal." Our definition of physical normality ("health") is not something we have strenuously to imagine or blindly to postulate, and there are obvious and sharp limits to possible disagreement; it is simply given to us because we are what we are. But psychoanalysis is in a more ambiguous position. Its definition of mental health has to be in good measure "thought up," and it must be done by men whose ideas are influenced by their lives and times. Psychoanalysis is always open to the accusation that its criteria of "neurosis" and "mental health" and "adjustment" have a cultural bias, and are influenced by political ideologies, national prejudices, and personal whims. To take the accusation in its most general form: Any psychoanalytical approach which, out of diplomatic cordiality toward religion, renounces its claim to an objective knowledge of human nature or to a lasting, true insight into the fundamental constitution of existence must admit that it is historically and socially conditioned. And once there is no objectively *true* human nature which is taken as the room, there is no possibility of general agreement on what it means to be "sick" and what it means to be "cured." We can then have communist analysts, Nazi analysts, democratic analysts, anarchist analysts, all with irreconcilable criteria of mental health.

Actually, the dilemma of the "revisionist" schools of psychoanalysis arises from their reluctance to abandon—at the same time that they drop all Freudian "metaphysics"—either of the two branches of psychoanalysis joined by Freud: the pathological and the general psychological. (This distinction is very lucidly made by Theodore Reik in *Listening with the Third Ear*.) Pathological psychology seems to have some intimate relation with the organic, intimate enough, in any case, for it to be a (still largely unexplored) subbranch of medicine. But in this field, psychoanalysis has to compare with formal psychiatry and neurology, both of which are closer to what is universally deemed medical science: Psychoanalysis can "explain" more than psychiatry only because it is less rigorously scientific. To be sure, psychoanalysis has effected cures of pathological cases. But cures have also been reached by treatments which have nothing to do with psychoanalysis, nor can psychoanalysis claim greater efficiency, greater rapidity, or any other advantage. Moreover, psychoanalysis is splintered into various schools, all of which claim to cure, and no way exists of deciding for or against any one of them, or of finding out whether they may work for reasons quite different from those given by all of them. In pathology, psychoanalysis stands to the ideal of medical science as the herb-doctor (whose herbs work too sometimes, and not entirely by chance) to a diagnostician.

Yet when psychoanalysis turns to nonpathological cases, and tries to fall back upon general psychology, upon its theory of human nature, for a warrant of competence, then it has to say what human nature rightfully *is*; it has to be explicit as to whether man prays to God or is trapped in an obsessional neurosis, it has to decide the question of truth before it dares raise the question of therapy. And this would involve it in those discussions about man and his place in the universe which would be fatal to its ambitious to live at peace with religion.

Freud, too, was faced with the problem that before one could aim at healing human nature it was necessary to decide what human nature in its undamaged state is, and in his analysis of dreams he stepped unhesitatingly from pathology to depth (general) psychology. The pathological and the abnormal were points of departure for the determination of the "really" normal, and Freud ceased to be a doctor and became a thinker.

Truth precedes healing—Freud's own italicized definition of the task of psychoanalysis was *"education to reality."* Where in all of his past history man had achieved only a self-deceptive self-consciousness, riddled with mythical projections of the unconscious, now man has acquired the ability to see the human situation as it really is.

Perhaps because of the verbal resonance of such terms as the "unconscious" and the "libido," and certainly because of his own harsh comments on various facile and optimistic beliefs, Freud is often viewed as a reaction to the nineteenth century's certainty that man was master of his fate and to its adoration of the goddess Reason. Freud himself, in certain passages, seemed to encourage this interpretation, as when he noted the three wounds inflicted by science on humanity's self-love: the cosmological blow of the Copernican revolution, the biological blow of Darwinian evolution, and the psychological blow of Freudianism. But such an interpretation of Freud would be erroneous, and Freud's remarks seeming to support it must be understood mainly as a not unflattering explanation of the hostility which his contemporaries directed at him.

Copernicus, Darwin, and Freud did not attack *man's* self-love, but only the *religious man's* self-respect. They diminished God (though, except for Freud, without intention) and aggrandized man as the rational animal. They did not undermine man's reason, but enthroned it, at the expense of the religious authority. Freud did not come to proclaim the law of Reason at an end—he came to fulfill it, at the same time explaining how previous efforts at fulfillment had been overly glib and superficial. Man, by virtue of Freud's work, was not less than he had been; he was infinitely more, facing for the first time the prospect of an authentic self-consciousness and self-control which would make him the true measure of all things. Though Freud, in comparison with his contemporaries, complicated human nature, it was the kind of theoretical complication (like Einsteinian physics) which makes possible the lucid solution of hitherto baffling problems; it is a gain for Reason, not a loss.

Freudianism was a legitimate son of nineteenth-century philosophy (Marxism was another) which declared that in all previous world history the human mind had not been free but had been enslaved to nature or society, and that now life according to true Reason (not ideological or neurotic rationalization) was within men's reach. The epoch of human history in which man's mind had been "alienated" from reality was approaching its end. And Freud was supremely a man of the nineteenth century in his idea of history as the development of the human race from infancy to adulthood, in his conceiving of the biography of humanity as entirely analogous to the biography of the individual, with religion as a childlike obsessional neurosis which the child had failed to outgrow and which the doctor was now hurrying to cure, so as to secure, in his own words, "the psychological ideal, the primacy of the intelligence."

Freud is of one mind with Spinoza, that to have a rational understanding of what our instincts (Spinoza called them passions) are up to is to make us master of them. The purpose of psychoanalysis is to redeem the ego from compulsive irrationality (neurosis) and to place the instinctual libido in the service of a rational ego, for it is not the instinctual unconscious itself which resists psychoanalytical treatment—its goal is to be discharged, into consciousness or action—but the irrational ego, the ego that has "solved" its problems by a nonrational adjustment (neurosis) and that desperately defends its precarious solution. This redemption of the rational ego is achieved in the three steps of the psychoanalytical treatment: (1) the "recall" of the repressed—a conscious awareness of what is behind the particular neurosis; (2) transference, or redirection of the libidinal force to the analyst, which gives the ego a chance to wrestle openly, through a transference neurosis, with the material raised from the unconscious; (3) mastery of the instinctual urges by the rational ego.

It is clear from this how absurd is the charge against Freud of being the high priest of the irrational, goading the instincts, especially the sexual instincts, into a coup d'état. (Monsignor Sheen seems to be of this opinion.) It would be more accurate to say that Freud was a supreme puritan. The tenor of Freud's writings is that the present sexual standards of respectability are maliciously provocative of nervous disorder. His plea for greater sexual freedom is the plea of a wise and experienced statesman, not the appeal of an irresponsible radical. For Freud, sex is the blind, powerful, and eternally rebellious subject of the legitimate despot Reason. Revolt means calamity: At the least, the established order is forced to share power with new tribunes, in an uneasy compromise; at the most, sheer anarchy prevails. It is because of his fear of the herd of sexual instincts that Freud would concede so much to them, would abrogate the existing sexual morality in favor of a less provocative one, would assure a free genital sexuality in order to provide protection to all those other zones threatened with erotic invasion. The localization in the genitals of the sexual urge is the necessary condition for the natural reign of Reason. The greater the liberty of the genitalia in satisfying this urge, the greater the security of the Rational state.

There are two fairly distinct trends in Freud's analysis of religion, both of them hostile, but corresponding, respectively, to his earlier mood of moderate hope and his later mood of only faintly relieved gloom. The second is more important in what it tells us about the ultimate destiny of psychoanalysis. The first is important too, however, in that it provided a crucial supplement to the rationalist refutation of religion. Though rationalists of the eighteenth and nineteenth centuries spoke of the slow education of human reason from superstition upward, from credulousness and helplessness to manly independence of spirit, it was Freud who came to show the psychological necessity of this evolutionary process. Freud's attack on religion cut more deeply than even that of Voltaire or Marx, for while Voltaire could expose the unreasonableness of religious dogmas, and Marx could show how religion mirrored the inauthenticity of man in the precommunist era, neither could satisfactorily explain the psychological mechanism by which human beings came to be so duped in the first place and why it lasted as long as it did.

According to Freud, religion is the price paid for the *blind* renunciation of inherent instincts. Religious prohibitions deprive sexuality of its due at the same time that religious creeds leave reason defenseless and feeble, so that sexuality is able to reappear in the disguise of neurotic behavior such as prayer, pilgrimage, theological speculation, and the like. Religions owe their obsessive character to "important happenings in the primeval history of the human family" and "derive their effect on mankind from the historical truth they contain"—a truth imprinted on the racial memory of every newborn child. The "happening" from which religion grew was the slaying and communal eating, in the primal horde, of the primal father by his sons, who had joined together in order to share the father's sexual prerogatives—the original Oedipal revolt, and one which each individual recapitulates in his own mental experience. But the victorious sons were tormented by anxiety about their portentous deed, and by fear of continual, bloody sexual rivalry. So there came into being, in these "ages of ignorance and intellectual weakness," the sense of guilt and sin, as well as moral codes and religious catechisms, to repress all sexual rivalry with the fathers, to appease the memory of the primal father who had been transformed into God, and to guarantee the existence of an orderly community. And each individual not only "remembers" the historic past, but in his own lifetime has to make some sort of adjustment to his own Oedipus complex, his impotence as a child to challenge the father for the mother's favors, his jealousy, and the anxious repression of it.

The history of religion is analogical to the history of neurosis in the growing child, its strength gathered from childhood anxieties and frustrations, and this strength dissipated with natural growth into adult rationality. The history of humanity, like the life-history of every one of its members, is a process of maturation in which the instinctual renunciations necessary for the stability of the community are rationally comprehended and lose their malevolent potential. Freud writes:

"We know that the human child cannot well complete its development towards culture without passing through a more or less distinct phase of neurosis. This is because the child is unable to suppress by rational mental effort so many of those instinctual impulsions which cannot later be turned into account, but has to check them by acts of repression, behind which there stands as a rule an anxiety motive. Most of these child neuroses are overcome spontaneously as one grows up, and especially is this the fate of the obsessional neuroses of childhood. The remainder can be cleared up later by psychoanalytical treatment." And in the same volume (*The Future of an Illusion*): "One might prophesy that the abandoning of religion must take place with the fateful inexorability of growth, and that we are just now in the middle of this phase of development."

By virtue of science and psychoanalysis, mankind begins to see the approaches to the Kingdom of Reason. The false knowledge of a supernatural Other, which was only an evasion of true self-knowledge, will be sloughed off like an outworn garment, and God, together with bibles, saints, and churches, will be consigned to the museum of human infancy.

What can religion reply to this? It is impossible to ask what *does* religion reply to this, for religion in our time for the most part does not reply at all. It either gives up the ghost and tries to show its social and psychological utility in an imperfect world where the triumph of Reason is not yet complete; or it utters grave twaddle about incorporating "the enduring insights" of psychoanalysis in a "larger perspective," as if its perspective were infinitely elastic. Religion is uncertain, does not know whether we were really on Sinai or whether it was only a dream.

Yet there are certain lines of argument, it seems to me, which religious thought, because it is religious, must take. Religion must agree with psychoanalysis that the world in which we live is sick, but where psychoanalysis asserts that religion is a symptom of this illness, religion must cling to its own diagnosis and see psychoanalysis itself as a symptom of a mind diseased. Religion has to deny the thesis of progressive human evolution, and must explain psychoanalysis, must explain it away, by tracing its genesis and showing that the error in which it is involved points to the truth which it denies.

Psychoanalysis, in the eyes of religion, is a historical passion of men obsessed with the death of God. Nietzsche proclaimed that God was dead, Freud followed with the news that we had eaten and devoured His human archetype, and that His spiritual existence had always been an illusion. Both were right, for the nineteenth and twentieth centuries have regarded God as a corpse whose essence has been appropriated by man—the so-called divine attributes have been made over into human possibilities. Yet in this era of humanism and godlessness, man found himself more than ever alienated: His flight from God has also been a flight from his true self, which had been made in His image. So it was that Freud could build a theory of human nature on the basis of his experience with hysterics and neurotics, a unique and strange achievement which testifies to our modern psychic equilibrium, whose fulcrum is at the edge of an abyss.

Religion cannot deny that psychoanalysis has discovered the unconscious. It can only say that the unconscious as such is a new phenomenon, the toll paid to God and nature for the presumptive effort to have man's conscious rationality prevail over all of existing reality—including divine reality; in the days when God's face was turned to man, the unconscious was integrated with consciousness and did not whirl madly free through psychic space. The age of Reason, through a series of strenuous introjections, has attempted to press all of religious reality into the rational intellect and to imprison God, cowering and sullen, behind the forehead. The reward of this effort is psychic fragmentation, for divine reality is not within the rational mind of man but outside it, and the mind which would encompass it bursts. Instead of a divine reality that was a great chain of being, there is now, for each man, only a hall of mirrors. Since man has cut all ties with divine reality, has indeed denied to it reality, his psyche has been sentenced to follow upon itself in a dark and unending maze.

Psychoanalysis, religion might say, comes not to remove insanity, but to inaugurate it.

It would seem that this debate between psychoanalysis and religion can continue indefinitely, until it is terminated by God speaking unequivocally or the Kingdom of Reason being attained. And since God is silent and the Kingdom of Reason unborn, the debate goes on, important but nonetheless wearisome. But it is not a debate without end—for that we have Freud's word. Freud's final and tragic message is that the truth is with Reason and against God, but it is a truth in which man probably cannot live. Rational self-consciousness is the avenue to perfect wisdom, which leads in most men to perfect despair. Though Reason still has the task of "reconciling men to civilization," it is an authority entirely vitiated by the fact that "man is a creature of weak intelligence who is governed by his instinctual needs."

This message is found in Freud's later "metapsychological" works, such as *Beyond the Pleasure Principle* and *Civilization and Its Discontents*. Many contemporary psychoanalysts, exercising the privilege of little minds to "revise" greater ones, casually dismiss these writings as deviations from the pure principles of science. But Freud was no eccentric, and if he went beyond the conventional limits of psychological science in his later works (just as he did, incidentally, in his earlier ones), he must have been of the serious opinion that the limits were too confining for the truth as he then saw it. In a letter to Einstein in 1932, in which he outlined his theory of the death instinct as the cause of war, Freud wrote: "All this may give you the impression that our theories amount to a species of mythology, and a gloomy one at that! But does not every natural science lead ultimately to this—a sort of mythology?"

Freud's final "mythology" involves a modification of the earlier postulated contradiction between sexual instincts and ego instincts into one between Eros and Thanatos, the life instinct and the death instinct. The concept of instinct is redefined as "a tendency innate in living organic matter impelling it towards the reinstatement of an earlier condition." What is this earlier condition? "It must be an ancient starting point, which the living being left long ago, and to which it harks back again by all the circuitous paths of development. If we may assume as an experience admitting of no exception that everything living dies from causes within itself, and returns to the inorganic, we can only say 'The goal of all life is death.' . . ." This drive toward extinction is countered by the sexual and reproductive instincts, which are the only ones which do not have as their aim the reinstatement of a previous condition, and which push to life, its extension and unification.*

Instead of being the evolution of Reason and its eventual enthronement, history is blind and its contradictions unresolvable: "And now, it seems to me, the meaning of the evolution of culture is no longer a riddle to us. It must present to us the struggle between Eros and Death, between the instincts of life and the instincts of destruction, as it works itself out in the human species." The death instinct, under the influence of Eros, is extroverted and becomes aggression. Civilization is a huge detour constructed by Eros so as to make the death instinct take the long way home.

Civilization tries to disarm the aggressive instinct by directing it against the ego, by making it over into the "superego" whose aggression against the ego takes the form of "conscience." This tension between the ego and the superego results in the sense of guilt, which while possibly neurotic by the absolute standard of Rational Man, is a normal quality of the human animal in the state of civilization. "The price of progress in civilization is paid in forfeiting happiness through the heightening of the sense of guilt."

Men who are loyal to the truths of Reason are doomed by their very natures to unhappiness. Happiness (but not *true* happiness, not happiness in the *truth*) is available only to those—the immense majority—who cannot face the truth of man's condition, who live with and by illusions, illusions of God, salvation, and the world to come. Freud's metapsychology concedes no more truth to religion than did his psychology. His "mythology" is a rational one. It is a mythology of rational despair.

The present attempts to wed a vulgarized psychoanalysis to a vulgarized religiosity are certain to fail: Between the two parties is stretched the sword of truth, and both are pledged to keep their backs to it. Sooner or later, the world will perceive the lineaments of frustration and will know that the union was never fully consummated. But this marital catastrophe is not

---

*There are important variations in Freud's formulations of his metapsychology. Thus, he seems to say at times that the sexual instinct too is conservative, and that it too aims at death. In *Beyond the Pleasure Principle* he makes use of the myth in Plato's *Symposium* of an original hermaphroditic nature which split into male and female, so that living matter, through sex, seeks a primordial unity.

inevitable—all the mates have to do is, acting together in full consciousness, stealthily to remove the sword of truth and hide it under the bed.

Oddly enough, it is only on the late-Freudian foundation of rational despair that psychoanalysis can be "reconciled" with religion—but at a price, a price that Freud, with his intense personal loyalty to the truth, could never pay. For there are a few men, very few, who are willing to look at life boldly as a bleak prelude to death, and at civilization as an enormous distraction from self-extinction. These men submit to the truths of Reason, because in them Reason is the master of the instincts and not its slave. But in the great mass of men, it is the opposite: Reason is the toy of instinct and happiness in untruth is preferred to truth.

If God does not exist, and if religion is an illusion that the majority of men cannot live without, then psychoanalysis and religion can be reconciled—if that is what one wishes—by the simple expedient of a double standard of truth. Let men believe in the lies of religion since they cannot do without them, and let the handful of sages, who know the truth and can live with it, keep it among themselves. Men are then divided into the wise and the foolish, the philosophers and the common men, and atheism becomes a guarded, esoteric doctrine—for if the illusions of religion were to be discredited, there is no telling with what madness men would be seized, with what uncontrollable anguish. It would indeed become the duty of the wise publicly to defend and support religion, even to call the police power to its aid, while reserving the truth for themselves and their chosen disciples.

Psychoanalysis itself, which assumes religion to be an illusion, would become a form of esoteric wisdom, and the psychoanalyst would, with regard to dreams, agree with Maimonides: "Persons whose mental capacity is not fully developed, and who have not attained intellectual perfection, must not take any notice of them."

Such a program is bound to sound unpleasant in the ears of twentieth-century Americans, though it does have the advantage of enabling many to do what they seem to want to do: to drive in two directions at once, in pursuit of peace of mind at any cost and in pursuit of rational truth. But, of course, there is always the further possibility that the truth is not with Freud and Reason, but with God, and that men *can* live in this truth and find their happiness—simply living in it, though it be a scandal to Reason. "Because the foolishness of God is wiser than men."

1949

35

Einstein: The Passion of Pure Reason

Arrows of hate have been shot at me too; but they never hit me, because somehow they belonged to another world, with which I have no connection whatsoever.
—ALBERT EINSTEIN

In Philipp Frank's biography, *Einstein: His Life and Times*, we read the following anecdote:

"Einstein was once told that a physicist whose intellectual capacities were rather mediocre had been run over by a bus and killed. He remarked sympathetically: 'Too bad about his body!'"

Of course it is probable that Einstein was having his own quiet little joke, making a gesture to the public image of himself as an abstracted, bloodless intellect floating languidly in the stellar spaces. And indeed, according to Einstein's way of thinking, body is body and mind is mind, and it is hard to think of a logical reason why one should have anything to do with the other. The body grows old, but that is hardly worth a thought: Einstein believes birthday celebrations are for children. The body perishes and is buried—of what interest is this to a mature mind? ("Attending funerals is something one does to please the people around us. In itself it is meaningless.") Men are prone to make spectacles of themselves, watching the calendar, meditating on their imminent dissolution into dust, but "the true value of a human being is determined primarily by the measure and the sense in which he has attained liberation

405

from the self."

A volume recently published in Einstein's honor* contains an auto-biographical sketch he wrote four years ago. It opens with the naked sentence: "Here I sit in order to write, at the age of sixty-seven, something like my own obituary." Then, with a few personal asides, there follow forty-five pages of physics and equations. The asides, to be sure, are illuminating. We learn that: "Even when I was a precocious quite young man I became vividly aware of the nothingness of the hopes and strivings that chase most men restlessly through life." Einstein's reaction to this discovery was a deep religiosity that ended abruptly at the age of twelve, giving way to a passion for science, which seemed more capable of freeing him from "the chains of the 'merely personal,' from an existence which is dominated by wishes, hopes, and primitive feelings." We are told all this briefly, in a few paragraphs quickly submerged in pages of technical discussion. But, on page 33, Einstein pulls himself up short, to dispel once and for all any confusion in the mind of the reader:

" 'Is this supposed to be an obituary?' the astonished reader will likely ask. I would like to reply: essentially yes. For the essential in the being of a man of my type lies precisely in what he thinks and how he thinks, not in what he does or suffers."

This, then, is how Einstein would like to see himself: no mournful pilgrim on earth, but the spirit of Pure Reason; not an anguished voice calling futilely from the depths, but a creative spirit hovering over the world of chaos; not a suffering creature, but a thinking creator, whose science is "the attempt at the posterior reconstruction of reality by the process of conceptualization," and whose duty it is "to arrive at those universal elementary laws from which the cosmos can be built up by pure deduction."

---

*Einstein: Philosopher-Scientist, ed. Paul Arthur Schilpp (Evanston, Illinois: The Library of Living Philosophers, 1949). This collection of essays by outstanding philosophers and physicists is most valuable for an understanding of Einstein. It can be read in conjunction with a collection of Einstein's more recent essays and addresses, Out of My Later Years (New York: Philosophical Library, 1950), and Leopold Infeld's Albert Einstein (New York: Scribner's, 1950); as well as Philipp Frank's biography, Einstein: His Life and Times, trans. George Rosen (New York: Knopf, 1947).

What is the path which the spirit must take to this "posterior recon-struction of reality"? On this point, Einstein is unequivocal: The path is through mathematics. And if one can "reconstruct" reality with the aid of mathematics, then it is clear that the original creation must have been according to formula. God is a mathematician, and mathematics is *imitatio Dei*. Of course, God is an exceptional mathematician and his creation is an exceptionally "well-designed puzzle." But not an insoluble puzzle, for God is just. *"Raffiniert is der Herrgott, aber böshaft ist er nicht"* ("God is subtle, but he is not malicious")—with such words Einstein consoles and encourages Princeton's mathematicians when they lounge in Fine Hall and read the inscription over the fireplace. God is not only not malicious, he is also divinely simple: "Our experience . . . justifies us in believing that nature is the realization of the simplest conceivable mathematical ideas."

And if one should inquisitively demand why God is, after all, a mathematician? Ah, that is the mystery, that "pure thought is competent to comprehend the real," that nature is intelligible.

Einstein is not involved in what have been, at different times, designated as the two major scandals of philosophy: the first, that philosophers have not yet been able to prove the existence of the external world; the second, that philosophers should ever have presumed to believe this to be their business. For Einstein, the real world simply is. Simply—is. For if its existence is not to be questioned by serious men, neither is its simplicity. This simplicity may not be apparent to those who are prisoners of their senses and have not been able to make the leap from the kingdom of the bodily self to the kingdom of selfless mind, which is the realm of mathematics and necessity. The world of the body's sense perception is real—but the realer world, the world of order behind the confusion of perceived existence, is the one which is also rational, that is, mathematical. When Einstein refers to the world that is both real and rational he uses the phrase "Physical Reality."

The way to physical reality is through the mathematical imagination, through an exercise of "musicality in the sphere of thought." Such exercises, giving birth to formulas, need to be verified by experiment in order to sift the true from the false; but this does not affect the fact that "the creative principle resides in mathematics." Sense experience is, in itself, chaotic; order is of the mind. "A theory can be tested by experience, but there is no way from experience to the setting up of a theory."

The "fateful" error is to entertain the belief that scientific concepts can be abstracted out of experience. They are "free inventions of the human mind." Fortunately for us, these free inventions of the human mind are found to be congruent with those free inventions of the divine mind which make up the real and rational world of Physical Reality.

One may well ask: What manner of scientist is this? He does not fit the popular image of a white-frocked manipulator of test tubes, or speak with the familiar accents of an apostle of "scientific method." He is, for instance, flatly in disagreement with the positivist Philipp Frank, who expresses what is probably the majority opinion of philosophers of science when he writes that "science cannot discover what actually happens in the world, but can only describe and combine the results of different observations." Einstein is old-fashioned, agreeing with most classical metaphysicians, and incidentally with the man in the street, that science aims to find out what *really* happens beyond the veil of appearance. Is Einstein a crank, his head filled with anachronistic jargon about God and physical reality, who by sheer luck stumbled upon some useful equations? Or is the inadequacy with a misinterpretation of scientific method?

If we examine the phrase "scientific method," we see that there is a studied ambiguity between a "method" of discovery and a "method" of verification, with "scientific method" presumably uniting the two. But, as Morris Raphael Cohen properly emphasized many years ago: "Science knows of methods of verification, but there are no methods of discovery. If there were such, all we need would be discovered, and we would not have to wait for rare men of genius." The universe of scientific discovery is ruled by an aristocracy of talent, not a democracy of method. All theories are in principle equal before the bar of verification, but only a few can gain seats in the house of truth, and there is no way of determining beforehand which these shall be. Genius is not reducible—to method or to anything else—and its very essence is to be uncommon, even exotic.

It is to be expected that men will be resentful of this state of affairs and attempt to circumvent it. The rise of modern science has been accompanied by an insistent philosophic effort at "the taming of the mind." Bacon set up his inductive method, whereby a scrupulous attention to the facts and the relation between facts would make an intelligent man a scientist; Descartes proposed his analytic method, by which "all those who observe its rules exactly would never suppose what is false to be true, and would come—without fatiguing themselves needlessly but in progressively furthering their science—to the true knowledge of all that can be known"; Dewey has sought to make science's "method of inquiry" a human habit, to divert men from "meaningless" metaphysical questions, and to encourage them to good works; and, most recently, logical positivism announced that science cannot hope to plumb the nature of things, but "can only describe and combine the results of different observations," a task for which genius is dispensable, though not entirely useless.

Yet in the actual history of science, discoveries have not been the offspring of any omnipotent "method." As often as not, private fancies have been more productive than the staid virtues of sobriety and skepticism. Men of genius—Galileo, Kepler, Newton, Einstein—have stubbornly gone their own way, possessed by metaphysical ideas of God and reality, perversely trying to plumb the depths of nature, passionate to the point of extravagance in their speculations. Descartes himself could be so certain of his method—and could make his mathematical contributions—only because he was convinced that the book of nature was in the script of geometry. The record of scientific thought gives us leave to say of science what Goethe said of poetry, that it "presupposes in the man who is to make it a certain good-natured simple-mindedness, in love with the Real as the hiding place of the Absolute."

So intimate has been the relation between scientific creativity and metaphysical (and theological) speculation that even so astringent a thinker as Bertrand Russell has wondered at the possibility of the wellsprings of science drying up in an era which deprecates metaphysical curiosity. Positivists, early in this century, were too well versed in scientific method to believe that atoms were "real," that they were more than a convenient intellectual construct by which one could "describe and combine the results of different observations"; but the atom was split nevertheless. Afterward, of course, the revelation of genius is taken as testimony to the virtue of scientific method, for it is not difficult to show—after the event—that by a proper extension of scientific method we could have known what we did not know, and to forget that we did not know it.

To this it might be retorted: What is of importance is the *result* of Einstein's work, not the idiosyncrasies that spurred him on to the job. Science is interested in what Einstein *does*, not in what he says.

If this were so, then Science would be an extremely discourteous mistress—as she has indeed often appeared to be. In actual fact, the relation between what Einstein says and what Einstein does is not so easily severed. It is true that *after* Einstein has done something, his work can be repeated by other physicists and mathematicians who will have no truck with anything called physical reality. The General Theory of Relativity can be used by anyone; it has no metaphysical patent any more than had Kepler's laws of planetary motion (which were also born of some very private fancies). It is also true, however, that it was Einstein who formulated the theory, and had he had none of these private fancies about physical reality there would not have been a General Theory of Relativity.

That it was Einstein who developed the Special Theory of Relativity in 1905 may be classified as an "accident." Physics was suffering a crisis in its foundations, experimental data refused to conform to prevailing theories, and a drastic revision of the Newtonian mechanical worldview was clearly in the offing. If there had been no Einstein, someone else probably would have thought up something similar to the special theory—though precious and painful years might have been wasted. But if Einstein had not devised the General Theory of Relativity, there is a good chance that it might never have been formulated at all. For the general theory was not needed by science to explain any baffling facts. It was needed by Einstein—and by him alone—to unite the basic concepts of inertia and gravitation in one formula, in order to approximate more closely to the divine mathematical simplicity of the universe.

This intimacy between Einstein's private metaphysics and his public science is dramatically revealed in his lonely position in contemporary quantum physics. Despite the fact that his early work on photoelectric phenomena (1905)—for which he won the Nobel prize—has been extremely important in the development of quantum theory, Einstein is today an isolated and somewhat embittered figure among physicists. He believes that quantum physics has gone off the right track and has deviated from "the programmatic aim of all physics," which is the description of any situation as it really is, regardless of the act of observation. For his own part, he toiled stubbornly during the past decades to construct his recently published Unified Field Theory, which covers electromagnetic as well as gravitational fields, and which would establish—in a nearly final form—the programmatic aim of physics. Never, perhaps, has any theory by so eminent a scientist been so thoroughly ignored by his colleagues. His Unified Field Theory is not even a subject for polemic—evoking only indifference. The newspapers, of course, gave it big play. In the laboratories, it was a topic for wisecracks. The quantum physicists feel that Einstein is exactly where he charges them with being: in a blind alley.

Einstein's reproach against quantum physics is similar—at least superficially—to that which the Catholic Church leveled against Copernicus's theory, or the conservative physicists against relativity: It is mathematically useful but not really, that is, metaphysically, true. Einstein sees the similarity but insists that the present situation is truly unique. For while the Copernican and Newtonian revolutions radically revised man's image of nature, and the relativity theory helped to substitute a mathematical model of nature for a mechanical one, the principles of quantum physics rule out the possibility of a model altogether. And this, Einstein believes, is the suicide of physics. His theory of relativity, he says, "teaches us the connection between different descriptions of one and the same reality." But the reality is there, and *physics must describe it.*

In a letter to the physicist Max Born, in 1944, Einstein wrote: "In our scientific expectation we have grown antipodes. You believe in God casting dice and I in perfect laws in the world of things existing as real objects, which I try to grasp in a wildly speculative way."

"God casting dice" is a picturesque but not inaccurate representation of how quantum physics conceives of physical reality. The statistical probability laws of quantum mechanics are not the kind of statistical laws one meets in actuarial work, for instance. In the latter, each individual event has its cause, even if statistics gives us only an average report. In quantum physics a detailed causal analysis of atomic phenomena is not only renounced for convenience, but excluded in principle. The very idea of causality does not pertain; all we know is the probability of the results of measurement at a given time.

Einstein concedes that quantum physics has made great progress with the aid of its probability statistics, but he will not admit that the present state of quantum theory is more than a stopgap. His aim is still a theory that represents "events themselves and not merely the probability of their occurrence"; he will not give up the principle of causality: He is convinced that the laws of the microscopic universe and of the macroscopic universe are continuous—nature is of one piece.

Obviously, science itself will ultimately decide whether Einstein's Unified Field Theory is relevant to the problems of modern physics—whether God casts dice or is subtle but still rational. The point here is that between Einstein as scientist and Einstein as thinker the relation is closer than some overly glib enthusiasts of scientific method consider decent.

Recently, the British positivist A. J. Ayer wrote (in *Partisan Review*) rather contemptuously of present-day intellectuals who turn to religion: "They want a form of explanation which will say something more than merely that this is how the world works. They have to be given a reason for its working as it does. . . . It is not enough to state what happens to be true; it has to be shown that it is necessarily true."

This may be taken as a fair summary of Einstein's philosophy of science. For Einstein is one of those—again in Ayer's words—"to whom it is intolerable that facts should be contingent, that things should just happen to be as they are."

Indeed, it can be said that it is not only Einstein's philosophy of science that Ayer has described, but the philosophy of science itself. For if it were not intolerable "that facts should be contingent, that things should just happen to be as they are," why should science ever have been born? In our epoch of technology, we tend to view the aim of science as prediction and control. But this is a modern belief that would have horrified the Greeks, Copernicus, Kepler, Descartes, and Newton, and which has been alien to the temper of Planck, Eddington, and Einstein, to name only a few contemporaries. For them, science has meant a passion for the rational truth which lies concealed behind all sense experience. Science in the West has been, and is, based on the assumption that what is factual and contingent has to be explained by what is rational and necessary, that statements of fact must be deduced from statements of mathematics, that matter is to be illuminated by Reason. Einstein is, par excellence, the scientist of the Western world, wedded to the belief that behind the particular and contingent there is the general and rational. The goal of science is a formula from which everything that ever happens can be logically and rigorously derived. Behind the All there is the One.

If we press further, and ask why Reason should have any success in comprehending physical reality, then, according to Einstein, we burst through science and philosophy together, and arrive at religion: "To the sphere of religion belongs the faith that the regulations valid for the world of existence are rational." This faith is not something tranquil and final; it is restless and perpetually dissatisfied, always goading Reason to convert it into a rational certitude.

God wills that the scientist—who is Reason incarnate—shall dissolve him into demonstrable theorems. Probably the dissolution will never be final, and Einstein has uttered some forlorn sentiments on the mystery of existence. But, as Henry Margenau has acutely pointed out, in the case of Einstein "a certain pathos for the unknown, though often displayed, always intimates the ultimately knowable character of existence, knowable in scientific terms." For God may be subtle but he does not deceive.

There are, according to Einstein, three ascending stages in the development of religion: the religion of fear, the religion of morality, and the religion of the cosmos.

The religion of fear is the product of primitive, self-centered, unenlightened men, of the kind we meet in the Pentateuch. These men believed in a personal God who was involved in their destinies, who rewarded and punished his creatures. The religion of fear not only did not free men from their bodily concerns and egocentric anxieties—it made these very concerns and anxieties an occasion for God's intervention in the workings of the world.

The religion of fear is superseded by the religion of morality, as embodied in some of the Jewish prophets and elaborated by the New Testament. Knowledge itself provides only the means, not the ends of life; religion—acting through the intuition of great teachers and radiant personalities—sets up the ultimate goals of life and provides the emotional context in which they can influence the individual. Men, left to shift for themselves, would see the ends of life to be ease and happiness; such a selfish ethic, dominated by elementary instincts, is "more proper for a herd of swine." A genuinely religious person is one who has "liberated himself from the fetters of his selfish desires and is preoccupied with thoughts, feelings, and aspirations to which he clings because of their super-personal value."

The religion of morality is the highest that the great mass of men can aspire to, and it is sufficient to tame their animal spirits. But for a select few there is something finer and more noble: the religion of the cosmos. For the wise man—and this is the very definition of his wisdom—ethical behavior needs no religious sanction; sympathy and love of humanity he finds to be sufficient unto themselves. His religion, as distinct from his morality, is the result of a unique religious event, the mystical experience of the rationality of the cosmos, in which the individual is annihilated. Of this experience Einstein writes: "The individual feels the nothingness of human desires and aims and the sublimity and marvelous order which reveal themselves both in nature and the world of thought. He looks upon individual existence as a sort of prison and wants to experience the universe as a single significant whole."

This experience is not reached by any Cabalistic practices. On the contrary: The *via mystica* is nothing other than the *via scientiae*. Science, at its greatest, is identical with religion, at its most sublime. Science provokes a "profound reverence for the rationality made manifest in existence." The scientist "achieves a far-reaching emancipation from the shackles of personal hopes and desires, and thereby attains that humble attitude of mind towards the grandeur of reason incarnate in existence." And just as science leads us to true religiosity, so does true religiosity lead us to science:

> The cosmic religious experience is the strongest and the noblest, driving scientific research from behind. No one who does not appreciate the terrific exertions, the devotion without which pioneer creation in scientific thought cannot come into being can judge the strength of the feeling out of which alone such work, turned away as it is from immediate practical life, can grow.
>
> What deep faith in the rationality of the structure of the world, what a longing to understand even a small glimpse of the reason revealed in the world, there must have been in Kepler and Newton.

When a Boston Catholic priest took it upon himself in 1929 to warn Americans of Einstein's "atheism," Rabbi Herbert S. Goldstein cabled Einstein: "Do you believe in God?" Einstein cabled back: "I believe in Spinoza's God, who reveals himself in the harmony of all Being, not in God who concerns himself with the fate and actions of men"—a statement which so affected Rabbi Goldstein as to make him predict hopefully that Einstein "would bring mankind a scientific formula for monotheism."

Instead of the worship of the God of Abraham, Isaac, and Jacob, we have—in the tradition of Maimonides, Spinoza, and Hermann Cohen—the *amor Dei intellectualis.* Instead of the Lord of Hosts, we have the God of the philosophers—the Logos, the Reason which governs the universe, the incorporeal meaning behind the chaos of concreteness.

Reason, which worships the God of Spinoza, begins with the *proposition* "all men are mortal," and is most interested in the immortal truth of this and other propositions. Biblical faith, which worships the God of Abraham, begins with the *fact* that "all men are mortal." The truths of Reason are true even if man does not exist; they are true, as Husserl remarked, for "men, angels, monsters, and gods." Faith is less concerned with the truths of Reason than with the fate of man—the mortal, finite creature who cannot volatilize himself into Reason. Reason is what we have gained by the eating of the Tree of Knowledge: We are like unto gods, sharing in divine omniscience. Faith is the human condition experiencing itself in its most naked actuality, for with the eating of the apple there goes the Fall, and we must surely die.

The struggle between the God of Abraham and the God of Spinoza is the central theme of the spiritual history of the Western world. Out of it there comes the Old Testament and the New, Greek philosophy and Gnosticism, medieval Scholasticism and Renaissance science, German Idealism and modern atheism.

And in this conflict the Jew is tensed and sundered. For he is of the Covenant of Abraham, whom God commanded; and he has also prominently been of the opinion of Philo and Spinoza, to whom the world is the garment of Reason.

Einstein was born in 1879 into a German-Jewish family whose Judaism had been pretty well eroded by the tide of assimilation. He was sent to a Catholic elementary school in Munich, and even here the fact of his being a Jew was in no way impressed on him. We are told in his autobiographical sketch about a preadolescent religious fervor, but it seems to have been in no way Jewish. At the Gymnasium, at the age of fourteen, he was instructed in the elements of Judaism; he was attracted to what he regarded as its elevated morality, repelled by its ritual codification. When Einstein was sixteen, his family moved to Milan from Munich for financial reasons; after six months, unable to bear the rigid discipline of the Gymnasium, Einstein joined them. In Milan he renounced both his

German citizenship—becoming stateless—and his membership in the Jewish community; only by such a double renunciation could the rational young man show his contempt for the idols of the herd.

Einstein formally became a Jew once again in 1910 when he accepted the chair of theoretical physics at the German University in Prague. Emperor Francis Joseph believed that only members of a recognized religious denomination were qualified to teach there, so Einstein had to register as a follower of the "Mosaic creed." More than half the German-speaking population of Prague were Jews, and the city at that time was witnessing, under the general influence of Martin Buber, a Jewish intellectual renaissance. Einstein came to know and be friendly with the active leaders in this movement, especially Hugo Bergmann and Max Brod. (He met Franz Kafka, too—one wonders what they had to say to each other.) But Einstein still refused to take being a Jew seriously.

In 1921, however, Einstein publicly declared himself to be a Zionist—to everyone's surprise and the consternation of not a few. The man who was known to despise nationalism as an excrescence of the herd mentality praised Zionism as "the embodiment of the reawakening corporate spirit of the Jewish nation." What happened to bring this "conversion" about? Nothing singular or dramatic so far as we know. Indeed, it is best understood as not a conversion at all, but as a relapse—from the religion of the cosmos to the religion of morality. It was apparently not possible to sustain forever the ecstasy of Reason; one had to return to the realm of matter and men, and there the best of all possible demeanors was an exalted, abstract morality. Einstein was able to announce that he found in Judaism an admirable ethical sensibility that demanded not faith but "the sanctification of life in a supraperson-al sense." Jewish morality, like Reason (though not so nobly), turned man from himself to the sanctification of life in general. He liked to quote Rathenau to the effect that "when a Jew says he's going hunting to amuse himself, he lies."

More to the point, one feels, is the tone and inflection with which he writes of his generations of ancestors, the ghetto Jews: "These obscure humble people had one great advantage over us; each of them belonged in every fiber of his being to a community in which he was completely absorbed."

Einstein's new Jewishness was not the result of his discovering a hidden Jewish self. It was, on the contrary, a new means of escaping from his self. The flight to Reason from the chaos of existence, which seemed to have succeeded so well, was now acknowledged to have been, at least in part, a failure. Something ponderable and indissoluble had been left behind: the flesh-and-blood Jew born of woman, the specific presence of the absentminded professor. And Einstein once again fled—into community, the ghetto, the warm mass of Jewry. What could not be transmuted into Reason would be absorbed into "the Jew."

And what could not be absorbed into the Jew would be once more etherealized—this time into the "world citizen."

Einstein's political and social opinions—so naive, so superficial, so bizarre—have baffled and disturbed his many admirers. They have usually sought to explain these opinions away with the statement that there is apparently no correlation between scientific and political intelligence. But this does less than justice to Einstein, who certainly would not concede the point. Moreover, it is possible to show that Einstein's political views are closely related to his entire outlook. He has applied to society that same rage for simplicity and love for the abstract that accomplished so much in his theoretical physics. But men cannot be so profitably transformed into clear and logical abstractions. The result of such an effort is confusion, contradiction, and, inevitably, an unpleasant impatience on the part of the thinker.

Thus, Einstein has always been a pacifist. His pacifism is bred of an intense hatred of the military, which he regards as the bestialization of man. But in so selfless a devotion to "Humanity" as Einstein's, strange things happen in one's relations to men. Sometimes, indeed, one cannot see men for Humanity. So it happened that Einstein not only vigorously supported the Second World War; he also defended the indiscriminate bombing of German cities as "morally justified," and urged that the Germans be "punished as a people" for their "collective guilt."

Einstein despises capitalism because it presupposes the existence of discrete, free, and autonomous selves in competition and even conflict. The individual's position in our society is such that "the egotistical drives in his make-up are constantly being accentuated, while his social drives, which are by nature weaker, progressively deteriorate. . . . Unknowingly prisoners of their own egotism, they [individuals] feel insecure, lonely, and deprived of the naive, simple, and unsophisticated enjoyment of life." Such a simple celebration of life can only come about when men have transcended their selves into Humanity, and the chaos of existing societies has been stilled into Community. Rejecting the idea of capitalism, Einstein elects for the idea of socialism.

The ideal community is the antithesis of the self-centered individual, and the perfect community, like the purified self, can only be won through Reason. But Reason has a way of discovering the "laws of society," the observance of which constitutes freedom. So there is the not uncommon sight of the radical rationalist—for example, George Bernard Shaw or the Webbs—who is favorably disposed to a society that suppresses the "self-seeking ego" (that is, the individual) in the name of a selfless *raison d'état*. Einstein's habit of sending messages to Communist-controlled "congresses of intellectuals" does not represent any sympathy for Russian totalitarianism—which he detests—but is rather a genuflection before the socialist idea, and an act of homage to those of vigorous intellect "who get things done," especially when they wish to "do things" for "peace." An international organization of the intellectual elite influencing the policies of nations has always been one of Einstein's fondest dreams.

The escape from the self into the Jew and Humanity, however, like the flight into Reason, has failed Einstein. Though he still signs petitions and sends encouraging communications, there is abundant evidence that his heart is not in them. Einstein's melancholic loneliness is the salient feature of his personality, as it is of his face.

> My passionate sense of social justice and social responsibility has always contrasted oddly with my pronounced freedom from the need for direct contact with other human beings and human communities. I have gone my own way and have never belonged to my country, my home, my friends, or even my immediate family, with my whole heart; in the face of all these ties I have never lost an obstinate sense of detachment.

Philipp Frank comments further: "He always has a certain feeling of being a stranger, and even a desire to be isolated. On the other hand, however, he has a great curiosity about everything human and a great sense of humor, with which he is able to derive a certain, perhaps artistic pleasure from everything that is strange and even unpleasant."

And: "His attitude in intercourse with other people, consequently, was on the whole one of amusement. He saw everyday matters in a somewhat comical light. . . . The laughter that welled up from the depths of his being was one of his characteristics that immediately attracted one's attention."

Einstein has not succeeded in becoming pure spirit or pure citizen or the selfless member of an organic community. He has ended up as simply more himself, laughing at his own presumption, though not for that the more content with man's condition and man's fate.

Einstein's gaiety, his informality of dress and manner, his quick sympathy—they [are] of that humanism which springs, not from love of fellowmen, but from compassion at the brutal fact that men exist at all. Perhaps if Einstein and Kafka—whose earthly self was amiable too, and from the same cause—had talked a while, they would have found more in common than one might expect! The Jew as Pure Reason and the Jew as Pure Alienation might have sensed in each other a kinship—perhaps even a secret identity, for the Kingdom of Reason can be as cold and infinitely empty as K.'s Kingdom of Nothingness; and both are as uninhabitable as the illusory world of the average sensual man. They might have smiled with a common irony at the world of matter and men, so complacent and blind in the ignorance of its own essential unreality. And they might have sighed, too, at being forever excluded from it.

1950

36

Is Jewish Humor Dead?

It is known that the surest way of killing a joke is to explain it, and humor has, in self-defense, made an especially comic figure of the man who would earnestly analyze it. Thus humor and seriousness contest the field, with all arbitration or appeasement ruled out, and with the possibility of rising above the battle simply unimaginable; one rises above the battle either through seriousness or humor—and then one is right back in the fight. It is an unequal struggle: Humor is more aggressive, more mobile, and has the more penetrating weapons. But in the end, humor loses and seriousness wins. Humorists die and dead men tell no jokes, and this, it must be admitted, is a serious matter.

Jewish humor died with its humorists when the Nazis killed off the Jews of Eastern Europe, though it seems likely that even without the intervention of Hitler this humor would not long have survived the disintegration of the ghetto community from which it drew its inspiration. This opinion is certain to be challenged, especially by those who, though willing to concede that persecution can wound the flesh, are reluctant to believe that it can murder the spirit or that the spirit can, by the erosion of time, simply wither and die. They will ask: Does not this humor still flourish in the Jewish communities of America and Israel? Is not Jewish humor a treasure in the perpetual custody of the Jewish people? The answer to both questions is, I think, no, and in the course of this essay I hope to show why. But first I would like to illustrate the defeat of humor with an anecdote that some will find amusing but that is really not a Jewish joke so much as the dying echo of one.

A group of Jewish refugees from Poland, recently arrived in the United States, visited one evening with their American-born relatives. One of the latter thought to lighten the conversation by telling an old Jewish joke:

A Jew in czarist Russia wished to buy a ticket that would permit him to enter the platform of a railroad station, and he was referred to a vending machine where such tickets were sold at ten kopecks each. The Jew eyed the machine curiously and mused, "Maybe you'll take five kopecks?" He inserted five kopecks and pressed the lever. No ticket came out. The Jew shrugged his shoulders and said, "Well, there was no harm in trying." He inserted another five kopecks, and pulled the lever. Nothing happened. As he stood there, bewildered, a Cossack brushed past him, inserted ten kopecks into the machine, pulled the lever, and got his ticket. The Jew flew into a rage, spat at the machine, and yelled: "Filthy anti-Semite! For a Cossack you give tickets, but for a Jew's ten kopecks you don't bother!"

To the narrator's pleasure, the newcomers laughed heartily at the joke though it is but an inferior specimen of the familiar genre of Jewish humor that pokes fun at the Jews for their propensity to gloss over their own shortcomings and blame the always available anti-Semite for their misfortunes.

Some weeks later there was another family gathering, this time to welcome some still newer arrivals from the DP [displaced person] camps. One of the refugees who had been present at the earlier meeting volunteered to tell the "very funny joke" that the *Amerikaner* had related. He told it as follows:

A Jew in czarist Russia wished to buy a ticket that would permit him to enter the platform of a railroad station, and he was referred to a vending machine where such tickets were sold at ten kopecks each. The Jew inserted his ten kopecks, but nothing happened. As he stood there, bewildered, a Cossack brushed past him, inserted ten kopecks into the machine, pulled the lever, and got his ticket. The Jew flew into a rage, spat at the machine, and yelled: "Filthy anti-Semite! For a Cossack you give tickets, but for a Jew's ten kopecks you don't bother!"

The laughter was every bit as hearty at this version of the joke, though the original point had been blunted and what had been a joke had really become a parable. Actually, these Jews from Poland were not laughing at any joke at all, but only at the way the story summarized their sense of a senseless persecution. The seriousness of the concentration camps had conquered.

It is true that in my telling of this incident the original point has been in part regained, for the butts of my story are Jews so sensitive to anti-Semitism that they have lost the detachment that is at the root of true humor. But it is a point that barely reaches the mark, and whatever smile it arouses is the mere shadow of a shadow. Too many corpses obstruct the comic perspective.

One recent anthologist of Jewish humor, doubtless expressing the sentiments of many, sees in the Jewish joke a victory gained by the Jewish spirit over centuries of adversity, an exultant defiance of persecution and harassment, an affirmation of the will to survival in the face of an ever-impending doom. It would surely be to the glory of the entire human race, and of the Jews in particular, if this were the case. And it is agreeable to note that there is some truth in this description. But not the whole truth.

Though the records are scanty, it seems safe to assert that the kind of humor we know came late to Jewish history, gaining ground in the seventeenth and eighteenth centuries and reaching its apogee in the nineteenth and early twentieth centuries. It is, then, a preeminently *modern* phenomenon. The Jews of an earlier day were rich in proverbs (some of them witty), parables, moralistic anecdotes—but not, it seems, in humor. This fact is no occasion for surprise if we cast a glance at the development of humor in the various Western Christian nations of the Middle Ages. There we see that humor could exist only in the interstices of a religious civilization (just as the Purim parodies existed within orthodox Judaism), that the religious authorities frowned upon it, and that it won popular affection to the extent that the dominion of religion became questionable, and that, indeed, one of its functions was to challenge this dominion. Humor needs to breathe the air of skepticism, and prior to the modern epoch the Jews were men of faith, piety, and hence sobriety. When one believes that this life on earth is implicated in eternal salvation or eternal damnation, there is little motive for levity.

Take, for example, the matter of *Galgenhumor* (gallows humor), which was elevated to such a fine art in the writings of the man who gaily signed himself Sholom Aleichem. Here is how Sholom Aleichem has one of his characters, Yisrolik of Kishenev, write to his friend Yankel in America after the Kishenev pogrom of 1903 (I use the version given by Maurice Samuel in his fine book *The World of Sholom Aleichem*):

Dear Yankel: You ask me to write at length, and I'd like to oblige, but there's really nothing to write about. The rich are still rich and the poor are dying of hunger, as they always do. What's new about that? And as far as the pogroms are concerned, thank God we have nothing more to fear, as we've already had ours—two of them, in fact, and a third wouldn't be worth while. . . . All our family got through it safely, except for Lippi, who was killed with his two sons, Noah and Mordecai; first-class artisans, all three of them. Oh yes, and except Hersh. Perel was found dead in the cellar together with the baby at her breast. But as Getzi used to say: "It might have been worse; don't think of the better, because there's no limit to that." You ask about Heshel. He's been out of work now for over half a year. The fact is they won't let him work in prison. . . . Mendel did a clever thing; he up and died. Some say of hunger, others of consumption. Personally, I think he died of both. I really don't know what else there is to write about, except the cholera, which is going great guns.

This is Sholom Aleichem at his best, which means that it is at the top rung of the world's literature of irony. Yet it is most improbable that a pious Jew who had, say, undergone the expulsion from Spain in 1492 would have found this letter as entertaining as did his descendants, or that he would have found it as "cathartic" as his own Cabalistic speculations. For him, death at the hands of persecutors was *kiddush ha-shem*, the sanctification of the Name. It was an affair in the realm of the sacred, and jesting was unthinkable. But for Sholom Aleichem death in a pogrom was a somewhat more ambiguous event. It might be *kiddush ha-shem*— Sholom Aleichem nowhere states that it is not. Or it might be nothing but bad luck ornamented with a high-sounding title. In this equivocation between the sacred and the profane, the eternal and the finite, the spark of humor is fanned.

It is interesting to note that fifty Jews were killed in the Kishenev pogrom and that the civilized world was shocked and horrified. Sholom Aleichem's irony was a harmonic counterpoint to this shock and horror. But when some six million Jews were slaughtered during World War II, the world was numbed by the enormity of the crime, and the victims themselves could not respond with the aesthetic freedom of Sholom Aleichem. The kinds of jokes that Jews brought forth from the concentration camps were mainly bitter thrusts at the idiocy of their oppressors. For just as humor cannot mature in a life of utter religious faith, so it cannot survive a life of sheer nihilism.

No pranks, no slapstick, no practical jokes—nothing that reduces the spiritual and human to the mechanical. Jewish humor is a humor of the spirit, not against the spirit.

What we call Jewish humor is Yiddish humor. It is the humor that was conceived and expressed in the Yiddish language, in a secular language of the marketplace that had as part of its everyday idiom a multitude of Hebrew phrases having to do with modes of Talmudic exegesis or with such nonsecular affairs as the world-to-come, the afterlife, and reincarnation; a language full of the chanting and inflections that accompanied the translation of holy texts and their memorization: a "knowing language," in Maurice Samuel's phrase, full of internal hints and esoteric references. It is the humor of a folk community of garrulous intellectuals and hairsplitters cut off from nature and animal life, intrigued only by the oddities of the human and the divine, taking as its frame of reference the complex structure of ghetto society, ghetto life, and Jewish tradition. It is, supremely, the humor of an intelligence running amok in the household of the gods without ever daring, or wanting, to set foot outside the open door.

Many of the specific jokes, of course, were borrowed from other peoples and other tongues, and have since been reclaimed with interest. Others have survived the long voyage to America or Israel and translation into English or modern Hebrew. But, with the wiping out of the Yiddish-speaking communities, the creative source of this humor is gone. To the extent that old habits and folkways persist among Jews in America, Europe, and Israel—especially insofar as they involve the family and the hazards of earning a living—slices of Yiddish humor will be appreciated (mother-in-law jokes, marriage-broker jokes, *luftmentsh* jokes). However, it is clear that a good part of the pleasure these jokes provide results from the warm nostalgia of merely hearing them. The old folkways are disappearing and Yiddish itself is on its way to becoming a dead language. The Jews of Israel prefer not to think of the ghetto, and their humor seems to be content with variations on Viennese café wit. (Example: Ben Gurion offers a friend the post of minister of colonies. "But we have no colonies," the friend protests. "So what?" replies Ben Gurion.

"Isn't Kaplan minister of finance?") American Jews are not so pressed to forget the ghetto, and Yiddish humor has for them a sentimental as well as comic value. But, though parts of the body have been preserved, even adorned and dressed as new, the soul is gone. The Jewish joke is no longer *important*. We are no longer in that world, and of that epoch, where the greatest of all Jewish writers was—one can even say, had to be—a humorist.

The "Jewish situation" that brought forth a humor unique in man's history has altered. What was that situation?

Stated briefly, the situation was one of godforsaken religiosity. And the humor of this situation is a humor of pious blasphemy, in which the religious emotion is siphoned off into explosive wit.

In one of Sholom Aleichem's stories, Tevyeh the dairyman, riding home hungry after a day's work, with one ruble in his pocket with which to sustain his nagging wife and seven thriving daughters, addresses God as follows:

"Thou hast made us a little lower than the angels. It depends upon what you call a little, isn't it? Lord, what is life, and what are we, and to what may a man be likened? A man may be likened to a carpenter; for a carpenter lives, and lives and lives, and finally dies. And so does a man."

The form of this speech is that of an edifying rabbinic discourse. The content is impudent and sophistical. But—and this is what is most significant—Sholom Aleichem is loyal at one and the same time to both the form and the content that controverts it. The Jews in their ages of faith had experienced the contradictions of life and the cosmos as revelation, as theophany; now they are only contradictions, existing side by side with a faith that cannot comprehend them.

The conflict between form and content can be seen in innumerable jokes, of which the following is a rather good representative:

If I have the right to take money out of my pocket, from which the other man has no right to take money, then is not my right all the greater to take money from *his* pocket, from which even he has the right to take money?

This "joke" is chanted in the melody usually reserved for Talmudic study, and the parody is further stressed by the fact that in the original Yiddish the two clauses are joined by the technical Hebrew phrase, which is the Talmudic counterpart to the logician's *a fortiori*. Indeed, the form is impeccably orthodox; only the content negates the purpose of this form, which in the Talmud aims at establishing the immutable principles of justice and piety. But though the form is negated it is not denied, for the jokester—assuming him to have been an average ghetto Jew—had no intention of substituting other and novel laws of thought: These laws were as good as any, it just happened that reality made an absurdity of them, and that was what was funny.

Ernst Simon has shown how the method of argument in the Talmud, and the singsong incantation of the unpunctuated text, lent itself to the uses of humor.* But before such use could be made, a measure of detachment had to be gained; the mind had to be able to stand apart from the sacred text, and to see itself as standing apart. The affective power of faith had to be stilled, replaced by what Bergson has called "a momentary anesthesia of the heart," and the world given over to pure intelligence. The life of faith is then seen as something absurd.

But, after that, Jewish humor takes another bold step: The world of nonfaith, of pure intelligence, is seen to be equally absurd.

Jewish humor is the humor of a rebellious rationalism. It is also the *reductio ad absurdum* of rationalism. Thus there is produced a distinctive quality of Jewish wit: its circularity.

Immanuel Olsvanger has recorded three versions—Arabic, Russian, and Jewish—of the same joke, which purports to reveal the "secret of Telegraphy":

Arabic—"Imagine a huge dog having its head in Beirut and its tail in Damascus. Pull the dog's tail in Damascus and the bark will be heard in Beirut."

Russian—First Russian: "Imagine a horse, its head in Moscow and its tail in Tula. Pinch the horse's nose in Moscow and it will wag its tail in Tula. And so it is with telegraphy." Second Russian: "Yes, but how do they telegraph from Tula to Moscow?"

Jewish—First Jew: "Imagine, instead of the wire, a dog, whose head is in Kovno and whose tail is in Vilna. Pull the tail in Vilna and the bark will be heard in Kovno." Second Jew: "But how does wireless telegraphy work?" First Jew: "The very same way but without the dog."

Here, rational explanation ends up by being identical with the original confession of ignorance, yet is offered as a proof. Now this circularity is

---

*In his article "Notes on Jewish Wit," in the *Jewish Frontier* (October 1948).

partly a sardonic and sophisticated mimicry of the naive circularity that is intrinsic to religious faith and that, for instance, permits the pious commentator to prove that Abraham wore a hat when he invited the angels into his tent—for would the patriarch Abraham *not* wear a hat? In the nineteenth century this mimicry was directed in particular against the "wonder-working" rabbis of Hasidism, as in the following:

Rabbi A., in Cracow, while praying, saw in a vision that Rabbi B., in Lemberg, had just died. He and his congregation went into mourning. Later, travelers from Lemberg reported that Rabbi B. was still alive and in good health. The critics of Rabbi A. took this opportunity to scoff at his supposed supernatural powers. To these the disciples of Rabbi A. retorted: "And isn't it miracle enough for you that our rabbi could see all the way from Cracow to Lemberg?"*

But if the reasoning of the devout is absurd, it is not ridiculous, for there is always one bit of evidence that makes sense out of the non-sense of faith: the pious man, who by his presence converts what is rationally absurd into something real. One must bear in mind to what extent the fullness of Jewish life was, for almost two millennia, devoted to what is rationally absurd, to what extent it was a dream-life, a sane type of madness. Jewish existence was grounded in a series of fantastic "make-believes." The Jews, seemingly the lowliest of the low, were God's chosen people. The Temple was destroyed but the routine of sacrifice was studied. On the last day of the Feast of Booths all Jews prayed for rain so that the nonexistent crops of Palestine's nonexistent Jewish settlements might prosper.

And here the Jewish jokester is in a dilemma. He is the child of a later age, and he believes that what is rationally absurd should be really absurd. He is, however, also close enough to the vitality of Jewish faith to be profoundly aware that the absurd can, through faith, become real. He *knows*, uncontrollably, and in every fiber of his being, that the Jew is the son of the covenant, even if such an idea is an outrage to enlightened intelligence. He becomes the victim of an exhilarating paranoia. Truth and reality diverge: What is true is rational, but what is real is the absurd. His reason finds itself impotent, and in the circular joke it proceeds to outwit itself.

---

*This is taken from Freud's *Jokes and Their Relation to the Unconscious*, which is still one of the best books on Jewish humor ever written.

A Jew, whose life had been one long trial and who was sustained only by the hope of compensation in the afterlife, lay dying. With his remaining breath he told his children, assembled round his bed, how he had suffered and with what joy he looked forward to the world-to-come. "But," he concluded, "what a joke it would be if there were nothing over there!"

The joke comes about if one ardently believes in a God who does not—and one secretly fears it—exist.

Jewish humor dances along a knife-edge that separates religious faith from sheer nihilism. It "knows" that the material world is the only true reality, but it also finds that this world makes no sense in its own terms and is impossible to live in, while the absurd world of Jewish faith, the one into which it was born and whose air it is accustomed to breathe, is no longer true. The intensity of Jewish humor derives from this double loyalty to incompatibles, to the sacred and the profane. Bergson has said that "a situation is invariably comic when it belongs simultaneously to two altogether independent series of events and is capable of being interpreted in two entirely different meanings at the same time." So it is that the European Jew, achieving self-consciousness in the Enlightenment, found himself at the point of intersection of faith and reason, in a comic situation he could master only with a joke.

Jewish humor is, consequently, also nostalgic. It looks backward to a state where the Jew did not know the comic, was incapable of wit, and did not need humor to make him laugh. Occasionally, its nostalgia is so acute that, as Theodor Reik has demonstrated, Jewish humor, especially in its self-aggression, strongly resembles psychopathic melancholia.

What is this but to say that Jewish humor is of the essence of modernity? Sholom Aleichem is a truly modern writer in the same sense that Dostoevski and Nietzsche are modern writers. He has eaten of the fruit of the tree of rational knowledge but he hungers for the fruit of the tree of religious life. And Sholom Aleichem's true heir is Franz Kafka, who used to laugh until the tears came to his eyes when he read his work aloud to friends. But Kafka does not make us laugh. That is a measure of the extent to which the modern situation, dissolving into murderous nihilism, robs Jewish humor of its victory.

1951

37

Christianity, Judaism, and Socialism

I want to say first what a privilege it is to have the opportunity to deliver a sermon to theologians, aspiring theologians, and theologians *manqués*.* This is not the first time I have performed that function. I can think of three occasions in the past five years when I have spoken to large bodies of "concerned clergy" in various American cities. I always say the same thing. I tell them to stop being so interested in politics, and I ask them why they don't take an interest in religion instead. Invariably, they are disinclined to take my advice.

I have been called a neoconservative—never mind precisely what that means, the term does suggest the general ideological posture from which I speak. I should make it clear that I also speak as a neo-orthodox Jew, in belief at least. That is, I am nonpracticing—or nonobservant as we say—but, in principle, very sympathetic to the spirit of orthodoxy. When I talk about religion, I talk as an insider, but when I talk about Christianity, I think it will be very clear that I talk as an outsider. When I say I am not a Christian, I do not say it polemically, of course. But whether one is Jewish or Christian does, it seems to me, affect one's attitude toward capitalism.

Orthodox Jews never have despised business; Christians have. The act

---

*This is the slightly revised text of a talk to professors and students of divinity, given at a conference sponsored by the American Enterprise Institute.

429

of commerce, the existence of a commercial society, has always been a problem for Christians. Commerce has never been much of a problem for Jews. I have never met an Orthodox Jew who despised business—though I have met some Reformed Jews who are businessmen and despise business.

Getting rich has never been regarded as being in any way sinful, degrading, or morally dubious within the Jewish religion, so long as such wealth is acquired legally and used responsibly. I was raised in a fairly Orthodox Jewish home, and everyone I knew was in business, including most of the rabbis. No one could make a living in those days as a rabbi, so rabbis ran shops, or their wives ran shops for them. It was generally assumed that the spirit of commerce is perfectly compatible with full religious faith and full religious practice. I think this is true in Islam as well, but it is not true in Christianity. The difference is that both Islam and Judaism are religions of the Law, and Christianity is a religion that has repealed the Law. This difference gives Christianity certain immense advantages over both Judaism and Islam in terms of spiritual energy; but in its application to the practical world, it creates enormous problems.

A year or so ago, I was chatting with a prominent rabbi, an old friend who heads a major institution of Jewish learning. He had just returned, sweating and angry, from a meeting with some of the faculty at Union Theological Seminary. He said he could not understand why they would talk about nothing but "prophetic Judaism" and "prophetic Christianity." At the end of the meeting, he told them that he was a rabbi, and asked why they would not talk about rabbinic Judaism, or rabbinic Christianity—to coin a phrase. They did not understand what he meant, or were not much interested in what he meant.

Now this dichotomy, this antagonism, I think, is absolutely crucial to an understanding of the relationship between any religion and the real world—the real world of politics, the real world of social life. The terms "prophetic" and "rabbinic," which come, of course, from the Jewish tradition, indicate the two poles within which the Jewish tradition operates. They are not two equal poles: The rabbinic is the stronger pole, always. In an Orthodox Hebrew school, the prophets are read only by those who are far advanced. The rest of the students read the first five books of the Bible, and no more. They learn the Law. The prophets are only for people who are advanced in their learning and not likely to be misled by prophetic fervor.

These two poles, of whatever different intensities, are present in all religions, so far as I have been able to determine. One may, adapting the concepts of Eric Voegelin, call the one pole orthodoxy and the other pole gnosticism. I think these are quite useful categories. I assume the tension between the prophetic and the rabbinic—or the orthodox and the gnostic—to be eternal.

We are talking about an eternal debate about the nature of reality, about the nature of human authenticity. When are human beings most perfectly human? When are they fulfilling their human potential to the utmost? The gnostic tends to say that the proper and truly authentic human response to a world of multiplicity, division, conflict, suffering, and death is some kind of indignant metaphysical rebellion, a rebellion that will liberate us from the prison of this world.

That thrust, that tendency, exists within Judaism, within Christianity, within Islam. It seems to be a natural human response to reality, because in some respects this world we live in is, in fact, a hell. Little children, as Dostoevski pointed out, suffer hideous pain—innocent little children die of cancer, of ghastly diseases. Is it not proper, then, for us to be indignant at the world and desire either to escape from it or to reconstruct it radically in some way?

This is the gnostic reaction to the existential reality in which we all have to live. The word "prophetic" may be misleading; in traditional Judaism, prophetic is not really the same as gnostic, since the ancient Prophets were law-observers, not law-repealers. But in recent decades the term "prophetic" has come to allude to a similar spiritual impulse.

These gnostic movements tend to be antinomian—that is, they tend to be hostile to all existing laws and to all existing institutions. They tend to engender a millenarian temper, to insist that this hell in which we live, this "unfair" world, can be radically corrected.

Orthodoxy, on the other hand, has a very different view of how human beings achieve their full human authenticity. The function of orthodoxy in all religions is to sanctify daily life and to urge us to achieve our fullest human potential through virtuous practice in our daily life, whether it be the fulfillment of the law in Judaism or Islam or *imitatio Christi* in Christianity.

Orthodoxy, in other words, naturally engenders a somewhat stoical temper toward the evils of the world. It says that evils exist, that we don't know why they exist, and that we have to have faith that, in some larger sense, they contribute to the glory of the world. Orthodoxy seriously concerns itself with the spiritual governance of human beings who have to live in this world and whose faith is being tested and tried every day. Orthodoxy has to do its best to give answers to questions that are unanswerable, that is, questions of why we live in a world that is "unfair," to use a term that has recently entered political discourse.

Christianity emerged out of a Jewish rebellion within Judaism. Christianity emerged out of what, I think, can fairly be called a Jewish gnostic movement. We know very little about it, but it seems evident that in the decades prior to the appearance of Jesus, there were all sorts of gnostic millenarian bubblings within Judaism. There were sects that were resentful of the Law, resentful of the world, promising to—or attempting to—achieve a radical reconstruction of reality, and a redemption of human beings from a condition that they perceived to be inhuman.

The trouble with gnosticism, however, is that it cannot ultimately win, because such radical reconstructions never do occur. Human nature and human reality are never transformed, so whether gnostic movements seem to win or lose, they always lose in a sense. The very different ways in which they lose, however, are terribly important. They can lose destructively, or they can lose constructively. A gnostic movement can mature into an orthodoxy, which from the gnostic point of view is a loss. From the world's point of view, however, a new orthodoxy is a good thing, if it is a genuine orthodoxy, one that people freely consent to. A gnostic rebellion can also spend itself, of course, in futile dissent, in revolution and bloodbaths, or whatnot.

For the first two centuries of the Christian era, the church fathers had to cope with precisely this problem: namely, how to take the gnostic temper of Christianity—so evident in the New Testament, as contrasted with the Old—and convert it into an orthodoxy. They had to convert it into a doctrine for the daily living of people, into something by which an institution could spiritually govern the people. I find it interesting to note that one of the ways the church fathers did this—and they did it in many ways—was by incorporating into Christian scripture the Old Testament.

I remember reading many years ago about the Marcionite heresy, the fearful dispute over whether or not the Old Testament should be included as part of Christian scripture. Marcion, who eventually lost, had a very good argument—why include the Old Testament when the New Testament transcends and repeals it? That seemed reasonable to me. Since the books did not say why the church fathers thought otherwise, why they insisted on including the Old Testament into Christian scripture, I did some desultory reading on the matter. It became clear that the church fathers needed the Old Testament to help convert what was originally a gnostic movement into a new creative orthodoxy, which they did brilliantly. They needed the Old Testament for certain key statements that are not found in the New Testament, or at least are not found there in an emphatic way, such as that when God created the world, he saw that "it was good." That is an Old Testament doctrine. It became a Christian doctrine, and it is crucial to any orthodoxy, in contrast to gnosticism, which says that no one knows who created the world—a demiurge or whatever—but that the world is certainly bad.

Another key statement needed for a new orthodoxy was the injunction to be fruitful and multiply, which is an Old Testament, not a New Testament, injunction. Again, this is crucial to any orthodoxy, any institutionalized religion that spiritually governs human beings and helps them cope with their inevitable and irresolvable existential problems. It affirms the goodness of life, in addition to the goodness of Being.

The reason why Christianity and Judaism both take the same controversial view toward homosexuality is not because they are narrow-minded, but because legitimization of homosexuality flouts the injunction to be fruitful and multiply. As a matter of fact, a gnostic movement can always be recognized by its reaction to that commandment. Gnostics are always interested in sex, since it is such a dominant human passion. Sometimes they become orgiastic; sometimes they become ascetic—the monastic movement was a form of gnostic asceticism that was co-opted by the church. It simply told the monks they could be ascetic so long as they did not go around teaching that everyone should be ascetic. But whether orgiastic or ascetic, gnostic sexuality rejects the injunction "be fruitful and multiply." In gnostic sexuality it is obscene for a woman to become pregnant in an orgy. Homosexuality contradicts that principle too, as does abortion at will.

The modern secular world, as it emerged after the Renaissance and the Reformation, is shot through with gnostic elements. Since the dissolution of the great Roman Catholic orthodoxy of medieval Europe, the modern world has oriented itself toward beliefs that premodern theologians, Christian or Jewish, would have quickly identified as heresy. In fact, the Catholic church, almost until yesterday, did regard them as heresy. I used to require my graduate class to read Pius IX's *Syllabus of Errors*, a wonderful statement of the credo of modernity. Pope Pius IX issued it in 1870 as a list of what it is anathema to believe, and he included just about everything that every one of my graduate students believes. They believe it all implicitly, as if it were natural and unarguable.

The Catholic church probably would not say quite the same things today. The *Syllabus* represents the premodern view. The modern view, to which the church increasingly leans, is much more gnostic in its lack of calm acceptance of the world. And, in its political versions, gnosticism takes the form of utopianism.

Modern thought has two characteristics not to be found in classical Christian thought or in classical Jewish thought. One is the absence of the idea, in any version, of original sin. This is crucial because a belief in progress, in the sense in which modernity believes in progress, is incompatible with a belief in original sin. (One must remember that a belief in the advancement of certain fine arts or technical arts is not quite the same as a secular faith in progress.) The modern way of thinking did not emerge fully until the doctrine of original sin—or whatever its counterpart would be in Judaism (and there is a counterpart)—had been abolished in favor of a doctrine of original innocence. The doctrine of original innocence meant that the potential for human transformation here on this earth was infinite, which is, of course, the basic gnostic hope.

The second element that made the modern secular world so gnostic-utopian by classical standards was the rise of science and technology, with the promise it gave of man's potential mastery over nature, and over human nature through something called the social sciences. The modern world, in its modes of thinking, has become so utopian that we do not even know when we are utopian or to what degree we are utopian. We utter utopian clichés in politics as if they really were clichés—for example, "a world without war." What would happen if a president of the United States said to us tomorrow: "I understand that previous presidents have told you that one of the aims of our foreign policy is to create a world without war. Well, let's face it, there will never be a world without war. Human beings have fought ever since the beginning of time, and human beings as we know them will not cease fighting. I will give you a world in which we will try to avoid war; if we get into war, we will try to limit the war; and if we get deeply into war, we will try to win the war. But I cannot promise you a world without war."

Can you imagine a president of the United States saying such a thing on television? Yet, everything that is said in that imaginary speech is true. The very notion of a world without war is fantastic. The lion shall lie down with the lamb, but not until the Second Coming.

The opening sentence of a very good book, *Political Messianism*, by J. L. Talmon, reads: "The present inquiry is concerned with the expectations of universal regeneration which animates men and movements in the first half of the nineteenth century." After I first looked at that, I asked the author whether his allusion to "expectations of universal regeneration" was meant to be ironic. He responded that this was a fair description of much of political thought in the first half of the nineteenth century—the thoughts of Saint-Simon, Comte, Fourier, Marx. Prior to the eighteenth century, anyone enunciating the notion that politics—politics, not religion—is concerned with the expectation of a universal regeneration of humanity, of the world, would have been regarded as mad. Regardless of political views, no one ever thought that politics could offer any such ambitious promise. It is only in our era that this conception begins to prevail. We even teach the Utopian Socialists in our history courses as if they were political philosophers, instead of religious fanatics of a peculiarly modern kind.

The major form which the expectation of universal regeneration takes is socialism. Modern political messianism or utopianism eventuates in the socialist movements of the last century and a half. These movements have been increasingly attractive to Christians and to Jews. The Jews who have played a prominent role in them are, on the whole, those who believe in what they call "prophetic" Judaism. These are Jews who rebel against rabbinic Judaism as something stale and decadent. They feel they have a historic mission to fulfill and then proceed to engage in the cardinal sin known to both Judaism and Christianity as "the hastening of the end"—the ushering in of the Messianic Age or the Second Coming through magic, or politics, or some other human contrivance.

Socialism also has a natural attraction to both Jews and Christians because of its emphasis on community, as distinct from a liberal society's

emphasis on individualism. In an individualistic society, voluntary communities can be created and sustained only with great difficulty. Indeed,
an individualist society is constantly subverting the voluntary communities the individuals themselves establish. This has been our own past
experience in the last hundred years with voluntary institutions, including churches. Individual initiative, simply on its own and without official
support, cannot satisfy the natural desire for community among human
beings. This happens to be one of the crucial weaknesses of the individualistic, liberal, capitalist society of the modern era.

I think the attraction of socialism also has something to do with the
decline of certain "primitive" aspects of both Christianity and Judaism.
Above all, there has been a decline in the belief in an afterlife in whatever form—the belief that, somehow or other, the "unfairness" of this
life in this world is somewhere remedied and that accounts are made
even. As more and more people cease to believe any such thing, they
demand that the injustice and unfairness of life be coped with here and
now. Inevitably this must be done by the government, since no one else
can claim a comparable power.

Capitalism and modern secular society encourage a rationalist way of
looking at the world that renders incredible any notion of an afterlife, of
eternity, or of a supernatural redress of experienced injustice. To the
degree that capitalism does this, it generates an avalanche of ever
greater expectations directed to the temporal power—demands which
no socioeconomic or political system can in fact meet. The consequence is that even a victorious socialist politics, arising out of these
urgent demands, can only survive by repressing them.

These seemingly inherent weaknesses of liberal capitalism unquestionably encourage people to turn toward socialism. But there is a way in
which socialism is peculiarly attractive on its own merits to Christians, or
people who have what are thought to be Christian impulses. The root of
all socialist economics is the separation of the distribution of wealth
from the production of wealth. Socialist economics assumes that there is
no problem of production, only a problem of distribution. This appeals
to Christians, or to people of Christian impulses, because Christianity, as
a religion, fares much better in a static society and in a static economy
than in a dynamic one. Moreover, socialist redistribution bears some
resemblance to Christian charity.

Now, it is true that, if there is no economic growth, and if distribution can be separated from production, then the question of distribution becomes an overwhelming moral issue. In my opinion, it is a trivial moral issue in our world because economic growth solves the problem—the problem of poverty—toward which redistribution aims. But Christianity has never much liked a commercial society that produces economic growth, a dynamic society in which everyone improves his condition. It prefers a static society in which Christian virtues are practiced, and the merits of that are not to be sneezed at. They have been eloquently expressed by T. S. Eliot in his *Idea of a Christian Society*.

The trouble, however, is that socialism offers a redistribution that only looks like Christian charity, and that socialist societies, when they come into being, are but grotesque parodies of a Christian community. One major reason why this is so is that the socialist promise is not truly a Christian promise. It offers redistribution *and* abundance—and on this promise it simply cannot deliver.

There is another reason why people who are experiencing a Christian impulse, an impulse toward the *imitatio Christi*, would lean naturally toward socialism, and that is the attitude of Christianity toward the poor. And here, again, I have to speak as a Jew. Traditional Judaism does not have Christianity's attitude toward the poor.

I know of no sacred Jewish writing that says it is particularly difficult for a rich man to get into heaven; it is just not in our tradition. But Christianity does begin, as I said, as a gnostic movement with the attitude that there is something especially good about poor people, that they are holy in a sense. They are God's children, in some special way, even though their poverty is not voluntary (one could understand voluntary poverty being regarded as such).

The result is interesting to watch today in our political attitudes toward poor people and toward movements that either speak in the name of the poor or, for that matter, may actually be representative of the poor. Let us imagine there is a revolution in Mexico in the name of poor people, one that may even be genuinely supported by them. I am giving myself the hardest possible case. Poor people, in fact, never make revolutions. They are made by professors and students and intellectuals in the name of the poor. But let us assume a case where it is really the poor who are making the revolution. We know, as students of political theory and history, that this revolution will only end in tyranny, in the ruin of the economy, and in a situation in which the poor themselves will be worse off than before, with the destruction of whatever liberties may have been provided by tradition, if not by liberal legislation.

If we know that, would we call this an unjust revolution? How many of us would really put ourselves flatly in opposition to a revolution of poor people, even if we had good reason to think that this revolution would lead to disastrous results? Not many, I think. And I believe the Christian attitude about the presumed special quality of poor people is part of the reason. One feels, somehow, that if the poor act this way, they must be doing it for good reason and we must respect that reason, even if it seems to us not really reasonable.

One of the difficulties of American foreign policy today in coping with so-called socialist and communist countries is the claim of those countries to represent the poor, and the claim of revolutionary movements in the so-called Third World to represent the poor. The claim is usually false, but it might in some instances be true. In my view, it would not matter whether it were true or false. But I suspect it would matter very much to most people, who would be most uncomfortable to find themselves opposing a majority composed of poor people. In terms of political philosophy, however, there is no reason why one should feel uncomfortable opposing a majority of poor people. There is no reason to think that poor people are wiser or nicer than any other people, or that they have an inherent sense of justice which other people do not have.

In the churches today, there is an attitude toward poor people that derives from Christianity, though it is in its profoundest sense anti-Christian. In Dostoevski's novel, *The Brothers Karamazov*, the Grand Inquisitor says that when the Antichrist comes, his message will be first to feed the people of the world, and then to ask of them virtue. But is that not the message that most Christian churches today preach?

Again, Judaism differs in this respect from Christianity. Judaism gives no exceptional status to the poor. Charity is a primary virtue, to be sure—Judaism is certainly not neglectful of the poor, as anyone who knows anything about Jewish communal life will agree. But no one can claim any exemption from any of the Jewish laws because he is poor. In contrast, the conventional Christian wisdom of today is that the poor— what we call underprivileged people—need not be expected to behave virtuously until their material situation has been remedied.

Socialism being an inherently gnostic movement—that is, trying to achieve the impossible in this world—always fails. The world remains unredeemed under socialism, as much as it was unredeemed under capitalism.

One can even see why and how the failure is inevitable. Socialism, like all gnostic movements, has a morphological structure. There is a group at the top—the "perfect" is the gnostic way of describing them. According to Marxist-Leninist dogma, this group would be the party leadership. Below that are the believers—the party; and below that the masses. All gnostic movements have this structure, and anyone with political experience would know that this structure must lead to a government of the perfect over the believers and the masses. And, since the believers and masses are not perfect, the perfect will have to coerce them in order to make them perfect. Our experience with human nature throughout history shows they will fail to make them perfect and that the coercion will, therefore, be permanent.

Even granting all conceivable good intentions to the communist movements of the Soviet Union, Eastern Europe, and China, that is precisely what has happened. A movement has to be led by a small group of people because they are the only ones who have *gnosis*, the arcane knowledge of how to reorganize the world, so as to make it a perfect place. And those high ideals then sanction the most Machiavellian means.

All of modern socialism is a movement that says it will create a good society, which will then create good people. I can think of no political doctrine more contemptuous of both the Jewish and Christian traditions, which say that there cannot be a good society unless there are good people.

It is true that a good government can improve the people somewhat, with difficulty. But the notion that a handful of true believers can, by manipulating the mass of the people, create a good society inhabited by good people is pernicious nonsense. All such movements end the same way, coercing people "for their own good" until, at a certain point, the people who are doing the coercing forget why they are doing it and come to regard the coercion, in and of itself, as legitimate.

Socialism today is a gnostic movement that has been unable to transform itself into an orthodoxy. It could not create a new orthodoxy, as Christianity did in its day through the creative brilliance of the church fathers who added a new dimension to man's religious experience.

Socialism evidently cannot do anything like that. What interesting social-ist book has come out of the Soviet Union in sixty years? There has not even been a decent biography of Karl Marx. There is no hagiography coming out of the Soviet Union, because no one wants to write it or read it. To discuss Marxism, go to Berlin, or to Paris, or to Rome, or to Berke-ley, but not to Moscow, where no one is interested in discussing Marxism. The doctrines of socialism are dead within the socialist world, as the Russian dissidents are showing us. There are no church fathers in modern socialist thought. There are some who tried to be, but they all ended up being denounced as heretics and driven from the fold.

In the area where it promised so much, namely economics, socialism has been a calamitous failure. That failure is due to its basic conception that production can be separated from distribution, that is, that produc-tion can be organized according to the dictates of whoever is running the state, and that distribution is a separate process also at the command of the state. But it turns out that there is a link between production and distribution, the link called human incentives. In order to distribute, there must be something to distribute. Production is not autonomous, and distribution is not autonomous. Human incentives are what create wealth, and to create affluence, as socialism promises, an economy must be respectful of human incentives.

Socialism says that we do not need that human incentive we call self-interest, that we can rely on altruism, on the pure spirit of fraternity. The experience of the world says, no—not in large societies. In the Israeli kibbutz, a self-selected elite may work altruistically for the common good for a generation or two. But this is not possible in a large heteroge-neous society. It is not only impossible; it is inherently absurd. To increase wealth, production must be increased through the use of mate-rialistic incentives. Without those materialistic incentives, there will be less and less to distribute, and any redistribution will become less effec-tive in bettering the material condition of human beings than was the capitalist system it replaced. Again, I think this is quite evident in the economies of all the socialist nations.

It is ironic to watch the churches, including large sections of my own religion, surrendering to the spirit of modernity at the very moment when modernity itself is undergoing a kind of spiritual collapse. If I may speak bluntly about the Catholic church, for which I have enormous respect, it is traumatic for someone who wishes that church well to see it modernize itself at this moment. Young people do not want to hear that the church is becoming modern. Go tell the young people that the message of the church is to wear sackcloth and ashes and to walk on nails to Rome, and they would do it. The church turned the wrong way. It went to modernity at the very moment when modernity was being challenged, when the secular gnostic impulse was already in the process of dissolution. Young people, especially, are looking for religion so desperately that they are inventing new ones. They should not have to invent new ones; the old religions are pretty good. New ones are being invented because the churches capitulated to modernity at the very moment when the rebellious, gnostic, self-confident spirit of modernity was entering a major crisis and was moving toward its own discreditation.

It is all very sad.

1979

38

The Future of American Jewry

For no other American ethnic group has the immigrant experience, including the experience of "Americanization," remained so vivid as for the Jews. Neither the Irish, the Italians, nor the Germans have produced a literature about this experience that is in any way comparable, in sheer bulk as in literary scope and scholarly depth. It is almost a century since the majority of Jews arrived on these shores, but the memories remain fresh—memories of economic hardship and economic success; of acculturation, assimilation, and the accompanying generational tensions; of triumphs and disappointments—sending your children to the nation's best universities and then watching them marry non-Jews.

Even in Israel, where immigration is so much more recent and the experience so much more traumatic, the past does not seem to be so present, so alive, so much in need of constant attention. The reason, of course, is that Jews in Israel feel that what immigration has done is to bring them "home." They do not doubt that they are where they ought to be, that the immigration experience is a narrative that comes to a proper—perhaps even a predestined—ending. American Jews have no such sense of an ending. For them, the immigration experience continues, and it continues because they cannot decide whether or not America is "home." They think that it is wonderful to be here, have no intention whatsoever of leaving for Israel or anywhere else, foresee their children and grandchildren and great-grandchildren as Americans—but somehow the idea of America as their "homeland" is one they find too slippery to cope with.

Not that they think they are in exile. An American Jew who goes to Israel, or who subscribes to the weekly edition of the Jerusalem *Post*, hears the status of American Jews described casually as "living in *galut*," "residing in the Diaspora." He hears those cant phrases but does not really listen to them. He has no sense whatsoever of living in *galut* or in something called the Diaspora—terms that American Jews under the age of twenty-five are not likely to comprehend. Indeed, it is probable that even among Israelis, those terms as applied to American Jews are by now empty of meaning, and are little more than linguistic survivals. Where, then, do American Jews live?

The answer, I would suggest, is that most American Jews see themselves as living in an imaginary country called "America." It was this imaginary country to which they immigrated—in this respect they certainly differed from other immigrants—and their long "immigrant experience" is a narrative of how they coped with living in two countries at once: an ideal America and an all-too-real America. It is this extraordinary phenomenon that accounts for so many specific and unique features of America Jewry—the powerful inclination to liberal politics as well as the strident "alienation" visible, for a century now, of Jewish intellectuals, writers, and artists. There is a Yiddish expression that used to be in common usage, *America goniff*, literally "America the thief," but in context meaning something like: "This is a wonderful country that takes as it gives." And so it does—as does life itself.

This dual life of American Jews was made possible by the fact that the ideal America and the actual America were in so many important respects convergent. The ideal America was (and is) indeed a homeland for American Jews, and the real America was sufficiently responsive to this ideal to encourage Jews to think of themselves as living in a homeland that existed *in potentia* if not yet in fact. The discrepancy between ideal and real, however, was always there, and existed to a degree that provoked Jews to a nervous and somewhat uneasy affirmation, as distinct from an easygoing and unequivocal one such as is to be found among other immigrant groups.

Most American Jews today are convinced—one should perhaps say they have persuaded themselves—that the trend toward convergence is stronger than ever. That is why they show signs of near-hysteria at any sign that suggests the contrary. The American Jewish community today is comfortable, secure, but lacking in self-confidence. It shows frequent symptoms of hypochondria and neurasthenia. It is a community very vulnerable to its own repressed anxieties and self-doubts.

It is right to be anxious because there are clear portents that we may, in fact, be entering an age of *divergence*, one in which the ideal America of the Jews will become more distant from the real America. But to get an insight into the processes of convergence and divergence, one must have a clear understanding of the fundamental forces at work. That understanding, it seems to me, is lacking because analysts of American Jewry look at their subject with a European paradigm in mind. But the United States is an exceptional country, and Jewish history elsewhere throws very little light on the American Jewish experience in the 20th century.

What is it, precisely, that has defined this experience? Can one call it "assimilation"? The word itself seems so inappropriate that, while used freely to apply to German or French or British Jews, it is not used nearly so often to refer to their American counterparts. "Assimilation" suggests a strong, longstanding national culture, with a marked Christian complexion, into which Jews melt as they shed their distinctly Jewish characteristics. One of these characteristics, of course, is religion. That is why "assimilation" is generally associated with conversion to Christianity, either formal or informal (i.e., "passing" for a Christian without benefit of conversion). We have seen something like this happening in a relatively small percentage of the American Jewish population, but the overwhelming majority do not fit this mold. For "Americanization" is not at all the same thing as "assimilation." Nor is it the same thing as "acculturation." If American Jews, in the course of the 20th century, have been "acculturated," so have all other Americans. American Jews have not changed more during this period than have American Catholics and American Protestants, of whatever ethnic group. Moreover, they have all moved, gradually but ineluctably, in the same direction.

What is this direction? Toward a far greater religious toleration, obviously, which has cheered all Jewish hearts. But what, more exactly, has been the basis for this extraordinary (by all historical standards) flowering of religious toleration? Here two explanations are commonly offered, one seemingly anachronistic, the other lacking in self-understanding.

The first explanation has to do with the historical origins of religious toleration in the United States. It is a matter of record that such toleration emerged out of the struggle of various Protestant sects for the freedom publicly to express their religious views and to have their constituents and their religious establishments free from official discrimination. This is what happened in the 18th century and the first half of the 19th. It is fair to say, along with Richard John Neuhaus, that religious tolerance in the United States originally derives from the tension among a multiplicity of religious allegiances.

But after the Civil War, and especially after 1900, a quite different climate of tolerance gradually developed. This had to do with a decline of religious intensity overall and with the growing popularity of the view that "religion is a private affair," by which is meant a purely personal affair. Toleration became a matter of relations among persons, not among religious denominations. Indeed, individuals and communities that seemed "excessively" interested in their religious beliefs and allowed these beliefs to shape their lives in uncommon ways were (and still are) regarded as somewhat "deviant," and sometimes even alien to "the American creed." This "American creed," now frequently referred to as our "civic religion," is a superficial and syncretistic compound of Judeo-Christian moral traditions with as much religious specificity as possible washed out. It is what John Dewey, the quintessential American philosopher of our century, meant by his phrase, "a common faith," an overriding, nondenominational faith to which all denominations are loyal and subservient. This common faith is what we have come to call "liberalism," its exemplary institution being the American Civil Liberties Union. To the extent that such a common faith has prevailed, religious tolerance is not an issue worthy of debate. It simply makes no sense not to be tolerant.

Historians call this phase of our intellectual history, now more than a century old, "secularization," and they point to analogous developments in other lands to sustain the thesis that secularization is an integral part of modernization. It is impossible to argue with this thesis, for which the evidence is overwhelming. But it is possible and legitimate to question the explanatory power of the concept of secularization. Something important happened, that is certain. Secularization is doubtless as good a shorthand term as any to *describe* what happened. It is not, however, a useful concept if one wishes to *explain* what happened. For what we call secularization is an idea that only makes sense from a point of view that regards traditional religions as survivals that can, at best, be adapted to a nonreligious society.

When we look at secularization without an ideological *parti pris*, we can fairly—and more accurately, I would suggest—describe it as the victory of a new, emergent religious impulse over the traditional biblical religions that formed the framework of Western civilization. Nor is there any mystery as to the identity of this new religious impulse. It is named, fairly and accurately, secular humanism. Merely because it incorporates the word "secular" in its self-identification does not mean that it cannot be seriously viewed as a competitive religion—though its adherents resent and resist any such ascription. Such resentment and resistance are, of course, a natural consequence of seeing the human world through "secularist" spectacles. Because secular humanism has, from the very beginning, incorporated the modern scientific view of the universe, it has always felt itself—and today still feels itself—"liberated" from any kind of religious perspective. But secular humanism is more than science, because it proceeds to make all kinds of inferences about the human condition and human possibilities that are not, in any authentic sense, scientific. Those inferences are metaphysical, and in the end theological.

There really is such a thing as secular humanism. The fact that many fundamentalist Protestants attack it in a mindless way, making it a kind of shibboleth, does not mean that it is, as some have been blandly saying, a straw man. It is not a straw man. As any respectable text in European intellectual history relates, "humanism," in the form of "Christian humanism," was born in the Renaissance, as a major shift occurred from an otherworldly to a this-worldly focus, and as a revived interest in Greco-Roman thought shouldered aside the narrow Christian-Aristotelian rationalism endorsed by the Church. At the same time, the Protestant Reformation weakened the Church as a religious institution and therewith undermined religious, intellectual, and moral authority in general. Christian humanism, moreover, did not long survive the near-simultaneous emergence of modern scientific modes of thinking about natural phenomena. By 1600, secular humanism as a coherent outlook was well-defined—Francis Bacon exemplifies it perfectly—though it was careful not to expose itself too candidly, lest it attract hostility from still-powerful religious establishments, Protestant as well as Catholic.

What, specifically, were (and are) the teachings of this new philosoph-ical-spiritual impulse? They can be summed up in one phrase: "Man makes himself." That is to say, the universe is bereft of transcendental meaning, it has no inherent teleology, and it is within the power of humanity to comprehend natural phenomena and to control and manip-ulate them so as to improve the human estate. Creativity, once a divine prerogative, becomes a distinctly human one. It is in this context that the modern idea of progress is born, and the modern reality of "progres-sive" societies takes shape. These are societies dominated, not by tradi-tion, but by a spirit of what F. A. Hayek calls "constructivism"—the self-confident application of rationality to all human problems, individ-ual and social alike.

What is "secular" about this movement is the fact that, though many people still go to church or synagogue for psychological reasons (conso-lation, hope, fear), very few educated people actually think that their immortal souls are at stake as a result of their beliefs or actions. Man's immortal soul has been a victim of progress, replaced by the temporal "self"—which he explores in such sciences as psychology and neurology, as well as in the modern novel, modern poetry, and modern psychology, all of which proceed without benefit of what, in traditional terms, was regarded as a religious dimension.

It is secular humanism that is the orthodox metaphysical-theological basis of the two modern political philosophies, socialism and liberalism. The two are continuous across the secular-humanist spectrum, with socialism being an atheistic, messianic extreme while liberalism is an agnostic, melioristic version. (This continuity explains why modern lib-eralism cannot help viewing its disagreement with socialism—with the "Left"—as a kind of family quarrel.) Nor is it only modern politics that has been so shaped. Christianity and Judaism have been infiltrated and profoundly influenced by the spirit of secular humanism. There are moments when, listening to the sermons of bishops, priests, and rabbis, one has the distinct impression that Christianity and Judaism today are, for the most part, different traditional vehicles for conveying, in varying accents, the same (or at least very similar) sentiments and worldviews. Of otherworldly views there is very little expression, except among the minority who are discredited (and dismissed) as "fundamentalist" or "ultra-Orthodox."

The impact of secular humanism on European Jews was far more striking than among Christians. It was the secular-humanist Left, after all, that agitated for (and won) Jewish emancipation and Jewish civic equality. Moreover, emancipation unleashed within the Jewish community latent messianic passions that pointed to a new era of fraternal "universalism" of belief for mankind. What is now called "prophetic Judaism" gradually edged out "rabbinic Judaism"—the distinction itself being a derivative of the secular-humanist impulse. By the time the mass of Jews, mostly Central and East European, came to the United States, they were already secular-humanist in their politics, i.e., somewhere Left of Center—if not in other respects. And, in time, as American Christianity and American culture also absorbed this secular-humanist impulse, Jews were encouraged to become more secular-humanist in other respects as well. They located themselves on the cutting edge of American acculturation to secular humanism as an integral part of their own Americanization.

That Jews should be liberal-to-Left in American politics is not surprising: They always have been so, and were ready to be so from the moment they set foot on these shores. What scholars and analysts take to be more interesting is that they remain so, even as they have prospered and achieved socioeconomic levels that, according to the socioeconomic determinism of contemporary sociology, should have made them more conservative. Aside from the fact that such determinism is always intellectually flawed to begin with, this overlooks the far more interesting phenomenon that American Jews have not only refused to become more conservative but have actually become more liberal-Left in their thinking about nonpolitical issues—what we today call "social" issues.

Take the question of abortion. The American people are divided on this issue, with 20 percent or so on the permissive "Left," another 20 percent on the restrictive "Right," and the majority flopping about in between these extremes. Jews, over the years, have moved disproportionately close to the permissive pole. Why? Why on earth should Hadassah or the National Council of Jewish Women be so passionately in favor of a woman's "freedom to choose"? There is absolutely nothing in the Jewish tradition that favors such a radical inclination. Nor is there anything in the experience of most American Jewish women that would explain it. (Out-of-wedlock births among American Jews are among the lowest in the nation, and married Jewish women are expert at birth control.) It is purely an ideological phenomenon, a reflection of the power of secular humanism within the Jewish community. After all, if "man makes himself," why should he (or she) not have the authority to unmake himself, if it is convenient to do so? Abortion (except in cases of endangerment to the life of the mother) was long forbidden to Jews for religious reasons. Today, it is taken to be permitted to Jews (always excepting the Orthodox) for religious reasons—but not Jewish religious reasons. Jews in America may belong to Jewish institutions, send their children to Sunday schools for Jewish instruction, proudly identify themselves as Jews—but their religion, for the most part, is only Jewish in its externals. At the core it is secular humanist.

Dedication to secular humanism is so congenial to American Jews because it has assured them of an unparalleled degree of comfort and security. It has done so because Christians in America have been moving in exactly the same direction, if more tardily. A secular-humanist America is "good for Jews" since it makes nonsense of anti-Semitism, and permits individual Jews a civic equality and equality of opportunity undreamed of by previous Jewish generations. It is natural, therefore, for American Jews to be, not only accepting of secular-humanist doctrines, but enthusiastic exponents. That explains why American Jews are so vigilant about removing all the signs and symbols of traditional religions from "the public square," so insistent that religion be merely a "private affair," so determined that separation of church and state be interpreted to mean the separation of all institutions from any signs of a connection with traditional religions. The spread of secular humanism throughout American life has been "good for Jews," no question about it. So the more, the better.

Well, perhaps this is a time for questioning whether more is better, and even whether what has been "good for Jews" will continue to be so. After all, the greatest single threat to the Jewish community today is not anti-Semitism but intermarriage, at a 30–40 percent rate. The Reform and Conservative rabbinates confront this problem with strong talk about the importance of Jewish survival. But it is absurd to think that young Jews, as individuals, are going to make their marital decisions on the basis of ancestral piety—a theme that modern rationalism cannot take seriously. Even if these young Jews approve of Jewish survival, as many do, they find it easy to assign this particular task to others. And, of course, there are an awful lot of Jews, young and not-so-young, who are less interested in Jewish survival than in the universal sovereignty of secular humanism, under which sovereignty Jews and Christians can live in fraternal peace, even though some may persist in older religious rituals which they find to have a therapeutic value as they cope with the stresses of secular modernity. One sees many such Jews in Reform and Conservative synagogues during the High Holidays.

But it is becoming ever more clear that what we are witnessing is not the advent of a brave new world in which religious orientation, like sexual orientation, will be largely a matter of taste. We are seeing, rather, the end of a major phase of American Jewish history, and of the history of Western civilization itself. American Jews, living in their suburban cocoons, are likely to be the last to know what is happening to them.

We have, in recent years, observed two major events that represent turning points in the history of the 20th century. The first is the death of socialism, both as an ideal and a political program, a death that has been duly recorded in our consciousness. The second is the collapse of secular humanism—the religious basis of socialism—as an ideal, but not yet as an ideological program, a way of life. The emphasis is on "not yet," for as the ideal is withering away, the real will sooner or later follow suit.

If one looks back at the intellectual history of this century, one sees the rationalist religion of secular humanism gradually losing its credibility even as it marches triumphantly through the institutions of our society—through the schools, the courts, the churches, the media. This loss of credibility flows from two fundamental flaws in secular humanism.

First, the philosophical rationalism of secular humanism can, at best, provide us with a statement of the necessary assumptions of a moral code, but it cannot deliver any such code itself. Moral codes evolve from the moral experience of communities, and can claim authority over behavior only to the degree that individuals are reared to look respectfully, even reverentially, on the moral traditions of their forefathers. It is the function of religion to instill such respect and reverence. Morality does not belong to a scientific mode of thought, or to a philosophical mode, or even to a theological mode, but to a practical-juridical mode. One accepts a moral code on faith—not on blind faith but on the faith that one's ancestors, over the generations, were not fools and that we have much to learn from them and their experience. Pure reason can offer a critique of moral beliefs but it cannot engender them.

For a long time now, the Western world has been leading a kind of schizophrenic existence, with a prevailing moral code inherited from the Judeo-Christian tradition and a set of secular-humanist beliefs about the nature and destiny of man to which that code is logically irrelevant. Inevitably, belief in the moral code has become more and more attenuated over time, as we have found ourselves baffled by the Nietzschean challenge: If God is really dead, by what authority do we say any particular practice is prohibited or permitted? Pure reason alone cannot tell us that incest is wrong (so long as there are no offspring), and one has had the opportunity to see a network TV program called *Incest: The Last Taboo*. Pure reason cannot tell us that bestiality is wrong; indeed, the only argument against bestiality these days is that, since we cannot know whether animals enjoy it or not, it is a violation of "animal rights." Reform Judaism has even legitimated homosexuality as "an alternative lifestyle," and some Conservative Jews are trying desperately to figure out why they should not go along. The biblical prohibition, which is unequivocal, is no longer powerful enough to withstand the "why not?" of secular-humanist inquiry.

The consequence of such moral disarray is confusion about the single most important questions that adults face: "How shall we raise our children? What kind of moral example should we set? What moral instruction should we convey?" A society that is impotent before such questions will breed restless, turbulent generations that, confronting their own children, will seek and find authoritative answers somewhere—somewhere, of some kind.

A second flaw in secular humanism is even more fundamental, since it is the source of a spiritual disarray that is at the root of moral chaos. If there is one indisputable fact about the human condition it is that no community can survive if it is persuaded—or even if it suspects—that its members are leading meaningless lives in a meaningless universe. Ever since the beginnings of the Romantic movement, the history of Western thought for over a century and a half now—in its philosophy, its poetry, its arts—has been a reaction to the implication of secular humanism that such is indeed the case. In fairness to secular humanism, it has to be said that it recognizes this challenge and encourages individuals to subdue it through self-mastery and mastery over nature. Human "autonomy" and human "creativity" are the prescription—but this only makes the doctors feel smug while helping the patient not at all. None of the powerful, interesting, and influential thinkers of the 20th century has remained loyal to secular humanism. The three dominant philosophers of our age are Nietzsche, Heidegger, and Sartre—a nihilist, a neopagan, an "anguished" existentialist. The main currents of thought in American universities today—postmodernism, deconstruction, varieties of structuralism—are all contemptuous of the universities' humanist heritage, which is dismissed as the accursed legacy of an "elite" of "dead white males." Secular humanism is brain dead even as its heart continues to pump energy into all of our institutions.

What does this portend for the future of American society? And for the future of Jews in this society?

The situation of American Jews is complicated by the fact that Israel, so crucial to the self-definition of American Jews, is facing exactly the same kind of crisis in secular humanism. Israel, after all, was founded by Jewish socialists for whom Judaism was but a "cultural heritage." Most Israelis still regard themselves as secular—but their secularism turns out to be different from, and more vulnerable than, American Jewish secularism. The very fact that their language is Hebrew and that their children read the Bible in school makes a significant difference. Orthodoxy in Israel is not a "saving remnant"; it is moving toward being the established religion of Israeli society, if not of the Israeli state, which remains technically secular. One out of every twenty eighteen-year-olds in Israel is studying in a yeshiva—i.e., is by American standards "ultra-Orthodox." These give an indication of which way the winds are blowing.

How will American Jews relate to this Israel? The answer, obviously, will depend on what happens to American society and to the place of Jews in it.

As the spirit of secular humanism loses its momentum, it is reasonable to anticipate that religion will play a more central role in American life. In theory, this religion need not be Christian. We see today all sorts of neopagan impulses bubbling up from below, filling an aching spiritual void. On our last Mother's Day, a few dozen people gathered in Central Park and uttered prayers to "Mother Earth" and her associated goddesses. The *New York Times*, in an editorial, thought this a perfectly appropriate way to mark the occasion. In general, what is loosely called "New Age" thinking—our bookshops now have special sections to cope with

"New Age" literature—represent versions of neopaganism, in which radical-feminist metaphysics plays an especially prominent role. Lesbianism, it turns out, is not so easily quarantined within the boundaries of an "alternative lifestyle."

Still, it is more reasonable to anticipate that the overwhelming majority of Americans, as they turn to religion, will turn to some version (perhaps in modified form) of Christianity. There is little point in speculating about the specific implications of any such development, but one general implication is unavoidable: As American society becomes more Christian, less secular, the "wall of separation between church and state" will become more porous. In all probability, we shall see a turning back of the clock, with the place of religion in the American "public square" more like that which prevailed in the 19th century, as against the 20th.

How will Jews react? In two ways, no doubt. The major Jewish organizations—including the majority of the rabbinate—will dig in their heels in defense of what we call a "liberal" society and "liberal" politics, by which is meant a society inclined to favor secular-humanist ideals and a corresponding set of official policies. At the same time, inevitably, Jews will perforce become "more Jewish," which at the very least will mean a firmer integration into the Jewish community, as well as becoming more observant, though not necessarily going all the way to strict Orthodoxy.

Is this picture of 21st-century America good or bad? Specifically, is it good for the Jews or bad for the Jews? The instinctive response of most Jews, committed to their secular liberalism at least as fervently as to their Judaism, will be that it is not merely bad but desperately bleak. One does get the impression that many American Jews would rather see Judaism vanish through intermarriage than hear the president say something nice about Jesus Christ. But this instinctive response is likely to be irrelevant. If America is going to become more Christian, Jews will have to adapt. That adaptation may involve changes in Jewish attitudes toward such matters as school prayer and the like; it would also surely imply a greater sensitivity to Christian feelings than has been evident in certain Jewish organizations in recent years.

In historical perspective, none of this is of major importance. After all, in the decades prior to World War II, American Jews were a lot less militant in their insistence on a secularist society, were indeed quite prudent in their approach to issues that crossed Christian sensibilities. Such prudence can be relearned.

The key question, inevitably, is whether a less secular, more religious society will mean an increase in anti-Semitism. Not official anti-Semitism, of course, which has always been alien to American democracy, but the kind of economic and social discrimination that was common before World War II. It may be noted in passing that such discrimination did not prevent Jews from acquiring wealth, education, and influence. It created hurdles, but not impossible barriers. In any case, while there may be a revival of such discrimination, it is unlikely. In our increasingly multiethnic society, it is hard to see why hostility to Jews should be a ruling passion for large numbers of Americans, especially since Jews are now so firmly established in the mainstream of American life. Insofar as opinion polls can be trusted, Americans display little paranoid distrust of Jews, and in fact are less interested in them than most Jews imagine.

So it is reasonable to believe that Jews will continue to be nervously "at home" in America, though in ways congenial to the 21st century rather than to the 20th. The real danger is not from a revived Christianity, which American Jews (if they are sensible) can cope with, but from an upsurge of antibiblical barbarism that will challenge Christianity, Judaism, and Western civilization altogether. The passing of secular humanism is already pointing to such a "shaking of the foundations." American Jews, alert to Christian anti-Semitism, are in danger of forgetting that it was the pagans—the Babylonians and the Romans—who destroyed the temples and twice imposed exile on the Jewish people.

1991

SECTION VII

Some Backward Glances

39

Memoirs of a "Cold Warrior"

Russell Lynes, authority on what is highbrow and lowbrow, in and out, recently wrote: "The new chic status symbol of the highbrow is to have been unknowingly on the CIA [Central Intelligence Agency] payroll." Well, perhaps; but I am not so sure. I have the feeling that, of late, I have not been really chic at all.

I have been getting that feeling because an awful lot of people— including some old (now former) friends—keep assuring me that the *Zeitgeist* has passed me by. I am a dropout from history, they murmur, and probably beyond the reach of retraining and rehabilitation. For I was a creature of the 1940s and 1950s, an anticommunist liberal, a political organism that is deemed to have suffered permanent damage from over-exposure to the subzero climate of the Cold War. In contrast, the "new breed" of the 1960s is genetically wholesome, intellectually incorrupt-ible, and securely possessed of the knowledge that "anticommunism" has never been anything but an elaborate con game on behalf of the power structure.

About this new breed itself, I shall have a few things to say. But first of all, I must recount the inside story of my involvement with the CIA. It is not a particularly interesting story, I hasten to warn. On the other hand, that fact in itself is interesting in a way. For it suggests that the ever-increasing appetite for political melodrama, in our time, is easily out-stripping the supply. The truth about the Cold War, when finally exposed

457

to historical scrutiny, is—in my opinion—not likely to be so very different from the conventional memories which we "cold warriors" carry
around in our heads.

I was cofounder (with Stephen Spender) of *Encounter* magazine, in London, in 1953, and remained coeditor until 1958. The magazine was
sponsored by the Congress for Cultural Freedom, a liberal anticommunist organization with headquarters in Paris. Had I known what has since
been revealed, that both the Congress and *Encounter* were subsidized by
the CIA, I would not have taken the job. Not, I hasten to add, because I
disapproved of the CIA or even of secret subsidies (at certain times, in
certain places, under certain conditions, for specific and limited purposes). Aside from the fact that the CIA, as a secret agency, seems to be
staffed to an extraordinary extent by incorrigible blabbermouths, I have
no more reason to despise it than, say, the Post Office. (Both are indispensable, both are exasperatingly inept.) No, I would have refused to go
for two reasons: First, because I was (and am) exceedingly jealous of my
reputation as an independent writer and thinker. Second, because, while
in the Army during World War II, I had taken a solemn oath to myself
that I would never, never again work as a functionary in a large organization, and especially not for the U.S. government. It is an oath I have so
far kept inviolate—except for those five years when I was unwittingly on
the CIA payroll.

But how could I have been so unwitting? Were there no signs of the
CIA presence? Were there not, during my time, rumors of secret governmental subventions? Why did I not believe them?

Rumors there were, but they were not particularly credible. Most of
these rumors issued from sources—left-wing, anti-American or both—
that would have been happy to circulate them, true or not, and one dis-
counted them in advance. Besides, as against such rumors there was the
fact of the Farfield Foundation, our ostensible sponsor, which subsidized
Encounter via a grant to the Congress for Cultural Freedom.

The Farfield Foundation was no shadowy or ghostly entity. Its president, Julius (Junky) Fleischmann—whose millions derived from yeast,
gin, and other profitable commodities—would float over to London
every now and then, on his yacht, and Spender would give a "London literary party" for him. There, he would be introduced as "the patron" of
Encounter, and he would acknowledge the introduction with a gracious

modesty that seemed very becoming, and was—we now know—even more becoming than it seemed.

On several occasions, both Spender and I questioned him about the rumors. He repudiated them indignantly, and said that if anyone dared to print the barest hint of such a libel, he would promptly institute legal proceedings. In the event, of course, they did, and he did not.

Mind you, I really bear no animosity toward Junky, and I doubt that Spender does, either. I am sure he was moved by patriotic motives, and it is even possible that *some* of the money came from his own pocket. (Like many such conduits, the Farfield Foundation was a mixture of bona fide philanthropy and CIA dollars.) Moreover, Junky himself unquestionably did, like so many millionaires, have a genuine passion for "Culture" and for culture heroes. I am sure he meant me no harm, though he ended by doing me no good. The only amends I believe he owes any of us is, perhaps, to reimburse Spender for those liquor bills of yesteryear.

There were other reasons, too, why we never could take those rumors seriously. To begin with, there was the editorial freedom that was granted by the Congress to its various magazines—*Encounter* in London, *Tempo Presente* in Italy, *Preuves* in Paris. The editors of *Tempo Presente* were Ignazio Silone and Nicola Chiaramonte—two men whose notorious and prickly independence of spirit intimidates even their friends. If I were running the CIA, I would be scared silly of entrusting them with *anything*. Even now, the mere imagining of it makes me retrospectively nervous, on behalf of the CIA.

In the case of *Encounter*, I can testify that the idea of any secret editorial wire-pulling by the CIA was not only unthinkable, it was literally impossible: Spender and I made our editorial decisions in London, and there just was not anyone around to look over our shoulders while we did so. The Congress had no office or representative in London. The only person who came close to filling this description was Malcolm Muggeridge, who was then—among many other things—president of the British Committee for Cultural Freedom, an offshoot of the Congress.

I would have drinks with Malcolm maybe twice a year, and our conversations would be about Muggeridge, not *Encounter*—especially they would be about the particular journalistic scandal Malcolm was at that moment busily creating. I do not recall a single discussion that touched on so solemn a matter as *Encounter*'s editorial policy. To tell the truth, I do not recall a single one of those conversations with Malcolm that could even be called sober.

Prior to going to *Encounter*, I had been managing editor of *Commentary*, then (and still) sponsored by the American Jewish Committee. The relations of the editors of *Encounter* to the Congress were in all respects comparable to those of the editors of *Commentary* to the Committee. In both cases, we had been hired because our views (including, of course, our political views) and talents were congenial to the sponsoring organization. We could always be fired, were our services unsatisfactory. Aside from that, our editorial freedom was complete.

To be sure, the American Jewish Committee would occasionally let it be known to the editors of *Commentary* that it might have less difficulty in fund-raising if the editors were a bit more solicitous of rabbinical opinion. Similarly, the Congress would let it occasionally be known that its work abroad would be made easier, and its overseas program would be strengthened, if *Encounter* found some Indian or Egyptian or Ghanaian writers to publish. In both cases, such gentle interventions were not entirely ignored; an independent editor need not be a prima donna. Spender and I did make an extra effort to publish Asian and African writers. The returns on this effort were, I fear, minimal.

But of anything resembling political censorship of *Encounter* by its sponsors, there was no trace. I may have been, technically, a "dupe" of the CIA; *Encounter* was not. Perhaps it will be said that my own frequently expressed political opinions were so clearly "safe," from the CIA's point of view, that censorship was superfluous. Maybe so.* On the other hand, it is not quite so simple as that, as the following incident will illustrate:

In 1955, Spender and I—for reasons I no longer recollect, and may never have comprehended—found that we were, as they say, "getting on each other's nerves." (We have, since this time, become good friends.) Stephen decided to do something about it—that is, replace me with a new American editor. He enlisted the support of Muggeridge *and* of the executive secretary of the Congress for Cultural Freedom—who had a

---

*Not long ago, I learned from an unimpeachable source that the CIA did contemplate approaching me to become a "witting" agent—but that, when the agency ran a security check on me, I failed to come up with a passing grade. So there are advantages to having been a young radical: It protects one against undesirable solicitations.

"writing" connection with the CIA, as he has since candidly admitted. At the very last moment, when my bags were packed and my boat tickets purchased, this seditious (from my point of view) movement petered out, as the result of interventions on my behalf by British and American friends. The man who was to have replaced me was Dwight Macdonald!*

Could the CIA really have "endorsed" him? Dwight has spent a fruitful life and a distinguished career purposefully being a security risk to just about everyone and everything within reach of his typewriter. If the agency had ever tried to run a check on him, the computers would have gone mad with anxiety. So what did the CIA have in mind?

I do not know. It could be that, most of the time, the CIA never had very much in its mind. Or possibly, someone, someday, will tell us the CIA's side of the story. From some recently published tidbits, one gathers that, during the McCarthy period, the CIA gathered unto itself a group of dispossessed liberals who, unable to shape the overseas public policy of the U.S. government, set out to shape its private policy. The ironies implicit in this situation are too numerous to count, and they should make a fascinating narrative for the lucky historian who first gets his hands on the agency's files. (Given the agency's adeptness at secrecy, these files will doubtless soon be auctioned off as government surplus property.) But, back in the early 1950s, one knew nothing about these shenanigans. Eisenhower was president, Dulles was secretary of state, and the idea that such an administration would secretly come to the support of the likes of me or Dwight Macdonald or Ignazio Silone or Bertrand Russell (then chairman of the Congress!) was too ridiculous to contemplate.

That is the way it was. In retrospect, of course, it is bound to look different. Apparently, it looks different now even to some people who lived through the events and participated in them. One writer, who was my house guest in London, and who has more recently been busy "exposing" the CIA in *Ramparts*, reports in his autobiography that he enjoyed my hospitality despite our political differences; I wonder why he forgot to mention those differences at the time. Another houseguest, now a prominent figure in book publishing (and, in the 1950s, a member in

---

*Indeed, as a result of the preliminary commitment that had been made to him, he did join the staff of *Encounter* for a year, as an associate editor.

good standing of the American Committee for Cultural Freedom), reports in the *New York Review of Books* that moral and intellectual corruption was rife among our crowd; at the time, he seemed to be rather enjoying the company he kept.

I am old enough, and hardened enough, not to be wounded (or even surprised) by this sort of thing. People change their views and, inevitably, rewrite their autobiographies—sometimes with no awareness of duplicity.

What does irritate me is the prevalence of the snide remarks about "an underground gravy train," "official limousines," "travel in style," and so on. I enjoy high living as much as the next man, and I suppose that if the Farfield Foundation (i.e., the CIA) had offered me a limousine, I might have thought it a very useful article. But it did not. The CIA may have been the last of the big spenders in other areas, but back in those days it was generally assumed by everyone (including, apparently, the CIA) that being an intellectual was not a way to make money.

My average annual salary during my five years at *Encounter* was $9,500. One could then live well in London on such a salary, and we did, so I am not complaining. Nor did I mind that my family and I flew tourist class, on the two home leaves that were granted me in those five years. Never having flown first class in my life, I did not know what I was missing. It does bother me, however, that all these $25,000-a-year men should now pontificate (at 10 cents or more a word) about the "corruption" that is supposed to have prevailed in the 1950s. (*Encounter*, incidentally, paid its contributors 3 cents a word.)

This notion of an intellectual class living high off the hog is, of course, part and parcel of a larger vision: of an intellectual class that was elevated into membership in the "ruling elite," the Establishment, in order to render service in the conduct of the Cold War. The idea that, in the late 1940s and early 1950s, there was a mass *trahison des clercs* by the liberal anticommunist intellectuals—a treason suitably rewarded with money, honors, and privileges of all kinds—is by now so widespread on the college campus that I despair of correcting it. Still, for the record, I'd like to attempt a reminder of what it was really like to be a liberal anticommunist in those days.

To begin with, it meant having practically no influence at all outside the hermetic universe of New York literary politics. The supposed connection between, say, the liberal intellectuals in New York and the political powers in Washington is wholly mythical.

When I left this country to join *Encounter*, I had been for five years an editor—in the end, managing editor—of *Commentary*, which was then the leading liberal anticommunist publication. My writings in *Commentary* had attracted a certain measure of attention. Yet I had never in my life been to Washington, D.C.; I had never seen a congressman or senator or high government official in the flesh; no agency of the American government had ever asked me for my opinion on *anything*.

My influence in the nation at large was of the same magnitude. I had never been invited by any foundation, to any conference, anywhere; I had never received a foundation grant (still have not, for that matter); I had never been invited to speak on any college campus; I had never been asked to write for such publications as *Harper's*, the *Atlantic Monthly*, the *New York Times Magazine*; I had never been asked even to review a book by anyone except the *New Leader* (another liberal anticommunist publication, of limited circulation, which paid no authors' fees). It is perhaps understandable, therefore, that I had no idea I was effecting a merger with the Establishment (*that* term did not even exist then) or the "power elite" (a term just beginning to get currency when I left for England). In those days, my moment of most intimate contact with the national purpose and national power came when I was introduced to Arthur Schlesinger, Jr., who had actually written a Book-of-the-Month-Club selection and was reported to know some very important people in the Democratic party.

Nor was my case a singular one. All of those who constituted the liberal anticommunist intellectual community in New York—and it could hardly have been said to exist elsewhere—had a similar experience. Many of these became very famous and distinguished people: Diana and Lionel Trilling, Daniel Bell, Mary McCarthy, the editors of *Partisan Review*, Dwight Macdonald, Leslie Fiedler, Sidney Hook, Nathan Glazer. But in the first decade after World War II, their fame and their distinction were limited to—and their talents appreciated by—a very small circle indeed. They wrote mainly for one another, not out of cliquishness but because no one else seemed much interested. Washington was a million light-years away, and one could no more influence it than one could influence the drift of the galaxies.

This state of affairs was in no way remarkable, or exceptional, or temporary. For close to two decades, liberal anticommunism was a minority movement among intellectuals. It had been so in the 1930s; it was still so in the 1940s; it was only a little less so in the 1950s. I do not mean, and emphatically do not wish to be taken to mean, that a majority—or even a significant proportion—of American liberals or American intellectuals were *pro*communist. They were not. They were, in the useful phrase invented, I think, by Sidney Hook, "anti-anticommunist."

What the phrase signifies is an aversion to the "excesses" of communism coupled with a profound reluctance to be unnecessarily nasty about communism per se. For instance, an anti-anticommunist would certainly be willing to censure the Soviet government for imprisoning rabbis and priests. But, being an "enlightened" and "progressive" person, he would not be particularly bothered by the fact that this government insisted that the tenets of "atheism" be officially taught in the schools, and that criticism of them not be permitted anywhere. Similarly, he might protest against the imprisonment of writers who violated the code of "Socialist realism." But the mass extermination of middle-class peasants ("kulaks") left him cold; these people were tainted with the profit motive and were therefore expendable.

I am sure we all know many such people. They have been with us a long while now—long enough to breed a generation of young men and women on our campuses to whom even the parents' anti-anticommunism is just another version of anticommunism.

One frequently hears it said, these days, in a completely matter-of-fact way, that liberal anticommunists during the 1950s were "obsessed" by the specter of communism. I find this an eccentric way of putting it. It touches the truth only to the extent that liberal anticommunists believed that the Soviet regime was contemptible, not only in what it specifically did, but in what it generally was—that is, Communist. (I still believe it.) Nevertheless, there would not have been a Cold War, for us or anyone, if this regime had not been engaged in a worldwide campaign of ideological belligerency against liberal nations, liberal values, and liberal institutions. And it is worth recalling that, together with this ideological belligerency, there went a great deal of vulgar, brutal, material terror.

There was nothing "spectral" about Communist activities during that period; they were as substantial as they were alarming. In the Soviet Union itself, an insane tyrant was busy relentlessly and senselessly persecuting the Russian people, dispatching them by the tens of thousands to concentration camps, arranging monstrous "show trials" at which children recited prefabricated indictments of their parents, silencing any writer or artist who showed a glimmer of originality, imposing a conformity of thought and opinion (even of rhetoric) to a degree unsurpassed in all of European history. Throughout Soviet-occupied Eastern Europe this same political paranoia became the established orthodoxy. And in Western Europe there existed large, well-organized Communist parties with the expressed intention of dragging their fellow citizens down this very same road.

Strangely enough, sections of the intellectual community in this country and in Europe were disinclined to believe their eyes. Incorrigibly optimistic about any regime that called itself "socialist" or "progressive," these people insisted that reports of Stalinist terror were either mendacious or exaggerated. Among the more sophisticated and "philosophical" of these intellectuals there emerged ingenious apologies for the "historical necessity" of every brutish act a Communist regime could perpetrate. (See the writings of Jean-Paul Sartre at this time.) This current of opinion—procommunist or anti-anticommunist—was powerful, influential, obdurate. We who were liberal anticommunists found our work depressing and unrewarding. There appeared to be no way to persuade our fellow intellectuals of truths that seemed to us then, as now, self-evident.

We never did persuade them. Khrushchev did that, with his famous "secret speech," in which he said about Stalinism everything that anticommunists had been saying for years. Did this vindicate anticommunism? Not at all. Those who had previously denied the existence of a Stalinist terror in Russia and East Europe now accepted the halfhearted repudiation of this terror as evidence that the Soviet regime was "evolving" toward a truer, higher, more humane version of Communism. This peculiar dialectic has continued ever since. Repeatedly, each new group of Communist leaders has denounced the crimes of its predecessors. Just as repeatedly, every such denunciation is taken as redounding to the credit of Communism itself.

Still, by the mid-1950s the "thaw" was under way, and liberal anticommunists had reason to think that history had taken a turn for the better. The Hungarian revolution of 1956 was a setback, but only a temporary one. I know that we at *Encounter*, and the other intellectuals associated with the Congress for Cultural Freedom, were as eager as anyone to "build bridges" to the East. So far from being obsessed with anticommunism, we too were fascinated with the potential for "liberalization" that seemed to have been released. We foresaw the "polycentric" impulse among the various national Communist parties, but we never imagined that "revisionism" in Asia and Latin America could take the reactionary forms it has assumed in, say, China and Cuba. We had Tito in mind, not Mao.

In those middle years of the 1950s, I had many occasions to meet East European intellectuals at meetings—formal and informal—in London, Paris, and elsewhere. There was never the slightest problem of "communication." Indeed, I cannot even recall having any serious political arguments with them. One simply assumed, at the outset, that the Communist system, as it had developed in Russia, was politically reprehensible and economically absurd. These intellectuals from the East were, of course, "Socialists"—but their main interest was in combining Socialism with political and even economic liberalism. This kind of Socialist one had always been at ease with. After all, among the contributors to *Encounter* had been Hugh Gaitskell, Denis Healey, Roy Jenkins, Anthony Crosland, and others of their persuasion in the Labor party.

The Russians, to be sure, were different. Not many Russian intellectuals were then permitted to visit the West—though, occasionally, some party functionaries were baptized "intellectuals" for the purpose of showing up at some conference or other. But over these past years, even this has changed. One does have the opportunity to meet and chat with real Russian intellectuals, either abroad or (more often) in Russia—and *they* have no particular complaints against the kind of liberal anticommunism that was represented by *Encounter* or me. Indeed, most of them strike me as being liberal anticommunist Communists. It is not an easy political philosophy to define or make sense of. But, then, neither are most of the political philosophies in the West.

What it comes down to is this: *My* cold war—the struggle against Stalinist terror in Russia, and against a neo-Stalinist, totalitarian, international movement—is largely over. True, the Soviet Union is a great power whose interests often conflict with those of the United States; this can make life dangerous and depressing (as in the recent Middle East conflict), but it is no kind of special problem for intellectuals. True, too, Russia remains an authoritarian and repressive regime. But, then, it always has been.

The main thing, from my point of view, is that what used to be called

"Communism" in Europe in the 1950s has spent most of its ideological force;* the international Communist movement has lost its monolithic character and structure; the Soviet Union no longer seems much interested in setting up "front" organizations of intellectuals or others; the intellectuals themselves in Russia and East Europe are engaged in courageous "confrontations" with their own regimes, and while they have my blessings, I do not see that they need or want my help.

These intellectuals may call themselves, and believe themselves to be, Communists. But they clearly want no cold war with me, and I reciprocate their sentiments. We still have important disagreements, but I really have little doubt that, if I were to spend an evening now with a representative group of Russian and East European intellectuals, we should talk mainly about the "new breed" of radicals who have sprouted up all over the world, and we would surely agree that they represent a threat to "our" civilization—even, perhaps, to "our" way of life.

The Russian writers I have met find the contents of *Encounter* (now under private ownership) far more to their taste than the neo-Castroism of the *New York Review of Books*. The ideological heroes of the New Left— Herbert Marcuse, Frantz Fanon, Régis Debray—evoke no response among the intellectuals of Communist Europe, and you find no blown-up photos of Che Guevara in the faculty offices of Moscow University. A Western "progressive" like Conor Cruise O'Brien might think that the persecution of Soviet intellectuals is, paradoxically, a sign that the Soviet regime is more elevated than our own, because *there* the authorities take ideas very seriously. A Russian intellectual finds this "sophisticated" proposition simply perverse, as indeed it is.

So I find it more than a little odd that I—and others like me—should be denounced as an obsessive anticommunist and an incorrigible cold warrior. But, then, I must admit that I find many things odd about the new radicalism in American intellectual and literary circles. I am confused by middle-aged radicals who insist, in one and the same breath, that the present distribution of income is horribly inequitable and that you cannot live decently in New York on less than $50,000 a year. I am

---

*A leading Polish Marxist philosopher who spent some weeks at Oxford was asked how he liked it. He responded with enthusiasm: "It's a marvelous place! Absolutely marvelous! Here you find people who are actually willing to talk about Marxism!" I can vouch for the truth of this anecdote.

bewildered by a highbrow left-wing magazine which proudly advertises that it is "cliquish" and "snobbish." I do not comprehend the merger that seems to have taken place between the literary Left and café society, or the calm assumption that writers are and ought to be "celebrities." I do not understand the view—becoming ever more popular—that mental illness in our decadent society is a positive sign of health, and that schizophrenics are in closer touch with ultimate reality than the rest of us. I do not think homosexuality is normal; I distrust drugs, and I do not find pornography all that readable.

No: Russell Lynes notwithstanding, and despite my unwitting connection with the CIA, I am not chic at all. Not in this country, not today. And there is still a sense, I suppose, in which I can fairly be called a cold warrior. What I mean is: I believe in individual liberty and representative democracy; I prefer a modified form of capitalism to any other proposed economic system; I am certain Castro is no good model for Latin American progress; I consider Maoism as detestable as fascism and not easily distinguishable from it; I do not see that the underdeveloped countries of the Third World represent any kind of wave of the future, and Che Guevara is not my idea of Robin Hood. But this is a new and different kind of cold war, in another time, for the most part in other places, and involving different ideologies. Looking back on the Cold War of the 1950s against Stalinism, I can at moments feel positively nostalgic for the relatively forthright way it posed unambiguous moral issues. No amount of revisionist rewriting will affect my view of these moral proprieties. It was, by every canon I recognize, a just war, and I am pleased to have had a small part in it.

1968

40

Memoirs of a Trotskyist

Not long ago, I passed through the Loeb Student Center, at New York University's Washington Square campus. It is a modern and luxurious building—to my eyes, definitely "posh"—with comfortable sofas and chairs, ample space and light and all those little amenities that correspond to our middle-class notions of "gracious living." On that particular day, the main lounge was half-empty; a few students were slumped in armchairs, reading or dozing, while here and there groups of two or three were chatting over cups of coffee. As I stood there gazing with wonder at the opulence of it all, and with puzzlement at the languor of it all, I was prompted once again to remember the physical squalor and mental energy of Alcove No. 1 at CCNY [City College of New York].

Such memories had been provoked more than once during the turbulent 1960s. Anyone who had been a student radical in the 1930s was bound to be moved to compare his own experiences (or the recollections of his own experiences) with the rebellions he observed a generation later. The danger of such an exercise, in the heat of the tumult, is the natural temptation toward the fogy's lament: "Why can't they be as we were?" In truth, that is a legitimate question—if it is meant seriously as a question, and not merely as a reproach.

Perhaps now that the wave of student radicalism has subsided, to be succeeded (temporarily at least) by a kind of sullen resignation, one can put those memories to paper without seeming patronizing or self-serving.

469

The student radicalism of the 1930s was indeed different from that of the 1960s, and different in ways that tell us something important, I think, about what happened to American society (and to the rebels against that society) in the intervening decades. And if the comparison is to the advantage of the earlier radicalism—as I admit right off it will be—it is because, in my opinion, the United States in the 1930s was in many ways a healthier (if materially far less prosperous) society than it has become, so that rebellion was healthier, too.

I was graduated from City College in the spring of 1940, and the honor I most prized was the fact that I was a member in good standing of the Young People's Socialist League (Fourth International). This organization was commonly, and correctly, designated as Trotskyist (not "Trotskyite," which was a term used only by the official Communists, or "Stalinists" as we called them, of the day). I have not set foot on the City College campus since my commencement. The present president of the college, Robert Marshak, has amiably urged me to come and see the place again—it is very different but still recognizable, he says. I have promised to go, but somehow I think I may never find the time.

It is not that my memories of CCNY are disagreeable. On the contrary: When I think back to those years, it is with a kind of nostalgia. It was at that place, and in that time, that I met the young men—there were no women at the uptown campus then—who became my lifelong friends. The education I got was pretty good, even if most of it was acquired outside the classroom. My personal life was no messier or more troubled than any adolescent's. True, I was poor—but so was everyone else, and I was by no means the poorest. True, too, it was not fun commuting by subway for more than an hour each way from and to Brooklyn, where I lived. But the memory of poverty and those tedious subway rides has faded with time, whereas what I now recollect most vividly is the incredible vivacity with which we all confronted the dismal 1930s.

Is it then perhaps my radical past, now so firmly disowned, that bothers me and makes CCNY unhallowed ground? I think not. I have no regret about that episode in my life. Joining a radical movement when one is young is very much like falling in love when one is young. The girl may turn out to be rotten, but the experience of love is so valuable it can never be entirely undone by the ultimate disenchantment.

But my feelings toward those radical days are even more positive than this kind of general reflection suggests. For the truth is that being a young radical was not simply part of my college experience; it was practically the whole of it. If I left City College with a better education than did many students at other and supposedly better colleges, it was because my involvement in radical politics put me in touch with people and ideas that prompted me to read and think and argue with a furious energy. This was not a typical experience—I am talking about a relatively small group of students, a particular kind of student radical. Going to City College meant, for me, being a member of this group. It was a privileged experience, and I know of no one who participated in it who does not look back upon it with some such sentiment.

So why have I never returned to visit the place? Perhaps because I know it is impossible. *That* place no longer exists. It has vanished with the time of which it was so integral a part. Whatever is now happening at City College, I doubt that I am likely to comprehend, much less enjoy, it. For what I have seen of student radicalism on various campuses over the past dozen years baffles and bothers me. It seems to be more a psychological than a truly political phenomenon. There is a desperate quest for self-identity, an evident and acute involvement of one's political beliefs with all kinds of personal anxieties and neuroses, a consequent cheerlessness and truculence.

The changing connotation of the term "alienated" tells us much. At City College in the 1930s we were familiar enough with the word and the idea behind it. But for us it was a sociological category and referred to the condition of the working class. We were not alienated. By virtue of being radical intellectuals, we had "transcended" alienation (to use another Marxist term). We experienced our radicalism as a privilege of rank, not as a burden imposed by a malignant fate. It would never have occurred to us to denounce anyone or anything as "elitist." The elite was us—the "happy few" who had been chosen by History to guide our fellow creatures toward a secular redemption.

Alcove No. 1 was located in the City College lunchroom, a vast ground-floor space which even we, who came from slums or near-slums, judged to be an especially slummy and smelly place. There was a small semicircular counter where one could buy franks or milk or coffee. I suppose they also sold some sandwiches, but I certainly never bought one, and I do not remember anyone else ever committing such an act of unmitigated profligacy. The less poor among us purchased a frank or two; the rest brought their lunches from home—hard-boiled egg sandwiches, cream-cheese sandwiches, peanut-butter sandwiches, once in a while even a chicken sandwich—and there was always a bit of sandwich swapping to enliven one's diet. There was also some sandwich scrounging by those who were *really* poor; one asked and gave without shame or reservation.

The center of the lunchroom, taking up most of the space, consisted of chest-high, wooden tables under a low, artificial ceiling. There, most of the students ate their lunches, standing up. (I looked upon this as being reasonable, since at Boys' High, in Brooklyn, we had had the same arrangement. To this day I find it as natural to eat a sandwich standing up as sitting down.) Around this central area there was a fairly wide and high-ceilinged aisle; and bordering the aisle, under large windows with small panes of glass that kept out as much light as they let in, were the alcoves—semicircular (or were they rectangular?), each with a bench fitted along the wall and a low, long refectory table in the middle. The first alcove on the right, as you entered the lunchroom, was Alcove No. 1, and this soon became most of what City College meant to me. It was there one ate lunch, played Ping-Pong (sometimes with a net, sometimes without), passed the time of day between and after classes, argued incessantly, and generally devoted oneself to solving the ultimate problems of the human race. The penultimate problems we figured could be left for our declining years, after we had graduated.

I would guess that, in all, there were more than a dozen alcoves, and just how rights of possession had been historically established was as obscure as the origins of the social contract itself. Once established, however, they endured, and in a manner typical of New York's "melting pot," each religious, ethnic, cultural, and political group had its own little alcove. There was a Catholic alcove, the "turf" of the Newman Society, a Zionist alcove, an Orthodox Jewish alcove; there was a black alcove for the handful of blacks then at CCNY, an alcove for members of the athletic teams, and so forth. But the only alcoves that mattered to me were No. 1 and No. 2, the alcoves of the anti-Stalinist Left and pro-Stalinist Left, respectively. It was between these two alcoves that the war of the worlds was fought, over the faceless bodies of the mass of students, whom we tried desperately to manipulate into "the right position" but about whom, to tell the truth, we knew little and cared less.

City College was known at the time as a "radical" institution, and in an era when most college students identified themselves as Republicans the ascription was not incorrect. If there were any Republicans at City— and there must have been some—I never met them, or even heard of their existence. Most of the students, from Jewish working-class or lower-middle-class backgrounds with a socialist tint, were spontaneously sympathetic to the New Deal and F.D.R. The really left-wing groups, though larger than elsewhere, were a distinct minority. Alcove No. 2, by far the most populous of the "political" alcoves, could rarely mobilize more than four hundred or five hundred out of a total enrollment of per- haps twenty thousand students for a protest rally, or "action"; we in Alcove No. 1 numbered about thirty "regulars" and were lucky to get an audience of fifty to one hundred for one of ours. But then, as now, stu- dent government and student politics were a minority affair, and what the passive majority thought really did not matter. What "happened" on campus was determined by *them*—the denizens of Alcove No. 2—or *us*. In truth, very little did happen; but at the time what did seemed terribly important. During my first three years, *they* controlled the college news- paper; in my last year, we got control. It was a glorious victory, and I do think that we went on to publish a slightly less mendacious newspaper— but I have not even a vague remembrance of what we were slightly less mendacious about.

I shall not say much about Alcove No. 2—the home of the pro-Stalin- ist Left—but, Lord, how dreary a bunch they seemed to be! I thought then, with a sectarian snobbery that comes so easily to young radicals, that they really did not and never would amount to much. And I must say—at the risk of being accused of smugness—that in all these inter- vening decades, only two names from Alcove No. 2 have come to my attention. One is now a scientist at a major university. The other was Julius Rosenberg.

I do believe their dreariness was a fact, and that this dreariness in turn had something to do with the political outlook they took it upon them- selves to espouse. These were young college students who, out of sympa- thy with Communism as officially established in the Soviet Union, had publicly to justify the Moscow trials and the bloody purge of old Bolshe- viks; had publicly to accept the self-glorification of Joseph Stalin as an exemplar of Communist virtue and wisdom; had publicly to deny that there were concentration camps in the Soviet Union, and so forth, and so forth. Moreover, since this was the period of the popular front, they had for the time to repudiate (by way of reinterpretation) most of the Marxist-Leninist teachings on which their movement was ostensibly founded.

Though I had no trouble understanding how a young man at that time could have joined the Young Communist League, or one of its "fronts," I did find it hard to imagine how he stayed there. Not everyone did stay, of course; many of the members of Alcove No. 1 had had their first political experience with a Stalinist group and had left in disillusionment. But those who did stay on for any length of time—well, it had to have deleterious effects on their quality of mind. After all, members of the congregation of Alcove No. 2 were actually forbidden, under pain of ostracism and exile, to enter into conversation or even argument with any member of Alcove No. 1! This prohibition was dutifully obeyed, and such mindless obedience could not fail to have its costs.

Which brings me to Alcove No. 1, where pure intellect—a certain kind of intellect, anyway—reigned unchallenged.

Alcove No. 1 was the place you went to if you wanted to be radical *and* have a theory as to the proper kind of radical you should be. When I say "theory," I mean that in the largest sense. We in Alcove No. 1 were terribly concerned with being "right" in politics, economics, sociology, philosophy, history, anthropology, and so forth. It was essential to be right in all of these fields of knowledge, lest a bit of information from one should casually collide with a theoretical edifice and bring the whole structure tumbling down. So all the little grouplets that joined together to make Alcove No. 1 their home were always in keen competition to come up with startling bits of information—or, better yet, obscure and disorienting quotations from Marx or Engels or Lenin or Trotsky—that would create intellectual trouble for the rest of the company.

The Trotskyists, with perhaps a dozen members, were one of the largest grouplets and unquestionably the most feverishly articulate. Almost as numerous, though considerably less noisy, were the Socialists, or "the Norman Thomas Socialists" as one called them, to distinguish them from other kinds of socialists. Among these other kinds, none of which ever had more than two or three representatives in Alcove No. 1, were the Social Democrats (or "right-wing socialists") who actually voted for F.D.R., and the "revolutionary socialists" who belonged to one or another "splinter group"—the Ohlerites, the Marlinites, the Field-

ites, the Lovestonites, and the who-can-remember-what-other-ites—
which, finding itself in "principled disagreement" with every other sect,
had its own little publication (usually called a "theoretical organ") and its
own special prescription for achieving *real* socialism. In addition, and
finally, there were a handful of "independents"—exasperating left-wing
individualists who either could not bring themselves to join any group or
else insisted on joining them all in succession. What held this crazy con-
glomeration together was, quite simply, the powerful presence of Alcove
No. 2, and, beyond that, the looming shadow of Stalinism with its threat
of so irrevocably debasing the socialist ideal as to rob humanity of what
we were certain was its last, best hope.

Obviously, in such a milieu certain intellectual qualities tended to be
emphasized at the expense of others. We were strongly inclined to celebrate the analytical powers of mind rather than the creative, and we paid
more heed to public philosophies than to private ones. It cannot be an
accident that so many graduates of Alcove No. 1 went on to become professors of social science; in a sense, what Alcove No. 1 provided was a
peculiarly intense undergraduate education in what is now called social
science but which we then called (more accurately, I sometimes think)
political ideology. Nor can it be an accident that none of the graduates of
Alcove No. 1—none who were there in my time, anyway—subsequently
achieved any kind of distinction in creative writing or the arts; in that
ideological hothouse, the personal vision and the personal accent withered for lack of nourishment.

So I do not want to be misunderstood as claiming superlative merits
for Alcove No. 1 as an educational milieu. On the other hand, it *was* an
authentic educational milieu. And this, I suppose, is why so many went
on to become professors—getting paid, as it were, for continuing to be
interested in the things they had always been interested in.

In some respects the quintessential representative of this milieu was Seymour Martin Lipset, now professor of sociology and political science at
Stanford—a kind of intellectual bumblebee, whose function it was to
spread the pollen of ideological doubt and political consternation over
all Alcove No. 1's flowering ideologies. Irving Howe, in contrast, was a
pillar of ideological rectitude. Thin, gangling, intense, always a little distant, his fingers incessantly and nervously twisting a cowlick as he enunciated sharp and authoritative opinions, Irving was the Trotskyist leader

and "theoretician." In the years since, he has gone on to become a famous literary critic and a professor of literature at the City University. But he has remained politically *engagé*, though slowly moving "right" from Trotskyism to democratic socialism (as represented in his journal, *Dissent*). Since I have abandoned my socialist beliefs altogether, I feel that I am still ahead of him politically.

Daniel Bell, now professor of sociology at Harvard, was at the opposite pole from Irving. He was that rarity of the 1930s: an honest-to-goodness social-democratic intellectual who believed in "a mixed economy," a two-party system based on the British model, and other liberal heresies. His evident skepticism toward all our ideologies would ordinarily have disqualified him from membership in Alcove No. 1. But he had an immense intellectual curiosity, a kind of amused fondness for sectarian dialectics, knew his radical texts as thoroughly as the most learned among us, and enjoyed "a good theoretical discussion" the way some enjoy a Turkish bath—so we counted him in. Over the years, his political views have probably changed less than those of the rest of us, with the result that, whereas his former classmates used to criticize him from the Left, they now criticize him from all points of the ideological compass.

Others who later found, to their pleasant surprise, that what they had been doing in Alcove No. 1 was what the academic world would come to recognize and generously reward as "social science" were Nathan Glazer (Harvard), Philip Selznick (Berkeley), Peter Rossi (Johns Hopkins), Morroe Berger (Princeton), I. Milton Sacks (Brandeis), Lawrence Krader and Bernard Bellush (City University), Seymour Melman (Columbia), Melvin J. Lasky (now editor of *Encounter*)—and others who may be just as pleased not to read their names in this context.

Bellush, a calm and obstinately moderate socialist of the Norman Thomas persuasion, was a most unlikely candidate to serve as a central symbol of student radicalism, and yet at one point he did. During an anti-ROTC [Reserve Officers' Training Corps] demonstration, Bernie was arrested for punching a police officer. The ensuing trial was a field day for us, as we "mobilized" the student body to attend protest rallies ("Cops off the campus!"), pack the courtroom, and so forth. Bernie was acquitted, and it was a moment of triumph. I must confess, however, that to this day I cannot honestly say whether or not he actually did punch that police officer; with typical radical disingenuousness, we studiously avoided asking either him or ourselves that question. Strange as it may sound to today's radical student, we really would have been disturbed had he been guilty as charged. At the very least, we would have been plunged into an endless debate on the finer points of "revolutionary morality." With the experience of Stalinism constantly in mind, we were extremely sensitive to the possibility that radical means could corrupt radical ends.

I certainly do not mean to suggest that membership in Alcove No. 1 was any kind of prerequisite for subsequent academic distinction. Kenneth Arrow, for instance, now a Nobel Prize-winning professor of economics at Harvard, and David Landes, now professor of history at Harvard, were contemporaries of mine at City who kept their distance from Alcove No. 1 and found other useful things (like studying) to do with their time. Nevertheless, it does seem clear to me that there was an academic impulse at work in Alcove No. 1, even if none of us understood its shaping force at the time. I mention this simply to emphasize the connection which was then possible—in many instances, probable—between student radicalism and intellectual vitality, a connection which seems to have been attenuated over the succeeding years.

Alcove No. 1 was, as I have said, where our real college education took place. Being a professor at City in those days was not a very attractive job. True, you had tenure and this counted for much in the 1930s. But you taught fifteen hours a week, had no private office, no faculty club, no library where you could do research; you commuted to the campus by subway, and, if you were a younger faculty member, your pay amounted to little more than pocket money. As a result, the very best professors left, if they could.

The Depression made it more difficult for many to do this, and the students benefited from their misfortune. But the fact remains that, for the bright, inquiring student, City College was a pretty dull educational place. The student who came seeking an intellectual community, in which the life of the mind was strenuously lived, had to create such a community and such a life for himself.

That an authentic educational process could exist outside of such a political community I discovered, to my amazement, at the University of Chicago, a couple of years after I left City. My wife had a graduate fellowship in history there, and I hung around the campus as a "nonstudent" for the better part of a year, working part-time as a freight handler

on the Illinois Central while waiting for my draft records to be transferred from New York. I still see that year as through a golden haze—
and I have never met a Chicago alumnus of that period who does not see
it likewise. Under the powerful leadership of Robert M. Hutchins and
Mortimer J. Adler, undergraduate education at Chicago centered on
reading "great books," thinking about them, arguing about them. And
the students did read, did think, did argue passionately. True, Chicago
also had its share of young anti-Stalinist radicals who constituted a counterpart—much more literary, much less political—to Alcove No. 1.
(Saul Bellow, Isaac Rosenfeld, Oscar Tarcov, H. J. Kaplan, and Leslie
Fiedler were members of that group.) But the point is that, at Chicago,
you did not *have* to be political to lead a vigorous intellectual life and be a
member of an authentic intellectual community.

Though the specifically political radicalism of Alcove No. 1 was conventional and coarse enough, what gave it its special quality was the fact that
it was intertwined with an intense interest in, and deference to, the
"highbrow" in culture, philosophy, and the arts. The two most influential journals in Alcove No. 1 were the *New International* and *Partisan
Review*. The first was the Trotskyist theoretical organ and, confined by
dogma though it certainly was, it was also full of a Marxist scholasticism
that was as rigorous and learned, in its way, as the Jesuit scholasticism it
so strikingly paralleled. Its contributors—Trotsky himself, Max Schachtman, James Burnham, Dwight Macdonald, C. L. R. James—were Marxist intellectuals. There were many important things one could not learn
from reading the *New International*; but one most emphatically did learn
how to read an intellectual discourse and several of us learned how to
write one.

Partisan Review, the journal of the anti-Stalinist, left-wing, cultural
avant-garde, was an intimidating presence in Alcove No. 1. Even simply
to understand it seemed a goal beyond reach. I would read each article at
least twice, in a state of awe and exasperation—excited to see such ele-
gance of style and profundity of mind, depressed at the realization that a
commoner like myself could never expect to rise into that intellectual
aristocracy, an aristocracy that included Lionel Trilling, Philip Rahv,
William Phillips, Sidney Hook, Mary McCarthy, Paul Goodman,
Clement Greenberg, Harold Rosenberg, Meyer Schapiro, and F. W.
Dupee. I have recently had occasion to reread some of these issues of

Partisan Review and, though I now see limitations then not visible to me, I also must affirm that it was a most remarkable magazine. The particular mission it set itself—to reconcile a socialist humanism with an individualistic "modernism" in the arts (the latter frequently being, in the 1930s, associated with "reactionary" political attitudes)—established a dialectic of challenge and response that released the finest creative energies. The effort at reconciliation eventually failed, in a quite unpredictable way, as the emerging "counterculture" gradually abolished the category of the highbrow altogether. But it was a bold, imaginative effort, and *Partisan Review* in its heyday was unquestionably one of the finest American cultural periodicals ever published—perhaps even the very finest.

In addition, there were the frequent debates which we attended. The term "debate" as used today really does not do them justice. To begin with, they ignored all conventional time limits. A speaker like Max Schachtman, the Trotskyist leader, or Gus Tyler of the Socialist party, could argue at a high pitch of moral and intellectual and rhetorical intensity for two, three, even four hours. (Since the Stalinists refused to debate with other left-wing groups, we were always debating among ourselves.) When, in 1940, the Trotskyists split into two factions, it was after a debate among four speakers that continued for two whole days. (The most succinct presentation, by James Burnham, lasted only two hours, and caused many of those present to question his "seriousness.") And, incredible as it may seem, the quality of the presentations was in all respects up to the quantity. They were—within the limits imposed by their socialist preconceptions—learned, witty, articulate, intellectually rigorous. I have never since seen or heard their equal, and, as a learning experience for college students, they were beyond comparison.

So far as I can see, universities today are not significantly better or worse than they were in the 1930s; they are not—as they were not—intellectual communities. But the rebellion against the "merely academic" has tended to take the form of a secession from the life of the mind altogether.

The radicalism of the 1930s was decidedly an adult movement, in which young people were permitted to participate. We young Trotskyists were as numerous as the adult party, but we unquestioningly accepted the authority of the latter. In contrast, the radicalism of the 1960s was a generational movement, bereft of adult models and adult guidance. It is not easy to understand just how this came about, but one thing is certain: The radicals of the 1960s were what they were because American society and American culture—which means we, the adults—permitted them (sometimes encouraged them) to grow up to be what they were. It is not, as some think, that we failed to impose our adult *beliefs* upon our children. That would be an absurd enterprise. What we failed to do is to transmit adult *values* to them—values affecting the way one holds beliefs, which would have encouraged them to take their own and others' beliefs seriously, and to think coherently about them. And precisely because we adults encouraged our twenty-year-old children to be "kids," their rebellion so often resembled a bewildering and self-destructive tantrum.

As to why American adults failed their children in this way—well, since some of my best friends are now social scientists, I will leave that for them to figure out.

1977

41

My Cold War

This past fall, in what used to be East Berlin, I attended a commemorative conference on "The Cold War and After." It was sponsored by the late, lamented *Encounter* magazine, which had been founded in London in 1953 by Stephen Spender and myself, and which ceased publication last year. Though I left the magazine at the end of 1958, to return to New York, I have always felt a special sense of solidarity with it.

Encounter was accused of being a "Cold War" magazine, which in a sense was true enough. It was published by the Congress for Cultural Freedom, which was later revealed to be financed by the CIA. As a cultural-political journal, it published many fine literary essays, literary criticism, art criticism, short stories, and poetry, and in sheer bulk they probably preponderated. But there is no doubt its ideological core—its "mission," as it were—was to counteract, insofar as it was possible, the anti-American, pro-Soviet views of a large segment of the intellectual elites in the Western democracies and in the English-speaking Commonwealth.

Just how large this segment was, and how influential, is now easily (and conveniently) forgotten. In France, it was practically impossible to work in the film industry unless you were a member of the Communist party or a reliable fellow-traveler. In Italy, it was not very different. In Germany, the dominant posture of intellectuals was "neutralist"—i.e., asserting a "moral equivalence" between the United States and the USSR.

Even in Britain and the United States, majority opinion in the intellectual elite was, when not fellow-travelling or "neutralist," insistent on distancing itself from America's Cold War policies as overly "militaristic."

This intellectual *Weltanschauung* derived from the fact that most intellectuals, everywhere, were generally on the Left of the political spectrum. It was therefore easier to give the benefit of all doubts to the Soviet Union or, say, Cuba which were nominally "socialist" and ideologically egalitarian than to a vigorously capitalist United States. Only among the so-called "right-wing Social Democrats" did one find a consistent "anticommunist" attitude—which was never, however, a simple pro-American one, for obvious reasons.

Under these circumstances, it is understandable that the political coloration of *Encounter* was, on the whole, right-wing Social Democratic—something which annoyed those of my American friends who felt that an unqualified pro-American position was incumbent on us. Though by this time I had become skeptical of Social Democrats or "liberals" in the American sense—they came to the same thing—I appreciated the clear strategic desirability (perhaps even necessity) of such an orientation. But I was less than enthusiastic about it and took some satisfaction in publishing a few articles by some of the younger, more gifted British Tories.

The truth is that, by the time I came to *Encounter*, anticommunism or anti-Marxism or anti-Marxist-Leninism or antitotalitarianism had pretty much ceased to interest me as an intellectual project. As a young Trotskyist in my college days, I had studied Marx and Lenin and Trotsky to the point of disillusionment. It was a useful inoculation that rendered me, not only immune, but positively indifferent to the ideological chatter around me. For almost half a century now, I have found it close to impossible even to read any apologia for a communist regime, any political analysis written from a procommunist point of view, or any socioeconomic analysis written from a Marxist or quasi-Marxist point of view. Only rarely did I feel moved to refute such writings. I was happy, for the most part, to leave that to others—scholars, journalists, publicists—being content to associate myself with their efforts to do God's work. I heartily approved of their Cold War but it was not my cold war.

My disillusionment with the Trotskyist version of radical socialism proceeded along its own path. I have never felt myself to be an "ex-Trotskyist" in the sense that some people conceive of themselves as "ex-communists." The experience was never that important to me, and my rightward drift commenced promptly upon its termination. I then defined myself as a "democratic socialist," though this was a movement so intellectually placid and politically inert that I am convinced I always understood it to be a convenient transitional phase.

In any case, my tepid loyalty to "democratic socialism" did not survive my experiences as an infantryman in the army. I entered military service with a prefabricated set of attitudes: The army was an authoritarian, hierarchical, mean-spirited, mindless machine—as later described by Norman Mailer in *The Naked and the Dead*—while the common soldiers, for all their human imperfections, represented the potential for a better future. Well, it turned out that, as a provincial from New York, I knew nothing about the American common man and even less about the army as an institution. Again and again, and to my surprise, I found reasons to think better of the army and less well of my fellow enlisted men. It is true that, since I was inducted in Chicago, my regiment was heavily populated by thugs or near-thugs from places like Cicero (Al Capone's old base), so my impressions may have been extreme. Nevertheless, my army experience permitted me to make an important political discovery: The idea of building socialism with the common man who actually existed— as distinct from his idealized version—was sheer fantasy, and therefore the prospects for "democratic socialism" were nil. The army may have radicalized Norman Mailer; it successfully de-radicalized me. It caused me to cease being a socialist.

But what was I, then? When, after the war, I joined the editorial staff of *Commentary*, I accepted, for want of a better term, the designation of "liberal." After all, members of the New York intellectual community were *all* "liberals," with not a conservative (not one!) among them. It didn't matter that much to me because, in the immediate postwar years, I wasn't particularly interested in politics. My own writings, in that period, encompassed religion, philosophy, and literature. I was a member in good standing of the anticommunist segment of that intellectual community—*Commentary*, after all, was one of its major organs—but I do not recall writing anything about communism. It was a period—it lasted almost five years—during which, as a liberal editor, nonliberal thoughts germinated in my mind and soul. I was far from being a conservative, had no interest in "market economics," and the notion of voting Republican was as foreign to me as attending a Catholic mass. I suppose that, in today's terms, I could be fairly described as a premature "neo-liberal"— with the emphasis most emphatically on the "neo."

The two intellectual godfathers of my neo-ism were Lionel Trilling and Reinhold Niebuhr. It was Trilling who, as early as my college years, and even while I was a Trotskyist, pointed to liberalism's dirty little secret—that there was something basically rotten about its progressive metaphysics that led to an impoverishment of the imagination and a dessication of the spirit. It was he who pointed out that among all the modern novelists and poets we admired, and which he taught in his Columbia University course, there was not one who could properly be called a liberal. This theme Trilling went on to develop and deepen in the decades that followed, and I greedily seized upon every word he wrote. Oddly enough, he never ceased to think of himself as a liberal, albeit a disturbed and dissident liberal, and while always respectful of religion, he was irredeemably secular in his sensibility. His mission as he saw it, apparently, was to liberate liberals from the confines of liberalism. But toward what, he could never say.

Reinhold Niebuhr could say. His two-volume *Nature and Destiny of Man* was the first theological work I had ever read and it pointed me beyond liberalism. To be sure, I had always had a vague, positive feeling about religion and was especially fond of religious poets (Donne, Hopkins, Eliot). Indeed, it may have been through poetry that my predisposition to religion was formed. But I had neither the intellectual vocabulary nor the intellectual grammar with which to *think* about religion. It was Niebuhr who introduced me to the idea of "the human condition" as something permanent, inevitable, transcultural, transhistorical, a transcendent finitude. To entertain seriously such a vision is already to have disengaged oneself from a crucial progressive-liberal piety. It also enables one to read the Book of Genesis with an appreciation that approaches awe. After Niebuhr, I plunged into theological literature with an ecumenical enthusiasm. By the late 1940s, religious thought was my most passionate interest—though, in the secular-liberal milieu in which I lived and worked, it was an interest to be revealed with prudence. The fact that Niebuhr, like Trilling, was generally regarded—and regarded himself to be—a member in good standing of the liberal intellectual community was reassuring to me. Perhaps it was possible, after all, to reject liberal metaphysics while remaining, to some degree and in some way, politically liberal. The following decades were to reveal to me how utterly impossible it was.

It was in 1951 that I started writing about politics again, if only intermittently. My first such effort was a book review of a prominent fellow-traveling liberal, in which I tried to analyze the rhetoric of this kind of liberalism—not so much to argue with this rhetoric as to demonstrate how it shaped an utterly false view of the world. This was the beginning of my cold war—a persistent critical inquiry into liberalism, trying to figure out what were the passions and the intellectual preconceptions that moved otherwise intelligent people to take a relatively benign view of communist tyranny in power and of communist movements that strove to establish such a tyranny. I was grappling with the phenomenon of left-wing political romanticism and utopianism that infected the intellectual classes of the West, and of the Westernized elites in the "Third World."

I was indeed a "Cold Warrior" (a "Cold War liberal" was the familiar ascription) but I was not engaged in any kind of crusade against communism. It was the fundamental assumptions of contemporary liberalism that were my enemy. For without the moral legitimation of communism provided by Western intellectuals—all the Soviet intellectuals had perished or were in prison camps—the "Cold War" was reduced to a raw, power conflict between totalitarian tyranny and constitutional democracy. This Cold War was a very serious business, as war always is. And there was certainly a crucial ideological dimension to the conflict. The Soviet rulers were authentic Marxist-Leninists, though the peoples they ruled were nothing of the sort. But there really was no good reason why the bizarre beliefs of communist leaders should have provoked ideological turmoil in the West, should have given rise to the notion that there were agonizing choices to be made. It was only the prevailing liberal ethos among intellectuals, academia, and the media that imported this complication into our lives.

In the decades that followed, this ethos moved consistently leftward as I moved consistently rightward. My liberal credentials became tattered, in my own eyes as well as in the eyes of others. Eventually, by the late 1960s and early 1970s, something that was to be called "neoconservatism" came into being as a new category of political identity for persons like myself. I found it a relief to be so designated and to be removed from that narrowing portion of the political spectrum labeled as "anti-communist liberal."

Anticommunism had long since ceased being an interesting intellectual issue for me. Resistance to the imperialist designs of communist totalitarianism was essential, of course. How to make such resistance maximally effective was a political challenge, as was resistance to the ever-mounting passion for appeasement evident in liberal circles. But what began to concern me more and more were the clear signs of rot and decadence germinating within American society—a rot and decadence that was no longer the consequence of liberalism but was the actual agenda of contemporary liberalism. And the more contemporary, the more candid and radical was this agenda.

For me, then, "neoconservatism" was an experience of moral, intellectual, and spiritual liberation. I no longer had to pretend to believe—what in my heart I could no longer believe—that liberals were wrong because they subscribe to this or that erroneous opinion on this or that topic. No—liberals were wrong, liberals are wrong, because they are liberals. What is wrong with liberalism is liberalism—a metaphysics and a mythology that is woefully blind to human and political reality. Becoming a neoconservative, then, was the high point of *my* cold war.

It is a cold war that, for the last twenty-five years, has engaged my attention and energy, and continues to do so. There is no "after the Cold War" for me. So far from having ended, my cold war has increased in intensity, as sector after sector of American life has been ruthlessly corrupted by the liberal ethos. It is an ethos that aims simultaneously at political and social collectivism on the one hand, and moral anarchy on the other. It cannot win, but it can make us all losers. We have, I do believe, reached a critical turning point in the history of the American democracy. Now that the other "Cold War" is over, the real cold war has begun. We are far less prepared for this cold war, far more vulnerable to our enemy, than was the case with our victorious war against a global communist threat. We are, I sometimes feel, starting from ground zero, and it is a conflict I shall be passing on to my children and grandchildren. But it is a far more interesting cold war—intellectually interesting, spiritually interesting—than the war we have so recently won, and I rather envy those young enough for the opportunities they will have to participate in it.

1993

INDEX OF NAMES

A NOTE ON THE AUTHOR

Irving Kristol was born in New York City and studied at the City College of New York. After service with the army in World War II, he became managing editor of *Commentary* magazine; in 1953 he founded *Encounter* magazine with Stephen Spender; in 1959 he briefly edited *The Reporter* magazine. After eight years as a vice-president of Basic Books, Mr. Kristol served from 1969 to 1985 as Professor of Social Thought in the Graduate School of Business Administration at New York University. He is now co-editor, with Nathan Glazer, of *The Public Interest* magazine and publisher of *The National Interest*, and is John M. Olin Distinguished Fellow at the American Enterprise Institute. His other books include *On the Democratic Idea in America*, *Two Cheers for Capitalism*, and *Reflections of a Neoconservative*.

ELEPHANT PAPERBACKS

American History and American Studies

Stephen Vincent Benét, *John Brown's Body*, EL10
Henry W. Berger, ed., *A William Appleman Williams Reader*, EL126
Andrew Bergman, *We're in the Money*, EL124
Paul Boyer, ed., *Reagan as President*, EL117
Robert V. Bruce, *1877: Year of Violence*, EL102
Philip Callow, *From Noon to Starry Night*, EL37
David Cowan and John Kuenster, *To Sleep with the Angels*, EL139
George Dangerfield, *The Era of Good Feelings*, EL110
Clarence Darrow, *Verdicts Out of Court*, EL2
Floyd Dell, *Intellectual Vagabondage*, EL13
Elisha P. Douglass, *Rebels and Democrats*, EL108
Theodore Draper, *The Roots of American Communism*, EL105
Joseph Epstein, *Ambition*, EL7
Lloyd C. Gardner, *Pay Any Price*, EL136
Lloyd C. Gardner, *Spheres of Influence*, EL131
Paul W. Glad, *McKinley, Bryan, and the People*, EL119
Sarah H. Gordon, *Passage to Union*, EL138
Daniel Horowitz, *The Morality of Spending*, EL122
Kenneth T. Jackson, *The Ku Klux Klan in the City, 1915–1930*, EL123
Edward Chase Kirkland, *Dream and Thought in the Business Community,
    1860–1900*, EL114
Herbert S Klein, *Slavery in the Americas*, EL103
Aileen S. Kraditor, *Means and Ends in American Abolitionism*, EL111
Irving Kristol, *Neoconservatism*, EL304
Leonard W. Levy, *Jefferson and Civil Liberties: The Darker Side*, EL107
Thomas J. McCormick, *China Market*, EL115
Walter Millis, *The Martial Spirit*, EL104
Nicolaus Mills, ed., *Culture in an Age of Money*, EL302
Nicolaus Mills, *Like a Holy Crusade*, EL129
Roderick Nash, *The Nervous Generation*, EL113
William L. O'Neill, ed., *Echoes of Revolt: The Masses, 1911–1917*, EL5
Gilbert Osofsky, *Harlem: The Making of a Ghetto*, EL133
Edward Pessen, *Losing Our Souls*, EL132
Glenn Porter and Harold C. Livesay, *Merchants and Manufacturers*, EL106
John Prados, *The Hidden History of the Vietnam War*, EL137
John Prados, *Presidents' Secret Wars*, EL134
Edward Reynolds, *Stand the Storm*, EL128
Richard Schickel, *The Disney Version*, EL135
Edward A. Shils, *The Torment of Secrecy*, EL303
Geoffrey S. Smith, *To Save a Nation*, EL125
Bernard Sternsher, ed., *Hitting Home: The Great Depression in Town and
    Country*, EL109
Bernard Sternsher, ed., *Hope Restored: How the New Deal Worked in Town
    and Country*, EL140
Athan Theoharis, *From the Secret Files of J. Edgar Hoover*, EL127
Nicholas von Hoffman, *We Are the People Our Parents Warned Us Against*,
    EL301
Norman Ware, *The Industrial Worker, 1840–1860*, EL116
Tom Wicker, *JFK and LBJ: The Influence of Personality upon Politics*, EL120
Robert H. Wiebe, *Businessmen and Reform*, EL101
T. Harry Williams, *McClellan, Sherman and Grant*, EL121
Miles Wolff, *Lunch at the 5 & 10*, EL118
Randall B. Woods and Howard Jones, *Dawning of the Cold War*, EL130

ELEPHANT PAPERBACKS

Literature and Letters
Walter Bagehot, *Physics and Politics,* EL305
Stephen Vincent Benét, *John Brown's Body,* EL10
Isaiah Berlin, *The Hedgehog and the Fox,* EL21
F. Bordewijk, *Character,* EL46
Robert Brustein, *Dumbocracy in America,* EL421
Anthony Burgess, *Shakespeare,* EL27
Philip Callow, *From Noon to Starry Night,* EL37
Philip Callow, *Son and Lover: The Young D. H. Lawrence,* EL14
Philip Callow, *Vincent Van Gogh,* EL38
Anton Chekhov, *The Comic Stories,* EL47
James Gould Cozzens, *Castaway,* EL6
James Gould Cozzens, *Men and Brethren,* EL3
Clarence Darrow, *Verdicts Out of Court,* EL2
Floyd Dell, *Intellectual Vagabondage,* EL13
Theodore Dreiser, *Best Short Stories,* EL1
Joseph Epstein, *Ambition,* EL7
André Gide, *Madeleine,* EL8
Gerald Graff, *Literature Against Itself,* EL35
John Gross, *The Rise and Fall of the Man of Letters,* EL18
Irving Howe, *William Faulkner,* EL15
Aldous Huxley, *After Many a Summer Dies the Swan,* EL20
Aldous Huxley, *Ape and Essence,* EL19
Aldous Huxley, *Collected Short Stories,* EL17
Roger Kimball, *Tenured Radicals,* EL43
F. R. Leavis, *Revaluation,* EL39
F. R. Leavis, *The Living Principle,* EL40
F. R. Leavis, *The Critic as Anti-Philosopher,* EL41
Sinclair Lewis, *Selected Short Stories,* EL9
William L. O'Neill, ed., *Echoes of Revolt: The Masses, 1911–1917,* EL5
Budd Schulberg, *The Harder They Fall,* EL36
Ramón J. Sender, *Seven Red Sundays,* EL11
Peter Shaw, *Recovering American Literature,* EL34
Tess Slesinger, *On Being Told That Her Second Husband Has Taken His First Lover, and Other Stories,* EL12
Donald Thomas, *Swinburne,* EL45
B. Traven, *The Bridge in the Jungle,* EL28
B. Traven, *The Carreta,* EL25
B. Traven, *The Cotton-Pickers,* EL32
B. Traven, *General from the Jungle,* EL33
B. Traven, *Government,* EL23
B. Traven, *March to the Montería,* EL26
B. Traven, *The Night Visitor and Other Stories,* EL24
B. Traven, *The Rebellion of the Hanged,* EL29
B. Traven, *Trozas,* EL44
Anthony Trollope, *Trollope the Traveller,* EL31
Rex Warner, *The Aerodrome,* EL22
Thomas Wolfe, *The Hills Beyond,* EL16
Wilhelm Worringer, *Abstraction and Empathy,* EL42